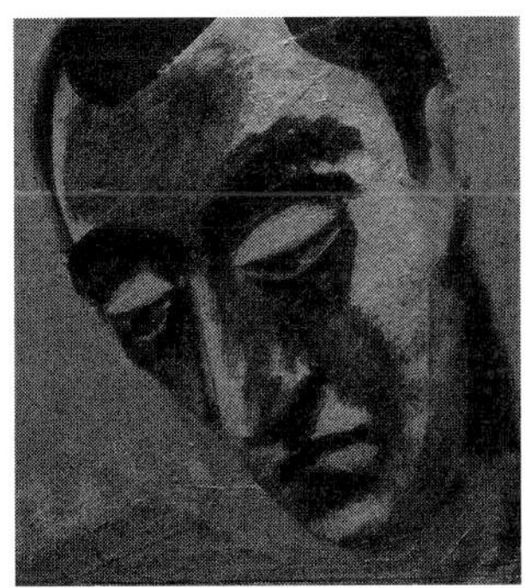

Rethinking
Arshile Gorky

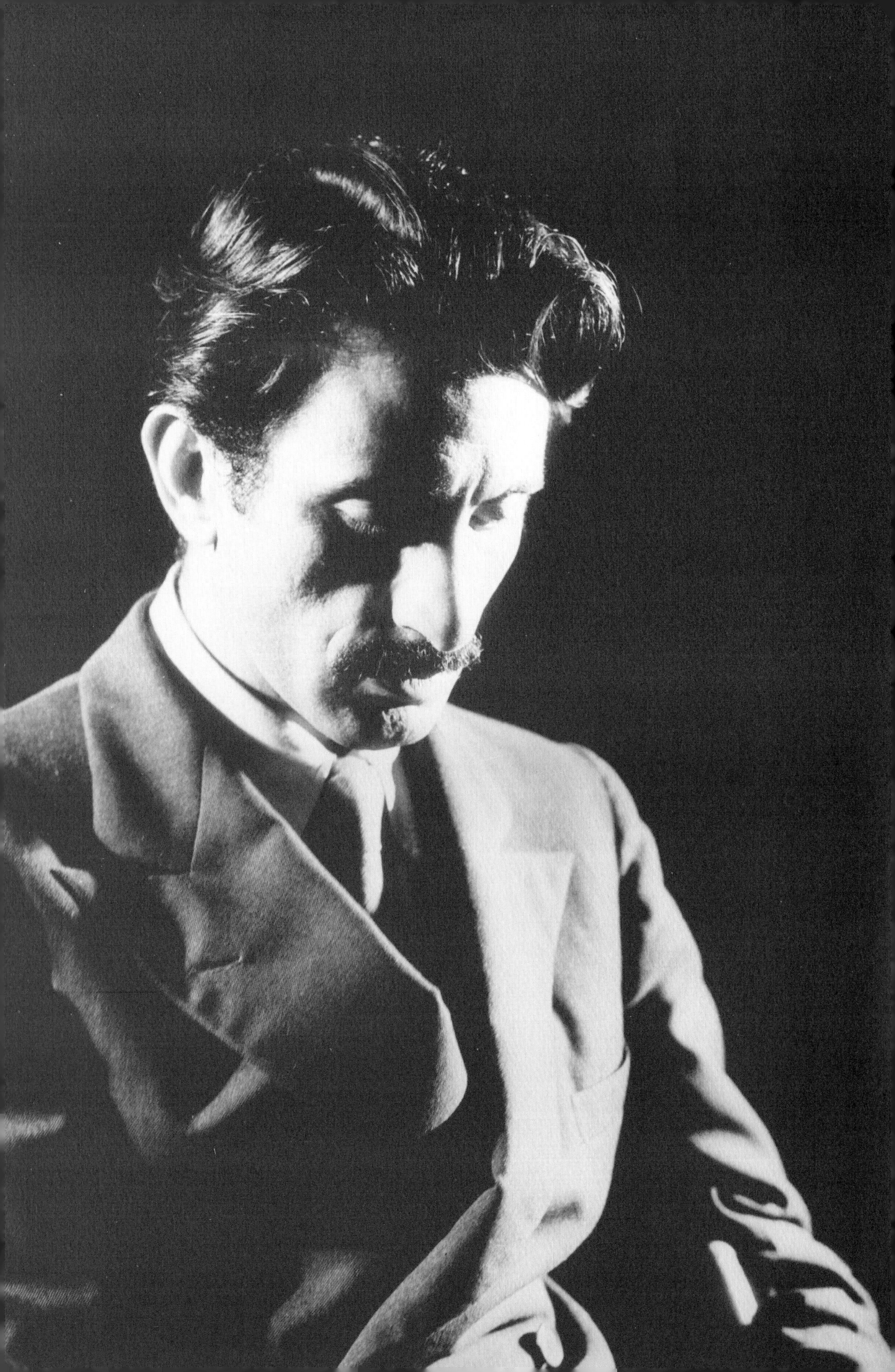

Rethinking Arshile Gorky

Kim S. Theriault

The Pennsylvania State
University Press
University Park, Pennsylvania

Library of Congress Cataloging-in-Publication Data

Theriault, Kim S.
Rethinking Arshile Gorky / Kim S. Theriault.
p. cm.
Includes bibliographical references and index.
Summary: "A reexamination of the art of Arshile Gorky (1904–1948), and an exploration of his role in the development of modern abstraction in America"—Provided by publisher.
ISBN 978-0-271-03647-2 (cloth : alk. paper)
ISBN 978-0-271-03646-5 (pbk. : alk. paper)
1. Gorky, Arshile, 1904–1948—Criticism and interpretation.
2. Painting, Abstract—United States.
3. Painting, American—20th century.
I. Title.

ND237.G613T48 2009
759.13—dc22 2009023727

Designed by Bessas & Ackerman, Guilford, CT
Printed in the United States of America
Published by The Pennsylvania State University Press, University Park, PA 16802–1003

It is the policy of The Pennsylvania State University Press to use acid-free paper. Publications on uncoated stock satisfy the minimum requirements of American National Standard for Information Sciences—Permanence of Paper for Printed Library Material, ANSI Z39.48–1992.

For my mother,
Rose Sielian Theriault

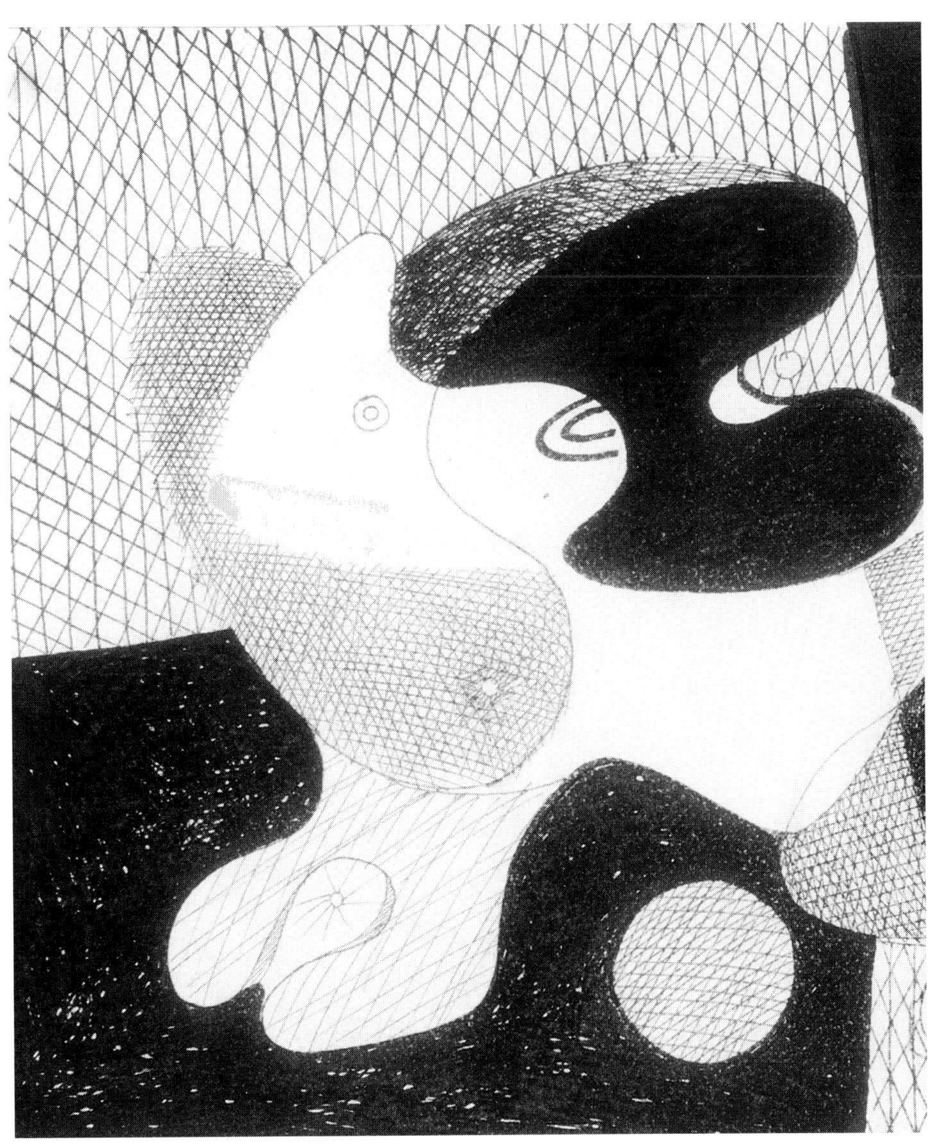

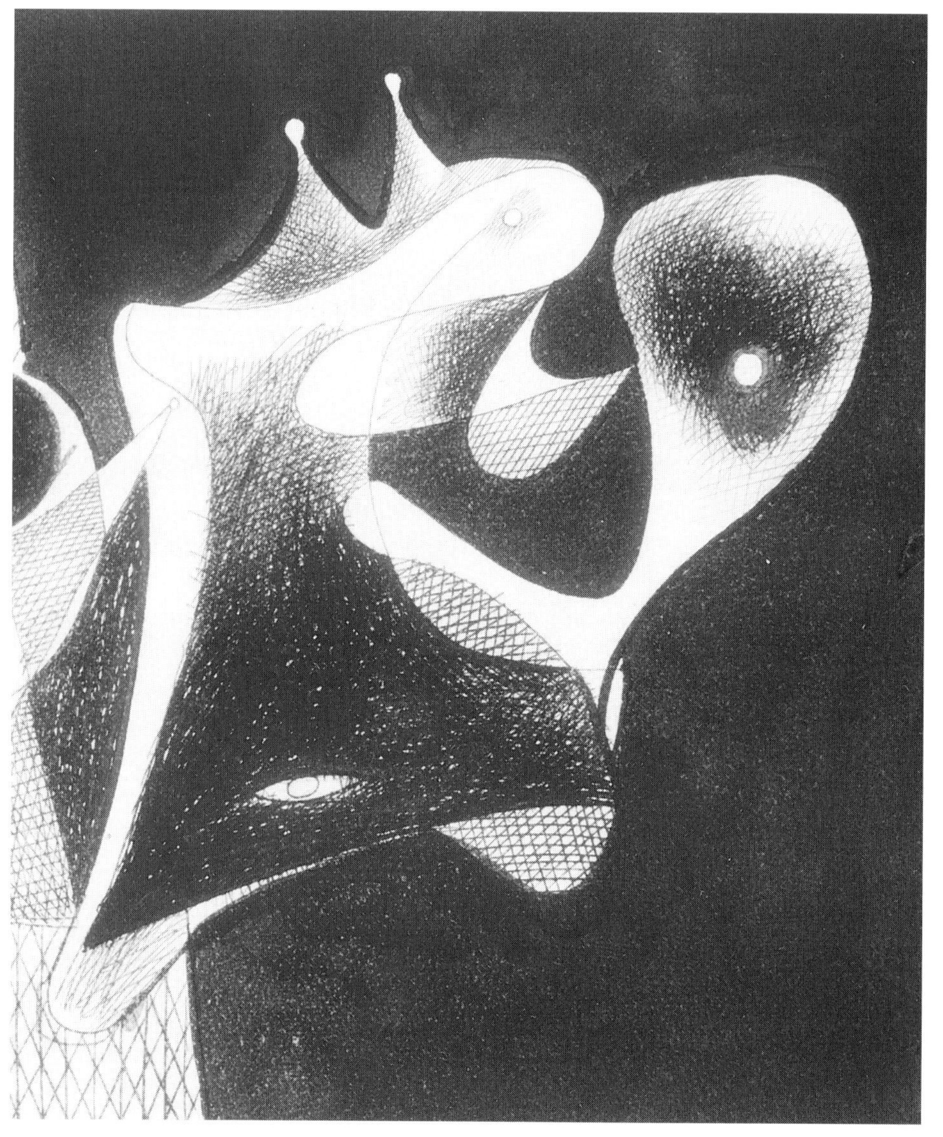

Contents

Illustrations

Color Plates

1 Arshile Gorky, *The Artist and His Mother,* ca. 1926–36. Oil on canvas, 60 × 50 in. (152.4 × 127 cm). Whitney Museum of American Art, New York. Gift of Julien Levy for Maro and Natasha Gorky in memory of their father, 50.17. © 2008 Artists Rights Society (ARS), New York.

2 Arshile Gorky, *The Artist and His Mother,* ca. 1926–ca. 1942. Oil on canvas, 60 × 50 in. National Gallery of Art, Washington, D.C. Ailsa Mellon Bruce Fund, 1979.13.1. Image courtesy of the Board of Trustees, National Gallery of Art, Washington, D.C. © 2008 Artists Rights Society (ARS), New York.

3 Arshile Gorky, *Self-Portrait,* 1937. Oil on canvas, 55½ × 23⅞ in. Private collection. Image courtesy of Gagosian Gallery, New York. © 2008 Artists Rights Society (ARS), New York.

4 Arshile Gorky, *Portrait of the Artist and His Imaginary Wife,* 1933. Oil on cardboard, 8½ × 14¼ in. Hirshhorn Museum and Sculpture Garden, Smithsonian Institution, Washington, D.C. Gift of the Joseph H. Hirshhorn Foundation, 1966. Photo: Lee Stalsworth. © 2008 Artists Rights Society (ARS), New York.

5 Arshile Gorky, *Portrait of Vartoosh,* 1933–34. Oil on canvas, 20 × 15 in. Hirshhorn Museum and Sculpture Garden, Smithsonian Institution, Washington, D.C. Gift of the Joseph H. Hirshhorn Foundation, 1966. Photo: Lee Stalsworth. © 2008 Artists Rights Society (ARS), New York.

6 Arshile Gorky, *Portrait of Ahko,* 1937. Oil on canvas, 19½ × 15 in. Private collection. Photo courtesy of Lennon, Weinberg, Inc., New York. © 2008 Artists Rights Society (ARS), New York.

7 Arshile Gorky, *Portrait of Mougouch,* 1941. Oil on canvas, 8 × 10 in. Private collection. Photo courtesy of the Allen Stone Gallery, New York. © 2008 Artists Rights Society (ARS), New York.

8 Arshile Gorky, *Landscape in the Manner of Cézanne,* 1927. Oil on canvas, 20 × 16 in. Private collection. © 2008 Artists Rights Society (ARS), New York.

9 Arshile Gorky, *Abstraction with a Palette,* ca. 1930. Oil on canvas, 48 × 35$\frac{15}{16}$ in. (121.9 × 91.3 cm). Philadelphia Museum of Art. Gift of Bernard Davis, 1942 (1942-64-3). Photo: The Philadelphia Museum of Art/Art Resource, New York. © 2008 Artists Rights Society (ARS), New York.

10 Arshile Gorky, *Organization,* 1933–36. Oil on canvas, 50 × 59$\frac{13}{16}$ in. (framed: 53 × 63 × 2¾). National Gallery of Art, Washington, D.C. Ailsa Mellon Bruce Fund, 1979.13.3. Image courtesy of the Board of Trustees, National Gallery of Art, Washington, D.C. © 2008 Artists Rights Society (ARS), New York.

11 Arshile Gorky, *Image in Khorkom,* 1934–36. Oil on canvas, 33 × 43 in. Private collection. Photo courtesy of Lennon, Weinberg, Inc., New York. © 2008 Artists Rights Society (ARS), New York.

12 Arshile Gorky, *Summation*, 1947. Pencil, pastel, and charcoal on buff paper mounted on composition board, 6 ft. 7⅝ in. × 8 ft. 5¾ in. The Museum of Modern Art, New York. Nina and Gordon Bunshaft Fund (234.1969). Digital image © The Museum of Modern Art/Licensed by SCALA/Art Resource, New York. © 2008 Artists Rights Society (ARS), New York.

13 Arshile Gorky, *Mechanics of Flying*, 1936–37. Oil on canvas, 111 × 136½ in. On extended loan from the Collection of The Port Authority of New York and New Jersey to the Newark Museum (L1.1983.2). © 2008 Artists Rights Society (ARS), New York.

14 Arshile Gorky, study for a mural for Administration Building, Newark Airport, New Jersey, 1935–36. Gouache on paper, 13⅝ × 29⅞ in. (34.6 × 75.9 cm). On extended loan from the United States WPA Program to The Museum of Modern Art, New York (EL1939.1811). Digital image © The Museum of Modern Art/Licensed by SCALA/Art Resource, New York. © 2008 Artists Rights Society (ARS), New York.

15 Arshile Gorky, *Nude*, 1946. Oil on canvas, 50⅛ × 38⅛ in. Hirshhorn Museum and Sculpture Garden, Smithsonian Institution, Washington, D.C. Gift of the Joseph H. Hirshhorn Foundation, 1966. Photo: Lee Stalsworth. © 2008 Artists Rights Society (ARS), New York.

16 Arshile Gorky, *Waterfall*, 1943. Oil on canvas, 153.7 × 113.0 cm. Tate Gallery, London. Photo: Tate, London/Art Resource, New York. © 2008 Artists Rights Society (ARS), New York.

17 Arshile Gorky, *The Liver Is the Cock's Comb*, 1944. Oil on canvas, framed: 75¼ × 100⅜ × 2¾ in. (191.135 × 254.9525 × 6.985 cm); support: 73¼ × 98" (186.05 × 248.92 cm). Albright-Knox Art Gallery, Buffalo, New York. Gift of Seymour H. Knox Jr., 1956. © 2008 Artists Rights Society (ARS), New York.

18 Arshile Gorky, *The Leaf of the Artichoke Is an Owl*, 1944. Oil on canvas, 28 × 35⅞ in. The Museum of Modern Art, New York. Sidney and Harriet Janis Collection Fund (632.1977). Digital image © The Museum of Modern Art/Licensed by SCALA/Art Resource, New York. © 2008 Artists Rights Society (ARS), New York.

19 Arshile Gorky, *Virginia Landscape*, 1943. Pencil and colored crayons on paper, 17 × 22 in. The Muriel Kallis Steinberg Newman Collection, The Metropolitan Museum of Art, New York. Gift of Muriel Kallis Newman, 2006 (2006. 32.20). Image © The Metropolitan Museum of Art. © 2008 Artists Rights Society (ARS), New York.

20 Arshile Gorky, *Garden in Sochi*, 1941. Oil on canvas, 44¼ × 62¼ in. (112.4 × 158.1 cm). The Museum of Modern Art, New York. Purchase Fund and gift of Mr. and Mrs. Wolfgang S. Schwabacher (by exchange) (335.1942). Digital image © The Museum of Modern Art/Licensed by SCALA/Art Resource, New York. © 2008 Artists Rights Society (ARS), New York.

21 Arshile Gorky, *Garden in Sochi*, ca. 1943. Oil on canvas, 31 × 39 in. The Museum of Modern Art, New York. Acquired through the Lillie P. Bliss

Figures

Mellon Fund, 1979.21.1. Image courtesy of the Board of Trustees, National Gallery of Art, Washington, D.C. © 2008 Artists Rights Society (ARS), New York.

30 Fernand Léger, *The City*, 1919. Oil on canvas, 91 × 117½ in. Philadelphia Museum of Art, A. E. Gallatin Collection. © 2008 Artists Rights Society (ARS), New York/ADAGP, Paris.

31 Marcel Duchamp, *The Passage from Virgin to Bride*, Munich, July–August 1912. Oil on canvas, 23⅜ × 21¼ in. The Museum of Modern Art, New York. Purchase (174.1945). Digital image © The Museum of Modern Art/Licensed by SCALA/Art Resource, New York. © 2008 Artists Rights Society (ARS), New York/ADAGP, Paris/Succession Marcel Duchamp.

32 Arshile Gorky, *Aerial Map*, 1936–37. Oil on canvas, 79 × 123½ in. On extended loan from the Collection of The Port Authority of New York and New Jersey to the Newark Museum, L1.1983.2. © 2008 Artists Rights Society (ARS), New York.

33 *Newark Ledger*, Thursday, June 10, 1937. Photographer unknown. Image courtesy of the Newark Museum Archives.

34 Arshile Gorky, *Man's Conquest of the Air*, 1939. Aviation Building, New York World's Fair. Destroyed. © 2008 Artists Rights Society (ARS), New York.

35 Arshile Gorky, *Mural Study for Ben Marden's Riviera Club*, ca. 1938–39. Gouache on paper, 13 × 18 15/16 in. Private collection. Photo: Luigi Pellettieri. © 2008 Artists Rights Society (ARS), New York.

36 Wassily Kandinsky, *Improvisation VII (Composition VII)*, 1913. 200 × 300 cm. Tretyakov Gallery, Moscow. Photo: Erich Lessing/Art Resource, New York. © 2008 Artists Rights Society (ARS), New York/ADAGP, Paris.

37 Andre Masson, *Battle of the Fishes*, 1926. Sand, gesso, oil, pencil, and charcoal on canvas, 14¼ × 28¾ in. The Museum of Modern Art, New York. Purchase (260.1937). Digital image © The Museum of Modern Art/Licensed by SCALA/Art Resource, New York. © 2008 Artists Rights Society (ARS), New York/ADAGP, Paris.

38 Arshile Gorky, *Water of the Flowery Mill*, 1944. Oil on canvas, 42¼ × 48¾ in. The Metropolitan Museum of Art, New York. George A. Hearn Fund, 1956 (56.205.1). Image © The Metropolitan Museum of Art. © 2008 Artists Rights Society (ARS), New York.

39 Joan Miró, *Le Carnaval d'Arlequin (Carnival of Harlequin)*, 1924–25. Oil on canvas, framed: 36¾ × 47 × 3¼ in. (93.3 × 119.38 × 8.25 cm); support: 26 × 35 5/8 in. (66.04 × 90.48 cm). Albright-Knox Art Gallery, Buffalo, New York. Room of Contemporary Art Fund, 1940. © 2008 Successió Miró/Artists Rights Society (ARS), New York/ADAGP, Paris.

40 Arshile Gorky, *Argula*, 1938. Oil on canvas, 15 × 24 in. The Museum of Modern Art, New York. Gift of Bernard Davis (323.1941). Digital image © The Museum of Modern Art/Licensed by SCALA/Art Resource, New York. © 2008 Artists Rights Society (ARS), New York.

Acknowledgments

When I began my research on Arshile Gorky, I never realized that this book would become as much a part of my history as art history. Throughout the years of research and writing, many have given me direction, inspiration, and company. There are some individuals to whom I wish to especially express my gratitude, but I offer heartfelt thanks to everyone who has been associated with this endeavor.

My mother, Rose Sielian Theriault, made this book possible. Her support has been infinite throughout my life, and I cannot thank her enough. In addition to incidents of financial support throughout the years, her unshakable belief in my potential and abilities and ever-present pride in my accomplishments have been priceless. Her sister, my aunt, Mary Sielian Harris, like a second parent after my father's death, has been crucial to particular junctures in my life, such as relocations, graduations, and finishing this manuscript. I appreciate the many lovingly prepared meals at Ann Sielian Donabedian's house while conversing with her about family history. That, along with early-life contact with my late grandmother, Servart Ayanian Sielian, and uncle, Henry Lazarus Sielian, contributed to my understanding of Gorky.

I am eternally grateful to Howard Singerman at the University of Virginia, who has continuously supported this book as well as my research and teaching career. An exceptional educator and scholar, he has had a huge hand in instigating what appears on the following pages. I am deeply indebted to Michael R. Taylor at the Philadelphia Museum of Art for his enthusiastic support of my manuscript and scholarship on the artist. I was honored by his invitation to write for the Arshile Gorky Retrospective Exhibition catalogue and feel very fortunate to have had the opportunity to organize a panel with him for the 96th College Art Association Annual Conference in 2008 as well as to watch him bring the Arshile Gorky Retrospective Exhibition to fruition. I would like to express my appreciation to the Penn State University Press's anonymous reader for substantial suggestions given on the original manuscript that contributed to this final product. Dominican University colleagues Samina Hadi-Tabassum, Liesl Orenic, and Susan Strawn also read the manuscript at that stage and gave constructive comments as well.

The Faculty Development Committee at Dominican University provided exceptional financial support for this publication in several forms, including a Summer Research Assistance Grant, a Special Support Grant, and a Publication Assistance Grant. I feel especially privileged to have been named a 2009 recipient of a Society for the Preservation of American Modernists Publication Grant.

Throughout the process of completing this book while negotiating the demands of teaching, my colleagues at Dominican University in the Department of Art, Art History, and Design remained steadfast in their support. Jeffery Cote de Luna, Javier Carmona, Bill Kerr, Jean Bevier, and Noelle Allen-Wright are a true joy to work with. The department kindly contributed from their budget toward the purchase of some images and supply costs related to manuscript preparation. The Dean of the Rosary College of Arts and Sciences, Jeff Carlson, has provided assistance in many ways and at many junctures since I arrived at Dominican University in 2004, and was especially generous in providing funding toward image copyright clearance for this book. I am grateful to Dominican University for granting me a leave of absence, which allowed me to dedicate myself to finishing this project.

I wish to thank my editor at Penn State University Press, Eleanor Goodman. Her persistence and belief in this project have been phenomenal, and I am grateful to have worked with her. I also wish to thank the editorial and production staff at Penn State University Press, especially manuscript editor John Morris for his insightful revisions, Jennifer Norton for shepherding the book design, and Patty Mitchell for bringing it to an audience in its final form. Three student assistants from Dominican University also helped at various stages of preparation. The first, Cristeana Bastian, was funded by the Faculty Development Committee early on. The Dominican University Partners in Scholarship program funded Marcela Andrade for one semester and Jacqueline R. Reich for two. These talented, intelligent, and organized individuals are a credit to the project, and I am glad to have worked with each of them. I am also especially grateful to Claire Howard at the Philadelphia Museum of Art, who worked on my behalf to obtain some key images and permissions for this publication.

Although some are far removed from it, a number of dedicated teachers contributed to the end result of this book. These include Stanley Moulton, who taught me how to research so long ago; Gregory Natt, who encouraged me to continue; George Brandon; Henry Taylor; and Edward Kessler, who taught me about thesis statements. At the University of New Hampshire, I was inspired by Margot Clark, and am perpetually appreciative of Mara Witzling, who has seen me through my entire art history career thus far. I am also especially grateful to Mel Lader, the first to complete substantial scholarship on the artist Arshile Gorky and whose kindness and friendship I still miss even years after his passing.

Throughout the years many friends have also been important to this book's completion, but a few in particular have been with it from the beginning and have endured throughout. Eileen Sullivan has given me great insight amidst the various stages of my research, writing, and life while keeping me in awe of her own achievements. I am grateful to Jack Nocera for his kindness, and for supporting my time spent with his family. The love and respect of their smart, unique, and generous children, Fiona Rose and Stuart Connor Sullivan Nocera, has always energized me. Renée Zettle-Sterling is a brilliant artist who has both offered suggestions for this project based on her own aesthetic inquiries and cheered for its completion throughout its many incarnations.

There are always more people to thank, and many of them are probably unaware of my gratitude. I have benefitted greatly from the support of Roger Stein, Lydia Csató Gasman, Paul Barolsky, Larry Goedde, Christopher Johns, Lucy Lippard, Deirdre Oakley, Ellen Handler Spitz, Kirsten Ringleberg, David Sokol, and Dominican University faculty and staff, including Ken Black, John Jenks, Lou Tenzis, Marion Weedermann, Jessica Cochran, Ken Orenic, Kitty Rhodes, Marlene Cozza, Emma Mims, Ellen McManus, and Becky Pliske, to only name a few. Thanks go to Laurie B., Jo W., Amberlee, Christina, Caitlyn, Samantha M., and the wealth of new and established writers with whom I came in contact while on leave in New Hampshire for contributing to happiness, diversion, or peace amidst the hard work of bringing this book to completion. Thank you also to the Dominican University Crown Library, the Public Library of Rochester, New Hampshire, Dimond Library at the University of New Hampshire, and the Dominican University Information Technology Department. All of my students, past and present and of all levels, have taught me much along the way, and I am grateful to them for their support of this project and tolerance while I was preoccupied with it.

I will close as I began—with my family. Thank you to my cousin, Richard Andrew Harris, who is like a second brother and whose rationality and blunt advice are rare in this world. I am grateful to my brother, Henry Charles Theriault, and my sister-in-law, Yoko Harumi, especially for his scholarship on the Armenian Genocide and human rights and for her enlightened perspective on culture and humanity. I greatly appreciate the love of, and time spent with, their intelligent, creative, and caring children, my niece Nairi Theriault Harumi and nephew Aram Theriault Harumi, who are an endless source of sunshine in my heart.

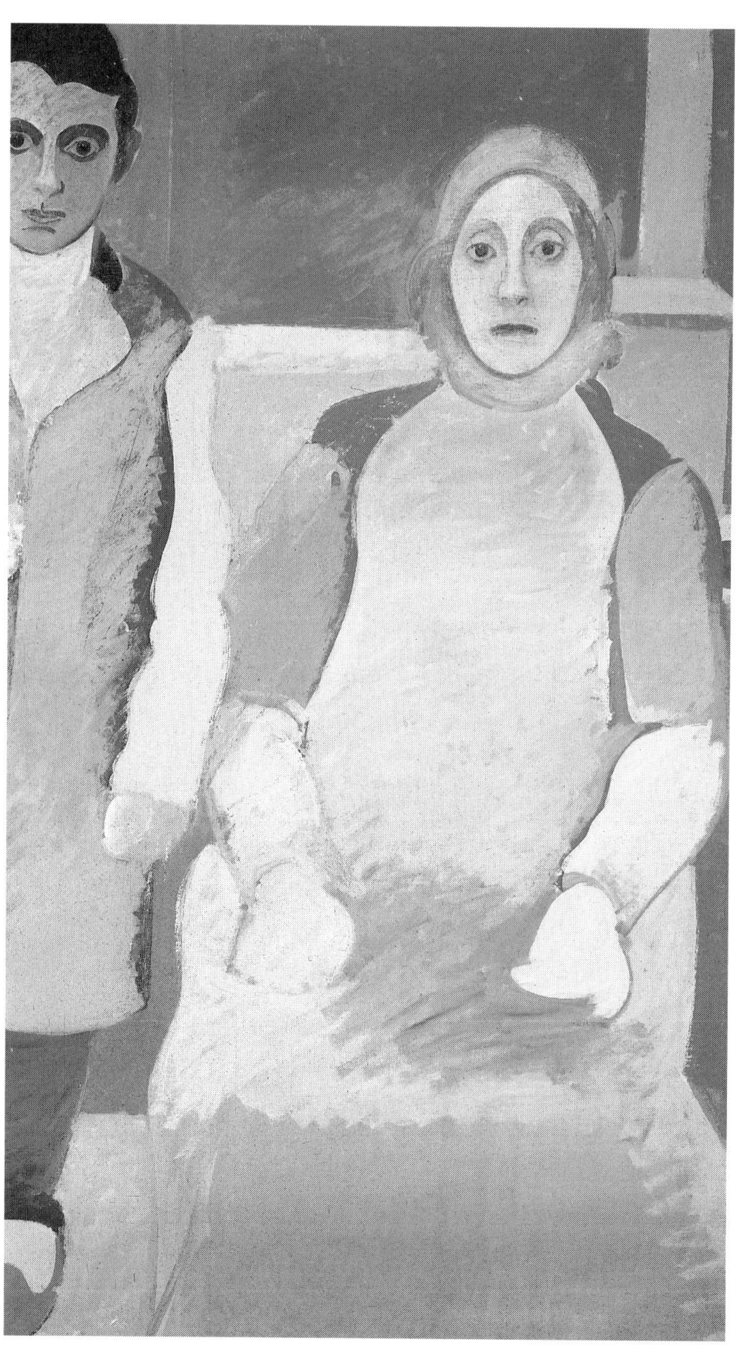

Introduction

A displaced, poor, and traumatized Armenian in a provincial New York, he could think of no more tractable project for himself than to join the seraphic ranks of the masters. Did he make it? We're not the ones to say, because our view of what constitutes greatness in art or anything else is so vexed, complicated, and ironic. The whole idea seems old-fashioned, even embarrassing. But Gorky's best art shows us the miracles that belief in it can work. And we are just the ones to appreciate his self-inventing, reckless grace. The attainment of individuality against ridiculous odds is right up our alley.

—PETER SCHJELDAHL, "THE GREAT GORKY"

Throughout the criticism, art-historical studies, and biographies of Arshile Gorky (ca. 1900–1948), the artist has remained an intriguing if not enigmatic figure. This book addresses Gorky's fascinating complexities by exploring the relationship of his artwork to his displacement as an immigrant in the United States, the characteristics and techniques of his style that contributed to the development of abstraction in America during the 1930s and 1940s, and the manner in which he is situated, evaluated, and read within the context of High Modernist art.

Long touted as a transitional figure, Arshile Gorky (fig. 1) appears as an interstice within art history's linear progression. Often referred to as the last Surrealist and first Abstract Expressionist,[1] Gorky, it has been claimed, embraced dream imagery in the tradition of the Surrealists, used all-over patterning before Jackson Pollock, promoted disembodied color before Mark Rothko, exploited the physicality of paint before Willem de Kooning, and anticipated stain painting.[2] Since the late 1990s, three biographies of the artist have been published,[3]

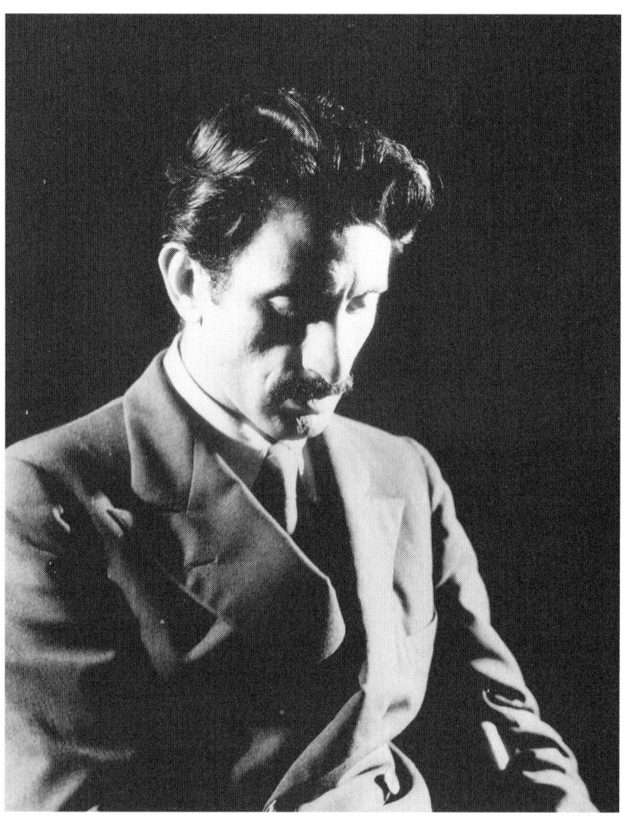

Opening image detail of plate 2.

FIGURE 1
Photograph of Arshile Gorky by Wyatt Davis.

varying somewhat in content and approach but each trying to assert an accurate narrative of the artist's life. To date, there have been almost as many biographies published as there have been serious art-historical books,[4] even though Gorky himself always preferred not to give too much specific information about his background, believing that after one is gone, it is predominantly the paintings that count.[5] Partially because of the Armenian Genocide and despite attempts by his biographers, much of Gorky's life story as we know it is inaccurate, unknown, or constructed by the artist, and "Arshile Gorky" is partially a performance based on an invented name and fictionalized background. Similarly, his artwork is a combination of observed and imagined space that has continually eluded description and definition.

Gorky was a survivor of the 1915 Armenian Genocide, a "starving artist" during the Depression, and a fixture in the developing New York City art scene during the second quarter of the twentieth century. His own tales about his background are a significant backstory to his artistic pursuits. "He was fond of telling his friends," said fellow painter and art writer Elaine de Kooning, "that he didn't speak until he was six years old. Before then he spoke only with the birds, he said. And unabashed by the most skeptical reactions (or, more likely, unaware of them), Gorky went on unfolding tale after tale of his childhood, of extraordinary peasants, customs, events and conversations."[6] Based in actual experience and founded in truth, tales of Gorky's dramatic persona and fantastic stories are ever-present in recountings of the artist's life and art, and Gorky himself loved a spectacle.[7] Therefore, the idea of "Arshile Gorky" as a figment of Modernism is often raised to mythic levels because it is complicated by our own stereotype of artists as brooding, mysterious, and often troubled geniuses—a classification into which Gorky's suicide in 1948 makes him fit all too well. Additionally, available art-historical literature about the artist can be problematic because it founds many of its theories on a cache of letters that Gorky's nephew and first biographer claims that Gorky authored, but have recently been called into question.[8]

Together, these components of Gorky's life and afterlife have drawn attention to the individual, while at the same time somewhat obfuscating the historic momentousness of his art. The irony seems to be that, contrary to what we understand of Gorky's practice and theories, the more he has been explained, the more his art has been disengaged from the viewer's direct experience. The larger art-historical challenge of this book, therefore, has been to decide what to include of biography and past analyses and when, how often, and to what extent in order to provoke new interpretations. Yet the necessity of this reexamination is evident: theoretically based endeavors like this study are almost nonexistent,[9] and there have been no single-author book-length scholarly investigations of the artist's work for almost thirty years.[10]

As a practitioner of modern art in America before it became widespread, Gorky appears as a one-man wrinkle in time, reflecting the social and cultural conditions of his era in addition to revealing art practices. Just as the molded separations that flank cement sidewalk sections both sever and preserve its continuity by allowing adaptation to changeable atmospheric conditions, Gorky's disjuncture is key to understanding his art.[11] This book rethinks Arshile Gorky's locus in art history by allowing, like the sidewalk fissures, expansion and contraction of extant knowledge and enlisting it as a solid foundation upon which to step forward and forge new interpretations of Gorky's place within the art-historical continuum. Ultimately, the multivalent possibilities posed for the artist's compositions reflect the indeterminate nature of American Modernism itself. For Gorky, art history is not entirely linear, and his artmaking does not necessarily follow a sequential trajectory. Indeed, it can be difficult to determine how some artworks fit into Gorky's career, because he was known to redate paintings, reuse earlier canvases, and repaint works while they inhabited his studio.[12]

The text and context of Gorky's art, therefore, cannot be separated. The conditions in which his art was produced, whether historical, biographical, sociological, or political, may have played a role in its development and manifestation, although not always in the way one might expect and usually in a covert manner, even when the obfuscation is not intentional. For instance, knowledge of the Armenian Genocide contextualizes Gorky's art, but the Genocide is not necessarily present in the works themselves through representative depiction or hyperbole. Rather, emotion is exposed through liminality, as we sense something ominous that is deep-seated and just under the painting's conceptual surface and arrangement of forms. Although the Armenian Genocide traumatized its victims, its residual effects on survivors were not always obvious, and triggered remembrances tend to be haphazard and rarely linear. In Gorky's case, the artist's deidentification with trauma—his refusal to discuss the Genocide—reverberates in his art and life through nuanced behaviors or bold attempts to achieve celebrity under an assumed name that denies his circumstances. Gorky's personality—he would execute energetic ethnic dances and chants at parties, grandly proclaim his debt to better-known artists, and diligently pursue his painting to the extent that he would often purchase art supplies with his limited funds instead of feeding himself—supports the claim that "even his least susceptible friends had to admit there was something fabulous about the man."[13]

Simultaneously interdisciplinary and dedisciplinary, this study explores expansive themes and multifaceted relationships between art, history, and society and reveals a continuous interplay between past and present, aesthetic heritage and Modernism, figural and abstract, and considers how individuals, beliefs, and movements may have influenced Gorky's placement within High Modernist art in America during the twentieth century. It seeks to complement extant critical evaluations of Gorky as a significant exponent of early twentieth-century painting and define him as an eminent Modernist innovator. By engaging sociopolitical, stylistic, and theoretical themes, it allows Gorky's unique relevance to the course of American artistic advances and his contributions to the art of the last century to become evident.

Locating Gorky within a conceptual framework of plurality to which he himself seems to have subscribed,[14] this study builds upon useful arguments, analyses, and components of earlier examinations of the artist.[15] Inserting a certain amount of academic rigor to attain a better understanding of the artist and his art while avoiding definitive claims that might limit future explanations, this project refuses strict parameters of theory, interpretation, and discipline and embraces the existentiality inherent within the space of art and life. Like Gorky himself, who drew upon multiple influences from a variety of art-historical eras, the study embraces, enlists, and entwines a diverse array of theorists and critics, few of which singly avert the characteristic pitfalls of Gorky's story that mythologize him as a tragic victim. Constructivist, Postcolonial, and Postmodern critiques coexist here with New Historicism, and theories of time, space, and memory offer new ways of envisioning Gorky's art. The relativity of this endeavor is in itself challenging because, as Hayden White has pointed out, writing history on some level is also inevitably plot-making.[16] The alternative emplotments introduced here might be more feasible than those structured in the past only when combined with the ultimate conclusion that Gorky and his art are imbued with a Modernist condition of indeterminacy. Additionally, regardless of any past, present, or future theories applied to his art and life, this study acknowledges that Gorky is anchored in making; that is, the process of making art and all of the actions, personal and professional, that manifest it.

Gorky lived during an exciting time in New York City. He understood the energy surrounding him, exclaiming, "The twentieth century—what intensity, what activity, what restless, nervous energy."[17] With the advent of so many private galleries and new museums, modern art was becoming established in the city's culture. In 1927, the A. E. Gallatin collection of contemporary European art was installed at the New York University Washington Square campus, within easy access of Gorky's studio. The Museum of Modern Art was founded in 1929 and expanded three times in the subsequent ten years. Throughout the 1930s, many artists like Gorky were employed through the government support program, the Works Progress Administration Federal Art Project, and among the burgeoning art schools was Hans Hofmann's, which, relocated from Munich, introduced a new generation of artists to Modernist practice. In 1936, the Museum of Modern Art highlighted the works of De Chirico, Miró, and Dalí, who had been fixtures in private galleries up to that point, in the exhibition Fantastic Art, Dada, Surrealism. A year later, the Museum of Non-Objective Painting (later to become the Solomon R. Guggenheim Museum) installed a permanent collection of European abstract art and the Museum of Modern Art placed Pablo Picasso's *Guernica* on display.

Throughout World War II, artists from Europe, including many Surrealists, such as the painter Max Ernst and the writer André Breton, sought refuge in the United States, complementing the pool of modern artists who had already relocated to America, such as André Masson, Piet Mondrian, Fernand Léger, and Amédée Ozenfant. Despite the constant influx of European art and artists, both the American-born and immigrant artists who made up the nucleus of the emerging New York School became increasingly interested in envisioning an American modern art.[18] Summing up their objectives in the 1946 catalogue for the Museum of Modern Art exhibition Fourteen Americans, in which Gorky was included, curator Dorothy Miller proclaimed that "these artists are concerned with communication even more than esthetics."[19] Gorky's work, as we shall see, is concerned with viewers' interpretations while insisting on exploring the formal elements of painting, a practice that later became the hallmark of the new modern American painting.

Rethinking Arshile Gorky begins by articulating Gorky's relationship to a prism of immigration in which the sociohistorical might be inscribed into his artmaking. Reflecting a Modernist tendency to link art and life, in his seminal essay "The American Action Painters," the critic and art writer Harold Rosenberg championed the idea that painting is an act, a kind of lived biography, making art and biography inseparable.[20] Chapter 1 posits that Gorky's background influenced his development as an artist while asserting that it did not define him. Gorky's practice was to some degree founded on his condition as a newcomer from outside the society in which he came to live, a refugee who had fled the Armenian Genocide and arrived in a xenophobic America in 1920. Gorky's status as a refugee may have enhanced his awareness of place, both literally, as a displaced person who physically relocated, and figuratively, as a person who as an immigrant was situated within a particular social schema.

When the young immigrant changed his name and moved to New York City in 1925 to become an artist, he began to make up stories about his artistic training.[21] The artist's transformation from the ethnic Vosdanig Manoug Adoian to "Arshile Gorky" redressed his foreignness.[22] While Gorky's self-fashioning may have functioned as an immigrant's attempt to legitimize himself within a largely unwelcoming early twentieth-century American society, it parallels the formation of his oeuvre and his development of a new aesthetic at a crucial point in American art history.[23] Reading Gorky's self-fashioning within this context elucidates identity as a prevalent theme in Modernist art, particularly for artists residing in the United States prior to and during World War II.[24] Identity construction was important to artists throughout the twentieth century; it is about the process of becoming and both Gorky and American art were transforming at a similar rate.

Chapter 2 continues upon the identity construction theme by examining Gorky's depictions of himself and his attempts to reconfigure human subjectivity. The chapter highlights how Gorky's self-portraits and images of women exemplify the dilemmas engendered by exile, the search for his own identity, and the development of his own visual language. Gorky's artistic vision was initially defined through modifications of his appearance in self-portraits to resemble other artists and in his reconfigurations of the women who were significant in his life. Through a refashioning process, applied both to himself and to his mother, sisters, and wife, he envisioned iconic representations of modern individuals through the use of a budding Modernist visual vocabulary. Gorky's portraiture presented a visual experience that is emotive in nature and that advanced the Modernist tenet that a picture need not be an accurate representation of or window to the world, but rather is so multidimensional that it transcends accurate identifications and temporal confinements.

An investigation into Gorky's refashioning is further substantiated in chapter 3, which considers more fully his reinterpretations of works of art that had been made by other artists. Often accused of parroting styles, Gorky migrated through techniques. By acquiring and adapting forms, he loosened their autonomy as if they were the vocabulary of a new language that he eventually recombined into his own sentences. This lexicon exposed broader themes prevalent in American Modernism, particularly those, such as originality, emphasized later in Abstract Expressionism. The art historian Meyer Schapiro claimed that because Gorky approached the art that he studied from completely outside of its tradition, he was "aware of Western Art in a way unlike other artists."[25] Gorky identified art that was useful, whether it hung in a museum or at an outdoor art fair.[26] His process of displacing forms resembles his own physical relocation and identity fashioning, ushering in a moment of modern art that is tied to physical and emotional execution and setting the stage for the Abstract Expressionist movement, in which art became imbued with the struggle of its own making. The French phenomenological philosopher Maurice Merleau-Ponty once wrote that the Postimpressionist painter Paul Cézanne sought depth, modes of space, and being,[27] mediated by an interest in how one perceives rather than what one perceives. Gorky, through his devotion to the elder artist, similarly endeavored to create a sense of place through the arrangement of compositional elements and belief in the superiority of the artist's conception of the world over the manner in which it actually existed.

Ultimately for Gorky, art could be the solution to the vexed problem of identity development in America and his desire to be recognized within the annals of art history as a serious and significant artist because of his unique perspective on the world. As the art critic Peter Schjeldahl alleges in the epigraph to this introduction, "the attainment of individuality against ridiculous odds is right up our alley."[28] The liberties that Gorky took with appearances, distorting them for the sake of pictorial, expressive, and emotive values, anticipated his abstract work, in which forms were subject to internal refinements. Chapter 4 explores Gorky's philosophy and process of abstraction, particularly through his mural works and in relation to his interpretations of other artists such as Léger, Mondrian, Matisse, Kandinsky, and the Surrealists. In his own art, Gorky created likenesses that were transmutations of the observed and the remembered, continuously shifting between the two, enabling a dialectic for representation and abstraction that forged a diacritical language of displacement and Modernism.

As the study progresses, the interplay between identity, originality, and likeness folds itself into hybridity. Chapter 5 discusses how Gorky's mature career art used objects, people, or scenes, such as the American landscape, as a point of departure, and united them with other places, spaces, or times, such as the western Armenia of his childhood memories. Gorky often referred to "my country," but in abstract terms so one could never be exactly sure of what country he was speaking. He was, in fact, referring to his Armenian homeland, which was under Turkish rule, thereby making the term a double dislocation. Gorky's late-career work of the 1940s, which reflected an abstract-surreal synthetic Modernism based in dislocation, was embraced for its phantasmagorical qualities. The Surrealist sovereign André Breton exclaimed that "those who love easy solutions will find slim pickings here . . . simply because they do not have the courage to recognize the fact that all human emotions tend to be precipitated in *hybrid* forms."[29] Breton's statement recognized that Gorky's art included emotional transfigurations of observed and remembered worlds.

Like great literature and poetry, whose meanings are often found between the lines, these codetermined hybrid forms of neither subject nor object operate so expansively that they also form a basis for social, cultural, psychological, ethnic, and contextual elaborations of the work. The term "hybrid," therefore, can be expanded to describe the many elements that operate simultaneously within each of Gorky's works. Combining both internal combinations and responses to outside influences and structures, Gorky created what might be better termed "displaced landscapes." These displaced landscapes can be viewed not as complete records of places that exist or had existed but as of both *place* and *displace-*

ment, functioning analogically. In this reinterpretation, objects and space are removed from their identity and made to function in a new manner. Gorky's own life was fractured: he came from a fractured place, spent his life displaced, and conjured places in a similarly fractured, displaced, figural-abstract manner. More simply, Gorky's work was derived from various sources, both observed and imagined, that were abstracted, rearticulated, and combined.

The discussion of Gorky's oeuvre continues in chapter 6, which re-places Gorky within twentieth-century Modernism by reinterpreting his attempts to create an identity in America as an artist through manifestations of memory in his art. The chapter introduces Gorky's practice of "re-membering," that is, recombining or putting together elements of images that Gorky observed at one point in time with those recalled through the memory that such scenes evoked, by which his art can be understood as synthesized compositions that surpass the basic belief that they are merely nostalgic recuperations. Memory itself is a collection of images that we have maintained from the past. Selective memory edits the past to escape or accentuate it. This embedding operates through abstraction, allowing for an interpretive resolution, which in Gorky's case navigated national identifications and temporal restrictions to construct what he seems to have hoped to be a simultaneously personal and expansive art, one described as driven and tragic, with "statements of sorrow, joy, passion and agony and, like an undertone to all but the most lyric canvases and nature drawings, a profound *Angst*."[30] The ramifications of Gorky's endeavor likely led to an abstract art that was a product of both physical and psychological displacement. In essence, Gorky composed according to a personal morphology that was haunted by his own individual history, interpretations of it, and imposed identities, but that might also evoke emotions and tones that are universally understood human conditions. His work was part of a shift in thinking that became central to Abstract Expressionism, and this chapter addresses Gorky's relationship to the burgeoning movement both during and after his death, situating him as instigator for it.

Acknowledging the cultural implications of Gorky's exilic status and the broader indeterminate nature of Modernist art, which denies labeling or rigid placement, we can recognize Gorky's mature abstract works as a resolution to the conflicts generated by displacement, while constituting one of the high moments of twentieth-century art. Gorky's background, it seems, situated him in a peculiar manner to a concept of "other." While he remade others, himself, and extant art compositions, he simultaneously removed and reinscribed his own Orientalization in the pursuit of being modern. In addition, Gorky was doubly inscribed because he and his art are also feminized. Chapter 7 investigates the reviews of Gorky's work and physical descriptions of him that feminized or primitivized him and treated him as an exotic. Such a tendency is also, on some level, part of the larger issue of the feminization of artists in general and ties into the Modernist embrace of the "primitive."

Finally, chapter 8 examines how the artist's image has developed after his death, particularly the way that Gorky's myth has evolved in his biographies because of confusion about his displacement, identity, and art.[31] Initially, very little was known about the artist's background and life, but now there is some question as to whether his biography has come to overshadow his art. This chapter elaborates upon viewpoints inherent in various versions of Gorky's life story through books and his representation in a feature film, versions that seem to manifest the conditions of their authors, rather than the artist who is the subject of their inquiry. Because of these popular culture representations, interest in Gorky is both useful, introducing people to his art, and problematic, enforcing a preeminence for biography and the myth of the tragic artist over individual responses to the art. Such an interpretation of the artist is reflective of our own "wound culture," which, coupled with continued denial of the Armenian Genocide, subjects Gorky's art to the risk of becoming unintelligible without the backstory of his life. The existential struggle of the artist that forever links his art and life is in itself an inherently Modernist process. Yet coupling the artist with tragedy was the antithesis of Gorky's direction and belief.

Because Gorky's identity was in flux, the incorporation of artistic technique became part of his struggle for an identity as an artist. And because of his displacement—his being from one place yet existing in another—Gorky's art was also in flux, and such indeterminacy encouraged an aesthetic that disengaged fixed forms and facilitated abstraction. Such fragmentation and restorying of loss in some ways propelled Gorky into Modernism and prompted him to create an aesthetic that is ultimately American because it consists of interwoven worlds, multidimensional space that blends and clashes, and fabrics of identity that reveal multivalent connotations. "Such art does not merely recall the past," says Postcolonial theorist Homi Bhabha, but rather refigures it "as a contingent 'in-between' space, that innovates and interrupts the performance of the present. The 'past–present' becomes part of the necessity, not the nostalgia, of living."[32] The in-between "past-present" is an important concept in understanding both Gorky's motivations and his art because, as we shall see, his art is a manifestation of this condition that is not always visible.

Interpreting the multiple layers present in both Gorky's art and life is complicated by what the artist did not speak of, left out of, or abstracted to the point of unrecognizability in his work, rather than what is present in it. Despite the ethereal qualities of his art, which mimic the spirit of the artist himself, Gorky's endeavors were clearly tied to questions about what it meant to be an artist in America during the mid-twentieth century, just at the moment when the focus of the art world, bound up with abstraction, was about to shift to the United States. Themes of historicity as justification for abstraction prompt this interdisciplinary and eclectic examination of Gorky's working method, tangential connection to other artists and movements, and use of abstraction.

Perhaps the best way to understand Gorky would be to view him as a punctum existing within a set of circumstances at a particular point and time, but influencing his art-related surroundings in a spherical rather than linear manner. The French literary and social theorist Roland Barthes' mechanism of the punctum provides a useful way to address both the artist and his art.[33] Although Barthes applies it as an explanation for a photograph that pricks or grabs the viewer's attention as a reference to the past, the relationship of the term "punctum" to the idea of punctuation applies to Gorky in many ways. A photograph punctuates the present with a reference to the past, but it also suggests that the past consisted of more than what is evident within the photographic frame. Gorky punctuates a transitional moment in art history: his work and his existence reference the past but also, through their abstracted composition, project onto the future because of the need for a viewer's interpretation or response to it. The most remarkable aspect of the device of the punctum, as it is applied to Gorky, is its power of expansion, in that it promotes the possibility that the artist's work can be understood in multiple contexts simultaneously.

Recognizing Gorky's art as a punctum also expands our comprehension of hi oeuvre. Within the entity of the punctum, what we know of Gorky and his art points toward many other outward elements. This is particularly true of Gorky's relationship to the Armenian Genocide, which is not something he addressed directly but is evident in his work partially through the personal and stylistic choices he made. A punctum is often evident only after the fact, and only now in retrospect, when we try to grapple with Gorky's meaning within art history and are left with the hole between two art movements that scholars have been trying to address for decades, can we determine Gorky's primacy to the era. The "blind field"[34] that results from the themes of this study increases vision, enhancing our understanding of the elements of a painting that relate to the life outside of it. Gorky's biography and self-fashioning in the past inform our interpretations of him in the present, and this in turn facilitates our interpretations of the art—both what the artist meant and our interpretation of it, and readings based upon our own experience with art and life.

Gorky's work itself is very much a punctum, containing both an absence because of what is unrecognizable, and something that grabs the viewer because of its familiarity. Often, amidst the unrecognizable and abstract shapes, we are enticed by an element that looks familiar—a bird, flower form, or partial body-like image—that has a synecdochic quality because it signifies both itself and the outside world. A work by Gorky is a punctum in its relating to its own internal composition, back to the work of the other artists, and to the landscapes or the sources upon which the composition was based. We can only fathom elements from the observed or remembered that exist in the works in retrospect, as they are an afterimage of sorts. Because Gorky's work is abstract and often undefined for the viewer, it exists also in a "blind field" in which the viewer completes it. Barthes says, "The *punctum*, then, is a kind of subtle *beyond*—as if the image launched desire beyond what it permits us to see: not only toward 'the rest' of the nakedness, not only toward the fantasy of a *praxis*, but toward the absolute excellence of a being, body and soul together."[35] Gorky's work, then, and even his biography, which is still being discussed, extend outwardly, forcing the viewer to adjudicate its meaning.

In the end, Gorky's is not the classic American tale of the triumphant outsider. Complicated and circuitous, his story, and the way it plays out and is interpreted in his art, is, as Schjeldahl says, right up our alley. Although one might muse about the direction of Gorky's art or what he might have produced or become, this book is about the fungible qualities inherent in Gorky's oeuvre—how, as a modern maker, he has reached mythic proportions, but also how this endeavor contributes to an understanding of his art that reflects contemporary concerns of self, difference, place, and space. By enlisting a combination of stylistic, historical, and theoretical knowledge and incorporating semiotic, psychoanalytical, philosophical, or sociological readings, we can synthesize the diverse attributes and meanings of Gorky's art. Explaining his art in terms of an ethnographic Modernism that reflects a teleological experience of twentieth-century America, while at the same time acknowledging that such endeavors expand beyond the examination of a singular artist at a particular juncture, induces plurality and multiple readings.

Neither Gorky nor his art is so provincial as to be concerned solely with hardships. "Tireless, fastidious and intolerant," as Elaine de Kooning described him, "Gorky reduced tragedy—his own or anyone else's—to the level of discomfort or irrelevancy, and in the light of his lack of sympathy, any misfortune lost its magnitude."[36] Never the victim, Gorky industriously learned techniques of art and being an artist. The struggle against displacement, to have an identity, and to produce abstraction is inherently about the need to produce art. Although Gorky's art offers no easy solutions, it is a tractable project to pursue its significance through the lens of these chapters, which, in turn, can assist each of us in attaining an individual understanding of it. This study, true to Gorky the entity and the manner in which his art functions, is a kind of sheaf, an assemblage with a complex structure that interlaces different threads and lines of meaning that go off in different directions just as they are about to be tied up.[37] The reader is left to determine what he or she wishes to rethink about Gorky and his art because its mutable meanings and indeterminate nature ultimately reflect Gorky's condition.

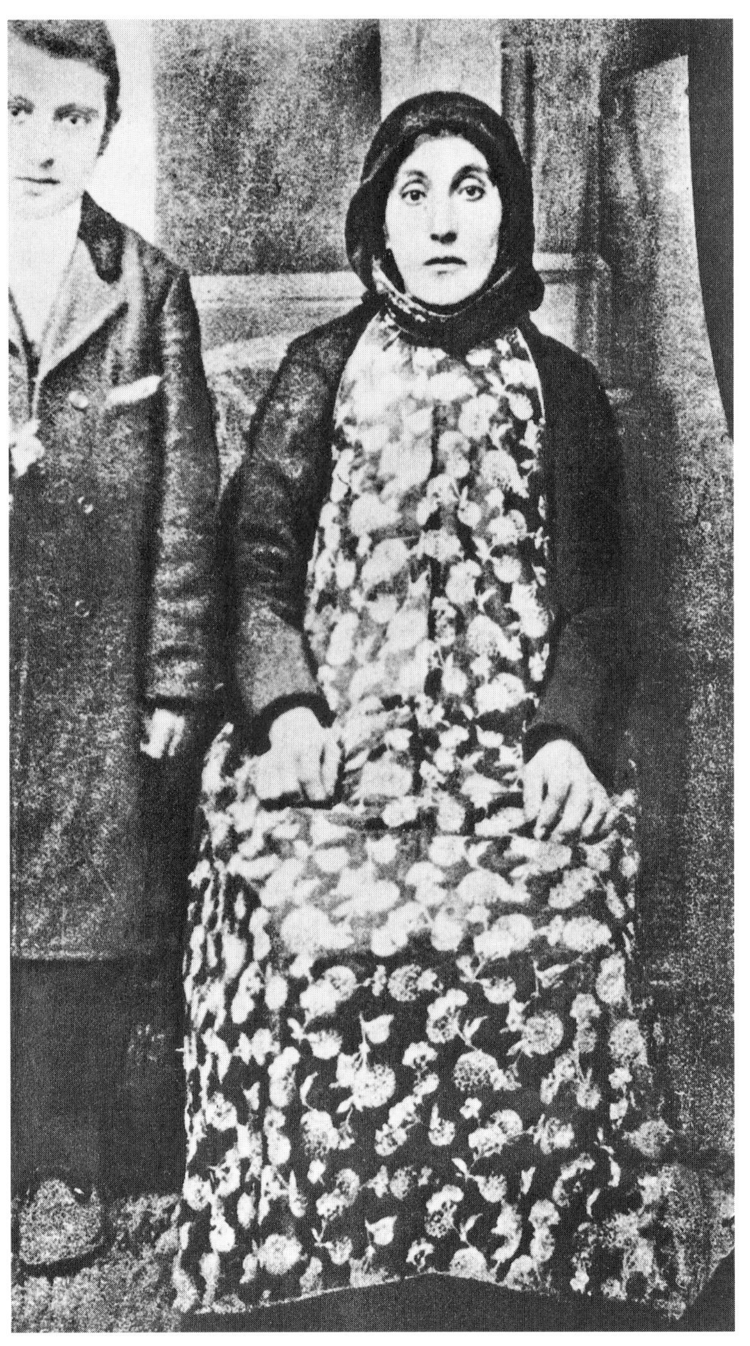

chapter 1

Genocide, Displacement, and Identity

Gorky's painting must be one of the great icons of immigration on which America was founded. It represents in all of its complexity the reality of which the Statue of Liberty is the symbol.

Gorky seems to be exploring his status as an outsider and the way in which this has made him an American. It is as though he had a heightened perception of the society and culture of which he had only recently become a part.

— DUNCAN MACMILLAN

Referring to Gorky's painting *The Artist and His Mother* (plate 1), the Scottish art writer Duncan Macmillan believed "that here for the first time was an art that was wholly American,"[1] precisely because it was painted by an immigrant who was conscious of his status as an outsider. The significance of Gorky's displacement is evident in the development of his artistic persona, which included abeying his origins, shifting his identity, and embracing the role of "artist". Considering Gorky as an exile or displaced person disengages him from Macmillan's romanticization, which casts Gorky as one of the huddled masses that the Statue of Liberty beckoned to become part of her ethnic stew. There is a certain *jouissance* in Gorky's work, a kind of being that begins with and eventually transcends the *Artist and His Mother* theme. Although this state of being involves identity, like Gorky's art, identity itself is fluid. In Gorky's case, identities—his own and those in his artwork—negotiate time, space, and place in a manner that serves the artist's method of self-instruction. As Howard Singerman has suggested, American art during Gorky's era was configured somewhat out of

Opening image detail of figure 5.

time and place because, in the absence of formal training provided through universities, learning about life was of seminal importance to the artist.[2]

Depending on context, the term "displacement" has numerous definitions, all of which, for the purposes of this discussion, it simultaneously embodies. The verb "displace" implies movement by external force, whether removal from a place or the act of replacing. Displacement, therefore, is the condition of having been displaced. In scientific terms, "displacement" is defined as a volume of air, water, or fluid that is displaced, moved, and then reoccupied by another object. In the Freudian psychoanalytic definition, "displacement" is a means by which an idea is made less painful or intense when it is transferred via a chain of associations. The Armenians were driven off their ancestral lands, which were then reoccupied by Muslims from Turkey and the Islamic world. Gorky immigrated to America and displaced observed or recognizable characteristics of works or scenes in front of him that triggered associations with his past. As we will see, Gorky's abstract compositions, through their reference to the recognizable world but failure to define it, produced compositions that have a displacing effect on the viewer.

Displacement, as Janet Wolff has effectively argued, can, in fact, "be quite strikingly productive" in a multitude of ways. "First," she says, "the marginalization entailed in forms of migration can generate new perceptions of place and, in some cases, of the relationship between places. Second, the same dislocation can also facilitate personal transformation, which may take the form of 'rewriting' the self, discarding the lifelong habits and practices of a constraining social education and discovering new forms of self-expression."[3] In other words, displacement precipitates the individual's volition for tending to physical and personal shifts, making biography mutable.[4]

Addressing sociohistorical fracturings like displacement caused by genocide elaborates Gorky's complicated triangulation of self-identification between exile, immigrant, and artist. E. H. Gombrich has noted that "no culture can be mapped out in its entirety, but no element of this culture can be understood in isolation."[5] Likewise, even though Gorky's background cannot be mapped out in its entirety, his art cannot be understood in isolation from it, particularly the seminal and brutal event of the Armenian Genocide.

Many factors, including economic, racial, and religious tensions, contributed to the Armenian Genocide.[6] The relationship between Turkey and the Armenians had been frequently strained since Turkic peoples overran the Armenian homeland, which had once included what became eastern Turkey, the Armenian Republic, and the northernmost tip of Iraq and upper northwest Iran. In addition, religious differences between the region's Muslim and Armenian Christian cultures were often emphasized as a cover for nationalistic and economic unrest. Hostility toward Armenians in Turkey expanded due to land claims in the eighteenth century and escalated in the late nineteenth and early twentieth centuries due to increased Armenian contact, trade, and cultural exchange with Europe. Initially, Armenian communities were victimized through exclusionary government policies, theft, murder, rape, and kidnapping by Turkish soldiers, citizens, and bands of nomadic Kurds, and included political oppression of Armenians by the Ottoman Empire from 1894 to 1896, when two hundred thousand Armenians were killed.[7]

In 1908, Gorky's father, Setrag, left his family, land, and home village of Khorkom on the shores of Lake Van in eastern Turkey and fled to America join his eldest son, Hagop, Gorky's half-brother, to avoid a military draft of Armenian men that often resulted in enslavement in brigades that worked the "soldiers" to death. In 1909, an additional twenty thousand Armenians were killed as a response to growing pan-Turkism, and in 1913 the ultranationalist Young Turk government came to power. Under the direction of the triumvirate pashas of Enver (minister of war), Talaat (minister of internal affairs), and Jemal (minister of the navy), Turkey killed over a million Armenians in 1915 through inhumane, unimaginable, or gruesome methods including mass murder, torture, starvation, rape, and enslavement.[8] Tribalism, ethnic boundaries, nationalism, and assertions of group identity likely played a role in the actions, but the obsession with killing and range of ways it was done perhaps suggests a group pathology that derived sadistic enjoyment from maximizing agony in a way that not only achieved simply death, but consumed the victims' humanity.[9] Despite worldwide acceptance of the Armenian Genocide as an unassailable fact, Turkey still refuses to acknowledge that it ever occurred, ignoring documented evidence, eyewitness accounts, and historical records. Such a refusal arguably perpetuates genocide and continues its assault on survivors, their offspring, and subsequent generations,[10] expanding both the human stain of the events and its trauma.

To escape the Armenian Genocide, like throngs of other Armenians, Gorky, his two older sisters, Akabi (Gorky's half-sister from his mother's first marriage, often also referred to as Ahko) and Satenig, his mother, Shushan, and his younger sister, Vartoosh, fled. They arrived in the easternmost region of the original Armenian kingdom, which was being overseen by the Russians. (The region was absorbed into the Soviet Union as the Armenian Union Republic and is now the nation of Armenia.) Gorky's father sent money to the family from America, but there was only enough to send the two older girls, with the additional help of Akabi's fiancé, to America to safety. Because the Turkish blockade of Armenia constrained food supplies from the West intended for the refugees (hence the infamous term "starving Armenians"), Gorky's mother died of starvation in 1919. Family lore states that she gave what little food she could to her children, especially Gorky as her only male offspring, and that she died while dictating a letter to Setrag saying that she could never leave her homeland.[11]

Biographies variously address Gorky's artistic training at this time, which may have consisted of drawing lessons in old country schools and exposure to art in an American missionary school, an Armenian secondary school in Yerevan, and limited knowledge gained in Tiflis before immigrating to America. With the help of family friends, Gorky and Vartoosh finally arrived in America on the S.S. *Presidente Wilson* in March 1920.[12] Reunited with Akabi and Satenig, they began living near Boston in Watertown, Massachusetts, an immigrant factory town with a large, concentrated Armenian population. Gorky did spend some time in Providence, Rhode Island, with his father and older half-brother, but it was not long before he became estranged from them.[13]

Like some Genocide survivors who experienced hardship while waiting to be rescued in Turkey, Gorky may have been angry that his father had, from his son's point of view, allowed family members to suffer and in particular, his mother to die.[14] In addition, Setrag also remarried, which reportedly angered Gorky, not only because he idolized his mother, but also likely because he felt it disrespectful to his mother's memory. For Setrag, widowed twice, it was his third marriage, which was not out of the ordinary for the time. Gorky's complicated status and family relations might be better understood through trauma theory and the application of writers such as Dominick LaCapra, who explains:

> The oceanic feeling, correlated with the presymbolic, pre-oedipal imaginary unity (or community) with the mother, would presumably also be lost by separation from the (m)other with the intervention of (the name of) the father and the institution of the symbolic under the sway of the phallus. When they are interpreted in a certain way, a similar conflation of absence and loss occurs with respect to the passage from nature to culture, the entry into language, the traumatic encounter with the "real," the alienation from species-being, the anxiety-ridden thrownness and fallenness of *Dasein,* the inevitable generation of the aporia, or the constitutive nature of melancholic loss in relation to the genesis of subjectivity.[15]

LaCapra refers to Heidegger's 1927 theory of *Dasein,* or "being there," which is a kind of authenticity. In addition, Gorky presumably experienced pre-Oedipal imaginary unity with his mother. The animosity toward his father, however, seems to invade the artist's psyche, perhaps contributing to his desire to change his name within years of their falling out.

Gorky's proximity to his patriarchal line becomes a traveling sign because of its relationship to his subsequent identity losses,[16] and his subjectivity, through the connection to his heritage, father, half-siblings, and sisters, and his roles as Armenian, son, and brother, travels throughout time. One can never be entirely sure, then, what Gorky signifies at any one moment. Such indeterminacy, however, is consistent with his identity as an Armenian, since, under Turkish rule and because of the Armenian Genocide, an Armenian's lineage itself was threatened. There was no recourse for Armenian women violated by Turkish men, and sometimes children resulted. Many Armenian women and children were given to Turkish families in order to keep them alive, but this effectively made them Turkish because they could no longer worship as Christians or identify with their Armenian culture without the danger of being identified as Armenian and risk losing their already tenuous social positions.[17] Assessing the effects of the Armenian Genocide on Armenians throughout time is difficult, but in Gorky's case, it influenced his identity and art.

Gorky was an exile, a particular kind of immigrant who was affected by transculturation and the impracticality of return.[18] Indeed, it was typical for some immigrants to move only temporarily to America to work at a time when there was less opportunity in their home countries, with the full intention of going back when they had made enough money or job availability or resources at home had improved. Literary theorist and cultural critic Edward Said's discussion of exile as a rupture is useful in considering Gorky's permanent predicament as an exile:

> Exile is strangely compelling to think about but terrible to experience. It is the unhealable rift forced between a human being and a native place, between the self and its true home: its essential sadness can never be surmounted. And while it is true that literature and history contain heroic, romantic, glorious, even triumphant episodes in an exile's life, these are no more than efforts meant to overcome the crippling sorrow of estrangement. The achievements of exile are permanently undermined by the loss of something left behind forever.[19]

There was, of course, no resolution for Gorky's exile during his lifetime, except, perhaps his own self-fashioning and artistic creation.

Gorky's displacement left him without a clear identity and may have prompted him to compensate for his succession of identity losses by pursuing art in America. Anny Bakalian, an expert on Armenian immigration matters and responsible for numerous studies and surveys, relates that Gorky's generation, fresh from and often haunted by a trauma they wished to forget, was concerned with getting a foothold in a new environment and did not consider themselves Americans.[20] Not only was "artist" a new identity, but it was one that addressed the condition of genocide itself. Genocide is an act that consumes humanity, yet creative acts like birth and art give back to humanity. Gorky's humanity had been threatened by genocide, and the option of working in a factory, arguably as a cog in a social and economic machine that also consumes humanity, was less likely to be rehumanizing than the act of painting. Furthermore, immersing oneself in any new experience was an alternative to feeling the trauma of the past life and identities attached to it. Trauma theorist Cathy Caruth has pointed out that trauma is not an event but a structure of experience,[21] and studies of

Armenian Genocide survivors have found that three out of four of them never spoke to anyone about their ordeal.[22] If, like Gorky, one changed subsequent experiences to those structured creatively, such as pursuing art, perhaps trauma could be overcome, or at least averted for awhile.

Looking at Gorky through the prism of immigration can inform an understanding of his identity construction, negotiation of the new world, development as an artist, and relationship to trauma. But immigration itself, the condition of being an immigrant in the United States in the modern industrial age, is complex. There had always been an antagonistic relationship in American society between native citizens and nonnative immigrants. The 1876 Centennial created an American self-image that discouraged difference,[23] and nativist thought increasingly veered toward racism. Immigrants have been discriminated against in various degrees continuously in America, with strong anti-immigrant movements since the 1880s. As the ever-expanding industrialization of America continued in the late nineteenth and early twentieth centuries, however, businesses and factories took on eager and inexpensive immigrant labor. To deal with these populations, moguls such as Henry Ford translated nationalist ideas into the "Americanization" (which might be read as "deprimitivization") of their workers by discouraging identification with their roots, "offering" to teach them English, and encouraging them to move out of the ethnic communities in which they lived.[24] Gorky's one-time friend Stuart Davis's remarks exemplify the attitude during the second quarter of the twentieth century, referring to immigrant children as "dirty hoodlum urchins from the reeking tenements" and "little beasts."[25]

Bakalian writes, "For some, assimilation into American society was a way of forgetting a painful past."[26] Certainly, individuals like Gorky who had experienced what he did—whether they were Armenians who had escaped the Genocide, Jews who had escaped pogroms in Russia, or Greeks who also had been targeted by the Turks—were placed in a precarious position when trying to build a new life. By leaving behind an often peasant background and ethnic roots, the immigrant embarked on the citizenship process and strove for an American ideal of upward mobility and embraced progress. Werner Sollors defines immigration as part of a codification of ethnicity in the United States and hypothesizes that ethnicity is in fact defined by difference.[27] The classifying term "ethnic" originated to explain differences between peoples. Throughout history this difference was often manifested by stereotyping and complicated by race. Therefore, difference, negatively tied to immigration, could be remedied in ways exemplified by Ford Industries.

Tactics enlisted in America to control immigration that could be considered exclusionary, xenophobic, or racist included a literacy requirement, which was finally enacted by Congress in 1917 after five defeats, and specific limitations on Asians, criminals, paupers, the diseased, and those deemed "immoral." The

1920s were a time of great social conflict, change, and backlash, with increasing nonnative populations subjected to more restrictive quotas. Just after Gorky arrived in March of 1920, the Red Scare was fueled in part by fear of foreign culture, ideas, and foreignness itself, as well as reports of "undesirables" fleeing wartorn Europe. In December 1920, just nine months after Gorky's arrival, the House of Representatives passed a bill to suspend all immigration for a year. The bill was rejected by the Senate, but the eventual outcome was the Immigration Act of 1924, which reduced quotas based on countries of origin under the auspices of making it easier to keep out undesirables, but whose result was to increase discrimination.

Against the backdrop of Prohibition, struggles between rural and big-city America, and mistrust among Protestant citizens of the largely Catholic immigrants, a naturalization debate also exposed the discriminatory nature of American society at the time. Armenians had to fight to retain naturalization status at the height of anti-immigration movements. The question first emerged in 1909, and in 1924 the government filed suit against the Armenians, claiming that they were not free white persons of Caucasian origin, but rather "mongoloid Turks." In addition to being racially targeted by the United States, Armenians must have found it painful to be doubly victimized by the Genocide in being denied access to freedom due to accusations that their identity was that of their oppressors. Eventually the courts determined that Armenians were Caucasian and thus should be allowed to stay in the country, but the presence of such a debate was evidence of the many layers of xenophobia that an immigrant such as Gorky must have been wary of in his new home.[28]

By becoming an artist, Gorky pursued culture as a strategy of survival. "Culture as a strategy of survival," Homi Bhabha writes, "is both transnational and translational. It is transnational because contemporary postcolonial discourses are rooted in specific histories of cultural displacement. . . . Culture is translational because such spatial histories of displacement . . . make the question of how culture signifies, or what is signified by *culture*, a rather complex issue."[29] Translation and negotiation is discontinuous. Because of the interruption of his culture, Gorky seemed on some level to embark on an attempt to balance his public and private identities to gain social capital. Gorky the immigrant had limited options within his scope of experience through which to gain capital in his new world. An immigrant could enter into his new world with economic capital, meaning finances, which Gorky did not have; human capital, in the form of education, of which Gorky had a sparse amount; and social capital, meaning some standing in society, of which most immigrants, by virtue of being immigrants, had little. Immigrants tended to strive for material security and education for themselves or their children, which then gave them some social standing. Gorky followed another route, opting to pursue social capital by becoming an artist, perhaps feeling it more readily available and attractive to him.[30]

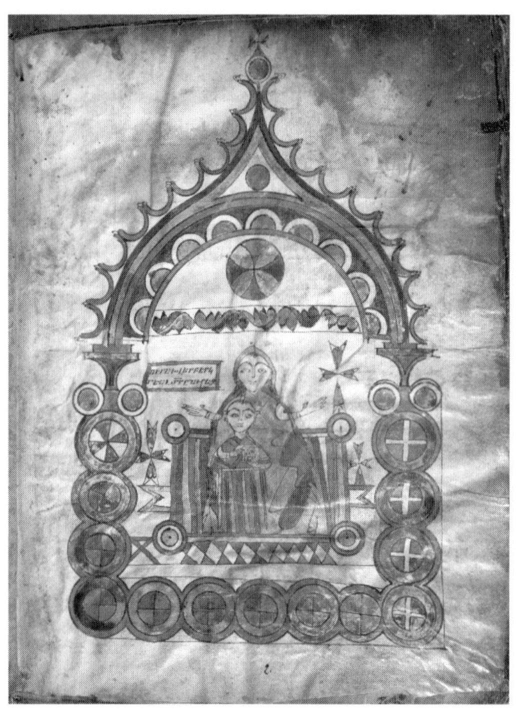

FIGURE 2
Anonymous, *Gospel of the Translators*, Armenian, nineteenth century. The Walters Art Museum, Baltimore.

A core question as to why Gorky decided to pursue art is inevitably related to, based upon, or somehow relevant to his status as an immigrant and/or determinations of race or ethnicity. Although Gorky's proclivity toward art may have stemmed from his formative years, when he viewed Armenian church art as a child and was exposed to art through the variety of jobs he held while in Armenia as an adolescent, or from encounters with it upon his arrival in the United States as a teenager, his reason or the impetus for his desire to practice art remains unclear. There is a long and proud tradition in Armenia of sculpture, mainly in the form of flat figural reliefs that adorn church exteriors and *khatchkars* (commemorative markers engraved with lattice-entwined crosses), similarly complicated jewelry and liturgical and ceremonial metal objects, or Byzantine wall or ceiling paintings much like those produced by the Armenian painters who traveled west to contribute to religious art during the medieval era. In Armenian art there was also an emphasis on manuscript painting, which could have been a source of Gorky's color choices, intricate abstracted design, and fluid lines, as a typical example reveals (fig. 2).

In the nineteenth century, the tradition continued of Armenian painters traveling to Europe or Russia to study in academies. The late nineteenth-century Armenian painter Gevorg Bashinjagyan left Signakhi, Georgia, to pursue art in Saint Petersburg. Hovhannes (Ivan) Aivazovsky,[31] who also studied in Saint Petersburg, was famous for his sea paintings; he was elected to numerous European academies, was respected by famous European painters such as Eugene Delacroix and J. M. W. Turner, and was awarded the French Legion of Honor. Martiros Saryan, a painter who worked primarily in watercolor and tempera beginning around the time of the inception of the Soviet Union, strove to represent nature symbolically as a "living entity." Gorky was therefore in some ways continuing an old-country tradition while resisting new-country cultural pressures.

It is possible that Gorky's artistic volition lends itself to a manner of negotiating the specific and global complications of immigration—that is, whether to assimilate or not. David Anfam has emphasized the difficulties inherent in Gorky's migration from one culture to another: "It was a remarkable leap to pass from an exotic, still almost feudal land in Asia Minor to a sophisticated technocratic Western nation at the start of the Jazz Age. Two choices met such immigrants who underwent America's so-called 'melting pot' experience. They could either assimilate themselves to their new destiny or retain the unwilling emigrant's longing for what had been left behind. Gorky was predisposed towards the second alternative."[32]

Always a bit of a loner, from 1920 to 1925 Gorky may have resisted assimilation into the new Armenian American subculture, characterized by industrialized shoemaking, textiles, and manufacturing, by painting pictures and looking at art in museums. Anny Bakalian characterizes the deliberate choices that immigrants make to balance their practical and cultural survival: "assimilation and ethnic maintenance do not just 'happen' to immigrant groups. Immigrants are not passive victims in the drama that forces them to make choices between their cultural survival and their mundane, existential survival. . . . The Armenian-American subculture is a creative adaptation to a new and different life."[33] Gorky's displacement, then, was both physical and ideological, and his behavior, in an attempt to gain social capital, could have been, at least initially, both an avoidance of and splitting off from his transient identity.

Gorky began painting shortly after arriving in America. The well-known tale about his being fired from the Hood Rubber Plant in Watertown for drawing on the warehouse ceiling or on the crates that were used to move shoe soles follows the format typical of the artist-genius myth that Ernst Kris and Otto Kurz discuss. In their overview of stories about artists and anecdotes about their training, they record the commonality of an artist's talent being described as innate and invariably manifesting itself in uncontrollable bursts of creativity that cannot be restrained by society or circumstances.[34] Gorky's insistence on making art, whatever his situation, might also have had deeper consequences or could be read in additional ways: as a conscious rebellion against the capitalist orientation of immigrant communities,[35] as a manifestation of Gorky's desire to shift his identity from immigrant or Armenian to artist, or as an adaptation to a new and different life that sought out social capital. Such a tale about Gorky's incessant drawing could also simply reveal the artist's desire to be an artist, which plays back into the myth of the artist that Kris and Kurtz define. Ironically, the pursuit of art seems to have resolved Gorky's employment dilemma, since by 1922 he was teaching art at Boston's New School of Design.

As a new artist in a new world, Gorky seems to have gained some economic and human capital through his pursuit of social capital. His role as an educator positioned him to gain credibility in the Armenian immigrant culture, from which he was becoming more distant. Within the Armenian community in the old country and by transference in the new, the profession of teaching was an acceptable alternative to factory work, the trades, and small business or shop ownership. Education had always been important to the culture. Despite harassment in Turkey, Armenians had continued to run schools or teach their children in an effort to remain literate. Gorky's identity as an educator, then, is a performance of cultural positionality.[36]

Moving away from his family and the tight-knit Armenian community in Watertown by 1925 and going to New York City to teach in New York, Gorky literally shifted his positionality. The purpose of the move was presumably to become an artist, and it made for Gorky the opportunity to start anew in terms of identity. "In choosing his vocation," says Harold Rosenberg, "the immigrant chooses whom he shall become."[37] Indeed, Gorky chose whom to become by fabricating a new name, thereby creating a fresh persona through which to act. Rosenberg has conceptualized naming as an extension of identity or self-creation. "The immigrant," Rosenberg explains, "is a self-made man. Making oneself (self-creation) is not, however, far distant from making oneself up (self-invention) and from make-up (self-disguise)."[38] According to Rosenberg, Gorky's choice to look, act, and live like an artist can be associated with an immigrant's actions of creation, invention, and disguise. The fabricated name, however, while it contributes to an imagined persona, is not necessarily a camouflage, as Rosenberg implies, but rather can be viewed as a manner of self-fashioning.

The creative act of self-fashioning, arguably, is part of an effort of rehumanization in the aftermath of genocide. It is a reassertion of a self after it has been displaced within a new world. Renaming represents one of the first steps in rebuilding one's life after displacement and trauma. The word "trauma" has been adapted from a medical term defining physical wounding. In many cases of medical trauma, repercussions can be permanent in the form of brain damage from head trauma or scarring from cuts in the skin. Gorky's self-fashioning, then, in this manner, is a scarring over, the organic result of traumatic displacement, rather than an outright disguise. Gorky's identity and his art cannot be separated from displacement and trauma, but are made up out of them in spite of any internal or external attempts to negate their impact.

Identity, if conceived as both an internal and external force—the way one conceptualizes oneself in the world and the way the world conceptualizes one—may have also been alienating. Self-identity, an important theme in Rosenberg's work, is an existential struggle, and one that can relate to ethnic self-definition. The art historian Matthew Baigell explains that Rosenberg, like fellow critic Clement Greenberg and Jewish artists in America after the Holocaust, was caught in the aftermath of being Jewish post–World War II: "By finding the basis of art making in existentialist activity, Rosenberg neatly sidestepped any question of confronting the Holocaust in art, of the artist bringing an agenda to his or her art or, in the instance of Jewish American artists, of wanting to identify themselves as Jews through their art. Indeed, it would seem that the artist should be bereft of everything on which to build an identity but his or her essential personality. Like Greenberg, Rosenberg, too, appeared to want to leave behind the parochial world of Jewish culture, history, and heritage."[39] According to Baigell, some post-Holocaust individuals loathed their prior identities.[40] Although the

Holocaust postdates the Armenian Genocide, the identity politics inherent in Gorky's renaming reflect Baigell's criticism of Rosenberg and Greenberg in that the artist's (or critic's) immersion in the idea of "art as self-creation" is an existential activity. Such a belief kept one's own culture, history, and heritage at bay. Gorky's denial, or omitting of his Armenian identity when among the general population, is consistent with studies of Armenian Genocide survivors who refused to identify with their own personal trauma.[41]

Self-identification itself refers to that punctal moment that the French poststructuralist psychoanalyst and psychiatrist Jacques Lacan describes when a child finally recognizes its reflection in a mirror. Yet, as Laura Mulvey has so aptly pointed out, this is a misrecognition because it adopts an alienated self-image, one that exists outside itself as an ideal ego and that constitutes a matrix of the imaginary.[42] Art as a means of self-identity became part of a complicated web of the modern experience. Arthur Danto, rethinking art within a postmodern framework, has proclaimed that self-definition is the "historical truth of Modernist art."[43] Modern art, therefore, is aware of its own identity. Perhaps, then, the primary motive of the modern artist is a self-conscious pursuit, but one that primarily exists in a matrix of the imaginary. Gorky's life, work, and career seem to affirm this assertion. In broader terms, the exchange between Gorky's ethnic origins and his identity as an artist is part of a larger human condition.

The imaginary matrix can also extend between the artist and his art. According to Rosenberg, during the modern era "the identity of the artist is a paramount theme. The concept of art as creation brings the artist literally into the picture."[44] As an immigrant, Rosenberg himself, as Baigell asserts, must have been aware of prejudice, in his case, anti-Semitism. Gorky's renaming, however, was not necessarily an attempt to hide from oneself, or the internal, as it seems to have been for Rosenberg,[45] but rather a way to address the external. Gorky might even have changed his name to a familiar Russian pseudonym in part to avoid bigotry toward obscure Middle Eastern nationalities, as evidenced in the 1924 naturalization controversy. Such self-fashioning became a way to formulate a new identity that perhaps avoided or escaped the past, making it a negotiation rather than a negation.

The artist's name, then, delineates a particular manner of existence and discourse.[46] Depending on how the name itself and Gorky's renaming are interpreted, it can also contribute to analyses of his art. Serving a purpose beyond descriptive, a name assigns a conventional identity, and, in doing so, may simultaneously exclude other identities. When multiple identities are considered together, the result is multivalent. Immigrants of Gorky's era had a peculiar relationship to names and naming. Some were renamed at Ellis Island because officials did not understand or know how to spell a name. Others renamed themselves in order to get jobs. For many it was easier to assume an anglicized name than to try to explain how to read or pronounce an ethnic one or elaborate upon its origins. That Gorky seems to have placed considerable emphasis on making and remaking his identity suggests additional interpretations and meanings for his renaming.

According to Anny Bakalian's research on Armenian American generations, "Genocide survivors undergo identity crises. They feel robbed of their faith and their patrimony,"[47] and they see no hope of ever returning 'home.'" More broadly, Edward Said states that exiles are "cut off from their roots, their land, their past."[48] Gorky's original Armenian surname, Adoian, was a referent for those roots, an indexical sign for a people who held certain lands or had a particular status or fixed identity within a region or group. Armenian surnames traditionally end in the suffix "ian" or "yan," meaning "of" or "from," which makes them a referent for one's origins.[49] The surname designates a family of or from a specific place, profession, or lineage. Gorky's first name, Vosdanig, which means "little Vosdan" or perhaps "sweet Vosdan," refers to his mother's ancestral home south of Lake Van.[50] At an early age, after his paternal grandfather Manoug's death and in his honor, his father's relatives began to call Vosdanig Manoug, which was also the boy's baptized name. Because Gorky was still called Vosdanig by his mother's relatives, he simultaneously had two names or two identities. Thus, Gorky's original name represented a culmination of family legacies, and he was in turn a living signifier of them.[51]

Displacement becomes a particular state of suspension and loss for men's traditional roles and familial rights. The literary critic and feminist theorist Susan Gubar speaks of Jewish men after the Holocaust in terms that apply to the case of male survivors of displaced peoples like the Armenians, who, "even if they inherited the patronymic[,] could never become the heirs of their fathers' places, properties, or positions and instead had to invent a line of inheritance quite distinct from one denied them in the process of dehumanization."[52] An invented name can mark uniqueness but can also forge the creation of an imagined self that is refigured after being drained of its humanity through ethnic cleansing. The French writer, philosopher, and literary theorist Maurice Blanchot suggests that one must detach from disaster as a manner of survival. "One cannot believe in it," Blanchot explains in his own disjunctive prose, "whether one lives or dies. Commensurate with it there is no faith, and at the same time a sort of disinterest, detached from disaster."[53] Gorky, because of his intermediate positionality and past trauma, needed to split from the past in order, like most Armenians, to make pain invisible in his new life.

Homi Bhabha's predicament of an "in-between" existence bracketed by binaries is a hybrid in which "private and public, past and present, the psyche and social develop an interstitial intimacy. It is an intimacy that questions binary divisions through which such spheres of social experience are often spatially opposed."[54] As an immigrant, Gorky was subject to a spatiality of the social that already existed within a binary system of insider and outsider, and he had already experienced rupture from the context of his original life and identity.[55] Art, or being an artist, could offer stability and be a means of negotiating the in-betweenness of his existence. It also seemed to be a way to negotiate the existence of an Armenian immigrant in the new world because as a teacher, he could be an economic contributor without working in a factory or selling items in a store, and as an artist, he could, in the creative endeavors through which he worked toward regaining his humanity, reflect the agrarian and simple existence of his past.

Gorky invested a significant amount of thought in selecting for his new identity a new name, which in some way had to be as relevant as the old one. Inspired by American Western movies, he considered taking the name Archie Gunn, but his eventual choice of an ethnic name may have served as a good cover for his accent and avoided complete assimilation. "Arshile" may be a form of the royal "Achilles," a variation of the Armenian king Arshak's name, or a derivative of the Armenian word "aysaharel," meaning possessed by evil but also likely used more affectionately and facetiously for a rambunctious individual, especially a mischievous child. It took Gorky some time to settle on the spelling of his new first name. Initially it was Arshel, Arshele, or Arshille, but these variations were most likely attempts to find the correct phonetic spelling. [56] For Gorky, identity was malleable and seemed to have both a public and private side. The payroll transcript from the General Service Administration Records, for instance, when he worked for the WPA Mural Division, lists him as Arsmile,[57] but it is not known whether this was the artist's doing or simply a typo on the government's part. At the same time, Gorky kept a bank account under the name Manuk Adoian (influenced by the Eastern Armenian translation of the name) while he was publicly Arshile Gorky.[58] Such deliberation on Gorky's part indicates a crucial consciousness of naming, labels, and titles and their relationship to history.

Names, as verbal objects, are endowed with their own figurality. Art historian Paul Barolsky, in a discussion of nomenclature, explains that names are, in fact, histories, not solely labels, and can have deeper meanings. Names can even be jests, Barolsky says, particularly in the case of renaming or nicknames that reveal physical attributes, detractions, or aspects of an individual's character. In this context, names even become iconic signs. "Names are, in short," says Barolsky, "the crystallization of history. They tell us about persons and places, about cities and streets, about anatomical and cartographical details, about professions and works, about personality and moral character, about the cultural values of an age, and about those who were once honored. Names are clues to history lived and history imagined."[59] Shakespearean scholar Stephen Greenblatt notes that sixteenth-century literary figures understood "the fashioning of human identity as a manipulable, artful process."[60] The idea of self-fashioning, then, is a historic one among artists, while also an artistic creation in and of itself.

Reemerging in a new country as a new person, Gorky poised himself for entry into a new community, that of artists. Kris and Kurz argue that artists created their own mythologies by recounting or creating stories about their artistic training, proficiency in art, or professional associations.[61] Building a new history for himself in America from scratch, "Arshile Gorky" asserted himself to be the cousin of writer Maxim Gorky and created a false pedigree of artistic training. Harold Rosenberg points out that Gorky "palmed himself off in a newspaper interview as the cousin of the famous writer and delivered himself of high-toned opinions about American women, skyscrapers, and the future of art in this materialistic country; incidentally, he claimed to have studied painting in Paris, like any good Russian." Maxim Gorky, whose real name was Alexei Maksimovich Peshkov, chose for himself a surname that meant in Russian "the bitter one." Therefore, Gorky's choice of another artist's surname, itself a pseudonym,[62] redoubles signification of the name as an artistic creation while accepting that its significance is sometimes imposed.

The artist Gorky had likely been familiar with the writer Gorky's works and may have noted similarities in their biographies, prompting a camaraderie that influenced the name choice.[63] English translations of Maxim's *The Mother* and *My Childhood* were available in the United States as early as 1907 and 1915, respectively, and the silent-film version of *The Mother* appeared in 1926.[64] *The Mother* is based on events that took place in the town of Sormovo involving a worker, Pyotr Andreyevich Zalomov, and his mother, Nilovna, who were devoted to the revolutionary cause. Gorky himself and his family took up arms against Turkish soldiers in Van City during their escape from Khorkom to Armenia.[65] *My Childhood* was the first of three autobiographical accounts by Maxim sometimes classified as an act of exorcism because they remember a difficult life. The early stages of Maxim's autobiography are akin to Arshile's life. *My Childhood* describes an absent father and brutal grandfather and leaving home at a young age, and *My Apprenticeship* (the Russian title was *In the World*) and *My Universities* describe an extensive self-education. Interestingly, much as Arshile is recognized as an impeccable draftsman, Maxim is revered as an acute observer with great descriptive powers.

Gallery owner Julien Levy insisted that Arshile created the connection to Maxim as a joke,[66] meaning that it was up to others to find the mistake. The act of taking on an identity that was also a pseudonym negated the significative quality of the name and actually referred back to the individual in a reflexive manner that *questioned* his identity. The referent, that is, the individual referred to as Arshile Gorky, therefore hovers between the literal and figurative, his identity fluid.[67] The significance of this in-betweenness, like the interstitial concept advocated by Bhabha, is quite in keeping with Gorky's position in Turkey as an Armenian even before his displacement to America. Armenians in Turkey were already a partial hybrid, often speaking a version of Armenian adulterated with

Turkish expressions, like contemporary Spanglish in America, and whose dances, food, and culture in some aspects were impurely Armenian, often intertwined with Turkish culture and Middle Eastern precedents.

Naming, or the art of renaming, can also be linked to rebirth, by which the name becomes both reinvention and resignification. Rebirth was a prevalent idea in American art, particularly leading up to Abstract Expressionism, the first internationally significant American art movement.[68] The idea of renaming as rebirth is worth considering. William Saroyan, a well known writer born in America to Armenian-immigrant parents, writes of rebirth as an important part of the artist's life:

> Everyone is born. The difference between artists and others . . . is that artists are born twice.
>
> The second birth takes place sometime before the artist dies, usually before he is twenty, in most cases much earlier, so that by the time an artist is thirty his art and his identity are inseparable. One acts on the other, art continuously seeking to purify identity, and identity, as a rule, insisting on making art more human, less lonely in dimension, as it were.[69]

In this passage, Saroyan formulates identity and rebirth as purification and as facilitators of self-realization. Saroyan's idea of rebirth, however, did not include changing one's name, which could be viewed as an act of assimilation, and he disapproved of Gorky for doing so.[70] Anny Bakalian claims that "assimilation and the changing nature of Armenianness are not acts of callous betrayal, but innovative responses to changing structural conditions and personal needs."[71] For Gorky, rebirth was also a cultural translation.

Changing an Armenian surname, as Gorky did, disconnected him from the dispersed members of the Armenian diaspora and made him unidentifiable as one of them. Saroyan felt that Gorky should not have tried to appear Russian but should have remained Armenian, so that his success reflected positively on all Armenians.[72] Conversely, failure, of which Gorky seems to have been afraid, could mar the family name and reputation as well as the ethnic one.[73] Ironically, the complete removal of an Armenian name, by figuratively wiping out an existence identified as Armenian, may actually have achieved the deracination that had been attempted by Turkey through genocide.

Renaming, however, also disassociated Gorky from his connection with the "starving Armenians," who, because of genocide and Turkish blockades, appeared as emaciated and downtrodden creatures in newspaper accounts. It also kept him from being identified as a hyphenated American, who at the time was typically a blue-collar factory worker subject to xenophobia. It is possible that if Gorky had been classified as Armenian during his career, it might have made his work more likely to be dismissed. Matthew Baigell identifies this same problem for Jewish artists, particularly after the Holocaust: "Very few wanted to be labeled 'a Jewish artist.' In calling attention to his or her Jewishness, such artists might be attacked or neglected and be likely to lose his or her supportive public."[74] Jewish artists, therefore, may have essentially denied their identities in order to survive in an unsympathetic world.

By changing his name, Gorky escaped identification as a victim and some level of discrimination,[75] but he also implied a connection to the Russians who saved Armenians at the siege of Van and allowed Gorky and his family to reach safety in Armenia. Gorky was also one of many Armenians at the time who saw hope for an Armenian nation in the area; it instead became a republic of the Soviet Union. Teaching at the New School of Design in New York, he earned respect from his students for his knowledge of art and his abilities. He spent time with John Graham and Willem de Kooning; frequented the Gypsy Tavern, where he met the photographer Wyatt Davis in 1927; encountered Isamu Noguchi in 1929 at a short-lived museum; and was a regular at the restaurant Romany Marie's two or three nights a week, where he met with Stuart Davis and whoever else dropped by. In the 1930s, the Works Project Administration provided Gorky a similarly supportive community of artists. Within these communities, he would be respected as an artist, regardless of his origins, as long as he proved himself a viable one.

These artists began a new legacy, choosing whom to become while forging a new American art. Many of Gorky's sometime companions and fellow immigrant artists had changed their names as well. Also making new identities for themselves in New York were the Armenian-born sculptor Raoul Hague, born Haig Heukelekian, and the Russian-born painter John Graham, born Ivan Dabrowski. Along with many artists in America in the first half of the twentieth century who came from elsewhere, such as the Lithuanian-Jewish Mark Rothko (Mark Rothkowitz) and the Dutch Willem de Kooning, these artists helped develop an aesthetic that catapulted New York into the center of the international art scene. Subjected to the persistent charge that modern art in America was a foreign import,[76] the group was interested in creating a visual language that would transcend individual and cultural boundaries. The aesthetic collectivity of modern American art that emerged from social contact, discussions of subjectivity and style, and ideological similarities was identified by critics in retrospect as Abstract Expressionism.

Relocation seems to have informed a language of Modernism. Cultural historian and theorist Raymond Williams, in writing of the passage from the rural to the urban, speaks of an immigrant's passage as well: "It cannot too often be emphasized how many of the major innovators were, in this precise sense, immigrants. . . . Liberated or breaking from their national or provincial cultures, placed in quite new relations to those other native languages or native visual traditions,

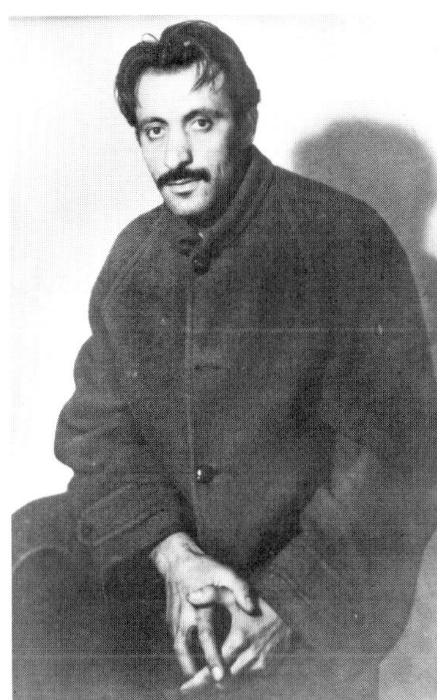

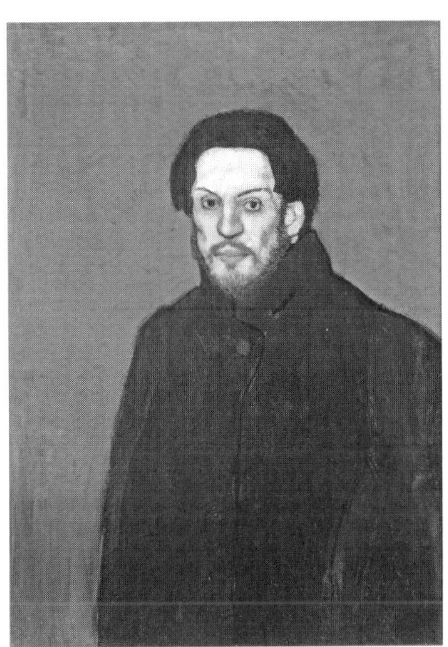

FIGURE 3
Photograph of Arshile Gorky, 1933.

FIGURE 4
Pablo Picasso, *Self-Portrait with Cloak,* 1901. Musée Picasso, Paris.

encountering meanwhile a novel and dynamic common environment . . . these artists and writers and thinkers . . . found the only community available to them: a community of the medium; of their own practices."[77] Gorky was attracted to masters of Modernism and the community of artists in New York City not only because of their modernity, but because of his displacement and theirs, which appears to have been both a bond to an old world and a method of negotiating a new one through modern visual precedents. By displacement I mean displacement from society as moderns who must find and form their own community within which to define themselves. As Williams indicates, this community is one based on their practices, in which Modernism substitutes for society.

In the role of artist, it seems, Gorky triumphed over being an involuntary immigrant. As fellow immigrant artist Milton Resnick has pointed out, "the thing about being an immigrant is that you're made to feel you're always in the wrong. The choice is: whether you want to cover that up, or whether you are going to pick up your head and spirit and have a little fun over it. If the latter is selected, then you know Gorky's way."[78] Gorky's friend Margaret Osborne has suggested that Gorky's dark hair, tall stature, and mustache encouraged a perception of him as a solemn, brooding artist. She explains that Gorky did not dress to play that role, but rather, "they cast him in one,"[79] making his identity the manifestation of both internal and external expectations. However, a comparison between a photograph of Gorky in his long, dark coat (fig. 3) and a 1901 Picasso self-portrait (fig. 4), of which Gorky was likely aware, suggests that artifice may have played a role in Gorky's identity construction. Stuart Davis explains that "Gorky himself provided the punch-line to this dramatic impact. Nature had provided him with a tall, dark

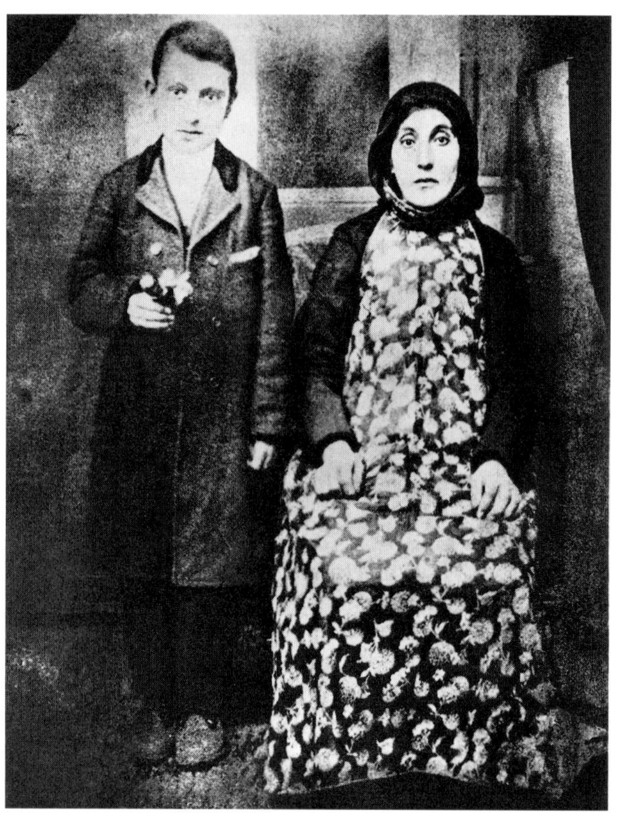

FIGURE 5
Photograph of the artist and his mother, 1912.

and impressive aspect easily identifiable with the 'artist-type' by persons who had taken the trouble to inform themselves on these matters."[80] This dramatic external appearance, coupled with his name, affixed to Gorky identities like costumes or masks.[81] It would seem that both aspects are true, with Gorky playing a role for which he was suitably cast and enacting the spectatorial. Apparently enamored by an audience, Gorky often welcomed visitors to his studio to watch him paint.[82] He may well have been aware of the difference in the way he viewed himself and the way others interpreted him and played up the latter, which then translated to his work. Although welcoming visitors into his studio was performative, it was also part of his genuine excitement with art and desire for his visitors to share his enthusiasm for materials, gesture, and line.

The roles of the artist channel into the role of cultural mediator, which ultimately filters down to the artist's work. Macmillan, writing in 1979, interprets Gorky's painting *The Artist and His Mother* as an icon of immigration and a vehicle through which the artist explores his status as an outsider. Rosenberg, in 1962, asserts that the portrait is an act of cultural exchange, although on a more personal level, one that reinscribes the significance of the name: "[Gorky] had to bridge the distance between the child named Vosdanig Adoian, shown in the photograph with his young mother in her flowered peasant apron, and the vanguard painter [fig. 5] of the Paris School (though he had never been to Paris) who called himself Gorky, after the Russian writer, whose 'Gorky' was also a pseudonym."[83] Gorky bridged the distance making his identity and performance as an artist a transfiguration of the worlds of the artist and viewer and playing the role of the displaced and disenfranchised foreigner and avant-garde visionary capable of unifying various national aesthetics into a more international one. Both Macmillan's and Rosenberg's views reflect hindsight in the aftermath of battles over pluralism and assimilation that morphed into an appreciation of the maverick qualities of Abstract Expressionism.

The transformation of the Armenian refugee Vosdanig Adoian into the persona known as Arshile Gorky is revealing for both Modernist art and twentieth-century history. Although no Horatio Alger story, the artist's life included a struggle to exist in a state of dislocation, which propelled him beyond individual consequence and toward a significance that can inform our readings of Modernist artists and the art they produced. The artists of American Modernism collected in New York City, a locus of industrial, commercial, and financial leadership, and their resolve to become artists seems to have fulfilled an existential need to reconcile past and present.[84]

While Gorky was negotiating the mental space of self-fashioning and artistic creation and the physical space of displacement and reentry into an artistic diaspora, he explored what became the existential dilemma of Abstract Expressionism: what it means to live, to be, in both a human and historical sense. From his early career in New York, Gorky was on the radar of Lloyd Goodrich at the Whitney Museum of American Art, and Alfred Barr, the Museum of Modern Art director, said that he remembered "hearing of Gorky late in 1929, the autumn our museum opened its doors." [85] Barr recalled going to Gorky's studio early in 1930 and being impressed immediately by "Arshile's seriousness as an artist and his charm as a person,"[86] to the extent that Barr included him in An Exhibition of Work of 46 Painters and Sculptors Under 35 Years of Age.

The bifurcated condition of displacement that had led Gorky to grapple with his placement in the new world came to be successfully applied to and expressed through, his art and the art of his time. As with the characters in Richard Hagopian's 1952 novel *Faraway the Spring*, the difficulty of Gorky's displacement plays out through his existence as an artist. In the novel, Doctor Danielian, the sick Setrak, and Maryam talk of life in the new world. Maryam observes, "It's a strange world that most of us have come to, a place we don't really understand. Perhaps that is why some of us behave the way we do." The doctor replies, "Of course it is different to be in one's own country, but when we have no country we must live as best we can."[87] Gorky lived as best he could through his art and, in doing so, contributed to the life of American Modernism.

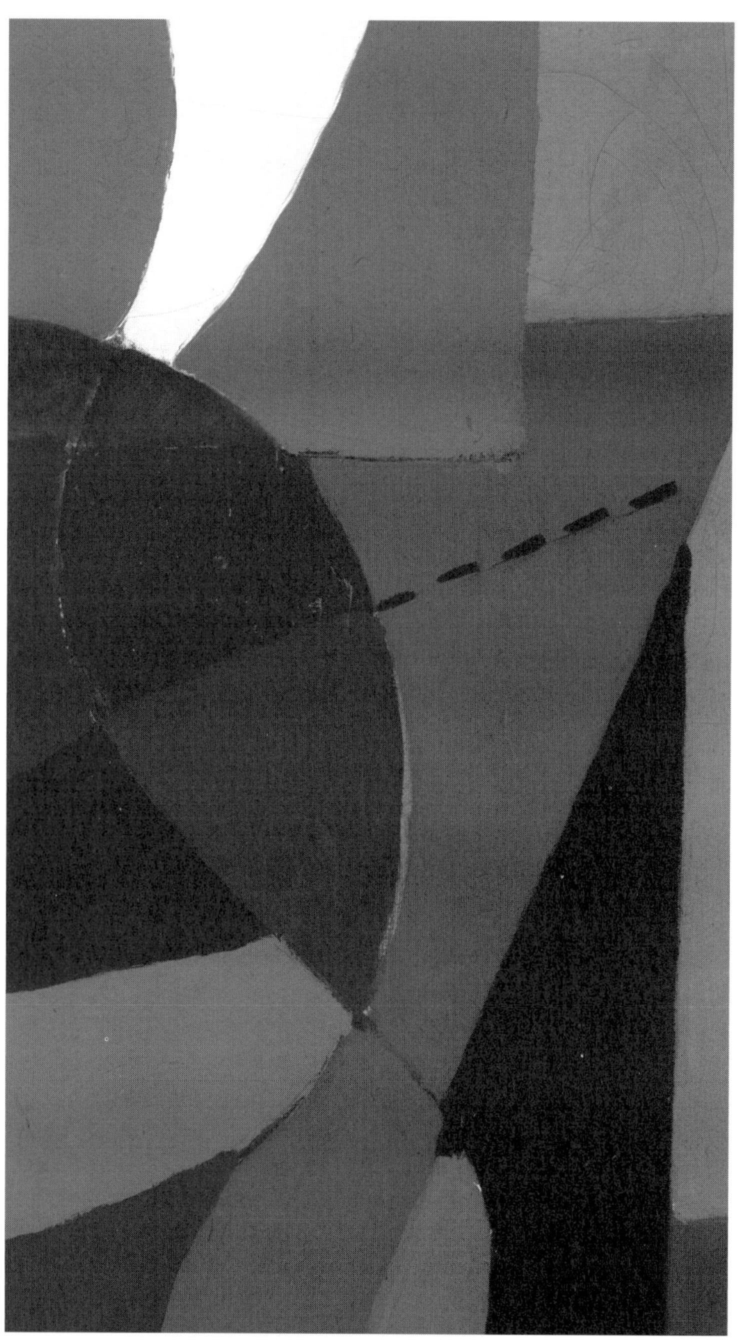

chapter 2

Constructions of Gender, Self, and Other

He had felt he could create a woman, as he had created his art. . . . He instinctively had tried to use the same process he had used in his work, a process of trial and error, infinitely patient renewed efforts toward the full-fleshed embodiment of an ideal perfection whose shadow lay cool, abstract and substanceless on the interior wall of his mind.

—ETHEL SCHWABACHER

Like many artists, Gorky related to the world primarily through his art. Although he is perhaps best known for his abstractions, Gorky's portraiture served an important purpose, particularly early in his career. Through it, he explored various art styles, pursued his own identity, and visually remade others. He often painted himself in the guise of famous artists, further adopting the persona of artist and shedding the predetermined role of immigrant. Gorky's portraits of his dead mother, immigrant sisters, unidentified women, and wife were complicated by his relationship to them, but these works simultaneously served the artist's development.

Ethel Schwabacher, Gorky's longtime student and the first to write at length about the artist, identified his tendency to remake the women in his life as if they were paintings. In the epigraph above, Schwabacher, whose own oeuvre reflects the influence of years of study with Gorky, notes that Gorky's revisions succeeded only within the paintings themselves. The formal motifs, however, such as the depictions of eyes, simplifications of contour lines, and

Opening image detail of plate 9.

dissipations of specific detail that recurred in his works, arguably became ideogrammatic. In Gorky's modifications of the observed, in this case the women in his life, he followed Modernist practice. By adapting visible form, he exemplified the Modernist mantra that the artist's conception takes precedence over anything that could actually be perceived. In addition, it seems that just as Gorky had considered several possibilities while deciding on his assumed name, he tested out several possible compositions for each painting, variably rethinking or emphasizing different parts.

The two versions of Arshile Gorky's *The Artist and His Mother,* one in the Whitney Museum of American Art in New York City and the other in the National Gallery of Art in Washington, D.C. (plate 2), loom large in discussions of the artist and his art. Two reasons for the attention paid to these images in an otherwise abstract artist's oeuvre are that recognizable images are more easily discerned and contemplated and that the artist worked on them fairly consistently in an organic manner throughout his career.[1] Gorky's process of creating each work, obsessing over its line, color, and form, became his existence, and it is precisely the nonillustrative qualities of the works that make them successful. By enumerating the way that he adapted the observed and recomposed it in different ways in different versions, these paintings also serve as a basis for Gorky's engagement with art, his past, his self-definition, and his aesthetic trajectory. Within the *Artist and His Mother* paintings are the seeds of Gorky's abstraction and the examples of cultural overlay and adaptation that were precipitated by his displacement and renaming.

The Whitney version of *The Artist and His Mother* consists of cool, muted blues and grays, and the figures look out from the picture plane with eyes slightly askew. The National Gallery version is washed with pinks and umbers, and the faces are flat and frontal, appearing to engage the viewer more directly. Visually accessible because of their representational form and the well-known photograph upon which they are based (see fig. 5), these works are a key to understanding Gorky's displacement, the stylistic underpinnings of his work, and the process of his artistic development. Through the subject of *The Artist and His Mother,* Gorky emphasized a pictorial composition through flattened shapes and deemphasized rendering in a manner that bridges his past and the Modernist formal concerns of his present.

Standing next to his seated, matronly mother, who wears a melancholic expression on her flat, disk-like face, Gorky as a young boy timidly holds a tiny bouquet of flowers, as if deciding whether or not to offer them to the viewer. Despite the works' debts to Ingres, such as the frontal pose, curvy female form, and large areas of color that construct the figures,[2] these are not portraits that meticulously depict their sitters. The hands are fingerless, almost bandaged-looking, and there are areas where figure is not differentiated from background. As in the works of other Modernist artists, such as Matisse and Picasso, details in

Gorky's works appear secondary to shape, color, and composition. Perhaps this moderate erasure underscores the power that the image invokes when complemented by the common knowledge that Gorky's mother died of starvation in his arms while escaping the twentieth century's first genocide. Indeed, this knowledge imbues the artwork with a narrative of duplicity and loss. The challenge of memory itself, or remembering, is therefore inherent in the Modernist conventions of the works' physical qualities.

Gorky's budding Modernist concern for conception over perception is evident in the way the forms in the paintings are reduced to essential parts and removed from the photograph upon which they were based. Although much may be read into the composition of these paintings, an unknown studio photographer posed the pair. The art historian and Gorky expert Melvin P. Lader has noted that in the compositions the artist has adjusted the size and location of his mother, who is painted larger and more forward than in the photograph, emphasizing the distance between them.[3] Setting the boy just slightly behind the mother makes clear that she is more significant. Gorky omitted details such as the pocket on the boy's overcoat and the floral print of the mother's dress, since unnecessary embellishments were opposed to Modernist composition. Even the faces are basic oval shapes and their features are iconic, reduced to the fundamentals of eyes, nose, and mouth.

In the Whitney Museum of American Art version, Gorky explored form by constructing the figures as blocks of subdued brown, ocher, and blue tones. Instead of the patterns and shading found in the photograph, the blocky background, together with the figures, creates a pattern. In the painting, but not the photograph, the boy's left arm is physically separated from the figure of his mother, but it is completed in similar tones as the mother's left arm.[4] The bright white of her apron, a fairly solid form at her chest that dissolves into rough strokes in her lap, is washed over the very lower left half of the young boy's leg, almost as a reflection or illumination. Because the figure of the boy turns away from his mother, the link through color is emphasized, yet overlapping and unfinished edges that lack shading and specific details somewhat meld the images into background space. This tendency is likely culled from Cézanne, as in such works as the *Large Bathers* (fig. 6), in which the artist, for the sake of compositional unity, omits parts of the enclosing contours of figures. In the Whitney *Artist and His Mother*, the boy's shoulder is dissolved into the frame of the sill and the mother's shoulder disappears because it is painted in exactly the same tone as the mantel-like fixture in the back.

The smooth, bluish-tan surface of the Whitney painting stands in stark contrast to the red undertones and pinks of the National Gallery version. The somewhat rough surface and dissipated color links of the latter are indirectly achieved by loose, dry brushwork, causing the abstracted figures to partially dissolve into the background. The color chords and the dematerialization of form

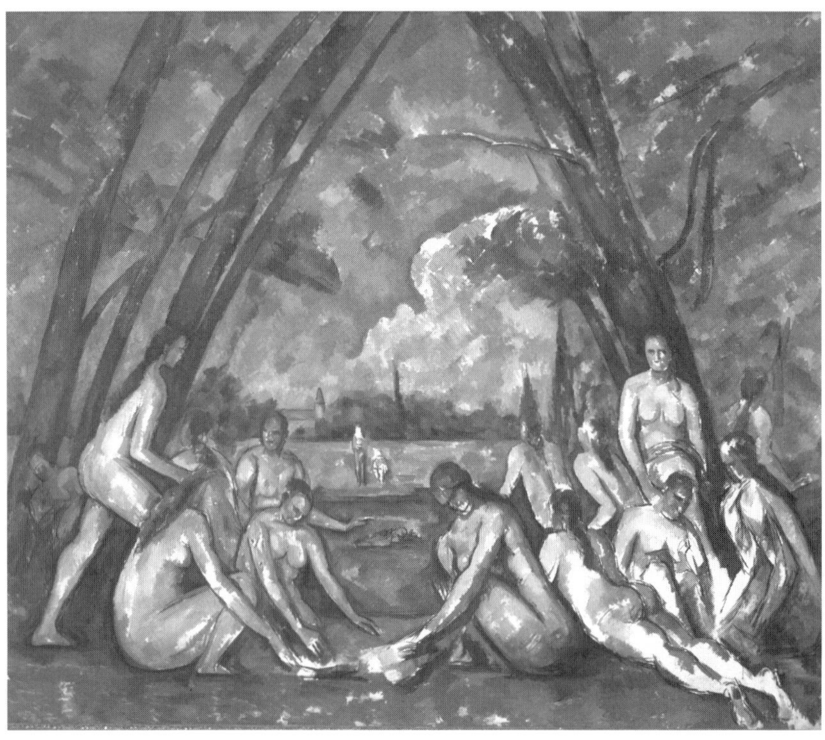

FIGURE 6
Paul Cezanne, *The Large Bathers*, 1906. Philadelphia Museum of Art.

give the illusion that the figures are floating in space despite a hint of ground line just below the bottom quarter of the composition. The boy's left arm is almost subsumed into the background mantel, which is a slightly darker gray. The color of the mother's amorphous apron washes over part of the boy's left foot and right hand, linking the physically separated figures and creating a visual trajectory around the composition. The mother's body has an ambiguity and a dissipating quality, and there is ambiguity as well in the way she is inserted into the space of painting—simultaneously on a floor to her left while up front in the picture plane and pressed back into the mantel. Gorky's apparent refusal to situate her entirely in real space underscores that she no longer exists and that she is perhaps a vestigial presence. The erasure of the hands in both versions, with fingers defined only by gradations of hue, acts as a formal element that also unmaps space, creating a slippage that is visual and temporal and that conflates absence and loss, the present and the remembered.

The mother's pale, white, mask-like visage, surrounded by a gray kerchief, reflects the original photograph, in which the almond-shaped eyes, long nose, and subtly frowning mouth are drained of expression. Willem de Kooning described this quality to Raphael Soyer by saying that "the trouble with Arshile, he had no blood," leading Soyer to admit that "from that time on, whenever I looked at Arshile Gorky, even of his portrait of himself and his mother, there's something anemic there. There's a certain amount of bloodlessness."[5] This comment, although it might appear derogatory, actually illustrates the Modernist concern with musicality. Postimpressionists such as Van Gogh desired to create musicality in their work so that colors could evoke emotion, saying that in *The Night Café* he had "tried to express the terrible passions of humanity by means of red and green."[6] The "bloodlessness" of Gorky's mother, therefore, is meant to evoke an undead quality; the image is caught between the photographic record of the past viewed in the present and the knowledge of her absence.

Although these works may be considered memorials to the artist's mother, or, as suggested by Lader, devotional paintings,[7] they are still very much concerned with explications of form that reflect Modernist iconicity and abstraction. The paintings are often compared to Egyptian or Fayum portraiture, which Gorky would have seen and studied in the Metropolitan Museum of Art, but visual precedents may also link back to his own cultural lineage. The composition resembles early medieval Armenian manuscripts such as the Walters Art Gallery manuscript of the Virgin and Child from a millennium earlier. Although less realistic and mostly outline, the abstraction of early medieval and Byzantine artwork underlies Gorky's modern composition. Armenian manuscripts and wall and ceiling painting were generally colorful, and Armenian architecture could be adorned with low-relief carvings and wall paintings of figures such as the Virgin and Child. The *Artist and His Mother* works are also related to memorial portraiture. In treading a thin line between representing his mother as living and dead, Gorky is perhaps enlisting visual precedents learned from Armenian, Egyptian, and medieval memorial portraiture. "Within ancient portraiture," Hans Belting explains, "the *memorial portrait*, which records the reality of a single life, contrasts with the *heroic image*, which represents an ideal beyond physical reality. The surviving examples either satisfy one ideal of portraiture at the expense of the other or strike a balance between the two, as they refer both to the temporal existence of a person and also to a realm beyond where the deceased dwell. The new existence of the afterlife requires the care and respect of the living."[8]

In his rendition of the theme, the boy's countenance is a dark flesh tone, almost brown, which contrasts sharply with his mother, as if to emphasize the opposition between living and dead. Gorky added shape to the boy's hair and a cleft to his chin so that he resembles more closely Gorky's appearance after he came to America than at the time the picture was taken. Indeed, it seems that while he was reflecting upon and portraying his identity as a boy, his adult identity crept in. The boy's hairline is less like that in the photograph and more like that of the aging artist's,[9] suggesting that within the painting the artist has collapsed time similarly to the way he has modified space and tone.

Replicating the photograph exactly was most likely never the artist's intent. Gorky himself was a cultural collage, and his in-betweenness is evident in the interplay between opposing qualities in this work: the two-dimensional and three-dimensional, gesture and stasis, line and field, and form and subject. The lack of accurate representation and the enhanced formal qualities imply that knowing the biographical details of the sitters is not really necessary for comprehending the essence of the picture. Roland Barthes has suggested that a photograph can replace the monument because it serves memory. "Earlier societies," he says, "managed so that memory, the substitute for life, was eternal and that at least the thing which spoke Death should itself be immortal: this was the Monument. But by making the (mortal) photograph into the general and somehow natural witness of 'what has been,' modern society has renounced the Monument."[10] By transcending the photograph, Gorky created a remembrance of his beloved mother and the circumstances of her death without referring to them in any narrative or specific way. Gorky's manner of painting forges an interpretation of absence or loss that is solidified by knowledge of genocide and death.[11] For exiles, says Edward Said, "expression . . . or activity in the new environment inevitably occur[s] against the memory of these things in another environment."[12] The visual elements of the *Artist and His Mother* paintings, such as the disconnection between the figures, the frontal stares, and the undefined hands, appear almost as apparitions within the picture plane, or reflections of an alternate world that combines past and present. The paintings derived from the photograph move beyond the concept of the photograph as a memorial; in essence, the paintings resurrect his mother while forever encasing her within the moment when the photograph was taken so many years ago.

It is commonly understood that when we lose something or someone with whom we are intimately linked, we are challenged to adapt in order to address our emotional reaction to the loss.[13] For Gorky, this meant developing an artistic process that relied upon a superstructure into which he spliced observations from his past, present, and imagined experiences. Gorky's repeated reworkings of *The Artist and His Mother* were perhaps a kind of incantation to resurrect her, at least visually, like an apparition. "By simplifying the forms, eliminating most of the detail, and emphasizing the broad areas of color," suggests Melvin Lader in his analysis of the National Gallery version of the painting, "Gorky gave this image a timeless quality. The spatial ambiguity he created by denying measurable and logical relationships between the forms leaves them floating and mysterious."[14] The floating and mysterious qualities to which Lader refers are a key component of the way Gorky envisions a composition as unbound to a specific time and place. They are also evident in a pencil drawing by Gorky of his mother that was perhaps a study for the paintings (fig. 7). His mother appears almost as an apparition out of the space of the paper, her youthful face wrapped in a scarf that separates it from her lightly sketched body.

Repetition itself perhaps serves to reduce trauma. Contemporary treatments for trauma suggest that the more one confronts the trauma, the less one is traumatized by it. As Hal Foster explains while discussing Andy Warhol's repeated representations of Marilyn Monroe, "Somehow in these repetitions, then, several contradictory things occur at the same time: a warding away of

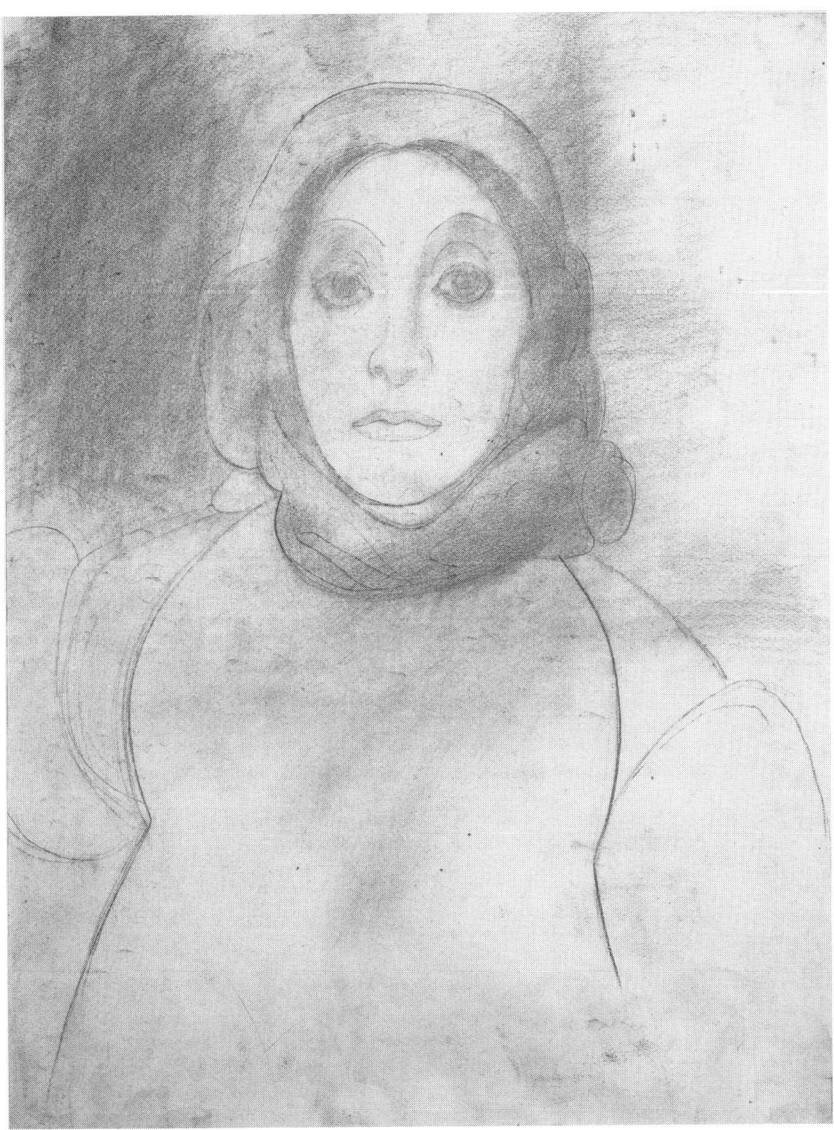

FIGURE 7
Arshile Gorky, *Study for Portrait of The Artist and His Mother*, ca. 1926–34. Private collection.

traumatic significance *and* an opening out to it, a defending against traumatic affect *and* a producing of it."[15] But the connection itself must be viewed as poetic, rather than literal.

Obtaining the photograph in America after his mother's death, muses Melvin Lader, "must have rekindled his already strong feelings for his deceased mother and revived memories of the hardships the 'fatherless' Adoian family had endured."[16] Schwabacher subtly suggests that Gorky's family's struggles to survive the Armenian Genocide "were felt too deeply by the susceptible boy, and passed into his life as a somewhat overbalanced sense of the unhappiness of things."[17] She believes that Shushan's abandonment by her husband forced Gorky into a role of protector, and that perhaps a premature feeling of responsibility coupled with the need to please her produced an idealized image of her in his memory. Gorky also may have had feelings of inadequacy because he had failed to save her.

Commentary by Ellen Handler Spitz may be helpful in understanding the possible impact of such events on Gorky. Spitz enlists a 1966 paper by Martha Wolfenstein that describes the impact of a parent's death on a child.[18] Enlisting Freud's *Mourning and Melancholia,* Wolfenstein compares the mourning processes of adults and children. According to Spitz, "she concludes that, even through adolescence, it is impossible for a young person to mourn in the sense in which we understand that process to occur in an adult: namely, the gradual acceptance of the finality of death on both a cognitive and an emotional level."[19] Spitz explains that Wolfenstein observes that children deal with the death of a parent in the form of denial, a splitting of the ego, in which the child can "verbally, superficially, acknowledge that the parent is dead, but he does not accept this terrible truth on a deeper level and denies it in manifestations of his fantasy life and behavior."[20] This condition, interestingly, is similar to the in-betweenness inherent in displacement.

It is possible that Gorky invokes this fantasy life while repainting his mother because it is based on a photograph from before they endured most of their hardships. The act of painting, then, could be a kind of erasure through recreation. This might be substantiated by Gorky's proclivity to repaint the paintings over an extended period of time, reworking them in interludes throughout much of his career. And yet Gorky did not necessarily start the images over—that is, he did not scrape down and repaint the entire picture, but only portions. In addition, he could not have completely started over because the properties of paint are like the past—you can try to remove the past or cover it over, but it is always present even through its invisibility or passing, and you can scrape paint down, but there is always a stain left behind on the canvas.

The action of painting, and repainting, is as much a part of the creative process, of perfecting the image, if not more so, as resurrecting the past or living in fantasy. In *The Pleasure of the Text,* Barthes describes a writer as one who plays with his mother's body. Of course, the body to which Barthes refers is the text itself, or in Gorky's case, the painting, but here, metaphorically, the mother's body becomes the act of painting itself. Perhaps the most beautiful and haunting image of Gorky's mother is a drawing with enough paint splatters on it that it may have been used as a study for the paintings (fig. 8).

Perhaps Gorky's continuous repainting gave him solace in that as long as he immersed himself in it, she was alive for him.[21] But the process did something more for him: it brought *him* to life, not only in the figurative sense of his renaming and identity construction, but in the existential struggle of production, fashioning, and regeneration, which suspended Gorky amidst the "in-between"

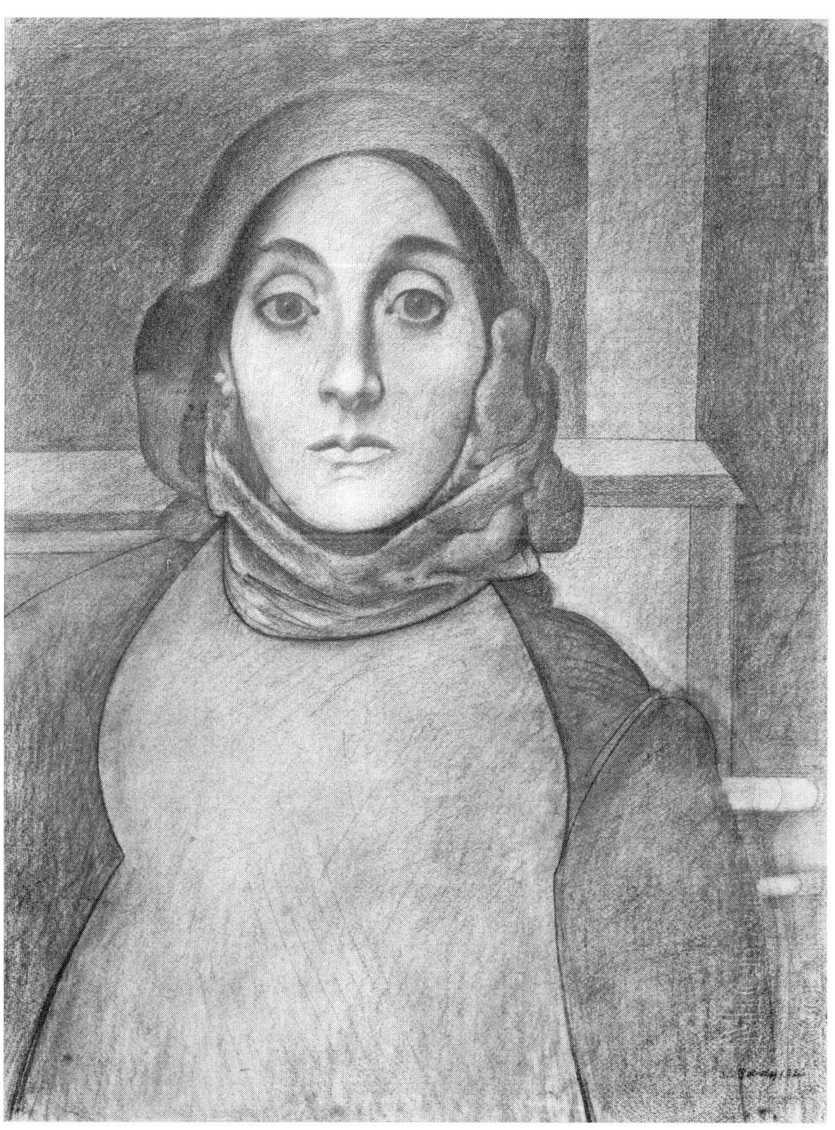

FIGURE 8
Arshile Gorky, *The Artist's Mother*, 1926 or 1936. The Art Institute of Chicago.

and "past-present" space and time that Homi Bhabha has defined. Jacob Kainen, among others, remembers seeing the Whitney portrait hanging in Gorky's studio, and, as discussed above, Gorky worked on versions of the composition for many years. The painting had been subjected to an intense technique in which the painter compulsively scraped the surface with a razor blade and rinsed it in the bathtub to produce a sheer, seamless finish. The National Gallery version is often considered unfinished, with Gorky taking it out for revisions as late as 1942.[22] Harold Rosenberg suggests that the fact "that Gorky failed to finish *The Artist and His Mother* had to do not with his usual manner of work-

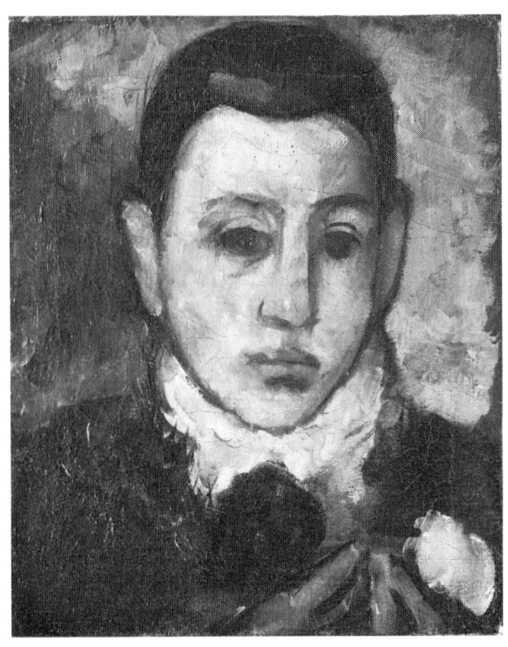

FIGURE 9
Arshile Gorky, *Self Portrait at the Age of Nine*, 1913, 1928. The Metropolitan Museum of Art, New York.

ing but with the subject he had chosen—that is to say, himself and his ancestry."[23] The unfinishedness, however, is also indicative of its in-betweenness, between living and dead, past and present, place and displacement.

In Gorky's work, time is as fluid as interpretation. Gorky tended to go backward and forward in time, completing, for instance, *Self-Portrait at the Age of Nine* (fig. 9) over a decade and a half after the age of nine. Whether the boy in the painting is depicted from memory or a young man who reminded Gorky of himself at that age is not clear, but the painting certainly illustrates the mutability of time and identity common to Gorky's practice. Furthermore, by removing compositions from the observed and redistributing them within the space of the canvas, he makes them more abstract and more readily malleable as artistic material. Harold Rosenberg explains, in reference to the "artist and his mother" theme, that Gorky spent years "*un*finishing the little photograph, changing the distant likenesses in it back into painting concepts in order to be able to take hold of these people as his own creation."[24] This *un*finishing is key to Gorky's working method. Such a practice might even be consistent with exile, since, as Said explains, "much of the exile's life is taken up with compensating for disorienting loss by creating a new world to rule."[25] Said implies that by becoming something else, like an artist, the exile can assert both mobility and skill and divorce himself from reliance on objects and places. "The exile's new world, logically enough," says Said, "is unnatural and its unreality resembles fiction."[26] Because of his history, the body/bodies of Gorky's life were both literally and figuratively mutilated, and what he created instead was a kind of fictional space on canvas that contained the observed, remembered, transcribed, and nonexistent.

The unfinishing and obsessive repainting, although indicative of Gorky's engagement with the tactility of paint, could also relate back to biography and the repercussions of a parent's death. If Wolfenstein's concept of fantasy applies, Gorky kept his mother alive and close in his studio for years, never quite accepting her death. Relating the way that parent-child trauma can insert itself into an artist's oeuvre, Spitz points out that at age thirteen Belgian Surrealist René Magritte lost his mother to suicide by drowning. When she was pulled from the water, the young boy witnessed her face covered by her nightgown, which became the basis for the many images Magritte later painted of headless female torsos or female bodies with their heads shrouded.[27]

Portraits of Gorky's mother might also be a fetishistic reclamation of the past and, by extension, imply that for Gorky his art became a remaking of his past. Despite having moved away from Armenian communities in America, Gorky maintained a mental tie to his homeland, particularly in the presence of other Armenians. Ruth French, a young Armenian woman who had changed her name from Sirun Mussikian to avoid association with her Armenian past, was an art-school model and Gorky's lover during 1929. She has explained Gorky's attitude toward his own heritage, and that Gorky's "painting memories were all of Armenia, nothing of America. Gorky thought everything in America was vulgar. That was his favorite word. He was really living in Armenia here in Greenwich Village."[28] Incorporating memories of Armenia, Gorky made paintings that adopted the art of the Western world while reflecting a sensitivity to Armenian and Byzantine aesthetics that he would have encountered before his exile.[29]

Not just a regurgitation of a tragic past, melancholic yearning, or modern or historic forms, the *Artist and His Mother* series exemplifies Gorky's oeuvre in other ways. One of few objects that Gorky saved from a 1946 barn fire, the photograph that served as the basis for the paintings was the only image he had of his mother.[30] Its translation into painted form transcends the biographical back-story that enlightens it in what Jack Ben-Levi has referred to as "the hinge that allows an interpretation with more disturbingly general implications to open out from the enclosure of a biographical analysis."[31] Even without the tragic story of Gorky's mother, however, the formal elements of each of the paintings—the color chords, generalized shapes, and flat faces—are compelling and even haunting. The overlapping arms of parent and child in the National Gallery version appear to be touching, yet seem disembodied. In the Whitney version, they do not touch, but the background creeps in between the two figures like a force field meant to keep them apart. The undefined hands serve as a compositional device. Their nondepiction actually enhances the overall and reductive hierarchy of the composition. The hinted fingers of the boy's right hand, holding the flowers in the Whitney version, are visually distracting because they pull the compositional weight of the painting toward that more specific detail. The National Gallery version has, because of its very unfinishedness, a subtlety is likely what the artist was trying to achieve.

Gorky mapped out the forms in the paintings based on the photograph, a kind of appropriation that became his signature working method.[32] While the image is haunted by a tragic past, and more explicitly reveals it when we delve into the artist's biography, it also became a means for Gorky to forge his future in Modernism. The image accounts for the relationship between the two figures in the painting as forms and objects, and the relationship of the figures to the viewer, in addition to the storying of Gorky's relationship to the painting. Observing the mask-like qualities of the mother image in the works, Schwabacher explains that the face does not communicate an objective view of the world, "but a sense of our emotional relationship to it."[33] Like his own in-between dilemma, the work simultaneously existed within Gorky's new and old worlds, while also currently existing between his and ours. Gorky traversed time and space and removed the work from the traditional genre of portraiture. Indeed, for Gorky a portrait was perhaps like a mask that represents both a looking out from the wearer's perspective, or Gorky's intention and connection to it, and a front presented to the world that thwarts identification, or the viewer's understanding of it. The tragedy of Gorky's mother can be read into the painting when we are aware of it, like the identity of a masked person, but the sense of something unsettling exists regardless, by virtue of being covered in the first place.

Gorky added to or took away from the painting as was necessary to evoke or emit his own conflicted feelings about it. He had the ability to create his mother's image and make her present, but also was aware of his loss of her. Dominick LaCapra discusses the difficulties that arise when absence and loss are conflated: "When mourning turns to absence and absence is conflated with loss, then mourning becomes impossible, endless, quasi-transcendental grieving, scarcely distinguishable (if at all) from interminable melancholy."[34] Because the painting is ultimately about composition, not replication, Gorky emphasized or deaccentuated certain elements and expanded others. Drawing the viewer's attention away from specifics toward an apprehensive state of suspension, the painting supposes emotionality even if the biographical details are not known. The undefined qualities of the iconic mother image in the paintings reflect our vision as much as Gorky's. If we do sense that the sitters staring out from the canvas want to speak to us about the trauma they endured between the time their picture was taken and the paintings were composed, the trauma becomes less specific to Gorky and his mother, or the genocide of the Armenians, and more indicative of a larger sense of human suffering that genocide produces and the global injury that each subsequent crime against humanity subjects us to. The paining truly does become the hinge that opens out from the enclosure of biographical analysis.

Peter Balakian, a poet who has also written on the history of the Armenian Genocide, drains the poetry and subtlety out of Gorky's paintings by subjecting them to literal interpretation. In his iconographic reading of the nondepiction of the matriarch's hands in both versions of *The Artist and His Mother,* Balakian insists that the "cut-off hands let us know that mother and child will never touch again" and continues by recounting the dismemberment in Turkish torture that he believes Gorky may have witnessed. "Both portraits transfigure this photograph and, it seems clear to me, disclose a single psychological process: the experience of a survivor confronting the nightmare of his past."[35] Although it is true that these works, by virtue of the fact that Gorky painted an image of his dead mother, confront the past, it is difficult to embrace the ambiguity of the hands as reflecting anything more than compositional and emotive concerns.

That ambiguity is a part of Gorky's Modernism, subsumed into the whole composition so as to be consistent with the iconic flat shapes that serve as basis of the works. Other paintings, such as Gorky's 1937 *Self-Portrait* (plate 3) and his *Portrait of Master Bill,* also have hand erasures, as Balakian himself points out.

The issue of the nondepicted hands, however, defines Gorky's overarching ability to compose in a manner that is itself interpretive and also lends itself to multiple interpretations. Gorky's experience and Balakian's interpretation of Gorky's experience, which derives from Balakian's own research on the Armenian Genocide and his intimate knowledge of it as an Armenian, is individualized, and therefore the interpretation and experience of the artwork for each viewer are not necessarily the same and do not have to be. This means that the *Artist and His Mother* compositions represent an emotionality that resonates for the viewer, as well as for someone such as Balakian who is highly sensitized to the subject of genocide and communes with the works on a personal level. The essence of the emotionality of the relationship between the two figures in the painting and the triangulation of that relationship with the viewer is Gorky's project.

As if underscoring the strain of being a displaced person caught between worlds, and accentuating this vantage point, *Portrait of Myself and My Imaginary Wife* (plate 4) relies upon the visual tension between the two figures and two existences even more directly than *The Artist and His Mother.* Gorky depicts himself with the cameo representation of a woman who overlooks his dark image as he gazes down with eyes half visible under heavy eyelids. She is slightly forward in the picture plane, but also extends back behind Gorky's ear. Her lightened skin tone illuminates the side of Gorky's face, and the color is repeated on the figures: the eyelids of the male image resemble the pigmentation of the woman's skin. The solid, almond-shaped lids are obvious on the male form, set against the shadow of Gorky's face. Many writers compare this painting to Picasso's 1907 *Tête de Marin,*[36] and Gorky may indeed have commented on that composition by adding to it, but his figure also clearly resembles Gorky's repose in the Wyatt Davis photograph. Although there are basic similarities in the shape and position of the male head in Gorky's and Picasso's paintings, Gorky's relies heavily on the relationship between the two figures. The hovering proximity of the female head unites both figures, even though Gorky's face looks away, as if unaware of the apparition behind him. If Gorky used the Picasso as a model, his introduction of the second figure indicates a willingness to modify and insert his own qualities into the work.

Portrait of Myself and My Imaginary Wife (1933–34) might be read as a lamentation for the life he could have had in Armenia if conditions had not forced his escape. Perhaps, then, this imaginary woman represents the idea of Gorky's wife as she might have been, and the sorrow in Gorky's depiction of himself stems from the realization that she is likely a casualty of genocide, or in any case, that she will never exist for him. She could also be a manifestation of

Gorky's shattered hopes for himself and Ruth French (Sirun Mussikion) because he could not have the life he had imagined with her. Numerous friends and biographers have noted that Gorky seemed very lonely for a wife, a woman who would be a worthy companion for him, so the painting may also represent that wish. She does seem to represent the ideal bride that Gorky's mother imagined for him, telling Gorky once, while making bread dough, that when he grew up he was to choose to marry a sweet Armenian girl with cheeks as soft and white as dough.[37]

Without these interpretations, the arrangement of *Portrait of Myself and My Imaginary Wife* also serves as a beacon for understanding Gorky's pictorial experience. The painting is a composition of simultaneous real and mystical space in which the images Gorky painted are caught, as he himself is, between an existence in America and a life no longer possible in Armenia. The color link between Gorky's eyelids and the woman's skin may recall an Armenian idiomatic phrase that translates as "you have been standing on my eyelids" or "you rest on my eyelids." The phrase constructs the eyelids as a repository of memory and connotes reflection and often a particular gravity related to deep-felt association with the thought of a loved one.

To further underscore the multiple layers of interpretation implied by the composition, the image embraces a modern connection for Gorky and indicates another conflation of the familiar and the new. The phrase "she is standing on my eyelids" appears in Paul Eluard's poem "The Beloved."[38] Gorky may have seen the poem prior to its 1936 appearance in Julien Levy's book *Surrealism*, where is was translated by Samuel Beckett as "Lady Love,"[39] but he used the phrase as late as 1936 in an August 24 letter to his lover and fellow artist Corinne, in which he liberally quotes from the poet:

> She is standing on my lids
> And her hair is in my hair
> She has the colour of my eye
> She has the body of my hand
> In my shade she is engulfed
> As a stone against the sky.

The visual emphasis on the eyelids and its relationship to both the Armenian idiom and to Eluard's surrealism—to both past and present—stipulates an imagined future, one in which Gorky's wife exists as she might have been had there been no Genocide and had he stayed in Armenia. What might be read as sorrow in Gorky's depiction of himself, then, stems from the realization that she is most likely dead, like his mother, and part of an unreachable past.[40] Still, the element of remaking is an art in itself. The reuse of the poet's words replaces a similar subject in a similar context, but ultimately makes it new. Even his doomed relationship with Corinne is overlaid with transmutations, since, at

Gorky's urging, she changed her name to Michael West, therefore reassigning identity and remaking her both to an artist and a him.

Re-placing the old life structure in the new is not uncommon for exiles. Gorky's dilemma is typified by Richard Kalinoski's 1992 play *Beast on the Moon*,[41] a story of two survivors of the Armenian Genocide who try to become a family in America. Ever-present on the stage is a black-and-white photograph of an Armenian family from 1914, just before the 1915 massacres, with the heads of father, mother, two teenage sons, and a daughter cut out of the picture. The face of one son occupies the space of the father's. Aram Tomasian, whom we come to know as the sole surviving family member, is a photographer who has just chosen as his bride a teenage orphan from Armenia.[42] Aram replaces his mother's head with a picture of his orphan-bride in preparation for the eventual replacement of all of the members of his past family with the members of the new family he wants to create.[43] This act of replacing is a way to fight the reality of displacement and loss by attempting to fit a new life into the old through the photographic images. One recaptures the old life by assuming that it continues in the new era with a different set of characters in the same roles. In order to integrate fully into his father's position, Aram manifests himself into an unfulfilling Oedipal act because despite what he overcomes, the present never fits perfectly into the past. Because he too is in the picture, as a boy, he destroys that part of his identity while taking over the others by force. The cultural collage is an attempt to control identity—that of himself and others—and like Gorky's, Aram's identification and disidentification create an uncanniness that is unnatural, seemingly desperate, and perhaps unnerving.

Gorky's own identity was a conception that kept past and present intact and developed a future. If the portraits of himself and his lost mother or imaginary wife revealed a Gorky subjected to loss, his solo self-portraits seem to represent the individual he was becoming in America, or at least, like Aram's remaking, the one he wanted to be. Roles and beliefs about people are often determined by appearances, and this was particularly true in early to mid-twentieth-century America, when people were so frequently judged by whether or not they looked foreign. This intertext between self and other creates a third space and refers back to Bhabha's concept of in-betweenness.[44] Although one is not necessarily "other," one's self and identification are called into question. Whether he was an immigrant, artist, or Modernist, Gorky's self-portraits seem to reveal that he was a very different person in the United States than he had been before. According to Carl Jung, appearance is not solely external; rather, "merely to establish the fact that certain people have this or that appearance is of no significance if it does not allow us to infer a psychic correlative."[45] Appearances in Gorky's artwork, therefore, are remarkably telling.

The art historian and biographer Hayden Herrera explains that Gorky's self-portraits portray "a precarious interaction between public image and private

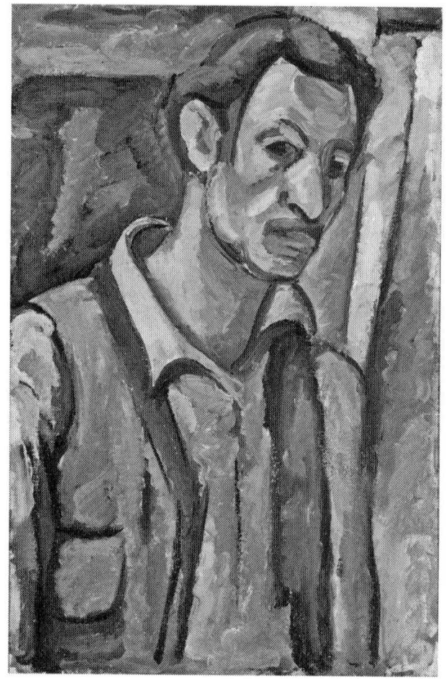

FIGURE 10
Arshile Gorky, *Self-Portrait*, ca. 1928. Los Angeles County Museum of Art.

sense of identity" and "simultaneously hide and reveal the artist's complex feelings about himself."[46] To develop this concept further, one could argue that as in the development of his name, Gorky's own self-identification in visual terms functioned as a means to traverse boundaries. American psychologist and philosopher William James explains such a phenomenon as a fragmenting and subsequent reassembling of a self otherwise ruptured:

> Properly speaking, a man has as many social selves as there are individuals who recognize him and carry an image of him in their mind. To wound any one of these images is to wound him. But as the individuals who carry the images fall naturally into classes, we may practically say that he has as many different social selves as there are distinct *groups* of persons about whose opinion he cares. He generally shows a different side of himself to each of these different groups . . . from this there results what practically is a division of the man into several selves; and this may be a discordant splitting . . . or it may be a perfectly harmonious division of labor.[47]

James's description supports conjectures about Gorky's identification with different roles, such as his exaggeration of the persona of artist. As a Cézannesque self-portrait of 1928 indicates (fig. 10), Gorky often depicted himself on canvas in the manner of other artists, trying on their identities and painting styles.[48] According to Melvin Lader, "Many self-portraits . . . depict Gorky in the style or image of the modern master he chose to emulate."[49] Being a chameleon by manipulating identity, either his own or others', in his paintings allowed for the simultaneous existence of many selves in a multitude of times, places, and spaces. Gorky's self-portraits, like those depicting him with his mother and imaginary wife, offer a different social self to the world. Each is a different Gorky—son, husband, and artist—but each of these existed within Gorky and each was perhaps equally fictive. Nevertheless, because Gorky's identities as exile, immigrant, and burgeoning artist were so precariously constructed in a simultaneic existence, removing any one of the identities would remove all of him because each is interconnected with the others.

There is certainly some power to be gained from reimagining the self. According to Stephen Greenblatt, "The power to impose a shape upon oneself is an aspect of the more general power to control identity—that of others as much as one's own."[50] Gorky's 1937 *Self-Portrait* shows him holding a palette

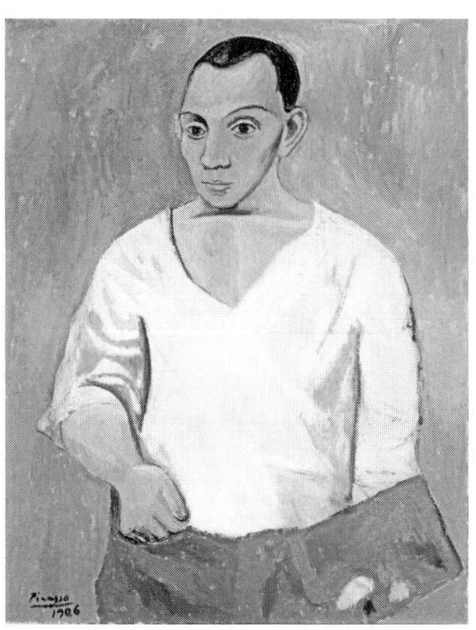

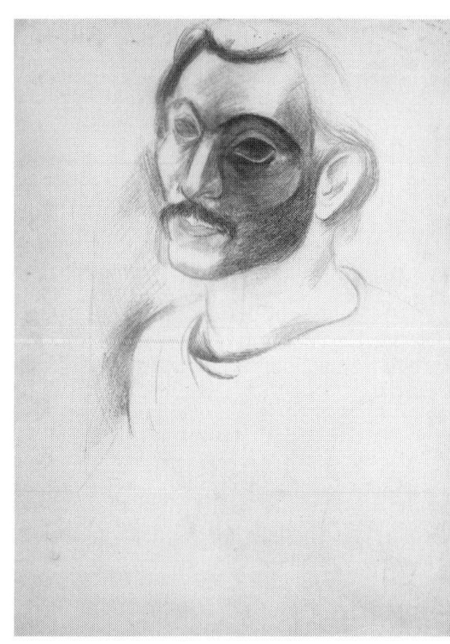

FIGURE 11
Pablo Picasso, *Self-Portrait*, 1906. Philadelphia Museum of Art.

FIGURE 12
Arshile Gorky, *Self-Portrait*, ca. 1933. Private collection.

FIGURE 13
Pablo Picasso, *Gertrude Stein*, 1906. The Metropolitan Museum of Art, New York.

much as Picasso does in a 1906 *Self-Portrait* (fig. 11), but such a pose is also a self-depiction traditionally made by artists to define themselves with the tools of their trade, and in Gorky's case was an iconic representation of what he wished to be and, by the time of this self-portrait, arguably was.[51] As an exercise in understanding visual composition, and entirely subsuming himself within an alternate identity, in another self-portrait (fig. 12) Gorky drew his left eye in a manner similar to the right eye in Picasso's 1905 *Portrait of Gertrude Stein* (fig. 13) but left the right half of the face indistinct. The stores of paint that he kept and his compulsive cleaning, especially of his studio floor, were a way of ordering the world, as was the creation and re-creation of himself in paint. Gorky's self-identification as an artist, combined with the way in which he painted versions of himself in the guise of past artists, was also perhaps a way to negate his otherness.

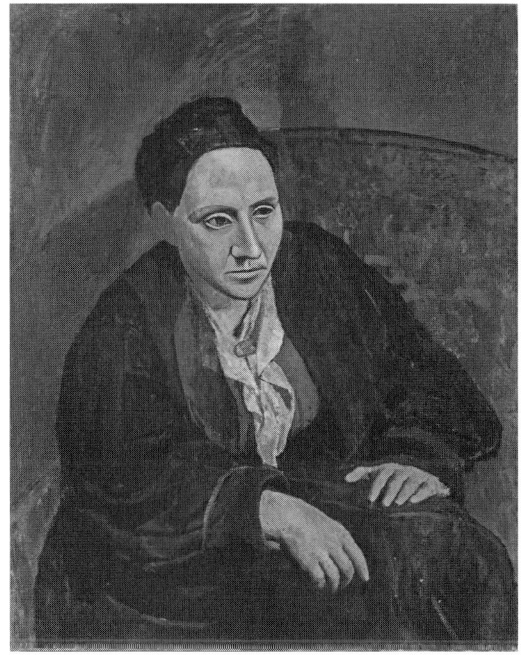

In his self-portraits, Gorky literally created his imagined self as an artist. This visual identity was a continuation of the revised identity he had created through his renaming. The self-portrait became an extension of the Lacanian mirror stage in which the artist identified with his double in the portraits by other artists, but because this misidentification occurred outside the individual, Gorky's self-portraits were a projection that was ultimately an abstraction of the self. Gorky created an elusion rather than an illusion in these works. The self-portrait was an objectification of the self, but without the self becoming an object; therefore Gorky conflated the self and other into an imaginary matrix.

Gorky's approach to the images he painted of other people was similar to that in his self-renditions, because Gorky really did not paint a portrait in the traditional sense. Observation-based pictorial structures were not discarded in these works, but reappropriated, and then reorganized around Modernist models. Defining relationships, depicted or imagined, between Gorky and his mother, his imaginary wife, or the artists he emulated, manifested in the way he painted portraits of the women in his life. In 1926, Gorky explained his distrust of traditional American portrait painting: "Too many artists paint portraits that are portraits of a New Yorker, not of the human being."[52] Perhaps Gorky is asserting that one must depict the essence of a human being above a singular identity. His modifications combine a specific vision that itself is not an exact physical depiction.[53] Gorky's images of women in particular may be part of an effort to create a new world in his art, but also in these works, memory is enacted through an imaginative alchemy. While the artist looked at reproductions of the works of Ingres, Picasso, and Matisse, he played Armenian and Russian music and recalled the Byzantine forms with which he was familiar.[54] Even the medieval concept of memory, to which the Armenian forms were related, was about content. Hans Belting has explained that "the present lies between two realities of far higher significance: the past and future self-revelation of God in history. People were always aware of time as moving between these two poles. Memory thus had a retrospective and, curious as it sounds, a prospective character. Its object was not only what had happened but what was promised. Outside religion, this kind of consciousness of time has become remote to us."[55] For Gorky, however, raised in an Orthodox world that in many ways still adhered to the past and whose sacred and secular lives intertwined with myth and folk tradition, memory could be as fluid as time.

Immigrants in America, whether displaced through exile, genocide, economic failure, or war, were actors, not victims. Displaced but not defeated, Gorky responded to the physical, psychological, spiritual, and intellectual dilemmas of his circumstances in a variety of ways, and his work became itself a melting pot of styles within the structure of his own existence and was in turn part of the melting pot of American society. John Ash explains that

> European painters resorted to non-Western traditions in order to arrive at the new. In Gorky's case the situation was different. Before arriving in America he can have known little of Western art. He apprenticed himself

> to the Renaissance masters in order to acquire the necessary technique; but it was his successive discoveries of Cézanne, Picasso, Kandinsky, Miró, et al. that gave him access to his past, through stylizations and distortions of form relating both to Modernism and to the medieval manuscript painters of Van, whose work he had first seen under his mother's tutelage at the age of six. The way forward was the way back.[56]

Gorky's forays are a combination of his stylistic past and present, as Ash suggests. Venturing into a kind of ethnographic Modernism, Gorky incorporated the stylizations and distortions of modern artists and their own interpretations of the art of other cultures into their aesthetic.[57]

Among the portraits of women that Gorky painted in the 1930s are numerous versions of his younger sister Vartoosh. Gorky and Vartoosh had both escaped the Genocide together, and she periodically lived with him in his New York studio. In the best-known version (plate 5), the greenish-tinted beige face looks off to the side rather than at the viewer, the hair is dark and pulled back, the eyes are dark and almond-shaped with high arching eyebrows, and the thin lips are closed and almost pursed. The flattened and stylized face, hairstyle lacking detail, and minimal distinction between figure and ground can be stylistically linked to both Armenian and Byzantine manuscript conventions and the Modernism of Matisse, as in Matisse's 1905 *The Green Stripe (Portrait of Madame Matisse)* (fig. 14).[58] This (dis)embodying is part of the authority of the Modernist artist's conception over perception. It is precisely the ambiguity, or duality, of the subject that makes Gorky's images of women a key indicator of his process.

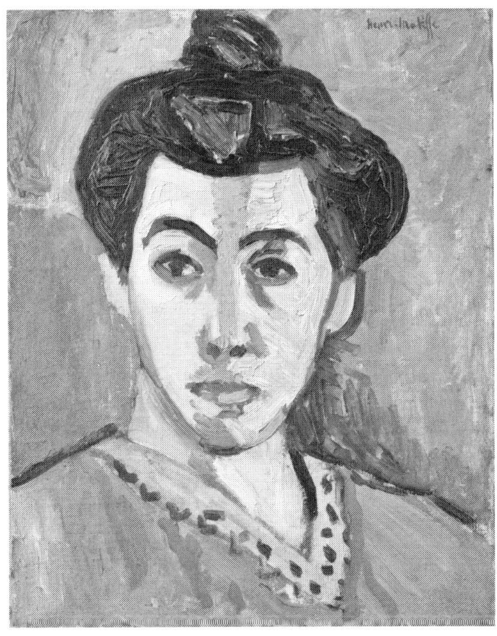

FIGURE 14 Henri Matisse, *Portrait of Madame Matisse*, 1905. Statens Museum for Kunst, Copenhagen. © 2008 Succession H. Matisse/Artists Rights Society (ARS), New York.

Rendered in light tones and constructed of flat, broad areas, the style of Gorky's portraiture has been classified by Lader as part of the Ingres revival of the 1930s and 1940s.[59] The large color blocks and simplifications of the face are similar to Ingres's and illustrate the manner in which many Modernist artists were looking to the earlier painter's style and subject matter. At the time, paintings by Ingres were moving into American museum collections and becoming available for examination by artists such as Gorky who frequented New York collections for study.[60] Lader points out that John Graham and

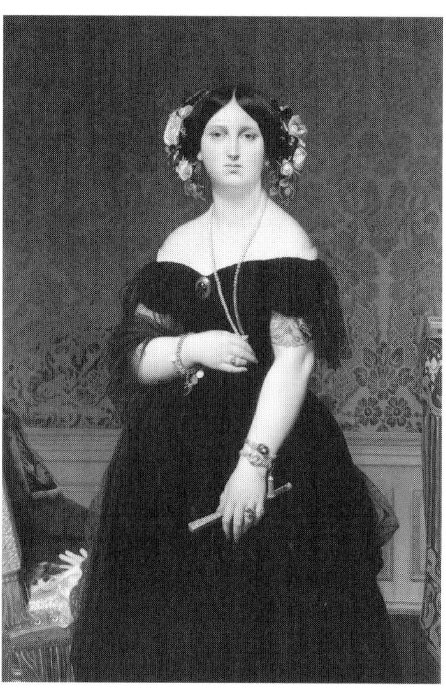

FIGURE 15
Jean-Auguste Dominique Ingres, *Madame Moitessier,* 1851. National Gallery of Art, Washington, D.C.

Willem de Kooning also were part of the Ingres revival, but that Gorky may have been aware of Ingres much earlier than the others.[61] Although the women depicted in Ingres's paintings functioned as exotic fantasies for nineteenth-century European men, and on a more metaphorical level represented the Orient, for Gorky they could have recalled the dark beauty of the Armenian, Turkish, and Kurdish women to which he was accustomed. Indeed, given the history of Turkish oppression, in which women from the peoples Turkey conquered were abducted into sexual slavery, it would stand to reason that the Orientalized women of Ingres's paintings might reflect Greek or Armenian ethnicity.

Gorky also read Ingres's paintings in a Modernist context as an assemblage of formal elements. John Graham insists that one must assemble "the features in order to bring out the character of plastic meaning of the face, grouping the eyes and nose close together in a poignant form or dispersing them or rearranging them at will in order to fit a preconceived composition."[62] Comparing *Vartoosh* to Ingres's *Madame Moitessier* of 1851 (fig. 15), Lader notes that *Vartoosh* bears similarities through the large flattened areas of shape created by contrasts of light and dark. But in portraits Ingres himself often Orientalized his sitters, as Carol Ockham has pointed out, emphasizing (as in the case of *Madame Moitessier*) the eyebrows, eyes, and dark hair of those who might be of Eastern origin.[63] Gorky truly admired Ingres, saying that he had "his own delicate line. At times I resent him. Can not accept him, but, oh, how I would like to draw like Ingres."[64] Gorky pays tribute to Ingres by avoiding outline on the head and facial features in *Vartoosh* and, in later works, by using the line as a connective thread between forms.

Vartoosh said that Gorky asked her to pose for him often "because he wanted to interpret Armenian eyes and sensitivity in portraits and believed, in particular, that the pure Armenian face provided the most expressiveness."[65] The essentialist nature of this comment suggests both a romanticization and a standard of ethnic purity, but because *Portrait of Vartoosh* also resembles works by Matisse such as *The Green Stripe,* we might say that Gorky integrated an Armenian face into a Modernist composition similarly to the way that the main character in *Beast on the Moon* inserts new faces into the spaces of the old. In the play, the new face replaces the old, but within the structure from the established past. And yet these "Armenian eyes," which recur in Gorky's portraits of his mother, sisters, and imaginary wife, are also applied to those of his future non-Armenian wife, yet again conflating past and present and imagined and existing worlds.[66]

In his paintings of women, Gorky evokes plastic meaning and pure form to such an extent that he makes the eyes a kind of ideogram. Gorky's images of women enlist Egyptian portraits,[67] Armenian portraits in a medieval tradition,[68] old master presentations, Ingres, Matisse, Picasso, and likely many others whose influence may be indiscernible. Gorky's knowledge of Western art and obsession with modern art was so complete that he very likely sifted these works through a visual vocabulary of Modernism and melded them together into a Modernist language of large, flat blocks of color and stylized representations. The tendency to simplify a sitter's characteristics is again supported by the theory of the time. As John Graham explains, "irrelevant obstructing frills and adornments are dispensed with[,] . . . permit[ting] the artist to work freely *within* pure form."[69] Graham comes to this understanding through his engagement with French avant-garde art, particularly Picasso.

In the history of art, women have been portrayed with varying degrees of accuracy, idealization, and desire. From the ancients to the enigma of the *Mona Lisa* and idealizations like the Pre-Raphaelite Rossetti's Elizabeth Siddal, women can embody for the artist his own conception of a particular woman, women in general, and even his views of life and art. Willem de Kooning and Pablo Picasso, like myriad other modern artists, distort the female image on the canvas. De Kooning was a long-time friend of Gorky's. His *Woman* series tracks the development of his own gestural style, but also his renditions of an iconic figure. De Kooning's grotesque 1950–52 *Woman I* (fig. 16) is constructed of harsh brushstrokes that resemble slashes on the canvas, effacing any conventional value of the feminine and undermining the traditional equation of woman with beauty. Read together, De Kooning's abstracted women, painted from the late forties into the early fifties, were about the subject of the female form rather than one specific woman. Picasso was one of the masters after whom Gorky modeled himself. His "weeping women," often depicted with faces that

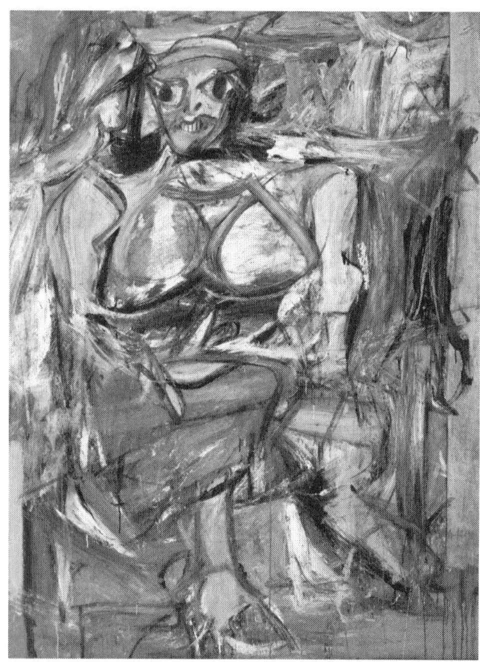

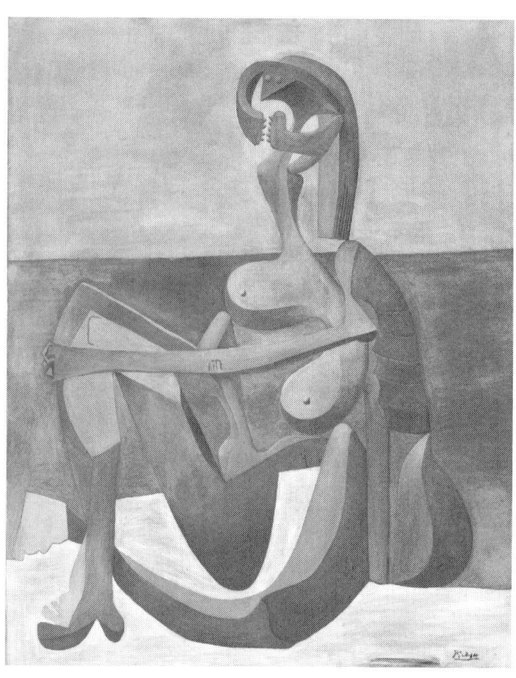

FIGURE 16
Willem De Kooning, *Woman I*, 1950–52. The Museum of Modern Art, New York.

FIGURE 17
Pablo Picasso, *Seated Bather (La Baigneuse)*, Paris, early 1930. The Museum of Modern Art, New York.

appear to be ripped apart, are both autobiographical and emblems of a tumultuous historical era.[70] For Picasso, works such as *Seated Bather* (fig. 17) were not only about a specific woman, but about his relationship to her.

In the 1937 *Portrait of Ahko* (plate 6), Gorky's older sister's body is generalized in a bulbous red dress, but the ethnic features of her Armenian face are emphasized, framed by dark hair and dominated by highly arched eyebrows and dark eyes. Ahko is portrayed as a collection of prioritized forms that tell the story about the image. These same forms are readable in images of Gorky's sister Vartoosh and of his mother as well. The schematic eyes that Gorky repeats also repeat a Modernist tendency. Picasso was inclined toward Iberian sculpture and Spanish Romanesque art, which in turn drew him to African masks because of their own degree of abstraction. The masks that Picasso depicted in *Les Demoiselles d'Avignon*, for instance, conflate tendencies and allegiances, both aesthetic and ethnic. The deep brown inlaid eyes with arching eyebrows that Gorky set into the faces of Vartoosh and Ahko are perhaps retrievals, like Picasso's Ibero-African quotations, related to Armenian folk culture or manuscript illuminations.[71] The "transformational value of change," Homi Bhabha explains, speaking of political change but in terms that apply here as well, "lies in the rearticulation, or translation, of elements that are *neither the One . . . nor the Other but something else besides*, which contests the terms and territories of both."[72]

Since Gorky paints, as an American modern artist, an image of his dead mother from an old photograph or a version of a wife he never knew, the illusion of presence, or rendered present, imagines composition, color, and form. This practice is related to what Jim Jordan terms "memory portraits." Jordan discusses the concept of memory portraits as a way to rectify the ambiguous dates that Gorky assigned his paintings. For instance, in the upper left-hand corner of *Portrait of Vartoosh*, Gorky has painted out a date and on the lower left-hand corner has added the date "XXII" (22). In addition, the portraits of Vartoosh do not always correspond to periods of time when she was with Gorky; Jordan believes that they are not entirely direct portraits, but memory portraits.[73] Memory portraits, Jordan explains, are images of one's family or past remembered, rather than paintings directly from a sitting model.[74] Paul Ricoeur notes that "remembering is not only welcoming, receiving an image of the past, it also searching for it, doing something."[75] In this remaking, the figural intervenes to punctuate the temporal. Such rememoration is perhaps a version of the changing same. In the simpler terms of Hegelian thesis/antithesis, Gorky takes the old and makes it new.

According to Jordan, such portraits were Gorky's remembrance or imagining of how a person looked or might have looked at a particular time earlier than the moment in which the portrait was painted. A prevalent conception of time during Gorky's era arises from Jung, as Martica Sawain explains: "The barriers that for our intelligence separate the different parts of time have shown their artificial character . . . the barriers dividing time into past, present and future must be broken down to give man a greater consciousness."[76] Another work featuring Ahko, *Portrait of Akabi,* although likely painted in the 1930s, was dated 1917 for an exhibition. That date was just before the time she left for America, and several years before Gorky himself arrived. There is little evidence that he painted so elaborately then or that he brought anything like this with him.[77] As Jordan suggests, it is much more likely that this is Gorky's remembrance of how Ahko looked in that particular year. As with *Portrait of Ahko*, Gorky paints a wedding headdress on her head much like the one she wore when she got married before leaving for America. Prompted when she sat for her portrait later in America, these images were resurrected from his memory.[78] It would appear, however, that Gorky also integrated present time with the resurrected image, therefore transgressing time or representing multiple dimensions of time simultaneously in a conceptually Cubist manner. The earlier dating was also perhaps a marketing ploy, like Gorky's name change and claim to have studied with Kandinsky, for the purpose of making him appear better trained and more knowledgeable in art history than the immigrant actually was.

Regardless of the date, however, it seems that Gorky needed a sitter or an image as a beginning point. Whether he relied on a photograph of a person, another artist's work, or a memory, Gorky continued to use this method throughout his career. Indeed, even his "imaginary wife" could have been based on some woman he had encountered. It is possible that the portraits of women, such as those of Vartoosh that Jordan questions, were developed from sketches Gorky made while the artist lived with his sisters before moving to New York City. Later Gorky perhaps combined his memory image with the drawn one and then expressed it in paint.[79] Although the dates and conditions surrounding these paintings are ambiguous, their characteristics are constant, suggesting that Gorky emphasized the most important aspects of his subject—both those that he remembered best, like the "Armenian eyes," and those based on Modernist portraiture, which did not emphasize details, shading, or personalized characteristics.

Since throughout his development Gorky did not repeat exactly what he saw, but sought to modify compositions, the modification of non-Armenian women is indicative of his desire not to re-create nature, but to create his own vision. This controlling tendency of conception over perception is also evident in Gorky's personal relationships with women. When Vartoosh had her hair curled at a friend's house, Gorky dumped a barrel of water over it and ordered her never wear her hair like that again.[80] Gorky's first wife, Marney George, a girl from the Midwest ten years the artist's junior, suggested that "Arshile wanted to form and mold me into the woman he wanted for his wife."[81] As the epigraph to this chapter suggests, Gorky, according to Schwabacher, thought that, like Pygmalion, he could mold and revise and create a vision of what he believed a woman should be. It is of course much more difficult to remake a human being than an image on canvas, but this idea follows the emphasis on Gorky's own remaking. Gorky even tended to repaint portions of his students' art rather than direct them to fix it themselves.[82]

At the same time that Gorky tried to remake the images of his sisters and students, he was dependent on them for his financial well-being. His sisters often sent him money during lean times. And for other women, Gorky had a certain charisma and exotic charm; he was, in many ways, like his own paintings, in which there was something familiar and endearing and at the same time something that resisted explanation and interpretation. While Gorky emitted brilliance and assuredness, women also felt a need to care for Gorky, and he survived during Depression with the help of women such as Mina Metzger, Jeanne Reynal, and Schwabacher, who took private lessons with him. They also occasionally purchased paintings as a way to funnel money to the artist without giving him handouts, which he was often too prideful to take. But despite Gorky's apparent command of the women in his life, his dependence on them for his survival may have been emasculating for him. Perhaps it repeated his dependence on his mother in the old country, while still feeling, as a male, that it was his responsibility to protect her, but at which he ultimately failed.

Gorky's conflict with his past was evident in his treatment of Sirun Mussikian, who came from his home region of Van. In their many discussions, it seemed that Gorky wanted to connect with the old world through her. Mussikian said that Gorky was frustrated by her lack of love and reverence for the old world. She remembered most vividly the terror of the Genocide rather than the pastoral existence to which Gorky referred, and like many she tried to forget it.[83] She left him when their relationship turned violent—he struck her on several occasions, partially because she did not romanticize Armenia as he did and because she would not conform to his ideal of an obedient Armenian woman.[84] Gorky's ideal woman quite possibly only existed in *Portrait of Myself and My Imaginary Wife*. Gorky's relationship with his first wife, Marney George, was just as tumultuous. George relates: "It seems the very moment we were married the battle began . . . 'ferocious as a giant, tender as a little child' he used to say of himself. How very true! Arshile tried to break the barriers, first with tenderness, then with force. But the barriers grew in direct relation to the violence. It was tragic for us both."[85] Although George attributes Gorky's violence to the stress of being poor, Schwabacher remarks that the relationship was complicated by displacement. "As a foreigner," she says, "he had no frame of reference by which to access the character of an American girl,"[86] and it was inevitable that misunderstanding and barriers grew and that Gorky, with a skewed perspective of relationships, emasculated by tragedy and with no real social power, resorted to violence and control over women. Gorky may have been overwhelmed by pressure or had limited tools with which to adapt because he was self-contained in his own displacement and self-construction, separated from his family and the Armenian diaspora, and was thoroughly invested in his art.

Gorky's second wife, Agnes Magruder, knew little about his past or Armenian identity, yet she was able to glean from her experience with him that the clash of his past and present was a source of deep trauma. She said after his death that "he steeped himself in western painting but he couldn't help his east . . . if only he had not felt the stigma of refugee if he could have been free and proud of his difference."[87] Perhaps because of that stigma, Gorky was drawn to her. He regarded the strong-willed admiral's daughter as fearless, and she, ill-suited to New York debutante circles, was perhaps drawn to his exoticism, brooding nature, and maybe even the romanticization of the artist image that Gorky worked so hard to portray. "I thought it was my abundance of health," she said, "psychological and physical that permitted me to dare to marry such a man."[88] She seemed in awe of Gorky's abilities, having studied art herself,[89] but Gorky lived a bohemian lifestyle that was very different from Agnes's conservative upbringing but quite consistent with her rebellious nature.[90]

Gorky chose to modify Agnes, pulling her into his world and simultaneously making her a bridge to the nonimmigrant world to which he had been continuously trying to gain access. At the same time, he projected outsider status onto her. First he renamed her, calling her "Mougouch," a term of endearment that adhered to her in such a way that others began referring to her by that name, which she came to prefer (and still does).[91] Even after Gorky's death, in a letter to Schwabacher, Agnes signed, "Devotedly Mougouch," which she then crossed out and re-signed "Agnes," commenting beside the revision, "me and my aliases."[92] She continues to manage Gorky's estate, and her own identity, despite subsequent marriages, remains linked to his. The name, although perhaps reflecting an Armenian pet name, such as "little mouse," was, Gorky explained to her, a Russian term meaning "my little one."[93] Gorky's giving his wife a Russian name reflects his own renaming. Although Gorky's drawing of his wife (fig. 18) is typical of his oeuvre in that the face is its most finished aspect, he emphasizes the eyes, giving them a hint of the glyphic Armenian/Byzantine/modern eye in his portraits of his Armenian mother and sisters. In a portrait of Agnes from 1941 (plate 7), the eyes, profile, and style are similar to *Portrait of Myself and My Imaginary Wife*. Gorky seemed to delight in having his wife sit for hours while he created many versions of her in a multitude of media. The paradox is that Gorky made her appear Armenian in these while he became more American through his marriage to her. The overlying conception of her identity, however, like that of himself and his sisters, is modern due to Gorky's belief that portraiture need not be specific to the person but should offer a representation of a human being.[94] In these works, Agnes is not entirely remade, but portrayed in a simultaneously iconic and modern manner through her remaking. These renditions of his wife reflect one of Willem de Kooning's observations on the artist, that "sometimes he painted in ways opposite to others. If he were painting you, he would look at you a long time and then move back away and he wouldn't see you, in essence, painting from memory."[95]

Mougouch was indeed central to Gorky's existence, not only as a muse, but as a cultural broker. With her help, Gorky negotiated the actual past and present in attempt to integrate as an artist and member of American society. As she became his wife and the mother of his children, she became even more central as a cultural intercessor. She recognized her unique role, writing from Paris in 1949, just over a year after Gorky's death, "I know this was one reason I was so important to him because he saw me as the Brooklyn Bridge, I was west."[96] Agnes admits, however, that unlike many artist's wives, she was not necessarily adept at managing the artist's finances and inventory. Despite her assistance in translating conversations with the famous French artists whom they spent time with in New York and Connecticut, Agnes realizes that she does not have flair in dealing with art dealers or running the household.[97]

Life with Gorky, however, was rarely stable; as Agnes describes it, it was "like riding a roller coaster, a huge dippy one to be sure but dizzy heights of elation that I can't describe for my heart is in my mouth."[98] With Gorky's financial, health, and professional problems, his temper would be uneven and he needed to be intensely focused when he painted. Agnes's strength and her recognition of his brilliance as an artist made her essential to his emotional stability and pro-

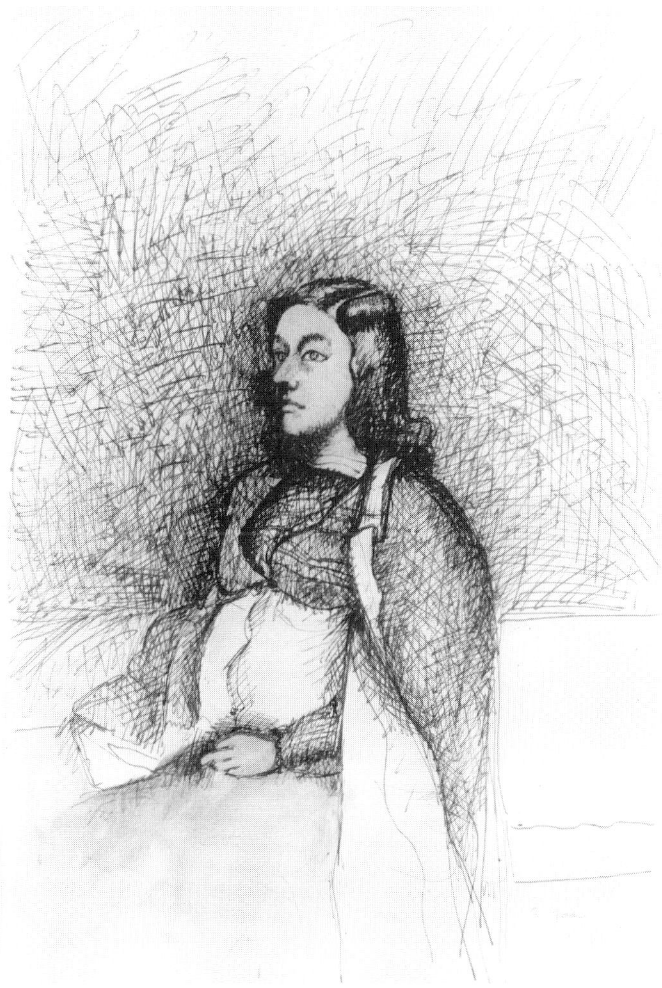

FIGURE 18
Arshile Gorky, *The Artist's Wife, Mougouch*, 1943. The Baltimore Museum of Art.

fessional success, and yet, the demands of family life could be distracting as much as it provided great comfort and joy to the lonely artist.

Elaine de Kooning, as both a painter and the wife of one, knew that for artists such as Milton Avery, Barnett Newman, and Adolph Gottlieb, who were all married to schoolteachers, "the wives were kind of shadows of the husbands."[99] Gorky was fascinated by his wife and needed her as a cultural broker, and despite her self-professed inexperience with the business end of Gorky's career, she did try to help and accommodate to the best of her abilities. In addition, it was she, both in giving him the joy of children, which dissipated his loneliness somewhat, and exposing him to her parents' farm, which helped yield his late-career abstraction. She also admits, however, that the pressure of being a father and trying to support a family with art took a toll on him.[100]

The cultural difference between Gorky and Agnes in addition to the pressure of providing for a family, may have played a role in the dissolution of the marriage. Gorky loved Agnes and the children, but had difficulty working with them in too close proximity.[101] Additionally, perhaps he wanted what his wife, as a nonimmigrant, had. Edward Said explains that "exiles look at non-exiles with resentment. *They* belong in their surroundings, you feel, whereas an exile is always out of place. What is it like to be born in a place, to stay and live there, to know that you are of it, more or less forever . . . ?"[102] Gorky's engagement with his past and modification of the present intruded into the relationship in such a way that Agnes could never have hoped to or been expected to negotiate his worlds. Indeed, it appears that Gorky never really even told her the truth of his origins or explained his existence beyond his passion for art.[103]

What emerged may have been, despite his love for Agnes, jealousy of her status as someone who belonged in America. Intrinsically, it was Agnes who had capital in America, not only because she was from there and Gorky was not, but because she had economic capital, even though her fairly well-to-do family had cut mostly cut her off; human capital, having had a fine education at upscale schools; and social capital because of her father's status as an admiral, which Gorky respected greatly due to the prominence the position held in both Armenian and American societies. Problems in the marriage were heightened by Gorky's deteriorating health in his later life, most notably due to cancer, and his insecurity about Agnes's devotion to him. Gorky's fears were confirmed by his wife's rendezvous with the Chilean Surrealist Roberto Sebastiano Antonio Matta Echaurren. Although it seems to have lasted only one evening and was her response to Gorky's rejection of her and impotence due to his colostomy, it devastated the artist.[104] As an Armenian male, like any male subjected to genocide, Gorky was in essence already castrated because he had been powerless to stop the injustices against him and his family. In addition, because he was an immigrant, much of his social capital, with the exception of that which had he obtained through his identity as an artist, was tied to his wife's. His marriage had shifted his position in America, but his belonging while struggling to be recognized more widely for his art was dependent on his association with her, and despite his trying to change her into his ideal woman by controlling his images of her, ultimately, because of her social capital, the control in the relationship was hers. The affair only accentuated their cultural differences. As Gorky's biographers explain, Agnes thought she was forcing a confrontation that would open communication with the increasingly brooding artist, but Gorky, coming from a patriarchal society in which women were supposed to obey and never consider such an act, viewed it as disobedience. And yet it had been Mougouch's independence and spirit that attracted him to her and allowed her to marry him, since she had a long history of opposing her parents and escaping her father's traditional expectations of her.

As Aram, in *Beast on the Moon*, replaced his mother's face with that of his bride, Gorky had tried to make a similar family unit, perhaps even to mitigate a sense of loss through re-placing. Just as Aram exclaimed, "I have a wife . . . my life can start now," so too could Gorky begin his life.[105] But through the act of reinterpreting his wife's features and renaming her, he underscored the continued presence of exile in his life and a desire to remake his present. As is visible in his self-portraits and images of his sisters and wife, not only did Gorky's portraiture have a teleological purpose, but as he continued to contemplate portraiture throughout his career, his process of remaking, re-placing, and integrating time and space became the methodology for the development of his abstracted compositions.

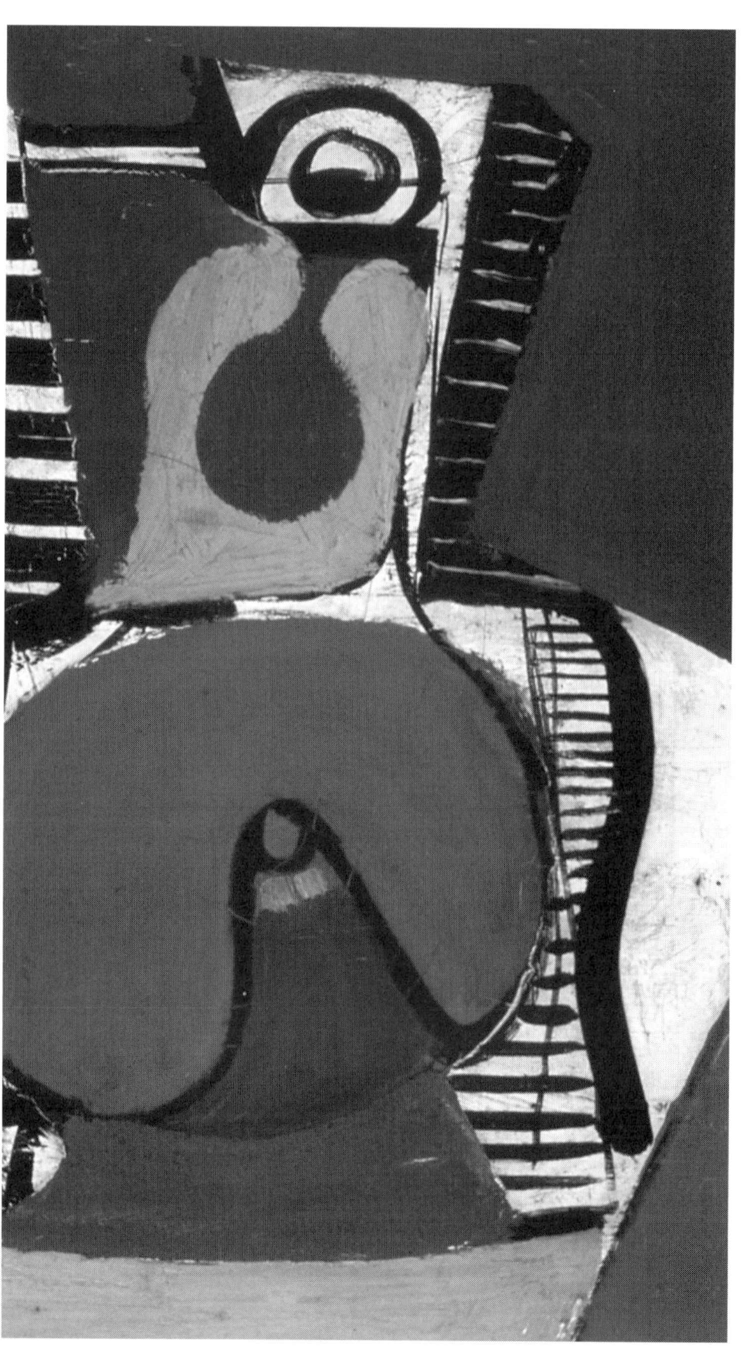

chapter 3

Language, Translation, and Diaspora

I was with *Cézanne for a long time, and now I am* with *Picasso.*

—ARSHILE GORKY

In New York City, Gorky had access to vast collections of traditional art, budding galleries of contemporary art, cutting-edge magazines and books about art, and a community of artists.[1] He analyzed compositions by Poussin and Ingres in the Metropolitan Museum of Art, studied the works of Pablo Picasso from reproductions in magazines like *Cahiers d'Art*,[2] attended exhibitions at progressive galleries such as A. E. Gallatin's Gallery of Living Art, where saw the works of such artists as Fernand Léger, and spent time at the Julien Levy Gallery, which opened in 1931 and a year later was the first to show the Surrealists in America. The newly established Museum of Modern Art became central to the young American artists in New York at the time, including Gorky, who exhibited there in 1930, just after it opened.

Gorky's persona as an artist solidified in New York City. According to Balcomb Greene, "Because of his spectacular appearance, he [Gorky] easily became a celebrity. He was better known than his paintings were. . . . Gorky's Celebrated Personality became very early an extension of him."[3] Greene, who

Opening image detail of figure 10.

often accompanied Gorky around the city, describes how, on one occasion, Gorky paused at a shop window to praise an English watercolor with such exuberance "that a crowd gathered to stare in awe and only faintly with amusement at this gesturing Titan," and later "at dead midnight commanded a group of us to stop in front of a fire hydrant, who cried out it was more beautiful than anything ever made by man."[3] Also shown in the scene Greene describes is Gorky's sensitivity to his surroundings, whether "fine" art, to which artists should appropriately be looking, or the viscera of the everyday and texture of the mundane. Gorky, it seemed, noticed every minutia and appreciated the aesthetic possibilities in the world around him.

In an effort to comprehend stylistic components and compositional methods, the self-taught Gorky transacted an aesthetic identity by trying on the styles of other artists in much the same way as he had tested out personal identities through pseudonyms and self-portraits.[4] David Anfam attributes Gorky's tendency to look at and absorb the work of others to insecurity, based in his being "caught between a lost past and an alien present."[5] The behavioral response that Anfam suggests as one of doubt and vulnerability is substantiated by Gorky's immigrant status. The loss of those who have witnessed our past undercuts our self-narrative, prompting revisions of our self-definitions could incite the need to "relearn the self" and "relearn the world."[6]

Gorky, therefore, mitigated his displacement somewhat by adopting a new self and new manner of negotiating the world. "Gorky, moving from mentor to mentor, searching for a new identity as soon as the old one became an 'act,'" says Donald Kuspit, "was perpetually destroying himself and being reborn as someone else until finally he was reborn as himself."[7] Just as Gorky was reborn by taking on a new name and becoming an artist, so too was he reborn, as an individual and artist, by adapting the art of others. The art world provided Gorky with generational mobility—being an artist gave Gorky social capital, and his use of other artists' styles gave him human capital. As Greene's story indicates, Gorky was also genuinely thrilled by each new discovery in his unfamiliar world and his aesthetic wardrobe changes seemed to be part of an earnest engagement with all that his environment had to offer.

Modernist creative minds have traditionally studied, appropriated, and adapted elements from other artists or cultures. Thus it was only natural for Gorky to do so within the macrocosm of America itself and the microcosm of his artistic diaspora. It is common for artists to paint in the style of others in order to understand how to reach similar conclusions in their art or understand how those techniques could be applied to their own compositions. Such a practice was a relatively practical way for an immigrant like Gorky to become an artist. Unlike European or American artists who had received formal training and been introduced to important artists by their teachers, Gorky sought out the artists who interested him and could inform his own work. These included old masters, nineteenth-century academic painters, and the European early Modernists and artists who fled World War II. Willem de Kooning referred to Gorky as a "Geiger counter of art. In a room in a museum, he always ran to the right painting, and in the painting he always picked the really interesting thing."[8] Gorky's heightened sensitivity, critical eye, or sixth sense about art may be related to displacement in a way that Edward Said describes:

> while it perhaps seems peculiar to speak of the pleasures of exile, there are some positive things to be said for a few of its conditions. Seeing "the entire world as a foreign land" makes possible originality of vision. Most people are principally aware of one culture, one setting, one home; exiles are aware of at least two, and this plurality of vision gives rise to an awareness of simultaneous dimensions, an awareness that—to borrow a phrase from music—is *contrapuntal.*
>
> For an exile, habits of life, expression, or activity in the new environment inevitably occur against the memory of these things in another environment. Thus both the new and the old environments are vivid, actual, occurring together contrapuntally. There is a unique pleasure in this sort of apprehension, especially if the exile is conscious of other contrapuntal juxtapositions that diminish orthodox judgment and elevate appreciative sympathy. There is also a particular sense of achievement in acting as if one were at home wherever one happens to be.[9]

Because of his status as an outsider, Gorky had a certain freedom and plural vision that Said enumerates as a byproduct of exile. Gorky could approach a museum or artwork with a fresh vision and without predetermined values. In addition, aspects of what he already knew informed his vision, that is, he connected to whatever familiar components existed in something that was otherwise foreign to him. Contrapuntally, Gorky's predisposition to Armenian folk arts, such as woodworking and Easter egg decoration, manuscript painting, and abstract rug patterns, combined simultaneously with his incorporation of certain stylistic elements such as saturated colors, flat, abstracted shapes, and distorted images in the work of artists such as Picasso and Matisse,[10] who liberally borrowed aesthetics from other cultures and time periods, or Ingres and his Orientalized women.

Gorky's awareness of cultures other than his own, particularly French and Russian, makes sense not only because of his exile in America but because of his experience before he arrived. Nineteenth-century Armenians in Turkey traded with Europe,[11] and late nineteenth-century Armenian writers were influenced by the numerous translations of French literature.[12] French missionaries had long frequented Armenian-populated areas of Turkey, bringing both their Catholic faith and their culture to the Armenians and the Turks.[13] According to Vahe

Oshagan, "to be an Armenian in 1900 was still to be very much an imitator, at best, a follower of foreign ways and literatures, especially French."[14] In Gorky's region of Van, Armenians used French culture as a form of rebellion against their Turkish oppressors by wearing soft felt hats derived from the French chapeaus that were the mark of proper bourgeois culture in early nineteenth-century France.[15]

It is probable that Gorky encountered French culture in Russian Armenia as well, particularly since Russians also embraced it. Russian art criticism was often written in French, and Russian literature acknowledged French literary forms. Even Tolstoy's seminal *War and Peace* begins in French: "Eh bien, mon prince."[16] Also, given Gorky's time in Armenia, which would eventually become part of the Soviet Union, Gorky's tendency toward things Russian was clear. Gorky's penchant for Russian culture may also explain his claim to have trained with Russian Wassily Kandinsky and his adoption of a Russian writer's surname.[17]

The French arts in particular were an international language, especially Modernist painting. Other artists with whom Gorky spent time, such as John Graham, Willem de Kooning, and Stuart Davis, likely contributed to his interest in French artists. Their cultures too (Russian, Dutch, American) were predisposed to France as a primary cultural center. France's Modernist leadership was promoted in the exhibitions that came to America, such as the 1913 Armory Show, the French exhibition catalogues and magazines that the young artists read, and training in and trips to Paris by artists like Graham and Davis. There was a long tradition of artists from America traveling to Paris to study art and importing styles such as Romanticism, Neoclassicism, Impressionism, and Cubism.[18] Looking at the work of artists such as Poussin, Ingres, Cézanne, and Picasso fast became a means for Gorky to connect with an emerging artistic community.[19] Picasso, although Spanish, not French, was part of Parisian Modernism. Gorky likely became interested in him because of his bold new conceptions of space developed through Cubism in Paris, his chameleon-like ability to move from one style to another, and even Picasso's own displacement. An expatriate living in Paris, Picasso himself integrated his folk culture and ethnic background into his work alongside his contemporary life and compositions.

Cubism was key to Gorky's development and the development of abstraction in Modernist American art; as Amédée Ozenfant explained as early as 1916, "Cubism was to fuse the regeneration of contemporary art with the great tradition of the formalists: Assyrians, Greeks, Chinese and the admirable anonymous 'Negro' artists."[20] The connection of Cubism to art with which Gorky was already familiar underscores the possibility that Gorky found something familiar in the Modernist movement. Gorky also would have become quite familiar with Russian and Slavic art and icons during his stay in Armenia, and the interest in socialist politics and culture after the 1917 Russian Revolution must also have engaged the artist.

As he learned English to survive from day to day, Gorky learned acquired a diachronic language of art that embraced the French, Russians, old masters, and new moderns. Language itself is a method of acquiring knowledge, and some level of mimicry is always part of its practice.[21] Learning new languages builds upon one's understanding of familiar objects and ideas by giving them new names, which is similar to the way that Gorky would have built upon any knowledge that he had of art prior to leaving his past life. Applying other artists' styles and embracing components of their compositions became a kind of vocabulary practice. Just as many immigrants kept vocabulary notebooks in which to record new words for future use, Gorky accumulated a syntax of surface, space, and color that formed his own visual sentences. As Homi Bhabha asserts, the displaced individual becomes subject to an interspatial temporality, so that "the inscription of this borderline existence inhabits a stillness of time and a strangeness of framing that creates the 'discursive' image at the crossroads of history and literature, bridging the home and world."[22] Gorky is known to have cut up prints of artworks that interested him, or examined them from various directions and angles to understand the components, or words, of their compositional sentences.

Language is an appropriate metaphor for Gorky's work, since it is intertwined with displacement and identity and is even a requisite of American immigration.[23] Stuart Davis described Gorky's use of language as contrived: "He expressed himself verbally in a complex personal jive that was extremely remote from accepted English," with an "earthquake-like effect on sentence structure."[24] As Greene recalled, however, Gorky only used broken English on occasion, and generally as part of a deliberate performance.[25] Gorky likely learned from his immigrant experience that sometimes it was to his advantage to play the exotic, the primitive, or the unaware immigrant because people might write him off as not knowing any better rather than hold him responsible for his actions, and that he might be given the latitude to push boundaries or go where not otherwise permitted.[26] The "personal jive" that Davis described is typical of the disjunctive grammar that results from the literal translation of Armenian, in which verbs are attached to a sentence's end, to English.[27] Because of interpretations of Gorky's actions like Davis's, and Gorky's actions themselves, such as donning a long black overcoat and dark hat, Margaret Osborne has argued that Gorky was as much cast or visualized in such a role by others as he played it.[28]

Despite Gorky's awkward English, Davis asked Gorky to write the essay for one of his early exhibitions. Although in retrospect Davis questioned whether Gorky actually wrote it himself,[29] phrases to describe Davis's work such as "mountain-like," which prompted ridicule from fellow artists, seem typical of Gorky.[30] His meaning was likely lost in translation; for Gorky, "mountain-like" would have been an extreme compliment to the sublime strength of Davis's composition, its immense impact on the viewer, and the pioneering quality of the artist's work. Such pastoral language did not seem flattering when written in English about a WASP city artist, but Gorky did address what he saw as Davis's new conceptions of space and the painter's intentional ambiguous symbols. These contributed to an effect that prevented people from making specific interpretations, which was exactly Gorky's goal for his art.

For Gorky, art escaped literal translation. He avoided artist statements that explained his own work as much as possible. Although this may have been partly due to the translation issue, it is more likely because Gorky preferred his work to speak for itself to each individual viewer. As his extensive library of art books—many of them in languages that he could not read and encompassing a range of countries and periods throughout art history—testified, his interest was largely formal.[31] It was the art itself, not how the visual could be described in words, to which Gorky was devoted. Gorky's own art was meant to operate on several levels at once and can be understood as bridging the in-betweenness of his existence. As Gorky's spoken language might indicate, his visual language was simultaneously past, present, and invented. Williams explains how this deconstruction and rearticulation of language became a medium for immigrants: "It was no longer, in the old sense, customary and naturalized, but in many ways arbitrary and conventional. To the immigrants especially, with their new second common language, language was more evident as a medium—a medium that could be shaped and reshaped—than as a social custom."[32] This vernacular disconnect is indicative of the passage from rural to urban of which Williams speaks, the conflicts between the small rural towns and big modern cities that were part of the American cultural landscape, and Gorky's own displacement from rural past and modern present.

Gorky meant his art to cross physical and temporal boundaries to get closer to the emotive. He believed that thought expressed through a medium could heighten emotion, intensity, and the musical qualities of art for the viewer. Gorky's borrowing became part of "a common language of painting, by associative reference. This way brings about an enrichment of the spectator's thought and brings him to see not only your thought but a further enrichment of your thought through allusions to the past."[33] Edward Sapir explained in 1924 that language could be a problem solver, but that it was part of a larger system within a group. "It is quite an illusion to imagine that one adjusts to reality essentially without the use of language and that language is merely an incidental means of solving specific problems of communication or reflection. The fact of the matter is that the 'real world' is to a large extent built up on the language habits of the group."[34] Current with Gorky's development, art as a language was taken up by the Bauhaus as a way to teach studio practice, so the idea of language as a problem solver—in the case of education, to teach art to those who have the talent or dexterity for it—was becoming more widespread and became a hallmark of teaching art in the American educational system. Without such instruction, however, Gorky proctored his own course.

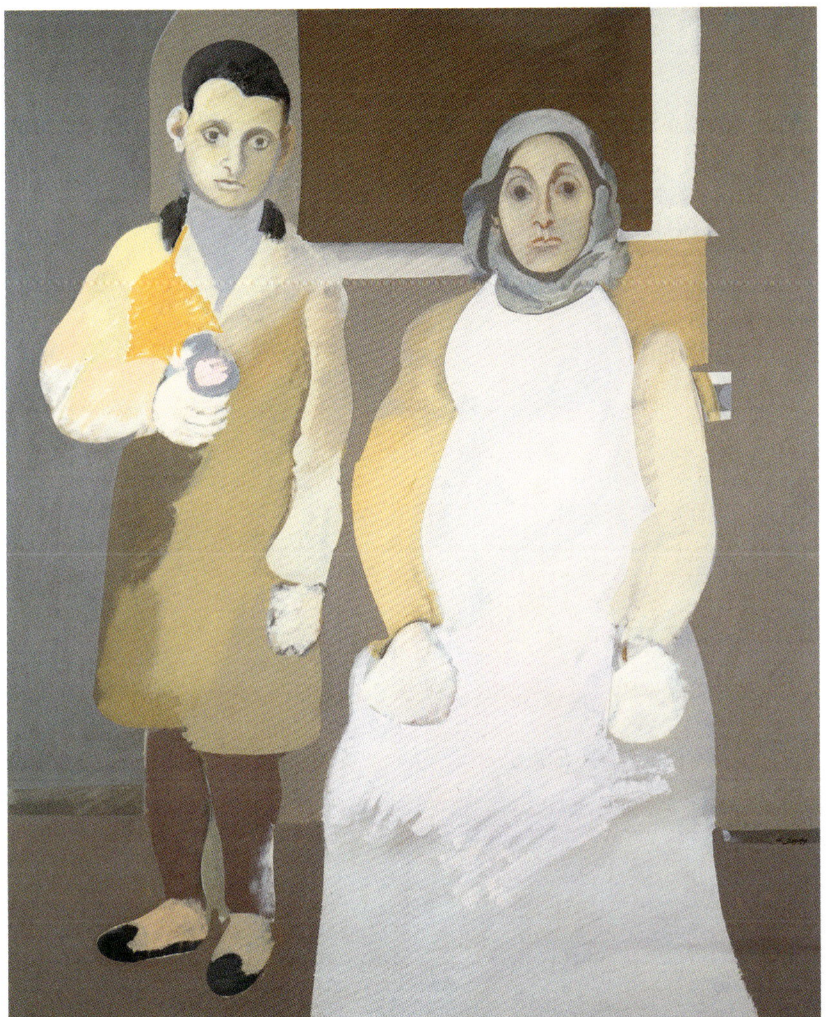

PLATE 1
Arshile Gorky, *The Artist and His Mother*, ca. 1926–36. Whitney Museum of American Art, New York.

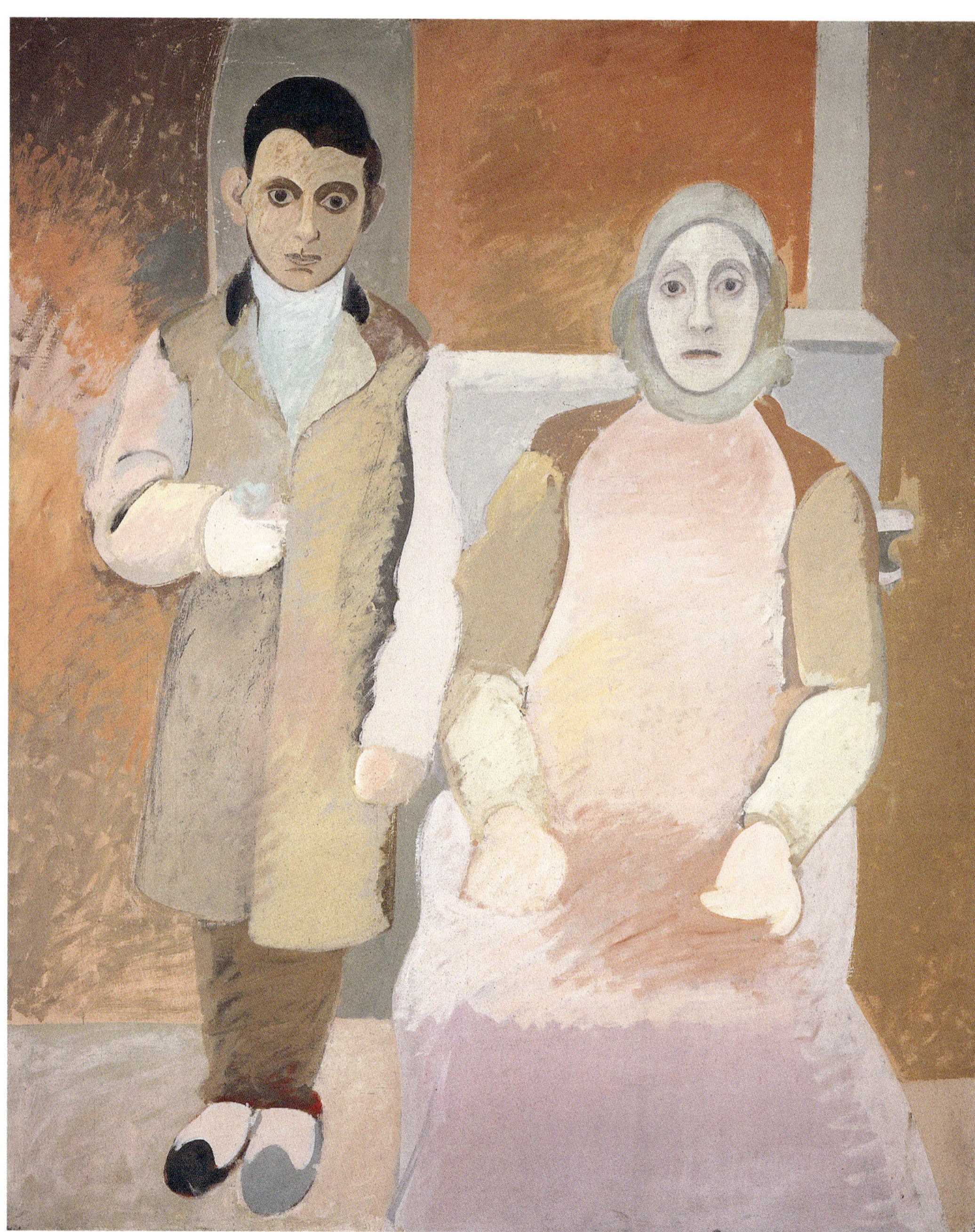

PLATE 2
Arshile Gorky, *The Artist and His Mother,* ca. 1926–ca. 1942. National Gallery of Art, Washington, D.C.

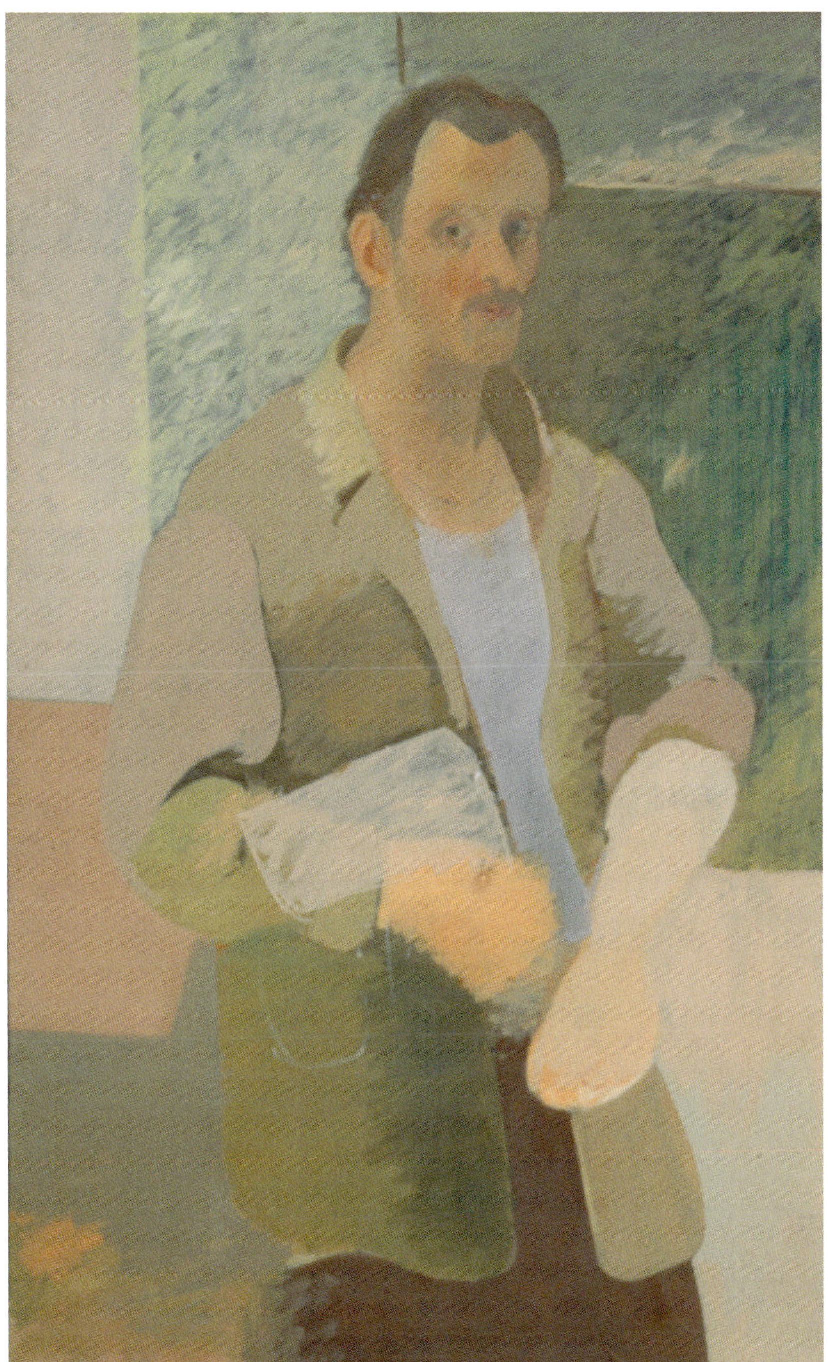

PLATE 3
Arshile Gorky, *Self-Portrait*, 1937. Private collection.

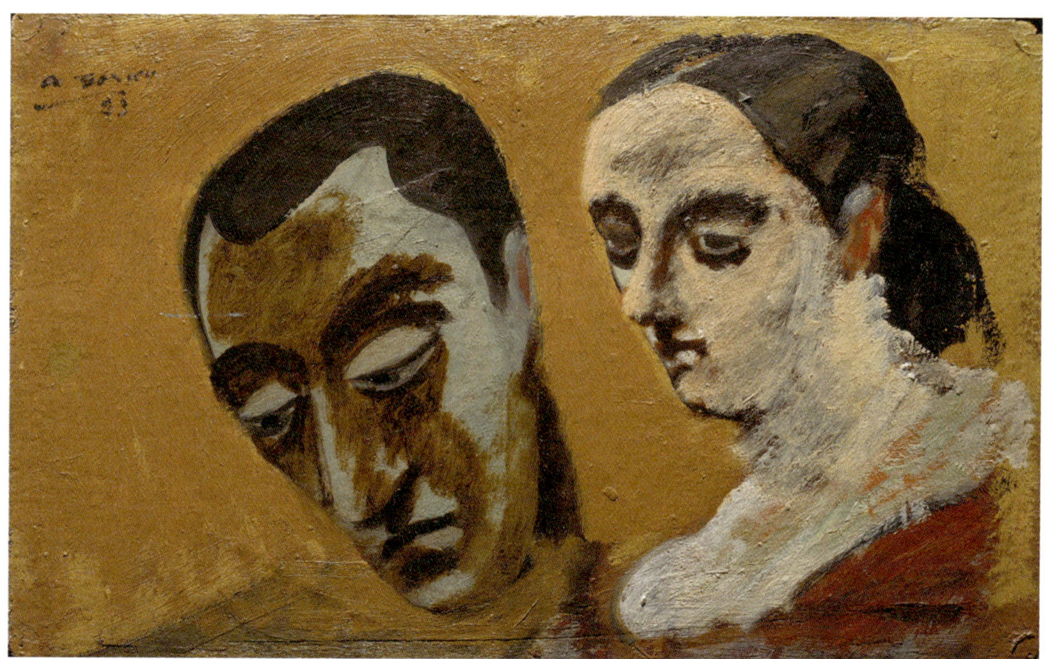

PLATE 4
Arshile Gorky, *Portrait of the Artist and His Imaginary Wife*, 1933. Hirshhorn Museum and Sculpture Garden, Smithsonian Institution, Washington, D.C.

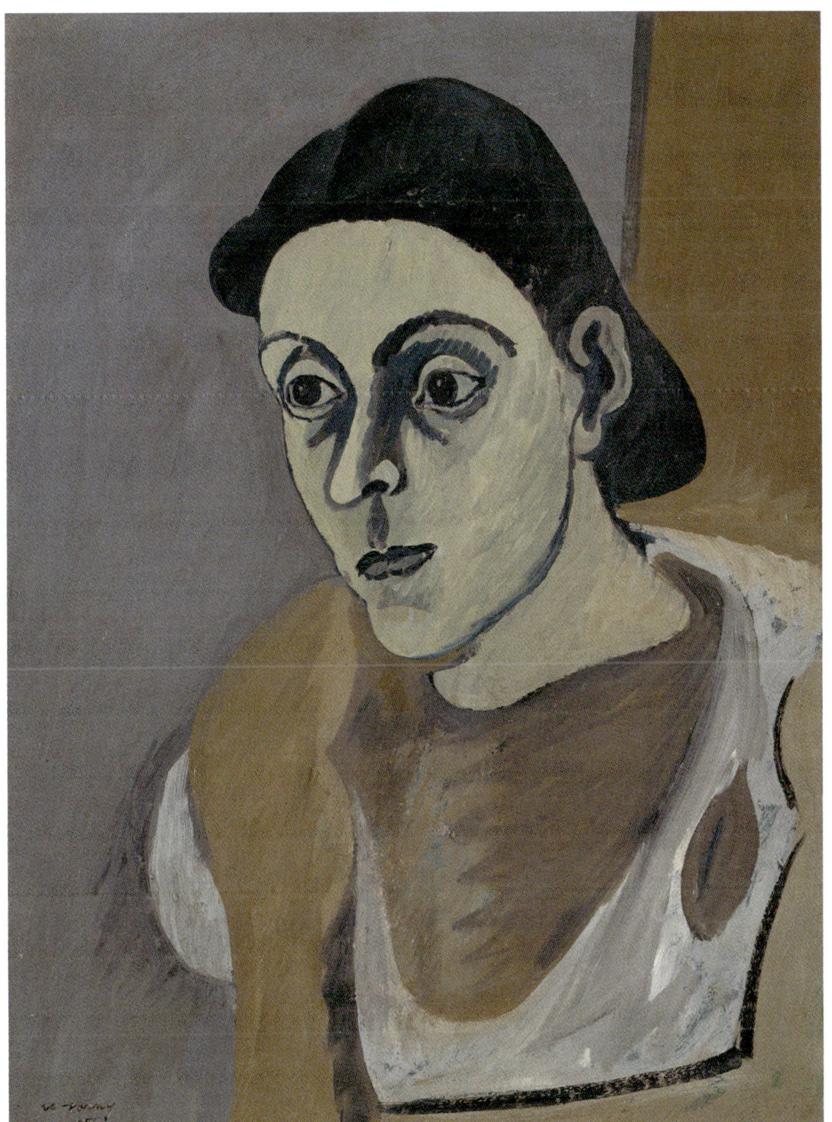

PLATE 5
Arshile Gorky, *Portrait of Vartoosh*, 1933–34. Hirshhorn Museum and Sculpture Garden, Smithsonian Institution, Washington, D.C.

PLATE 6
Arshile Gorky, *Portrait of Ahko*, 1937. Private collection.

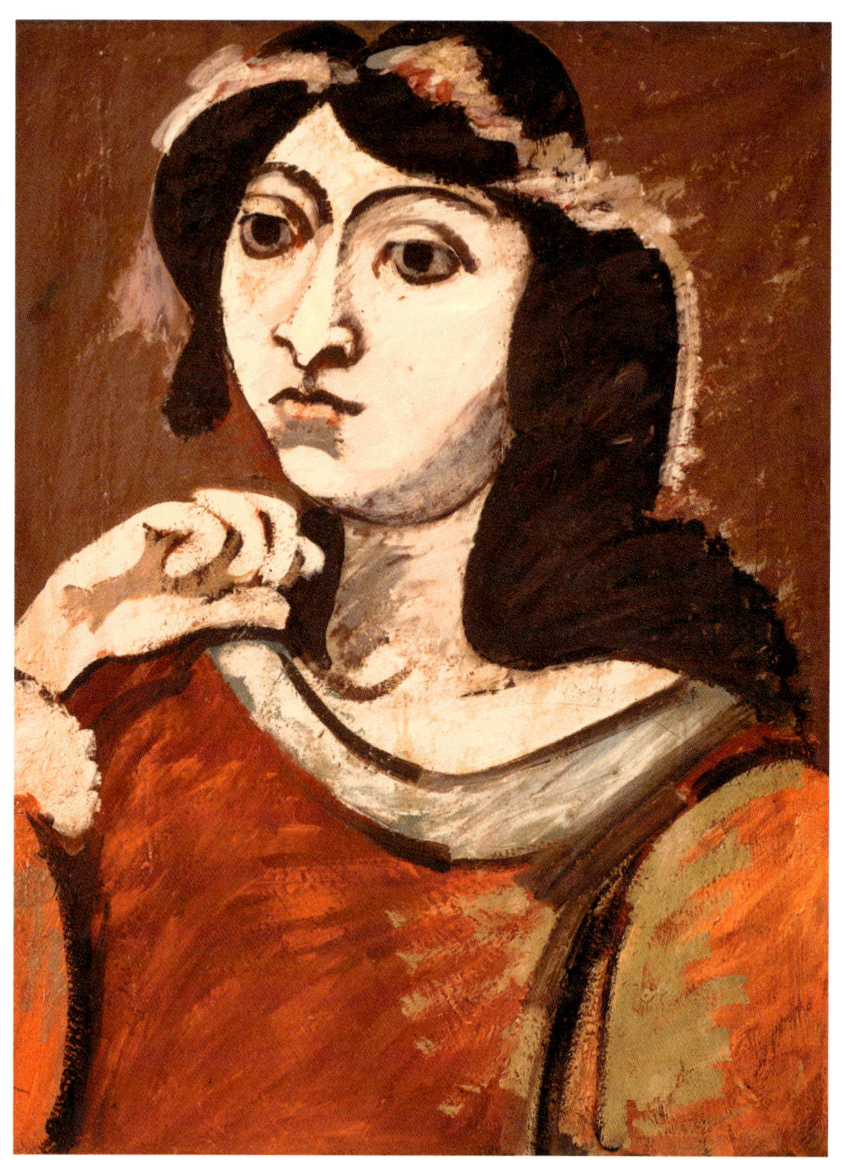

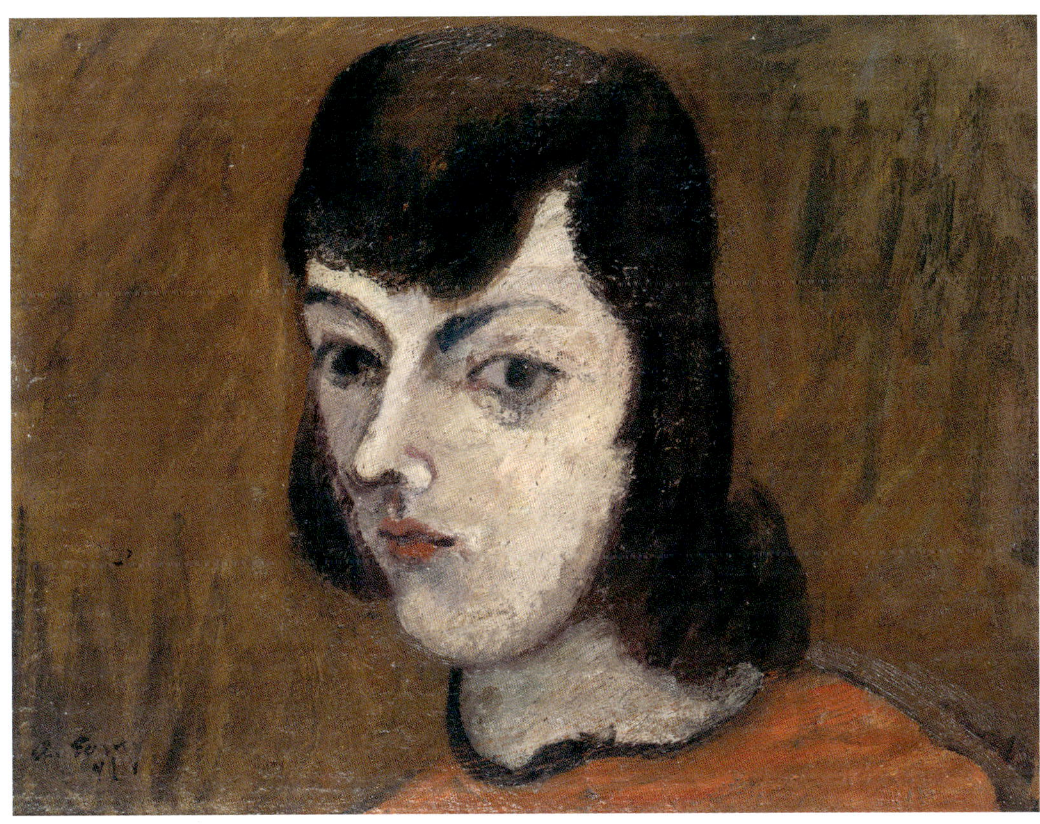

PLATE 7
Arshile Gorky, *Portrait of Mougouch*, 1941. Private collection.

PLATE 8
Arshile Gorky, *Landscape in the Manner of Cézanne*, 1927. Private collection.

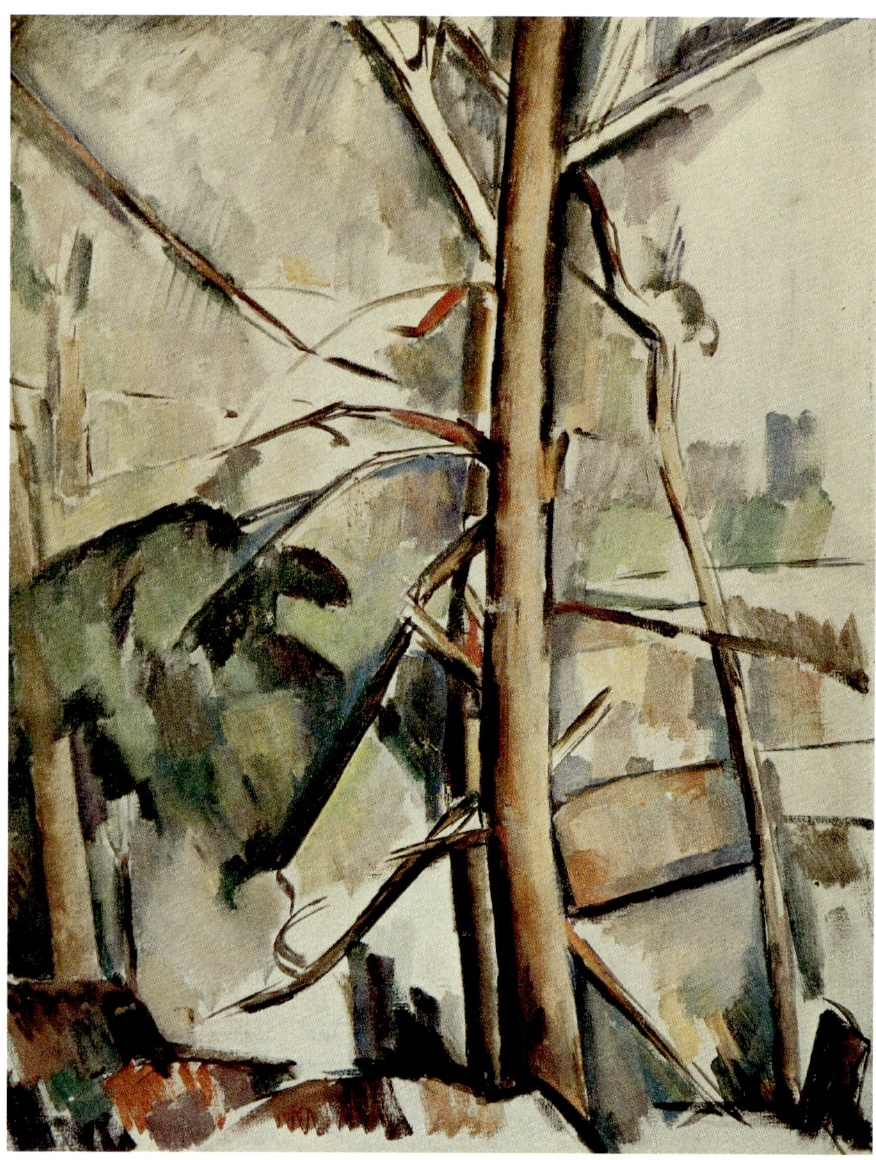

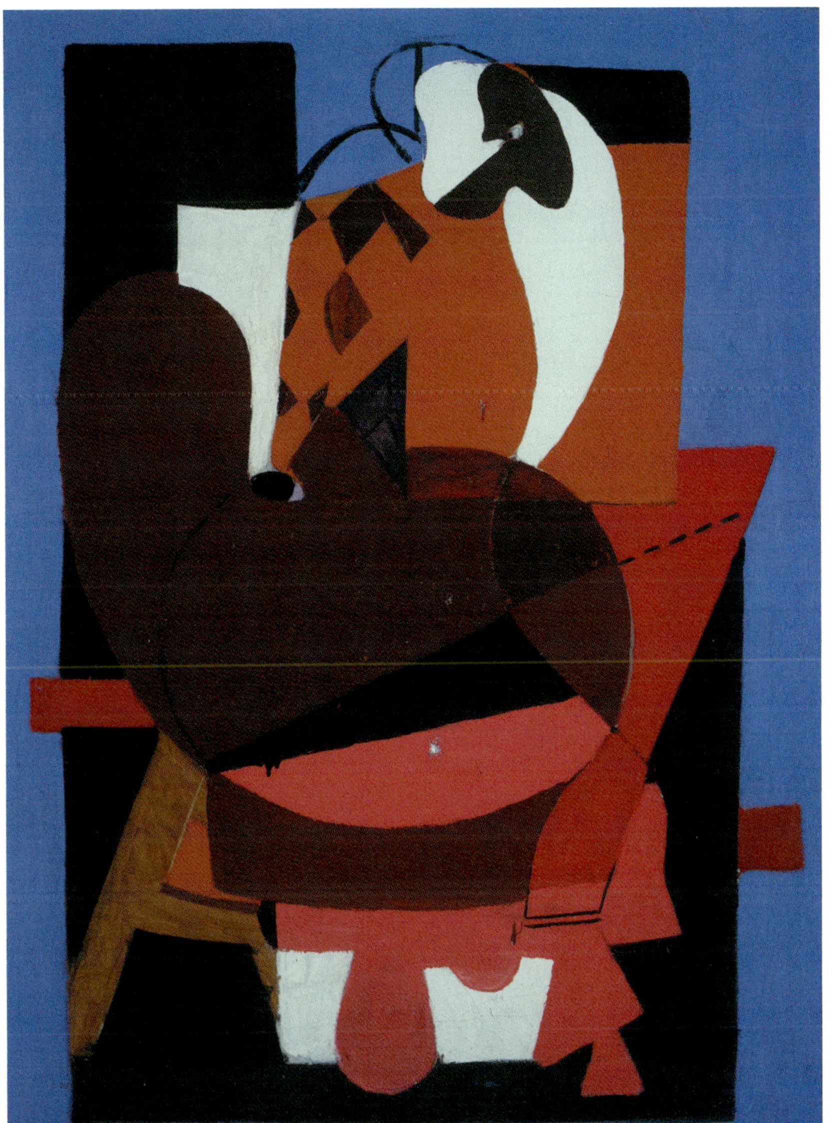

PLATE 9
Arshile Gorky, *Abstraction with a Palette*, ca. 1930. Philadelphia Museum of Art.

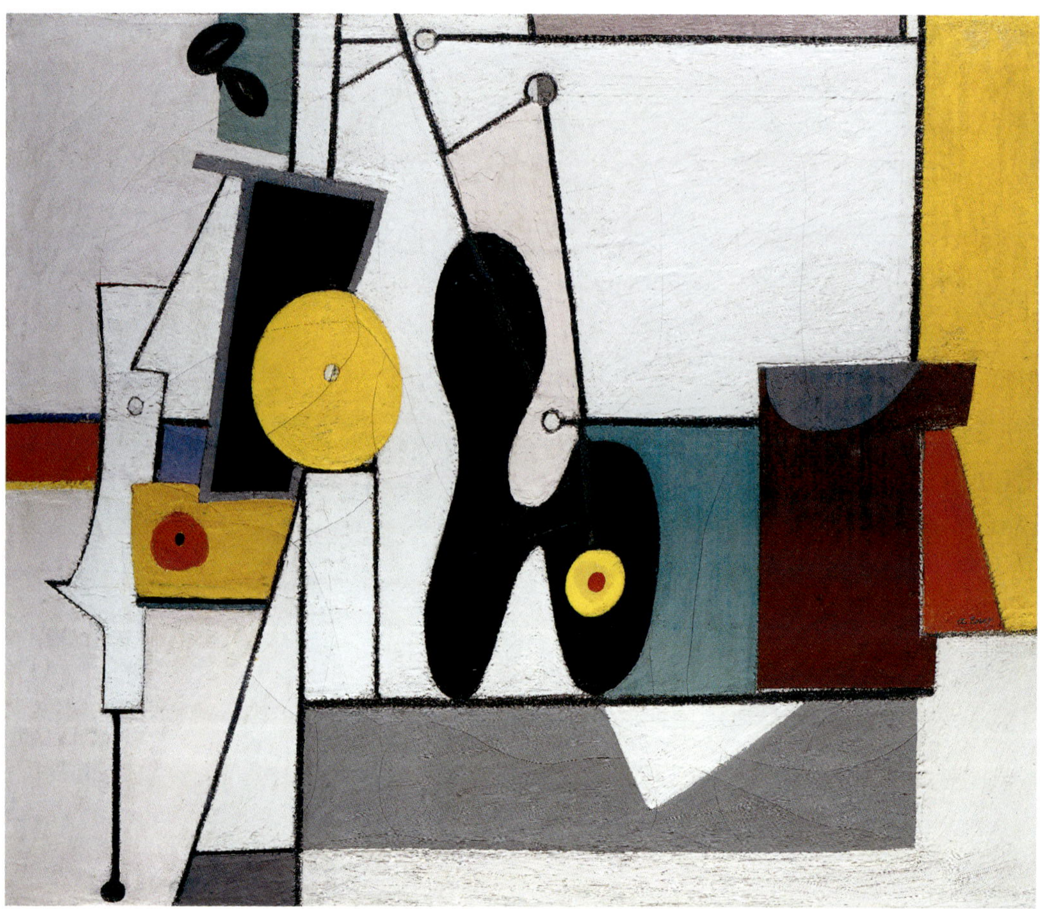

PLATE 10
Arshile Gorky,
Organization, 1933–36.
National Gallery of
Art, Washington, D.C.

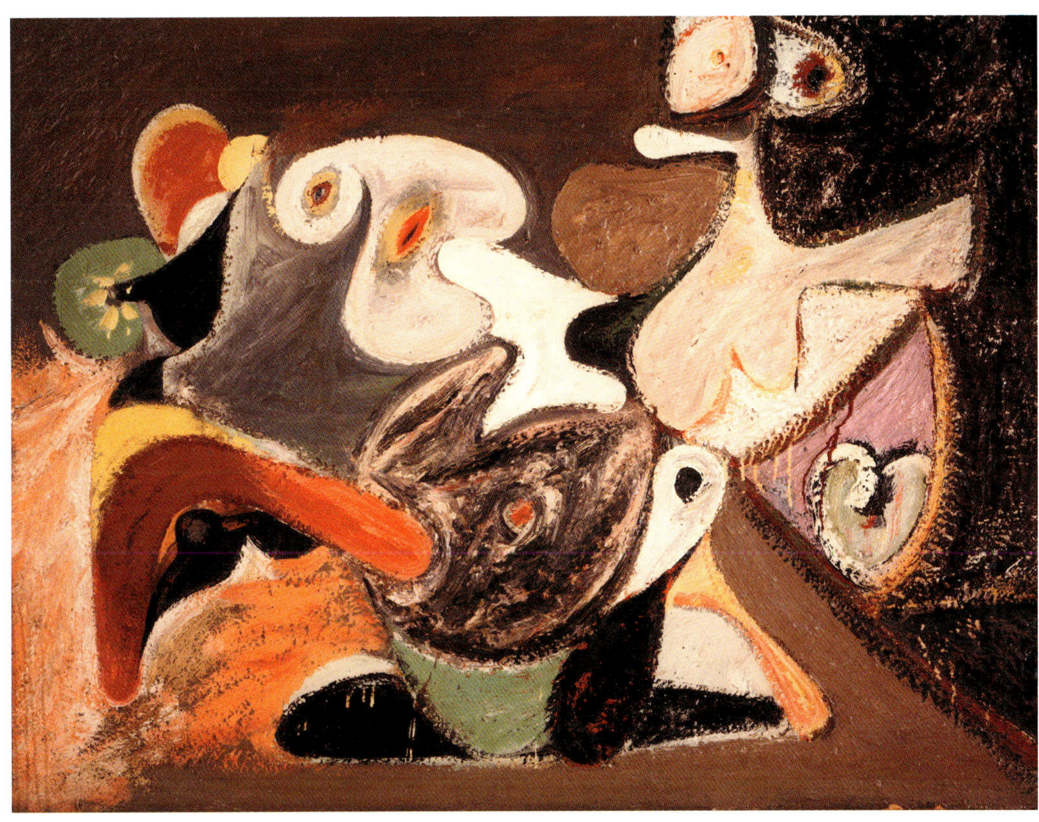

PLATE 11
Arshile Gorky, *Image in Khorkom*, 1934–36. Private collection.

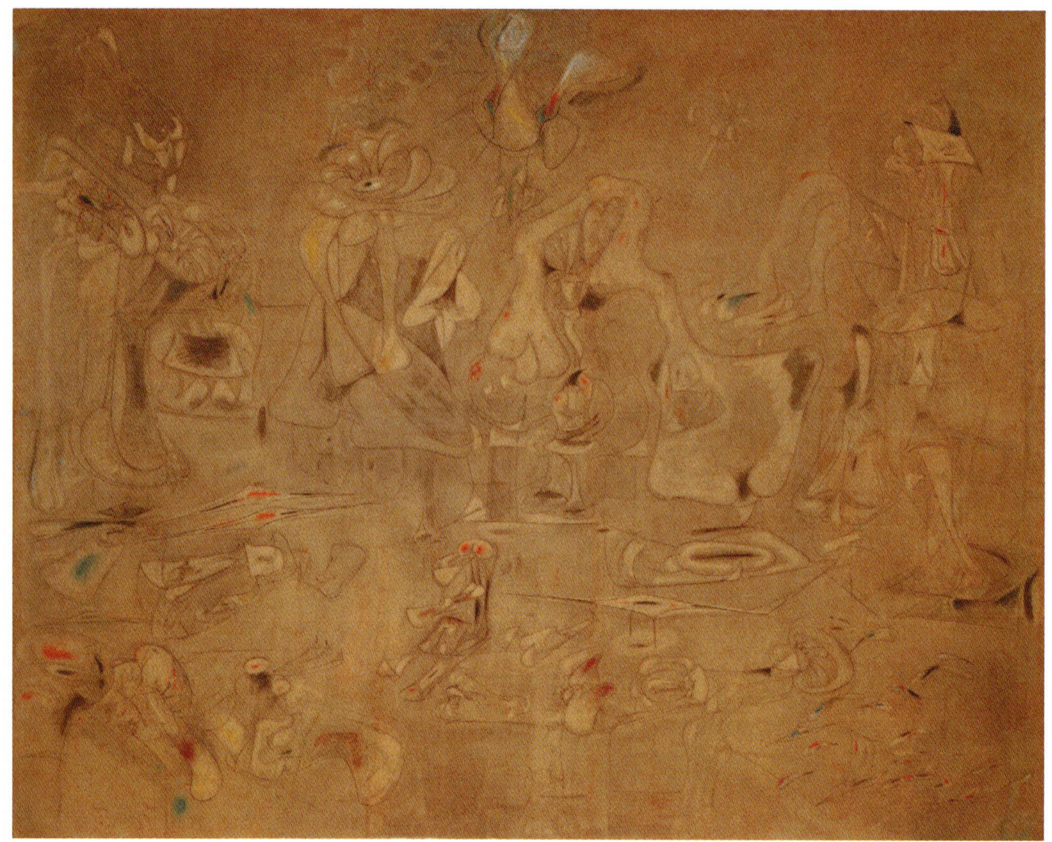

PLATE 12
Arshile Gorky,
Summation, 1947.
The Museum of
Modern Art, New York.

Opposite top:
PLATE 13
Arshile Gorky,
Mechanics of Flying,
1936–37. On extended
loan from the
Collection of The Port
Authority of New York
and New Jersey to the
Newark Museum.

Opposite bottom:
PLATE 14
Arshile Gorky, study for a
mural panel, *Activities on
the Field*, for Admini-
stration Building, Newark
Airport, New Jersey,
1935–36. On extended
loan from the United
States WPA Program to
The Museum of Modern
Art, New York.

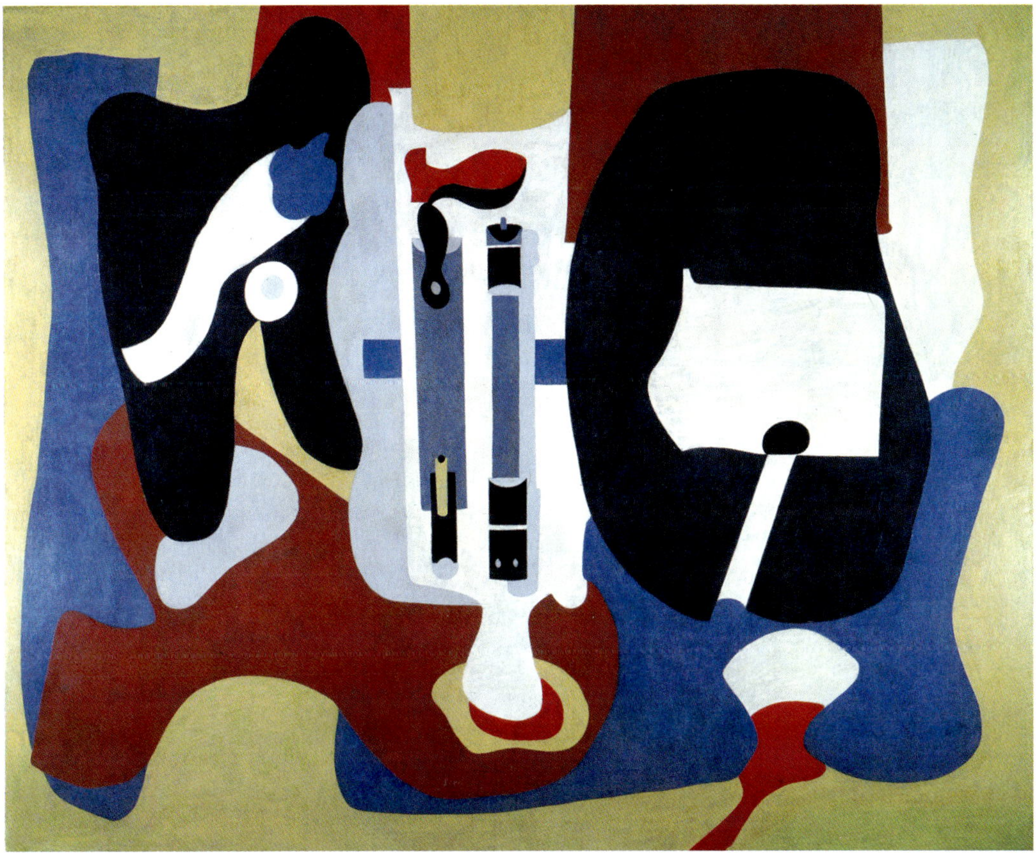

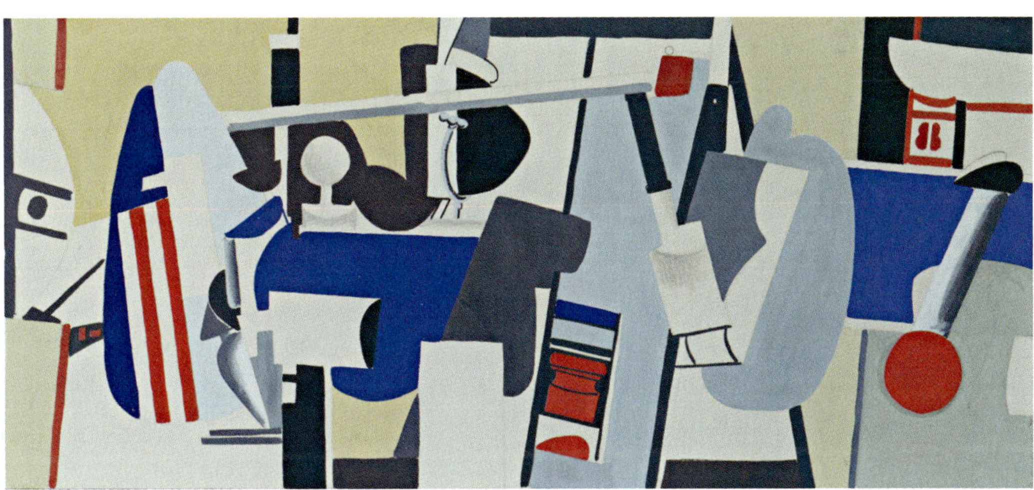

PLATE 15
Arshile Gorky, *Nude*, 1946. Hirshhorn Museum and Sculpture Garden, Smithsonian Institution, Washington, D.C.

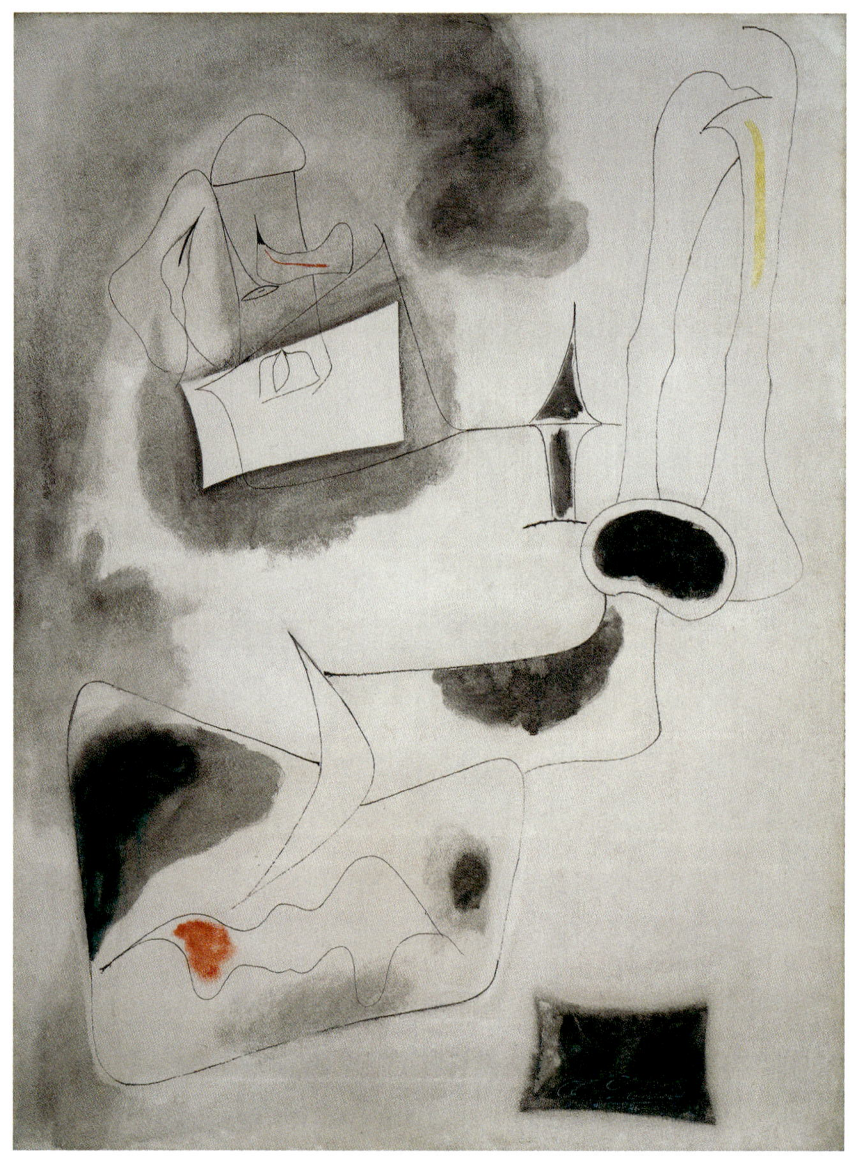

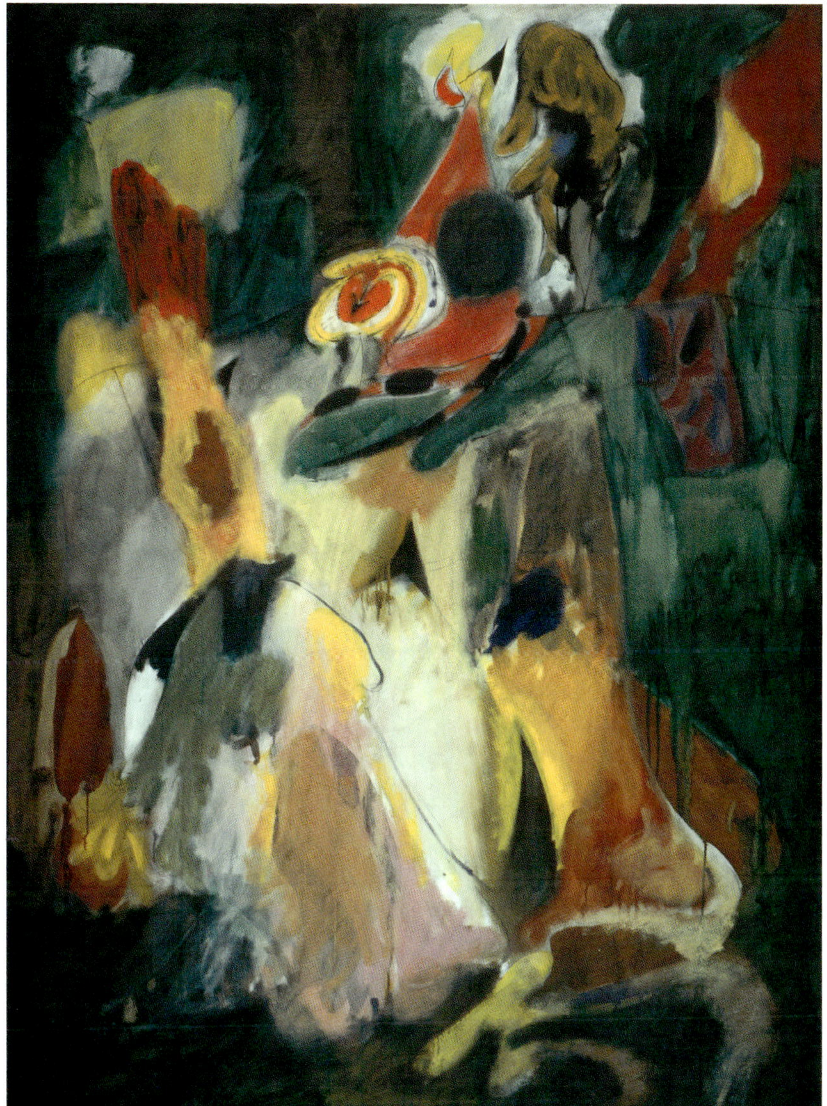

PLATE 16
Arshile Gorky, *Waterfall*, 1943. Tate Gallery, London.

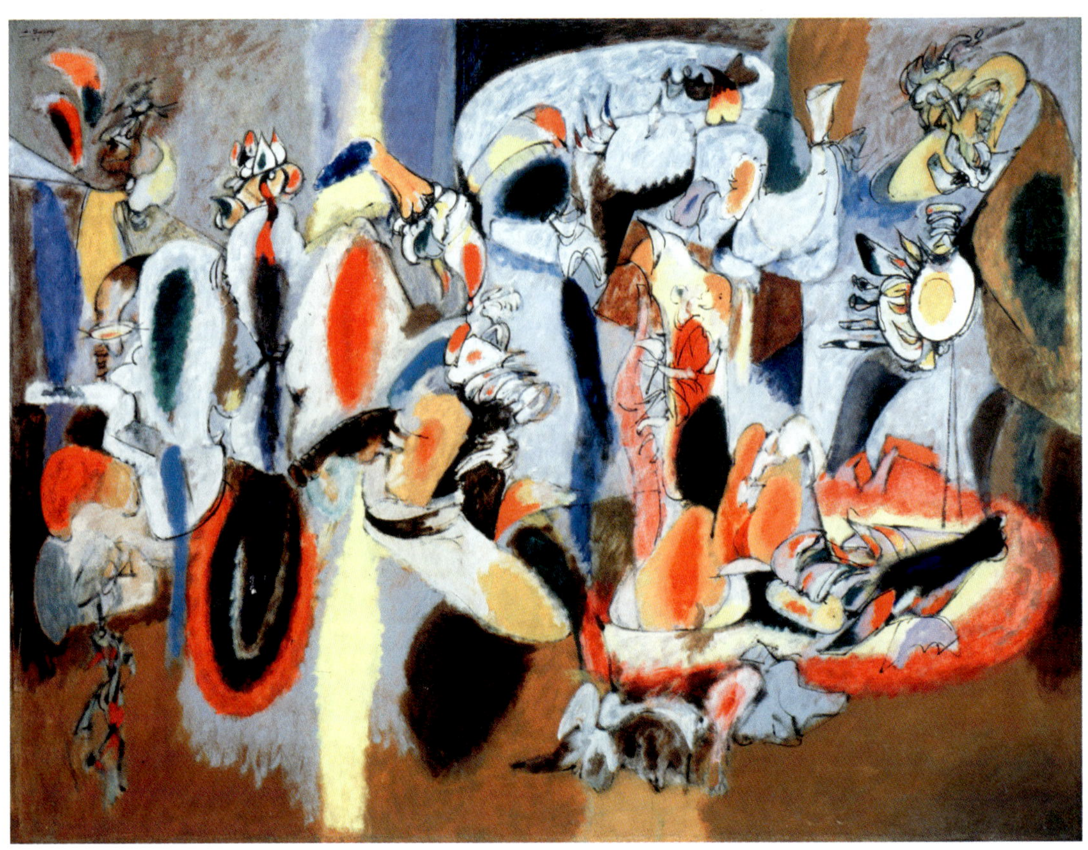

PLATE 17
Arshile Gorky, *The Liver Is the Cock's Comb*, 1944. Albright-Knox Art Gallery, Buffalo, N.Y.

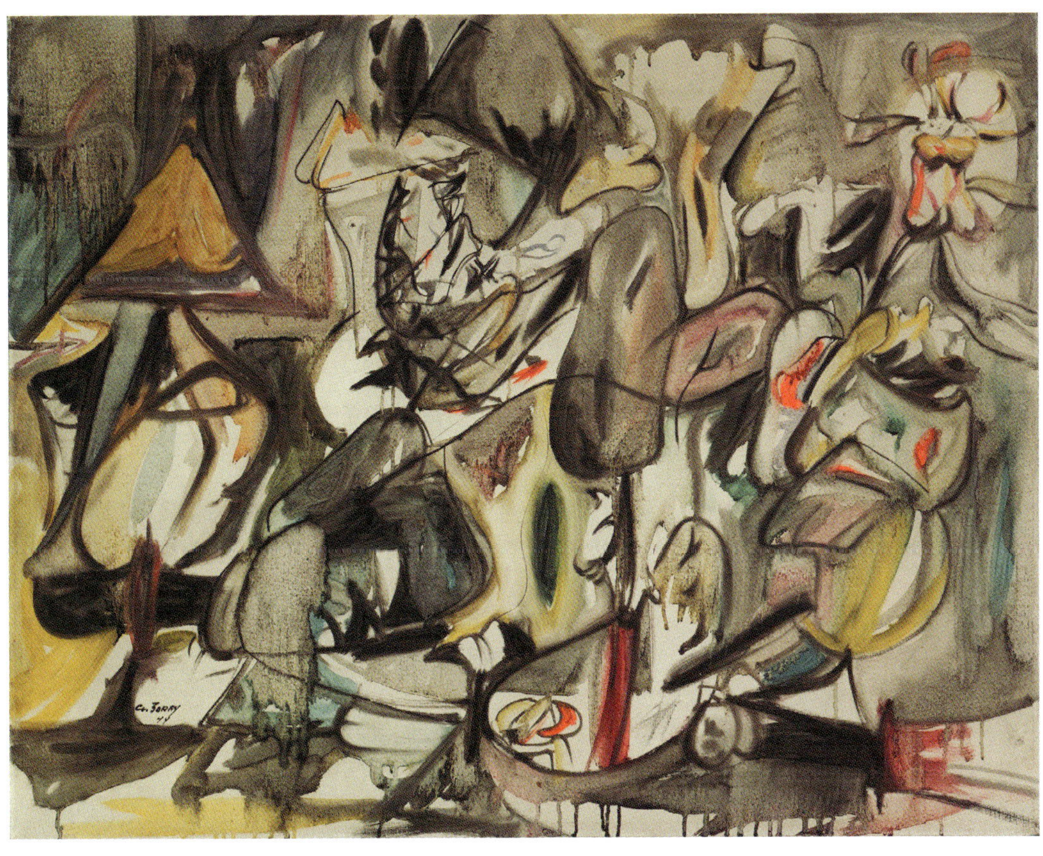

PLATE 18
Arshile Gorky, *The Leaf of the Artichoke Is an Owl*, 1944. The Museum of Modern Art, New York.

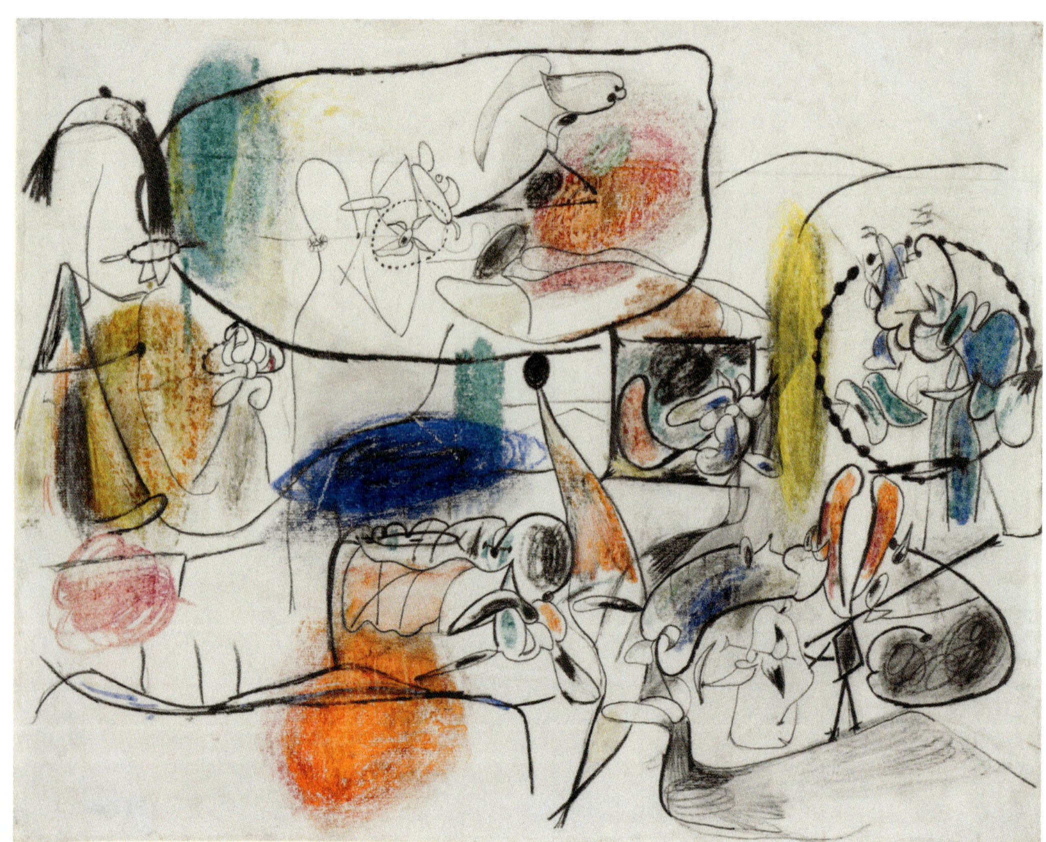

PLATE 19
Arshile Gorky, *Virginia Landscape,* 1943. The Metropolitan Museum of Art, New York.

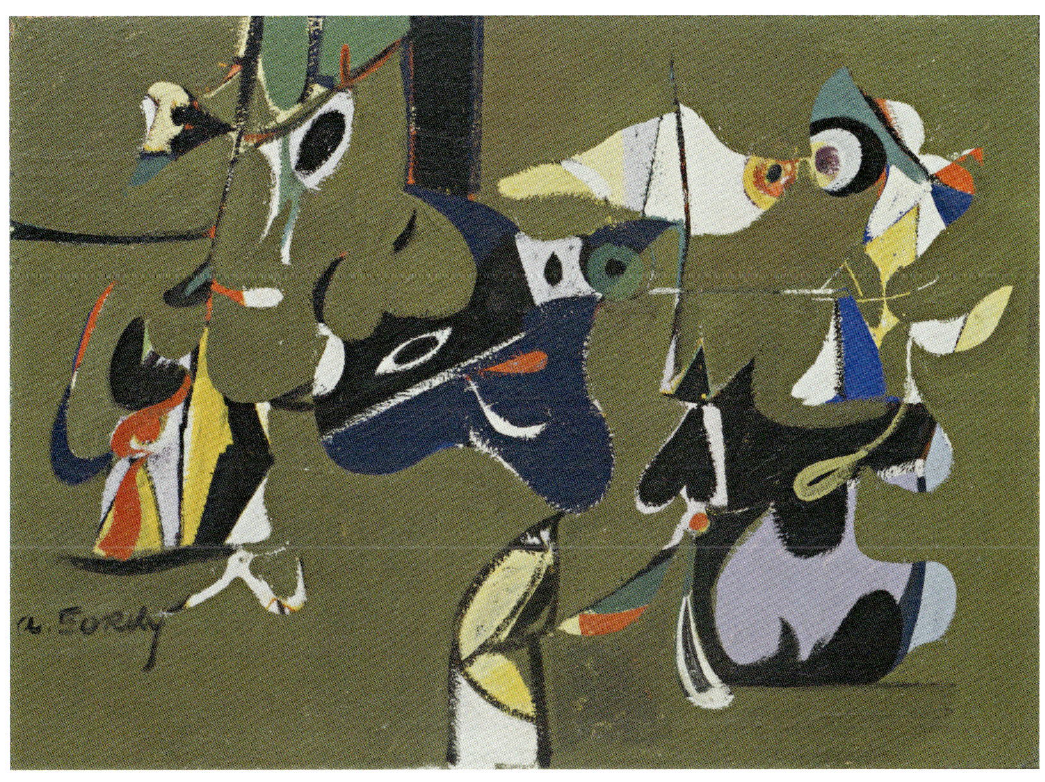

PLATE 20
Arshile Gorky, *Garden in Sochi*, 1941. The Museum of Modern Art, New York.

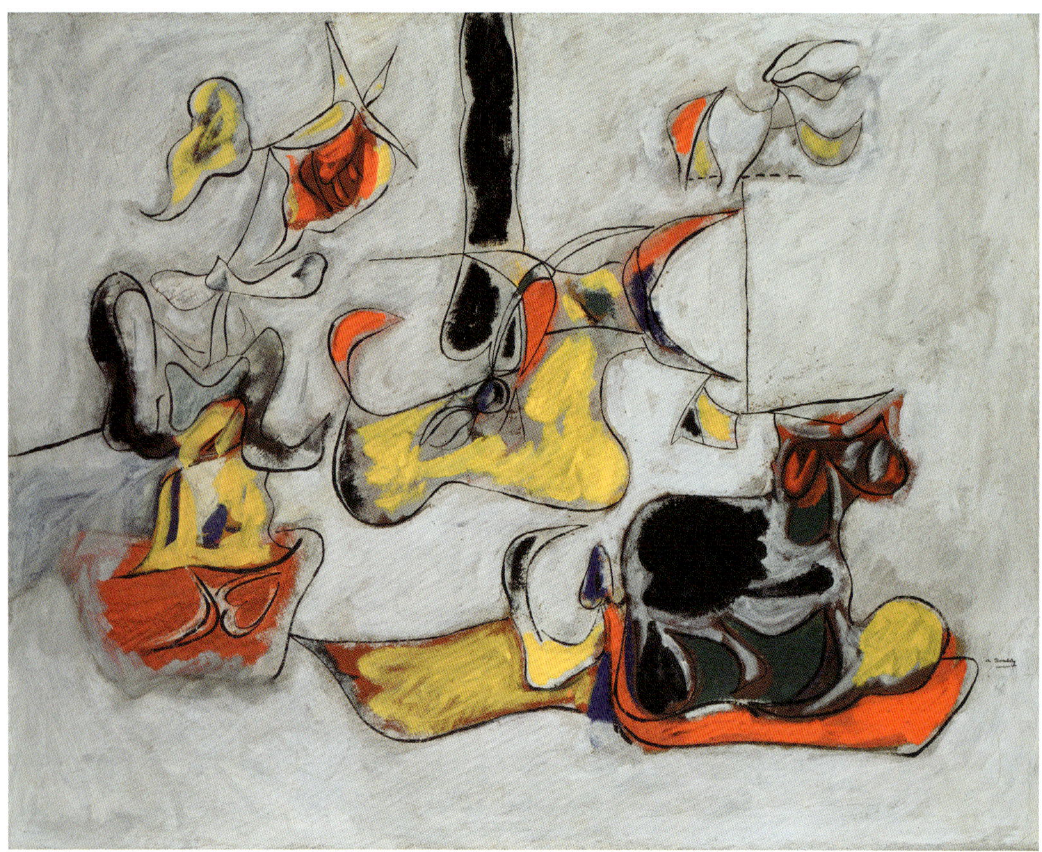

PLATE 21
Arshile Gorky, *Garden in Sochi*, ca. 1943. The Museum of Modern Art, New York.

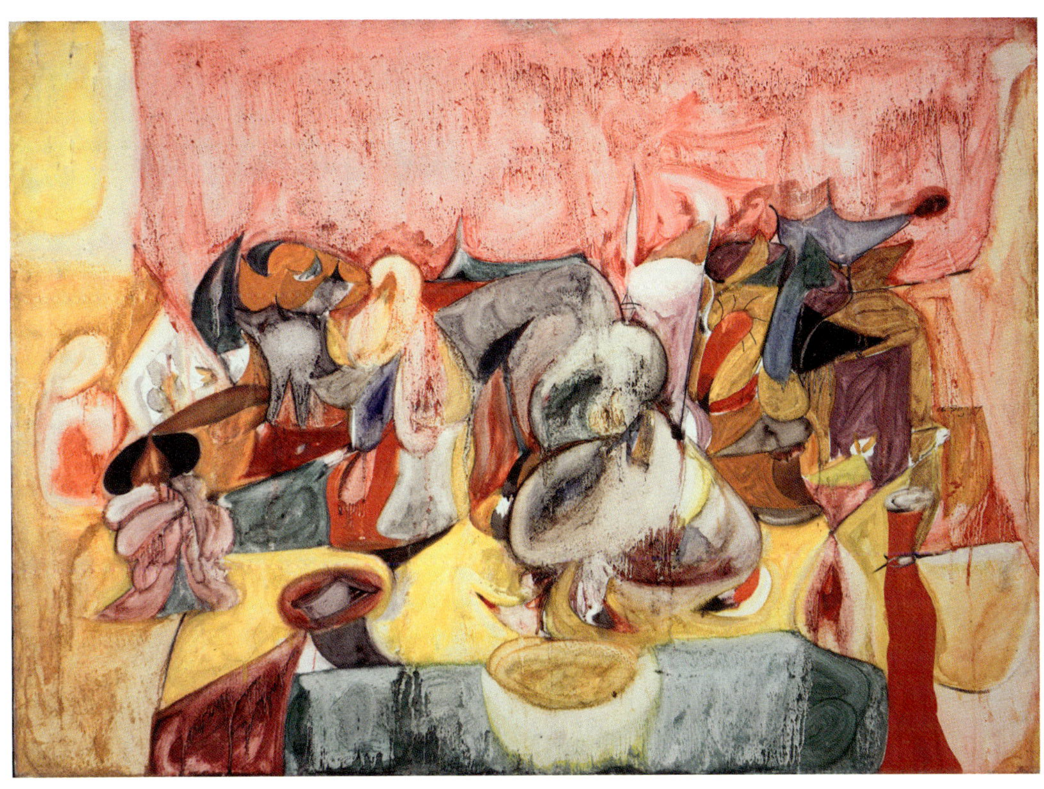

PLATE 22
Arshile Gorky, *Scent of Apricots on the Fields*, 1944. Private collection.

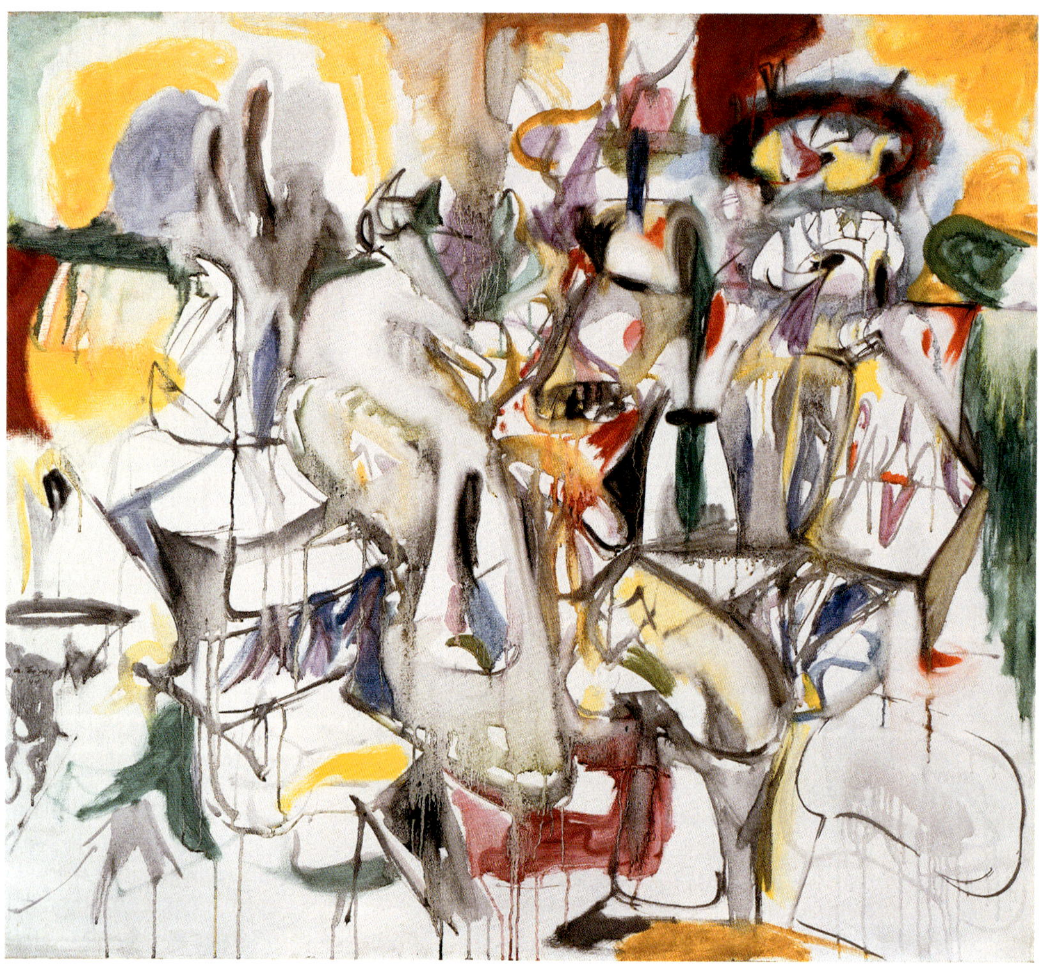

PLATE 23
Arshile Gorky, *How My Mother's Embroidered Apron Unfolds in My Life*, 1944. Seattle Art Museum.

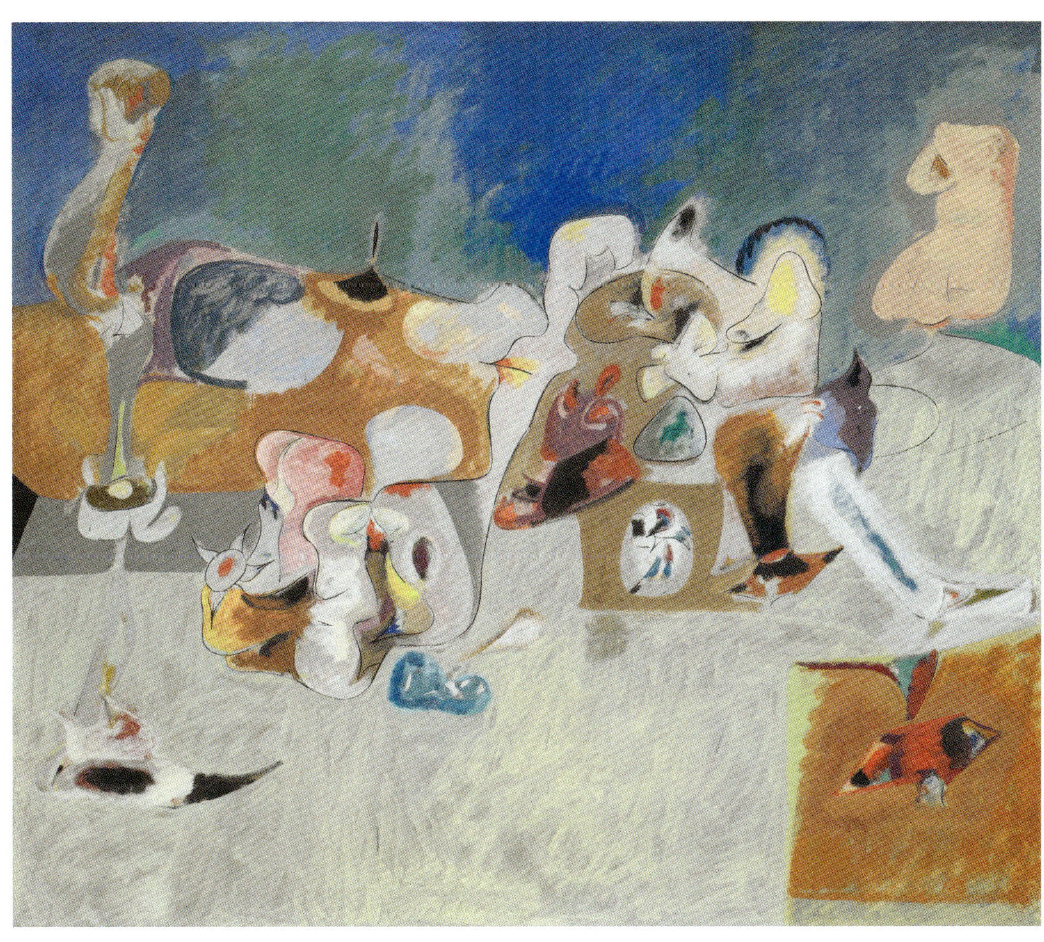

PLATE 24
Arshile Gorky, *The Plow and the Song* (II), 1946. The Art Institute of Chicago.

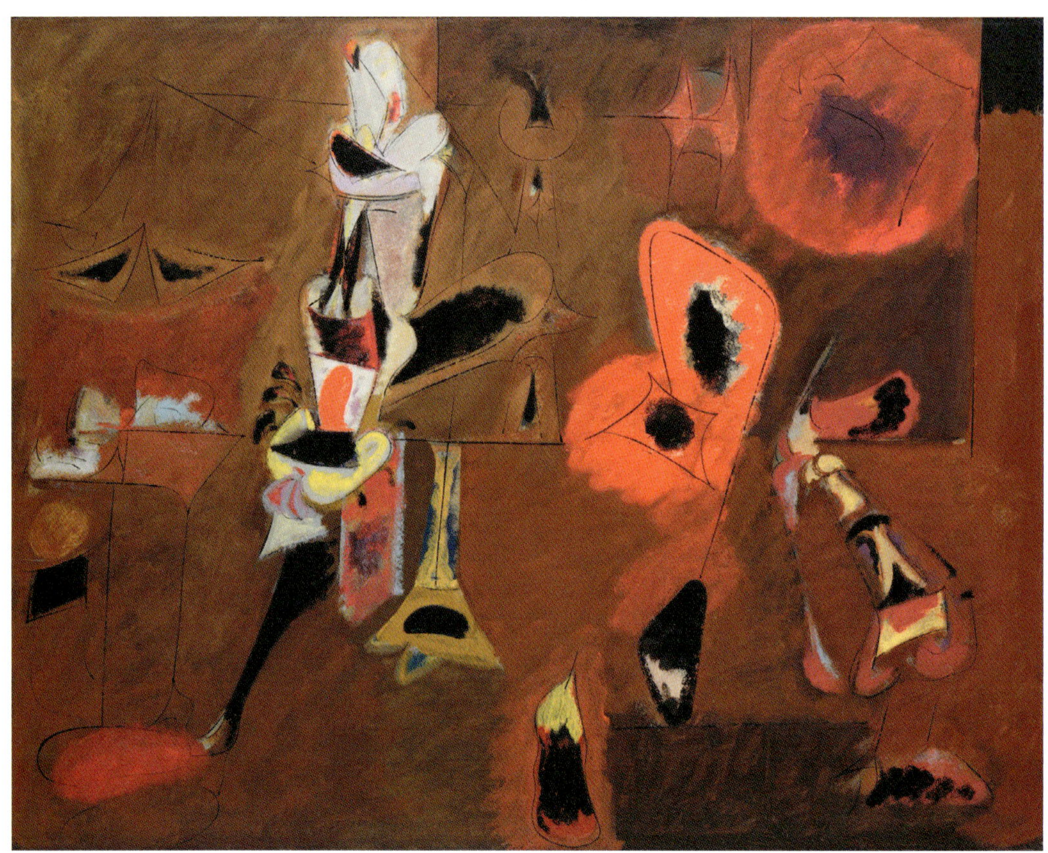

PLATE 25
Arshile Gorky, *Agony*, 1947. The Museum of Modern Art, New York.

Accompanying Gorky and Graham on a typical outing to the Metropolitan Museum of Art, Gorky's young contemporary Jacob Kainen explained one of the habits of Gorky's group: "Graham and Gorky took that painting [Poussin's *Triumph of Bacchus*] apart in detail, traced the spiral movement spinning off from the wheel of the chariot, followed the verticals, horizontals, and diagonals and related all the spaces, shapes, and colors and their cunning echoes."[35] After observing a set of relationships like this in a composition that interested him, actually acquiring this second language, Gorky went back to his studio and translated them into his own work. Gorky kept seeing possibilities in the visual languages he observed, but everything was a possibility within the larger system of Modernism and abstraction of which he was becoming a part.

Because his interests were highly technical, Gorky liked to reenvision spatial relationships. At Western movies, for instance, much to the dismay of surrounding patrons, Gorky would continually point out, shot by shot, visual patterns, such as how the shape of a hill was the opposite of an indentation in a saddle or was related to the shadow of a galloping horse.[36] Gorky was seemingly incapable of not viewing the world in terms of shapes, forms, and layers. He evaluated all aspects of life with a spatial intelligence, reading the visual language that surrounded him constantly and then incessantly trying to work it out or replicate it in some form on his canvas. In his work, Gorky was the cinematographer who created a world with natural laws that he himself controlled. Ethel Schwabacher, who spent much time in the artist's studio as a student and colleague, suggests that Gorky's "method was to relate all distances between objects and himself to an imaginary point; he held a matchbox up before his eyes (literally, not figuratively) and to this fixed point he related the world in front of him."[37] Gorky tried to create likeness though working directly from images of paintings by other artists, by remaking images of women, and later by creating analogies between his own observations of nature and memory. Gorky meant to engage the viewer by enticing him or her with familiar forms, but as in the technique of early cinema, indices in Gorky's art were only revealed in a montage.

Gorky considered how each form functioned in its compositional setting and how it could be applied to or altered in his own. Edward Said's borrowed term "contrapuntal" applies because both the new and the old occur simultaneously in Gorky's work, reflecting the artist's own self-fashioning. "To Gorky at the time," notes Harold Rosenberg, "nothing was more fenced off than his own self. In his work he did his best to assume not only the style of painting of the master he was imitating but the style of his personality as well."[38] Melvin Lader has argued that Gorky "never executed an exact copy. Rather, Gorky examined his sources for their inner structure and meaning. We often find that the variations he made on a source are a valuable stylistic comment on the original."[39] Gorky's work interpreted the original in a manner that reflected his own translation.

The idea of translation is supported by Gorky's use of styles that solved certain visual problems at particular junctures in his career. Paul Cézanne, whom Gorky greatly admired, had segued nineteenth-century art into twentieth-century abstraction, and it seems that Gorky was poised to do the same by translating European art into something American. In *Landscape in the Manner of Cézanne* (plate 8), for instance, Gorky uses Cézannesque precedent to develop some of the building blocks of his later work.[40] Gorky adapts Cézanne's subtle differencing of value and color through thickness, direction, and length of brushstroke rather than through manipulating tonality. Pictorial space is formed from the division and analysis of the painted image of the tree in large sections and from multiple directions, a technique of Cézanne's that informed Cubism, while other sections of the canvas are left free of pigment. This accentuates negative space and transports the eye throughout the composition in a disorienting manner. The light, unpainted areas, mostly in the background, are juxtaposed against the darker depiction of the tree, forcing multiple fractures in the picture plane by pushing the secondary characteristics of the painting forward and the subject back. Like Gorky's identity, the referent of the painting, the tree, becomes fluid within its surrounding space. George Dennison connects this fluidity to the creative act: "The self-awareness of the creative act, entering directly and structurally into the work, can be seen in a great deal of modern art. Gorky has drawn upon it in an extreme and unprecedented way. All that is sensuous is revealed in its departure from shapes and the process of shaping, and is made to exist so primordially that it manifests something of the mysterious *élan* of inchoate energies."[41]

This self-awareness of the creative act follows from the artist's self-creation, and the visual malleability of a work becomes a characteristic of the work itself. Gorky may also have felt a kinship with Cézanne similar to that he felt with Picasso. Picasso's Iberian roots and respect of the form and superstition in the "primitive" art that he adopted drew Gorky to him, and Cézanne's simplicity and unconventionality likely attracted Gorky as well. Like Gorky, Cezanne had not been formally schooled, which some believed allowed him to "see" in a very genuine way. Cézanne, says Howard Singerman, became an artist by virtue of his own "inability and redefined the terms of artistic success."[42] Singerman has described, in his analysis of the development in the way artists are trained, that Cézanne as a failure became a theme of modern art for the first half of twentieth century, and it was this "failure" that allowed Cézanne to be an individual artist.[43] Critic Maurice Denis explained that Cézanne's trajectory was one of adaptation or mimicry. "His originality grows in his contact with those whom he imitates or is impressed by; thence comes his persistent *gaucherie,* his happy *naïveté.*"[44] This second eye of Modernism, the "innocent eye," framed as a childish perception that allowed one to see flat colors, was first identified by John Ruskin in his *Elements of Drawing*, but carried over into the lore of Cézanne. Before developing writing and speech skills and a fundamental expression that separates image from thing and image from language, one is believed to have an innocent and simplified vision and concept development, like the innocence of childhood vision itself.[45] The untrained Cézanne broke into a new dimension in art because he was uninhibited by the expectations placed on artists at the time and saw with a unique vision, which is exactly what can be argued for Gorky as well.

Although evaluating and building upon the manner in which others structured their work became one of Gorky's trademarks, it was almost his downfall. Similarities to Picasso and Cézanne were often seen merely as imitations. But Gorky was not the only artist charged with imitation. In 1930, Stuart Davis was similarly accused. Dore Ashton comments that in fact, "many artists of Gorky's generation attempted to emulate modern masters, but they were not as good at it."[46] Donald Kuspit writes that "not only was Gorky not an imitator of the Modernist elders in his thirties works, but he was already beginning to move beyond their ideas, which they themselves had reified into clichés."[47] Gorky's art, then, was an invigoration of the staid state of Modernism at the time, and it existed within an American aesthetic that was not and never had really been independent of European artists. In Davis's retort to those accusations, he eloquently notes that few significant American artists had developed independently from European influence and that he himself "did not spring into the world fully equipped to paint the kind of pictures I want to paint."[48] Davis asks why, since America consists almost entirely of hyphenated Americans, artists cannot be similarly hyphenated in terms of their stylistic influences, as long as they ultimately develop their own language.

Through Gorky's visual language, he formed a dialogue with tradition by creating an aesthetic synthesis that is contrapuntal in nature. Without appropriating Western art or being appropriated by it, he extracted fundamental contextual elements of form, color, and line that served as a basis for his own work. As an active participant in this very particular mimetic creative process, Gorky established an expressive format that served as a foundation for himself as an artist from outside the culture in which he practiced and for other American artists who succeeded him. Gorky contended that the son is always killing the father, meaning that new ages or generations extinguish older ones in order to live. But because art, which he loved, was his father, Gorky could not kill it. "Since I as a son," he said, "cannot kill my father—that is my past, the past of art—then I have to die because I am born to art and cannot deny my father and cannot murder him."[49] Gorky admitted that he was destined to follow art's tradition because he was born to a parent whom he greatly loved. As much as one might deny a father, it is impossible to do so because one's existence is evidence of having had one. However, one can change one's ancestry by taking on a new name, as Gorky did, or adopting and modifying the styles of previous artists.

It makes sense that while Gorky communicated in English as his second language, he expressed himself in a new visual language as well. It was common for writers of Armenian descent, such as William Saroyan, Dickran Kouyoumdjian, and Michael Arlen, to write in a language other than that of their heritage.[50] In their stories, they often translated their intercultural experiences. Saroyan, for example, wrote in English of his hyphenated Armenian experience in America. It stands to reason, then, that in his new world Gorky would embrace the language of Modernism insofar as it translated his existential existence. If Davis's commentary is characteristic of the historic moment, to see Gorky's volition as inescapably derived from displacement would be to denigrate his achievements as an artist within the diaspora. Rather, Gorky's process, while a component of his displacement and informed by it, was contrapuntal.

The manifestations of Gorky's actions are visible in the 1930 *Abstraction with a Palette* (plate 9). Contemporaneous with Davis's work, as noted above, Gorky flattened objects and distorted them into a combination of viewpoints that recalled Picasso and Braque. Gorky often painted several versions of one Picasso composition, each emphasizing a different element of the work, and borrowed from Cubism "the idea that painting is the establishment of flat, essentially parallel, overlapping and hard-edged planes of color which may refer to actual objects, but are independent of them."[51] At the same time, Gorky integrated and recalled images that reflected his worlds. The argyle pattern in *Abstraction with a Palette* is often linked to Picasso's harlequins, but it can also be likened to a sweater that Gorky owned (fig. 19). Further, the image hints at a stool leg in the lower left quadrant, palette in the center,[52] and table-like form jutting out into the lower right. In works such as *Harmony* (fig. 20), from 1930–31, characteristic of what is informally called Gorky's "striped period," the artist worked through Cubist spatial construction, defining shape with striped, solid, and lined patterns that differentiate planes within the picture. Gorky's drawn and painted works exhibit the artist's keen awareness of the way in which images are layered one over another to create spatial illusion. Recognition and reference are multidimensional, drawing upon various motifs—his sweaters, Picasso's conventions, and adaptations of formal elements.

Gorky's visual mapping incorporates line that is not necessarily a barrier and color that is not always a coherent form. Gorky was "always looking and making decisions about what he saw,"[53] often producing his own works by cutting up prints by others and working from them as if they were still lifes. In this way, there is mimicry, but the dismemberment and rearticulation destroy the authority of the original works, leaving only traces of the original reference. This hint at Postmodern splitting—decentering, dislocating, and fragmenting—remains modern, since the meaning is determined by the formal structure of the work. In addition, Gorky's debt to Cubism also transgresses time and space because the spiritual and spatial aspects of Cubism are sometimes linked to a concept of the fourth dimension. This means that a Cubist composition repre-

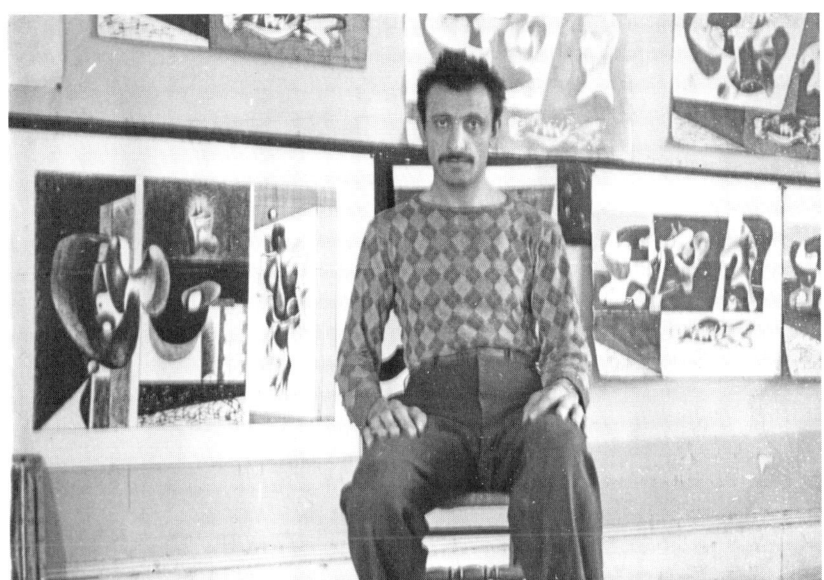

FIGURE 19
Photograph of Arshile Gorky by Alexander Sandow.

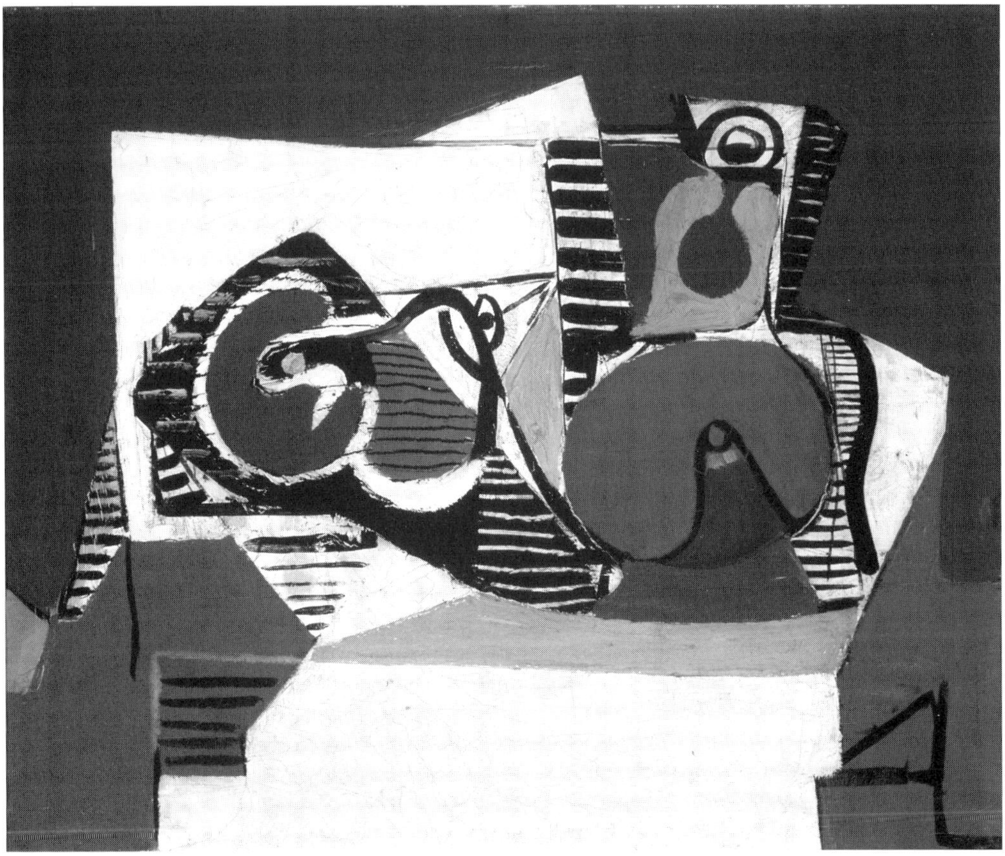

FIGURE 20
Arshile Gorky, *Harmony*, 1931.

sents simultaneity through the multiple views of an internal object depicted all at once and through its references to aspects of the outside world. Richard Wollheim, in summarizing the crucial position of the fragment in the contemporary artist Kitaj's work, has explained that "the fragment serves three purposes. It attaches the work of art to its past by embedding some of the past in the present: it reproduces the condition of modern life, and, in particular, of modern urban life, to which Modernist art is wedded; and it allows the artist to capture intimations of the uncanny, and the daemonic and the dreamlike, which are integral to any art of a confessional kind, which modern art is committed to being."[54] The fractal identities that Modernist painting develops are crucial to both its technical and philosophical elements.

It is the concern for space, layered but still illusory, that may have prevented Gorky from pursuing collage after his experimentations with the medium.[55] Jim Jordan has viewed Gorky's attempt at collage as a possible pun upon the Cubist invention, even though Gorky was never one to treat art, especially that of artists he revered, lightly, and insisted that the artist abandoned his exploration because he entirely disliked the idea.[56] More likely, Gorky rejected collage because of its constraints. Objects were too immediately referential to the real world and could not be manipulated and transformed in the same manner as those that were painted,[57] such as the argyle sweater in *Abstraction with a Palette* that also referred to Picasso and the palette shape that recurs and transforms throughout his career.[58] For Gorky the space of the painting subordinated the identifiability of objects, allowing them to act as pseudonyms. Therefore, collage-like elements ultimately become about the act of artmaking, not object representation, which was Gorky's ultimate project. In this sense, the idea of collage that shifted and layered shapes and severed objects served a useful purpose for Gorky because it *re*-presents objects that we experience with a singular perception into something that is metaphoric and associative, like Gorky's art. Gorky's collage-like painting creates a discourse between the recognizable and abstract, the identifiable and poetic, and becomes a transmutation that functions as a sign.

As well, Gorky did not necessarily need the identifiable or three-dimensional in his work. He viewed the medium of paint as having an integrity of its own, using its own depth and layering to assist in defining or defying spatial relationships or object identification, much like the push-pull of color, form, and texture that immigrant Hans Hofmann taught in his classes in New York and of which Gorky was aware. Hofmann asserted that the essence of the picture exists only within the picture plane and that there is a movement and countermovement, or push-pull, between the two-dimensional plane and three-dimensional space, which is devoid of illusion.[59] *Abstraction with a Palette* also serves as a outstanding example of Gorky's process. The surface is thick with paint, and the large, brown central palette is sculpted in very flat relief.

The palpability of oil paint became an exciting part of Gorky's aesthetic.

His painting *Organization* (plate 10) further illustrates his investment in a picture's texture as well as its composition, and is a good example of how Gorky began to translate form into his own visual language. Over four feet high and five feet wide, *Organization* consists of a thick impasto that incorporates so many layers of reworked paint that it has cracked extensively due to weight. Black lines cage its numerous semigeometric shapes, distributed within a broad, white background. In addition to orange and yellow circles that act as halos around small points of color and a biomorphic black form in the center of the work, an assortment of rectangular shapes and incomplete triangles is situated parallel to the painting's edges. The shapes have their own properties (or perhaps identities) from the color and texture of the paint.

Surface treatment gives each of the shapes its own minute physical height or depth. For instance, the white area just right of center consist of brushstrokes read horizontally, whereas more vertical strokes line the painting's left side. Layers of swirling brushstrokes define the circular forms, such as the large yellow orb. The central black biomorphic form is also thick with paint. It is both on top of, and in, the painting, its edges forming a ridge that cuts into the shapes around it. The black lines too are incised into the background, both marking color on top, as the edges feather into the surrounding shapes, and scraping it up because the action of creating the lines disturbed the drying surface of the canvas like a plow turning up dry earth. Gorky was known to leave his palettes uncovered for days until the blobs of paint that had been squeezed straight from the tube became gummy or formed a thin, blister-like skin that he would pop and then use on the canvas, making a pasty film.[60] Such working, reworking, and mixing of textures gave the picture plane many diverse physical elements that mimicked the outside world. While living in New York City, the artist was captivated by textures that marked the urban landscape. Jacob Kainen explains how, in his excitement with tactile surfaces, Gorky "pointed to unplanned, nature-made felicities of texture and pattern on mud-spattered walls; surprising color combinations on painted surfaces worn by wind and rain; cracks and other vicissitudes on pavements and curbs."[61] Legibility of the painted surface is modern in that it moves the artist away from accurate representation and metaphorically relates to landscape.[62]

Other artists shared Gorky's fascination with the surfaces around them. "Beauty is everywhere," said Fernand Léger, "in the arrangement of your pots and pans, on the white wall of your kitchen."[63] Gorky's passion for the physical qualities of the painting surface anticipated the all-over painting of Abstract Expressionists such as Willem de Kooning, a frequent visitor to Gorky's studio, and Jackson Pollock, who was familiar with Gorky's art through encounters at artist gatherings and from his wife, Lee Krasner, who was well connected in artist circles and who had briefly painted in the style of Arshile Gorky.[64] Although the extent of Gorky's direct impact on these artists is unknown, as part of the artistic diaspora of New York at the time, he was working in potentially influential ways, including laying his canvas on the floor to paint and pouring paint onto it, foreshadowing both Pollock's drip painting and Helen Frankenthaler's stain painting, which soon followed. Nan Greacen explains that "there came a moment when Gorky poured [the paint] on like cement, by the bucketful. I saw him do it. The canvas was on the floor, edged with boards. He mixed the paint in basins, then stood up and poured it into a mold. I am not sure if the canvas actually had a mold on it, but that's what it looked like. I'm not absolutely sure that what he used was paint, even. All I can tell you is that, whatever it was, he poured it onto the canvas when it was flat, and there was a lot of it."[65] Gorky's sensitivity to materials and the sculptural qualities that such techniques describe is evident in works such as *Image in Khorkom* (plate 11). The center area, about the size and relief of a dinner plate, looks to have been created in the manner Greacen describes and shows Gorky's tendency to use thickened paint from his partially dried palettes. This process likely served a gratifying purpose for the artist as well. As described in reference to the paintings of himself and his mother, painting for Gorky was a state of suspended animation where time, space, and place were subject to the act and the existence of the artist. Indeed, since the subject of the painting, his home village of Khorkom, was part of his lost-imaginary past and he was painting it in America, his transposition was complete.[66]

Gorky evoked Khorkom through interlocking shapes and surfaces whose heavy impasto culminated in the thick, plate-sized mold of paint in the center. Even in his drawings, Gorky created tangible surfaces, which helped to express the image. He layered different types of pencil strokes and then washed over or erased them, only to add more drawing before finishing. His constant reworking produced a terrain whose topography became an integral element in the work. The surface, Ethel Schwabacher has noted, "suggests the erosion of mountains, the slow filtering down of layers of soil on the earth. In this patient way nature creates a new typography. Gorky imitated nature's processes."[67] Gorky's filtering process is part of both his art and life. In his earlier art, he filtered the images or beings of others. In life, he filtered emotions and memory. Later his mature work was a slow filtering down of layers of memory recall and emotion—a new typography on the canvas.[68]

The huge drawing *Summation* (plate 12), now in the Museum of Modern Art in New York, is a superb example of this technique. In it, Gorky layered multiple pencil drawings over each other and then rubbed back into them with his eraser. The effect of the blended layers creates ambiguous space because each successive stage of the drawing is part of earlier or later ones. The constant erasure eroded the paper and displaced the normal hierarchy of drawing. The drawing is no longer *on* the paper, but the paper is *in* the drawing. Like the past, which can be covered but remains ever-present, something of the original draw-

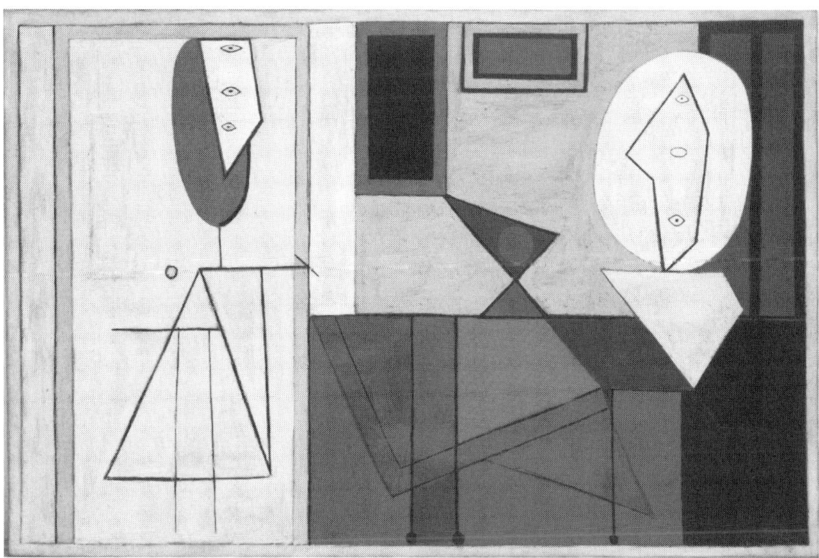

FIGURE 21
Pablo Picasso, *The Studio*, Paris, winter 1927–28; dated 1928. The Museum of Modern Art, New York.

ing, through the distress that erasure caused to the surface of the paper or the ghost image of the graphite residue, is always left on the surface. The viewer experiences the work through its textures as much as its form because the friction of the process becomes as evident as the friction between background and foreground, concept and space, and image and abstraction. The textures, which reflect those found in the natural world, are familiar to the viewer.

The effect of this mimetic landscaping process is even more pronounced in Gorky's painting than in his drawing. Brushstrokes are visible, and ridges and paint masses of varying levels break up entire areas of a single color that should read visually as two-dimensional. As in *Organization*, Gorky used the medium as an independent element, not solely as a vehicle to define form. Many of Gorky's canvases are laden with numerous layers of paint that have been scraped, dried, and reworked extensively. This process creates a dialectic of brute materiality. The surface of the work is physically evident, becoming itself a body where irruptive and disruptive forces collide in a manner that literally rebuilds and reestablishes the work.

Gorky's working and reworking and mixtures of textures and forms in a discursive manner gave the picture plane its own topography. A painting can be defined as one composition, but the multiple surfaces that exist simultaneously differentiate the forms on the surface, eliding a singular reading of the work. The shapes in Gorky's *Organization* are often compared to those in Pablo Picasso's 1928 *Studio* (fig. 21). While they share an underlying structure defined by black lines, the objects in *Organization* are flat on the picture plane, whereas *Studio* defines a particular interior architectural space. Picasso's black lines

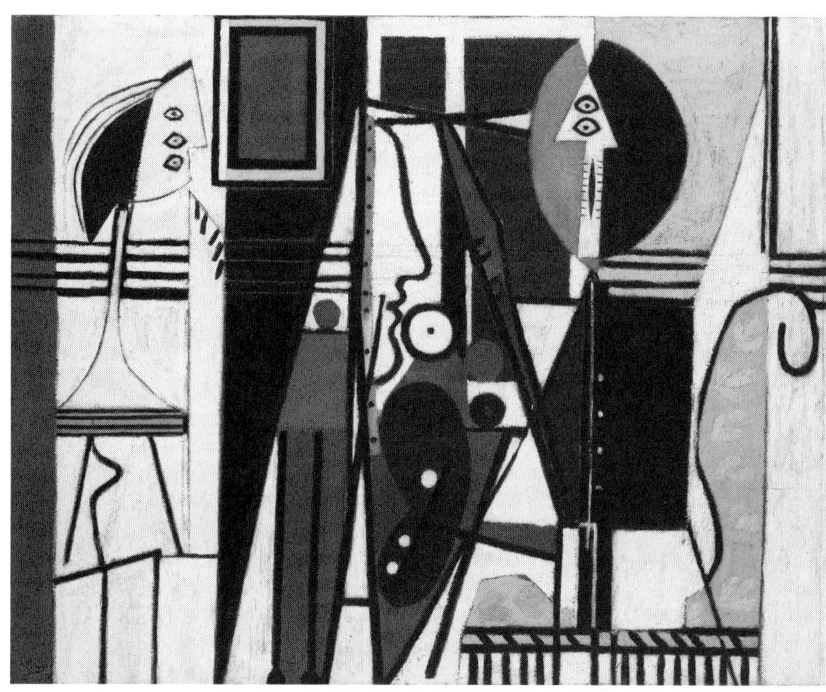

FIGURE 22
Pablo Picasso, *Painter and Model*, Paris, 1928. The Museum of Modern Art, New York.

frame a room with a door on the left, a back wall hung with pictures, and a table in the center with a bust placed on a table at the right; a figure stands in front of the door. Gorky's process of translation is evident here as well. In *Organization*, Gorky dissolved the representational space by removing elements of the composition piece by piece from Picasso's context so it was no longer necessary to identify them by situating them in an architectural space. Gorky adopted the motif of Picasso's doorknobs, seen on *Studio*'s left side, but redistributed them as points that accent and exploit the compositional structure of the painting because they connect the black line at intersections or endpoints. Gorky translates the Picasso more fully into the language of abstraction because space is made ambiguous and the elements of the Picasso lose their context while still leaving indexical traces. The resulting picture by Gorky is a disfiguration rather than an appropriation, and, whether one looks at the original Picasso with knowledge of the Gorky or the Gorky with the knowledge of its basis in the Picasso, the act of looking becomes one of rediscovery.

Gorky rarely incorporated only one work at a time as a model, but combined the elements of many that he melded together in his reinterpretation. *Organization* has also been compared to Picasso's 1928 painting *Painter and Model* (fig. 22). Gorky conflated his vision of Picasso's two works and metamorphosed them into *Organization*, where he actually *organized* aesthetics by compressing figure and ground. The internal balance in the composition may also incorporate a translation of classic Piet Mondrian paintings that have verticals and horizontals designated by black lines and white spaces graphed and balanced with cubes and rectangles of color. In essence, Gorky's visual language reflects both the rupture caused by the fragmenting of experience at the heart of his own physical displacement and his pursuit of modern art, by displacing selected elements of Picasso's works and translating them into his own composition.[69]

According to Roland Barthes, speaking of writing but in terms we can extend to painting, such a practice creates a "multidimensional space in which a variety of writings, none of them original, blend and clash." Barthes goes on to speak of "tissues of quotations" that mix writings and translate them.[70] Gorky's practice in visual terms is a flirtation with the real. Gorky was, in a way, creating a kind of alternate universe in his painting in much the same way that the Cubists had. Cubism was very much attuned to conceptions of science, such as quantum theory, articulated by Max Planck in 1900, Einstein's 1905 theory of relativity, the development of the motion picture, the idea that objects were built up from components called atoms, and considerations of the fourth dimension. "When Braque and Picasso stopped trying to imitate the normal appearance of a wineglass," explained Clement Greenberg, "and tried instead to approximate, by *analogy*, the way nature opposed verticals in general to horizontals in general—at this point, art caught up with the new conception and feeling of reality that was already emerging in general sensibility as well as in science."[71] The Cubists fractured objects and spliced them into space, opening up the closed form of painting. The multiple perspectives in Cubist works acted like graphed coordinates that varied with relative motion; therefore, the artist's interpretations of different events, impressions, and feelings were recorded simultaneously, and both the artist's and viewer's relation to the painting could vary as well.

Following the work of such artists, Gorky's art is also a window into multiple worlds and simultaneity, and the idea that when Gorky painted he was transcended into a state of being within the canvas is not all that farfetched. Picasso painted *Studio* and *Painter and Model* after his Analytical, High Analytical, and Synthetic Cubist stages, so that their space was informed by the alterations of Cubism, in that it was flattened, mixed figure and ground, and analyzed objects from a perspective that Gorky further adjusted in *Organization*. Gorky's *Organization* is the multidimensional space of which Barthes speaks, and the "tissues of quotations" or visual cues such as the palette shape, displaced doorknobs, and globe-breast-circles serve as multiple referents for the viewer.

Inherent in Cubist works were the semiotic clues of the recognizable world. Picasso's High Analytical *Ma Jolie* from the winter of 1911–12 (fig. 23), for instance, has buried in it iconic and reductive representations of hair, guitar strings, and fingers that act as synecdoches for the real person who is its initial subject. Like the space of the fourth dimension that opens up corners and curves allowing for the simultaneous viewing of multiple perspectives, *Ma Jolie*, although based on a representation of Picasso's lover "Eva" (Marcelle Humbert), encompasses, by virtue of the title emblazoned across it, multiple references to the outside world. These are autobiographical references and nods to

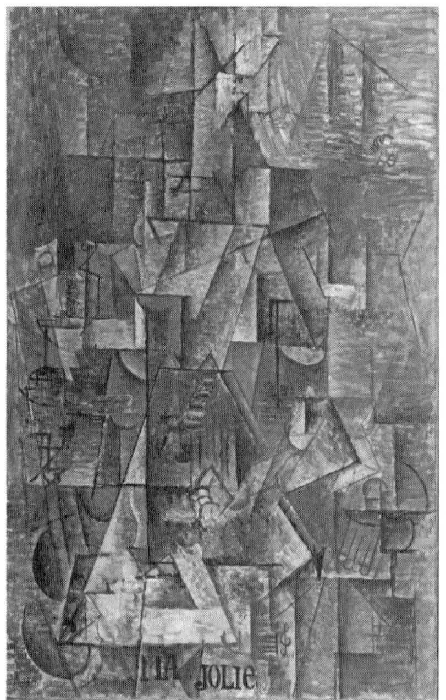

FIGURE 23 Pablo Picasso, *Ma Jolie (Woman with a Zither or Guitar)*, Paris, winter 1911–12. The Museum of Modern Art, New York.

the urban landscape and cultural metropolis of Paris in which the Cubists lived. "Ma Jolie," meaning "my pretty one" or "my pretty girl," was Picasso's pet name for Eva, and was also the name of a popular song of the era. In Picasso's case, the title signifies the subject of the painting, but as one moves from European to American art and the development of Cubism moves toward Abstract Expressionism, the artist's identity also comes into play. The painting's subjectivity becomes tied to the artist's identity through abstraction because the work becomes a record of the artist's existence in addition to a depiction of references to it.

Gorky's existence, identity, and subjectivity are also tied to authorship. He seldom signed his work without being asked to do so, and often signed on the back of the canvas or on the frames. On the front of paintings Gorky regularly signed in ways that blended with the composition. The signature in *Organization*, for instance, is in a triangular area halfway up the canvas. The name, therefore, is malleable and dependent on the composition, as Gorky's identity was tied to his role as an artist. The signature is displaced, like Gorky, without a stable home. Yet when the signature is buried in the composition, it further integrates the identity of the artist with the art itself. The signature "A. Gorky" can be read as "a Gorky" or as a surrogate for the artist himself. The artist's name, then, defines both the artist and a body of work. Harold Rosenberg linked artist and work to the extent that during Abstract Expressionism one no longer bought a painting by Jackson Pollock, but "a Jackson Pollock," making the name of an artist synonymous with the work itself. This implies the inherent connection between the artist and his work that Rosenberg believed became an emblem of the personal struggle of the era, so that "I have bought an 'O' (rather than a painting by O) becomes literally true. The man who started to remake himself has made himself into a commodity with a trademark."[72] In essence, the artist and the work of art, as defined by its style, become one and the same.[73]

The concept of authorship is also tied to originality. Gorky was always very open about his allegiances to different artists and did not try to disguise his inspirations. According to Jacob Kainen, he "wasn't ashamed of his sources which is more than you can say for a lot of other artists who deny everything."[74] Gorky transformed his sources, cutting up prints, rearranging the fragments by turning them upside down or sideways, and working from them as if the fragments themselves were a still life to be rendered.[75] According to Melvin Lader, one of the first to assert adamantly that Gorky was not copying, Gorky's process was

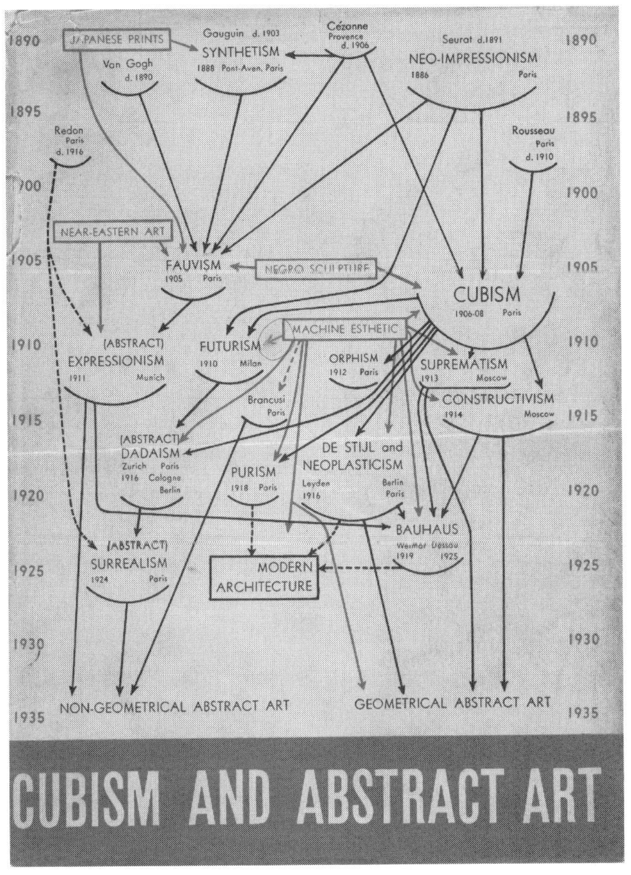

FIGURE 24
Alfred H. Barr, cover of the exhibition catalogue *Cubism and Abstract Art* (New York: Museum of Modern Art, 1936).

akin to apprenticing because it "reflect[ed] Gorky's view that art is a succession of links in an unbroken chain, in which all art evolves from past styles and artists."[76] Such an understanding is characteristic of Modernist beliefs. John Graham wrote of art as a succession of styles,[77] and Clement Greenberg's seminal "Modernist Painting" justifies American Modernism and Abstract Expressionism by tying it to the decisive moments and better-known artists in the history of modern art. Demonstrating the unbroken link between European and American Modernism was a way to remedy the tribulations of Modernism's leap over the ocean to an American avant-garde, the classification of so many immigrants who were part of it, and Gorky's individual displacement. Situating American art in the larger context of modern art, and Gorky within that context, gives him, like other immigrants, status and a place in the world, despite his displacement. Gorky's concept of past art, however, is more akin to that in Alfred H. Barr Jr.'s diagram on the front cover of the catalogue for the 1936 Museum of Modern Art exhibition Cubism and abstract art, which suggests a circuitous and cross-pollinating rather than linear development of modern art (fig. 24).

Art historian Ann Eden Gibson points out that originality was an "attribute [that] was wielded like a critical club."[78] It could be used to enforce a classification of artists that was a subversive adaptation of ethnic classifications. According to Ethel Schwabacher, Gorky was repeatedly singled out and devalued for his practice of emulating aspects of others' works. He was "tormented by this. People tortured him with this."[79] Raymond Williams has stated that for the displaced artist, any measure of mimicry was liberating because the targets were *new* visual traditions for the immigrant, even though they were not new to art history.[80] Gorky's practice, therefore, although original to him, was at odds with the perceived originality of other artists. It seemed, however, that Gorky understood that the concept of originality itself was flawed, or at least overrated. "Gorky used to say, 'very original' about some of my work," Willem de Kooning explained, "but the way he said it didn't sound so good . . . because you have a lot of original art which is not very good art. There's a difference between being original and being a great artist, or being original and breaking the rules."[81]

Elaine de Kooning noted that Gorky "never entertained the provincial (but popular) concept that the originality in art is measured in terms of rejection of tradition."[82] Rosenberg explained that Gorky's motivations were based on the whole history of painting that "contained endless inventions which the living painter could make his own. Even inventing a thing that had already been invented was an act of creation."[83] Meyer Schapiro points out that the nature of Gorky's copying was quite original because he was "one of the rare people who appreciated something very new and difficult, and who resolved to assimilate it in a continually searching way, and doing it with passion. Now, that in its time is highly original."[84] To be an apprentice to modern artists at the time was original because, with the exception of those within Gorky's diasporic community, like John Graham and Stuart Davis, American artists were not necessarily so attuned to modern art. According to Albert Camus, "Art is neither a complete rejection or acceptance of what is. It is simultaneously rejection and acceptance, and this is why it must be a perpetually renewed by wrenching apart. The artist constantly lives in such a state of ambiguity, incapable of negating the real and yet eternally bound to question it in its eternally unfinished aspects."[85] This dilemma applies very strongly to Gorky—it is the ambiguity and the unfinished that Gorky embraced by enlisting what he viewed, but he wrenched it apart to fit formally and physically into his own composition.

Lee Krasner, recognizing Gorky's cutting-edge approach, tried to advance her art in the same manner by emulating Gorky. Her 1943 work *Composition* (fig. 25) closely follows the style and format of Gorky's 1936–37 *Composition with Head* (fig. 26). Anne Wagner explains that there was a certain safety in emulation. Krasner, as a woman who insisted that she was not "other," painted "like a man—like Arshile Gorky, to name one—in a way that bespeaks less a lack of originality than a certain confidence, inherited from Cubism, in a shared and

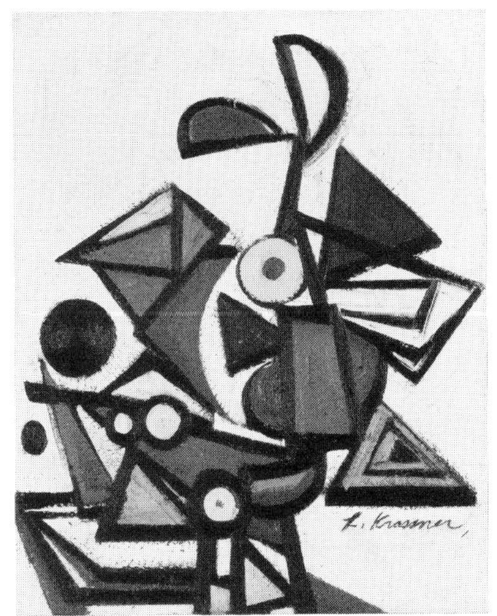

FIGURE 25
Lee Krasner, *Composition*, 1943. Smithsonian American Art Museum.

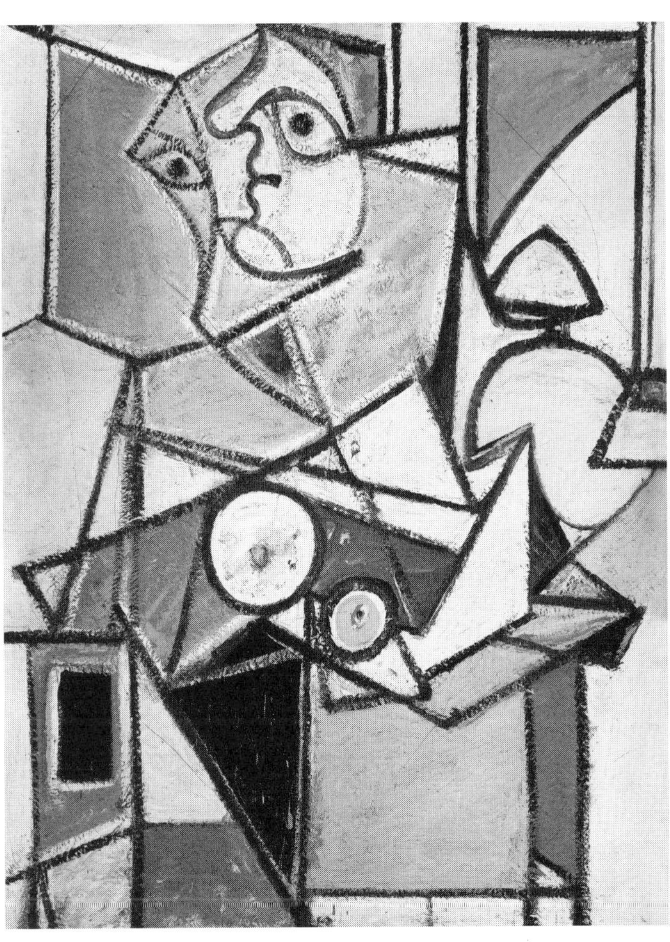

FIGURE 26
Arshile Gorky, *Composition with Head*, 1936–37. Donald L. Bryant Jr. Collection.

usable abstract style uniting a community of practitioners."[86] If one believed that art was a historically determined succession of styles, then Cubism represented a necessary rather than arbitrary mode. Because, for Krasner, Gorky was at the forefront of art's progression, his art was the next to emulate.

As Gorky's own art developed, he relied less and less on the work of others and more on his immediate surroundings and memories. Ellen Handler Spitz has noted that every artist needs to "maintain continuity of self in terms of the traditions of his art . . . and, at times equally or more urgently, to risk rupture, to break utterly with such continuities."[87] Gorky continuously pushed his art forward, maintaining aspects of the compositions he invoked, but still also rupturing what he had observed. "With Gorky," said Nicholas Calas, "one can understand how art is neither invention nor imitation but primarily an assertion of existence."[88] Gorky's art should be viewed as a negotiation of diaspora that reflects his life situation. Very few Armenians would have left their homeland if not driven out by persecution. Consistent with his presence in the United States, Gorky's art relates to life as an immigrant integrating into a new culture. Clinging to threads from his old world and grasping strings in the new, Gorky created a multivalent identity. The identities that he chose to pursue were calculated to enable him to become part of an artistic diaspora. These mutable identities carried over into Gorky's work as he displaced visual elements and collaged them together to create identities that were referents to many others.

By viewing Gorky in broad cultural terms, it is possible to see him as an international painter—a one-man stylistic melting pot. This tendency, born out of displacement, is transnationalist in nature. In other words, just as the elements of Gorky's art are not confined to a single national or ethnic aesthetic, but rather in a collage-like manner extend over and operate within several, his art also seeks to bypass a specific, fixed reading of the artist and his work.[89] Gorky's art is a collage of physical, stylistic, and temporal elements that should be read together. Ethel Schwabacher urged such a reading even back in 1951 in her text for the Arshile Gorky Memorial Exhibition and again in her 1957 book on the artist, saying, "America has been singularly capable of assimilating foreign ideas and blood and so she has accepted such artists as Gorky, who might more accurately be called an international painter."[90] Modern art, to Gorky, was "the greatest the world has ever known,"[91] and he was a hinge who helped to facilitate the movement between European and American and traditional and modern art. Perhaps the best way to view Gorky would be contrapuntally, both in Modernist practice and his position within modern art.

Gorky accessed a reservoir of images adapted from other artists and became a bridge for abstraction—the epitome of translation. Gorky emphasized the idea of art as translation, saying, "I am in entire sympathy with the modern European movement to the exclusion always of those moderns who belong to the other class, those who invent things instead of translating them."[92] In his later work, Gorky combined his collection of forms and applications of paint and conjectured internally complex compositions. Yet these compositions still reflect his displacement while simultaneously being modern because he was self-aware of the creative act. When Gorky declared to Julien Levy, "I was *with* Cézanne and now I am *with* Picasso," Levy replied, "When you are *with* Arshile Gorky, give me a call." This statement, in retrospect, is ironic because "Arshile Gorky" was literally and figuratively a pseudonym—a construction that manifested itself through the creation of art.

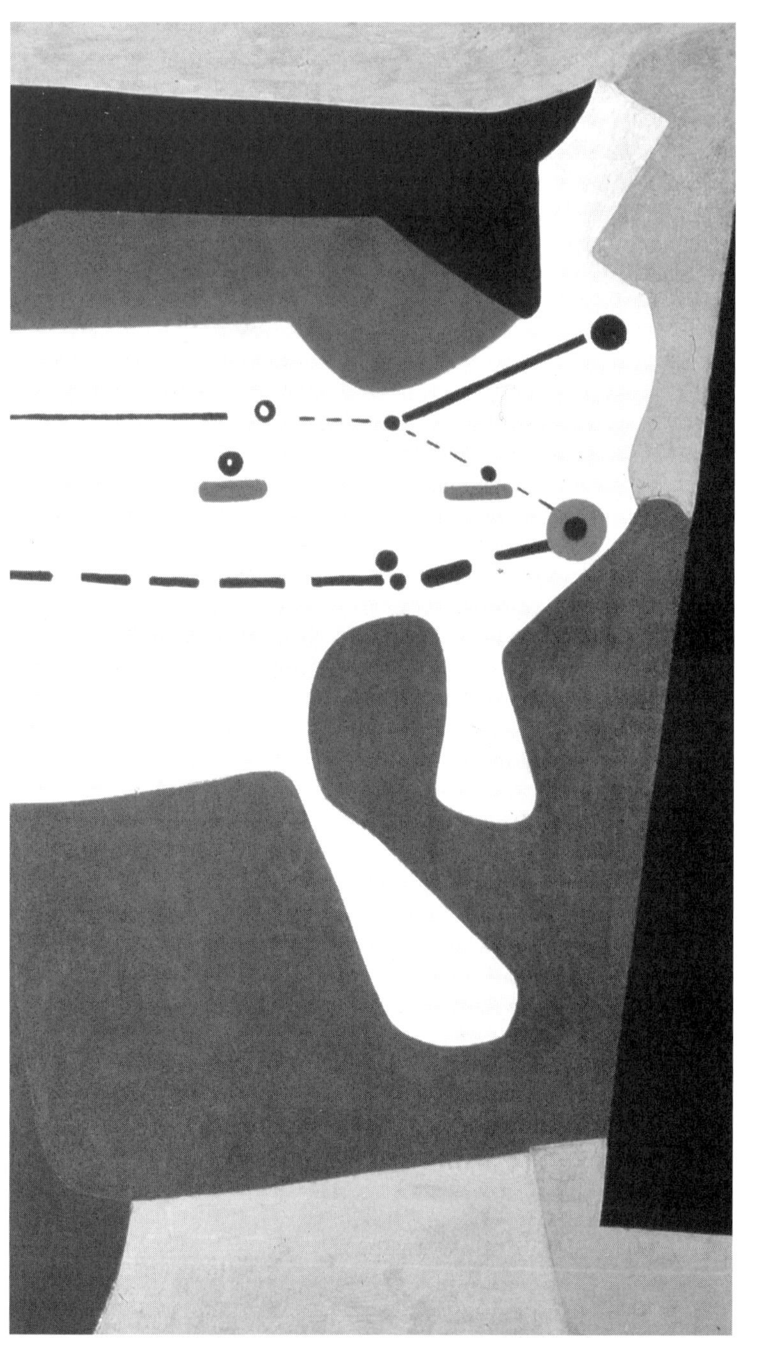

chapter 4

Exile, Abstraction, and Nonobjectivity

The passage from the pre-modern to modern is always understood as a rupture and separation, whether of a rational self from a disenfranchised world, of producers from their means of production, or of nature and population from the processes of technological control and social planning. Each of these so-called ruptures is a way of accounting for a world increasingly staged according to the schema of object and subject, process and plan, real and representation.

—TIMOTHY MITCHELL

Arshile Gorky's constant negotiation of object and subject, process and plan, and real and representation mimics the passage of premodern to modern of which Timothy Mitchell speaks. Viewing Gorky's method of remaking as a diacritical language of displacement leads to a deeper understanding of his abstraction. When abstraction is read within the context of displacement, it functions in a manner that evokes the artist's struggles, but is not entirely determined by them. The existentialism that became an emblem of the Abstract Expressionist movement is imbued in Arshile Gorky's practice, and yet, like Gorky, the Abstract Expressionists were driven more by their desire to create art than their personal trauma, even though the assertion of existence played a palpable role.

Gorky's aesthetic is evident in a series of over fifty drawings entitled *Nighttime, Enigma and Nostalgia* (fig. 27), whose 1929–34 dates reveal Gorky's focus on drawing, rather than the more expensive medium of painting, during the Depression. The works appear to be initially based on Giorgio de Chirico's *The Fatal Temple*[1] (fig. 28), yet, consistent with his method, Gorky adapted and

Opening image detail of figure 32.

transformed the composition throughout his series. It is almost as if Gorky were exploring all of the possible versions that could be manifested by changing particular elements in the image. Harking back to the paintings of his mother, sisters, and wife, Gorky's own self-portraits, and his renditions of other artist's works, Gorky's repetition, reworking, and revising became a process of differentiation, not replication. Gorky inflected abstraction, biomorphism, and hatching in such a way that positive and negative forms hovered between recognizability and artifice, thereby activating the composition for the viewer. In considering Gorky's eventual relationship to the Surrealists, Dickran Tashjian explains, "Visual ambiguities abound. The pictorial space might be interior or exterior or both, with biomorphic shapes that are fixed in the darkness of their 'nighttime.' Our eyes strain to make them out—hence the 'enigma.'"[2] By the process of trying to identify abstract shapes that have been displaced and made to function in a new manner, Tashjian, as the viewer, approaches an enigmatic state. The strength of Gorky's rendition is in its enigmatic qualities and the way it captures the essence of a moment or mood, rather than depicts it. In doing so, he reflects ideas developed by his friend John Graham, who advocated painting as an evocation of feeling and the enigma of emotion that was beyond literal representation. Such views fit Gorky's goals and processes perfectly; Gorky embraced the eloquent enunciations of Graham while executing them in paint.

Ethel Schwabacher claims that it was in the *Nighttime, Enigma and Nostalgia* series that Gorky first set forth the "themes of fertilization and of labyrinth which continued to obsess him throughout his life."[3] With a backdrop of organic Art Deco and Art Nouveau in New York City skyscrapers that melded with the geometry of the International Style, or perhaps as a rejection of the rigid nature of the built environment, Gorky's work began to blend structure and nature using the gridding methods of the Cubists, Matisse, and Léger. Restructuring fragmented compositions and objects, Gorky continued to develop his reductive and repetitive processes. Using washable ink, Gorky sponged down the compositions to blur edges and worked back into them with cross-hatching. Indeed, many drawings in the series (fig. 29) exhibit the same kind of working and reworking as found in *Summation* and *Image in Khorkom*.

Gorky's revision processes were always crucial to the completion of works, and particularly in this series. "Always prodigal of time and effort," explained Elaine de Kooning, "once when he had finished one of these drawings, the artist, eager to get his final effect, precipitously rubbed a soaking sponge over it, smearing two weeks' work before he realized that he had used ordinary ink. Horrified at first, he shrugged his shoulders characteristically and said, 'Oh well, I didn't like it anyway,' and immediately began on another."[4] Gorky's exploitation of media through many versions of works allowed the artist to experiment with an idea and explore the variables encountered when even a single aspect of the

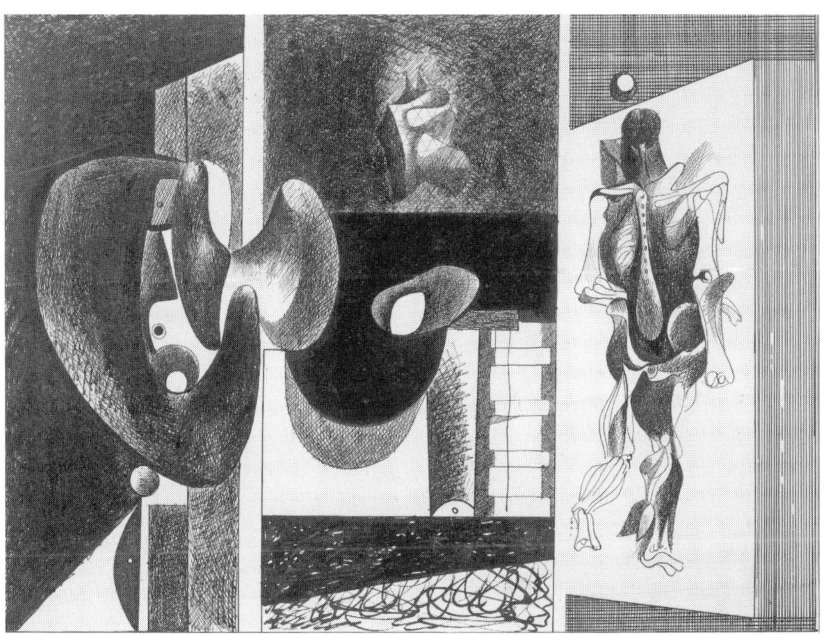

FIGURE 27
Arshile Gorky, *Nighttime, Enigma and Nostalgia*, ca. 1931–1932. Whitney Museum of American Art, New York.

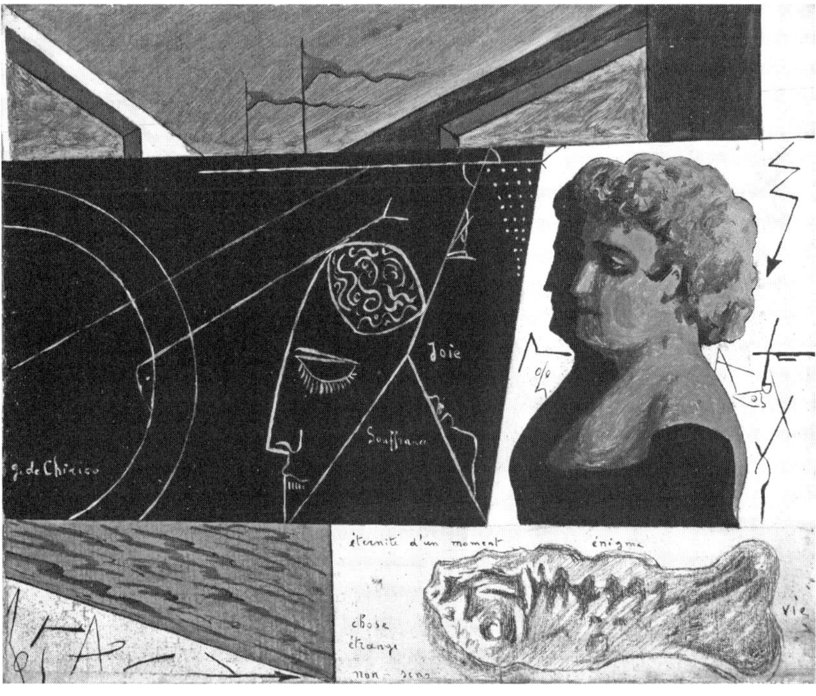

FIGURE 28
Giorgio de Chirico, *The Fatal Temple*, 1914. Philadelphia Museum of Art.

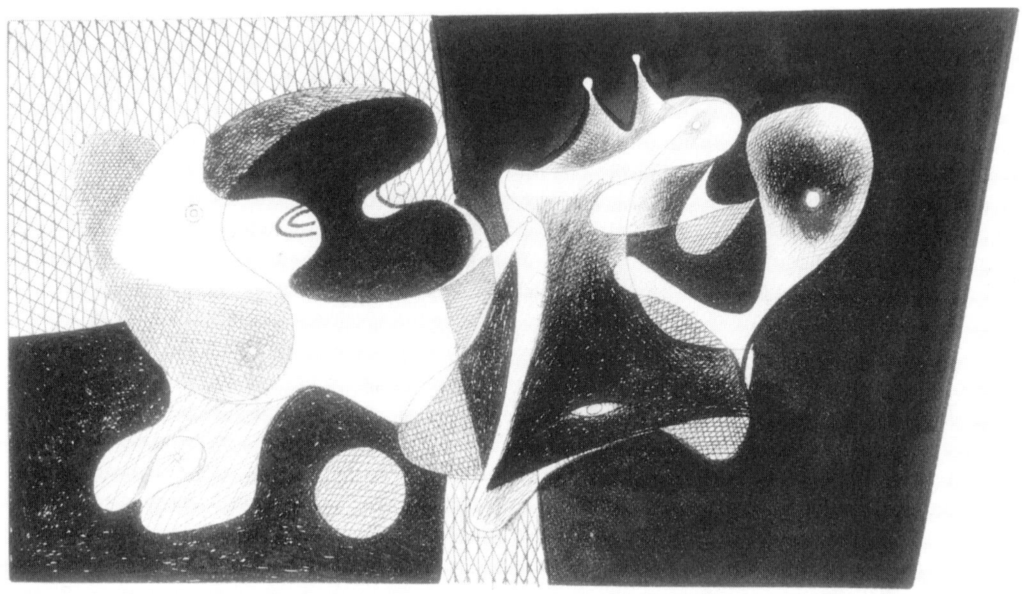

FIGURE 29
Arshile Gorky, *Nighttime, Enigma, and Nostalgia*, ca. 1932–1934. National Gallery of Art, Washington, D.C.

composition was shifted, thereby changing its internal balance or emphasis.[5] Such repetition was one of mastery, if not a little compulsive.

The meaning of the *Nighttime, Enigma and Nostalgia* series, it seems, is caught up in the process of Gorky's making and our attempts to decipher it, which is in keeping with Gorky's intentions. If the series is about process, if making art is its subject, then, regardless of our effort, it will remain an enigma and we can only experience it as far as we can sense the trajectory of the artist and our own understanding imposed upon it. The more that the artwork maintains its enigma, the more it maintains its integrity, but also the more it replicates the artist's revelatory process of making for the viewer, disclosing itself slowly. According to Maurice Blanchot in his writings about trauma, "the enigma (the secret) is precisely the *absence* of any question."[6] Asked by the Museum of Modern Art in 1941 about the sources of a drawing from the series that they had recently purchased, Gorky replied, "Wounded birds, poverty and a whole week of rain."[7] The association with trauma is intriguing, particularly within the context of genocide, but the passage is not definitive or descriptive of genocide in detail. Enigma is, in fact, a state of mind, not a literal illustration in the image, and the drawing is perhaps meant to invoke such a mood. Because there is no question that the artist is asking or answering, the subject is interpretative and readings are emotive for the viewer.

Following this drawing series and between his allegiance to Cézanne and Picasso and his subsequent encounter with the Surrealists, Gorky became interested in a particular attitude toward abstraction introduced by the Dutch De Stijl artists and the French Purists. Like De Stijl, Gorky began to reduce natural objects to abstract essentials. In an attempt to order nature, Piet Mondrian essentialized trees into vertical and horizontal patterns and Theo van Doesberg transformed a cow into a geometric abstraction. Like Fernand Léger and Purist artists Le Corbusier (Charles-Édouard Jeanneret) and Amédée Ozenfant, Gorky formed objects into an abstract composition by simplifying edges and shapes into flat, geometricized planes.

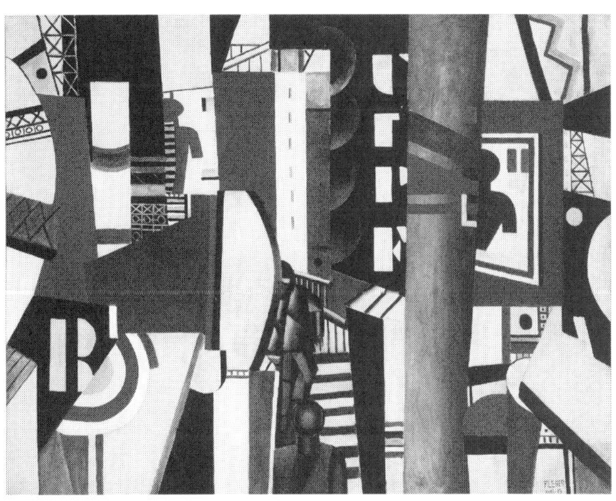

FIGURE 30
Fernand Léger, *The City*, 1919. Philadelphia Museum of Art.

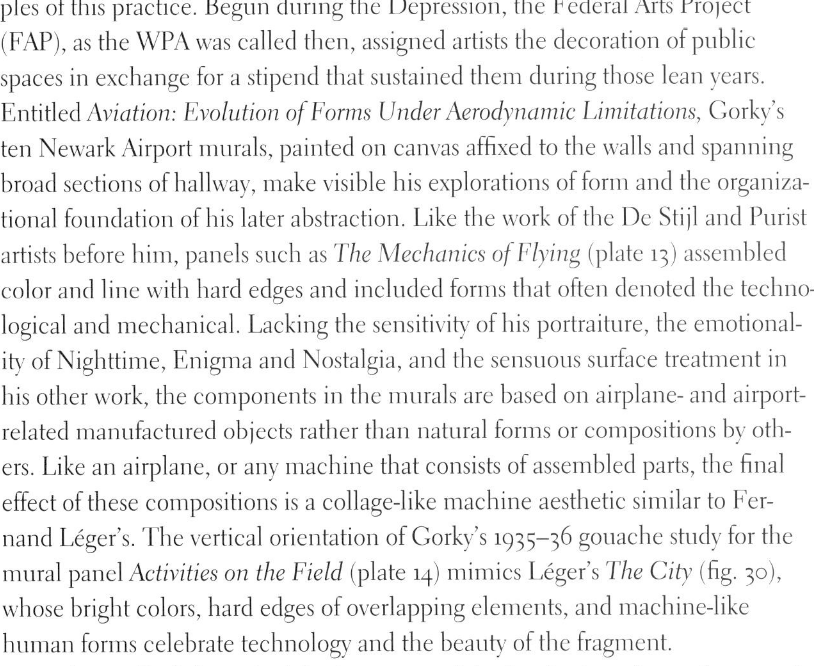

Gorky's mural works, particularly those that were part of the government-sponsored work-relief program the Works Project Administration (WPA), are examples of this practice. Begun during the Depression, the Federal Arts Project (FAP), as the WPA was called then, assigned artists the decoration of public spaces in exchange for a stipend that sustained them during those lean years. Entitled *Aviation: Evolution of Forms Under Aerodynamic Limitations*, Gorky's ten Newark Airport murals, painted on canvas affixed to the walls and spanning broad sections of hallway, make visible his explorations of form and the organizational foundation of his later abstraction. Like the work of the De Stijl and Purist artists before him, panels such as *The Mechanics of Flying* (plate 13) assembled color and line with hard edges and included forms that often denoted the technological and mechanical. Lacking the sensitivity of his portraiture, the emotionality of Nighttime, Enigma and Nostalgia, and the sensuous surface treatment in his other work, the components in the murals are based on airplane- and airport-related manufactured objects rather than natural forms or compositions by others. Like an airplane, or any machine that consists of assembled parts, the final effect of these compositions is a collage-like machine aesthetic similar to Fernand Léger's. The vertical orientation of Gorky's 1935–36 gouache study for the mural panel *Activities on the Field* (plate 14) mimics Léger's *The City* (fig. 30), whose bright colors, hard edges of overlapping elements, and machine-like human forms celebrate technology and the beauty of the fragment.

As was Gorky's method, he incorporated the inspiration of several compositions and artists simultaneously into his work. He was aware of the large-scale productions being rendered in Siqueiros's workshop in Union Square and had visited Ozenfant's studio numerous times in the 1930s while the artist lived in New York City.[8] After visiting, Gorky went back to his own easel and, "picking up some brushes similar to Ozenfant's, immediately began to experiment with that artist's method of applying paint."[9] Gorky also studied a reproduction of Duchamp's painting the *Passage of the Virgin to the Bride* (fig. 31), suggesting an interest in a kineticized Cubist structure.[10] Basing his work in observation, Gorky encrypted

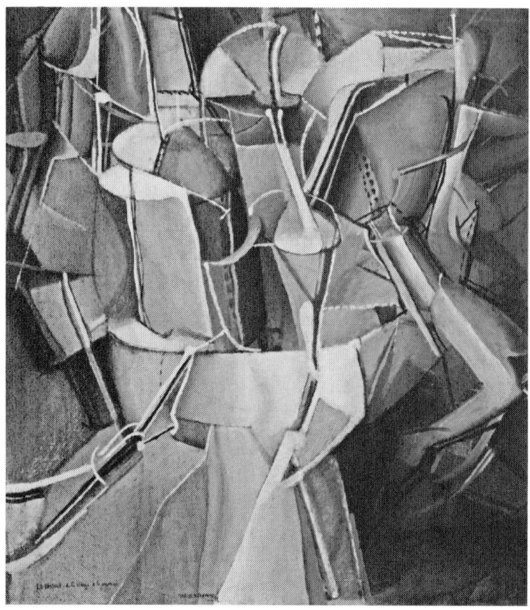

the real like the Cubist and Purist artists he had studied, cutting forms into contours or formulating them as apertures into a space with the objective of transforming objects rather than concealing them. In accordance with the tendency of the era, in which the picture plane was envisioned as a total object and represented space as a total object,[11] Gorky expanded his composition across the entire space of his canvas. He often studied the scale of his works, stepping back and considering whether the composition held from a distance.[12] Indeed, it was Gorky's interest in painting's plastic qualities and the possibilities such views might hold for the medium of painting that caused his split from friend Stuart Davis and the Artist's Union. Gorky severed these relationships, "declaiming like a prophet about plastic qualities in paint. . . . When in reference to social-content art, he coined the phrase 'poor painting for poor people.'"[13] Gorky recognized, however, the implications of the space of the painting as literal space, a space of culture, and as a space for discourse.

FIGURE 31
Marcel Duchamp, *The Passage from Virgin to Bride*, Munich, July–August 1912. The Museum of Modern Art, New York.

In his Newark Airport murals, a government work-relief commission based in technological advancement, Gorky revealed space as a mediator between intellectual and social activity.[14] At the left of the gouache, a tailfin is in the process of being welded or attended to by a figure to its right. With a clear relationship to other art styles and artists, such as Fernand Léger, whose *The City* includes robotic human forms making their way up stairs, Gorky's forms are similarly integrated into his composition. Toward the center, searchlight shapes appear with a lever-like structure that also resembles an aerial view of a car on a runway. The upper right-hand corner of Gorky's work recalls signage, similar to the portions of letters found in the Léger. Gorky visually collaged painted forms over each other in flat layers and used a limited palette of repeating red, blue, white, and black throughout the composition, both following Léger's lead and emulating the Oriental carpets produced in his native land.

Gorky's unpublished essay about the murals, although filtered through two editors,[15] provides a record of Gorky's approach to the works at the time and is one of the few statements of his aesthetic theories: "A plastic operation is imperative, and that is why, in the first panel of 'Activities on the Field' I dissected an airplane into its constituent parts. An airplane is composed of a variety of shapes and forms and I have used such elemental forms as a rudder, a wing, a wheel and a searchlight to create not only numerical interest but also to invent within a given wall space plastic symbols of aviation."[16] Gorky's discussion of the dissection of the airplane into parts, as well as the whole statement itself, echoes Léger's theories. In his 1924 essay "The Aesthetic of the Machine," Léger explained that "plastic beauty in general is totally independent of sentimental, descriptive, or imitative values. Every object, picture, piece of architecture, or ornamental organization has a value in itself; it is strictly absolute and independent of anything it may happen to represent."[17] In 1926, Léger published "A New Realism—the Object," in which he explained a technique to "isolate the object or the fragment of an object and to present it on the screen in close-ups of the largest possible scale."[18] Gorky's own repeated use of the word "plastic" is significant because it mirrors ideas present in the artistic repertoire at the time. Although not published until 1937, after the mural project, Piet Mondrian's ideas about figurative and nonfigurative art would have been making their way around the New York art scene. In "Plastic Art and Pure Plastic Art," Mondrian discusses such questions as the subjective versus the objective and the relationships between forms as universal versus individual.[19] For Mondrian, a passage in a composition may have been derived from the recognizable, but when disembodied from that object-bound existence, it functions in a new manner as a component in a work of art and becomes something different than it might have been originally. Its plastic nature, therefore, allows its identity to be malleable.

In Gorky's description of his murals, he explains that he wished to visually dissect the airplane into elemental forms and then reconstitute it in partially invented symbols that represented aviation. Such plasticity, like the malleability of his own identity, the identities of women he portrayed, and the works of other artists, allows the objects to be unfixed. In the Newark murals, airplane parts function compositionally, not mechanically, in their new identities. Similar to that moment when the wheels of an airplane come off the ground and it begins to take flight, but remains close enough to the landscape for scenery to be discerned, the abstraction of the murals becomes airborne. Like a plane in flight, subjected to the dimensions of pitch and yaw in addition to the forward, back, and side-to-side of its existence on the ground, Gorky's art begins to further expand the limits of space that the Cubists pushed outward a quarter-century before.

The statement also refers back Gorky's homeland. One fleeting moment of memory established for Gorky his means of approach, since he had never actually been in an airplane himself. Gorky titles the statement *an* interpretation, and it begins with a description set in an unnamed homeland:

> The walls of the house were made of clay blocks, deprived of all detail, with a roof of rude timber.
>
> It was here, in my childhood, that I witnessed, for the first time, that most poetic image of operations—the elevation of the object. This was a structural substitute for a calendar.

> In this culture, the seasons manifested themselves, therefore there was no need, with the exception of the Lental period, for a formal calendar. The people, with the imagery of their extravagantly tender, almost innocently direct concept of Space and Time conceived of the following:
>
> In the ceiling was a round aperture to permit the emission of smoke. Over it was placed a wooden cross from which was suspended by a string an onion into which seven feathers had been plunged. As each Sunday elapsed, a feather was removed, thus denoting a passage of Time.
>
> As I have mentioned above, through these elevated objects, floating feather and onion, was revealed to me, for the first time, the marvel of making from the common the uncommon![20]

In this passage Gorky exposes concerns with time, space, and making the common uncommon. His lost culture is an interesting juxtaposition to the mechanical elements of the work, but what Gorky is actually describing is the poetic process of artmaking and interpretation, his ultimate concerns, in addition to the fluidity of space and time. Despite the new location and new name and any performance he might give or life he might lead, Gorky remains essentially the same person. He looks more dramatic and the way that he is identified has shifted, but essentially Gorky remains the same individual at the core, the sum of all the heritage and experiences that led him to traverse space to begin with.

The metaphor of the airplane is effective since flight, like Gorky's artworks, compresses and expands time and accesses alternate space. Air travel allows for traversing time (zones) and switching places (crossing the country) while remaining in one space, that is, in one's seat on the airplane. Through flight, one becomes immediately but temporarily displaced. Such a global concept—the way the microcosm of a specific experience is part of a macrocosmic simultaneity—is something of which Gorky was acutely aware. Evident in his "memory portraits" and renditions of space in his modern-master-inspired studies, the two surviving panels of the Newark Airport murals speak to these characteristics. *Aerial Map* (fig. 32) contains flight routes that span a schematized chart of the country superimposed over abstract shapes of buildings and nature as seen from the air.

In these murals, Gorky's abstraction is conceived as a system of relationships between objects and space in which parts are removed from their identity, made to function in a new manner, and then reorganized. The multiple implications of each work—the way it can be read semeiotically[21]—make it challenging for both the artist and the viewer. Like Gorky the exile, the objects in the murals hover between their original purpose and their role in the composition, intercessors between the recognizable and the abstract. Such detaching and recontextualizing is clearly part of both Gorky's life and art because both are examples of how Gorky argues *against* legibility. He says: "In 'Mechanics of Flying' I have used morphic shapes. The objects portrayed, a thermometer, hygrometer, anemometer, an air-

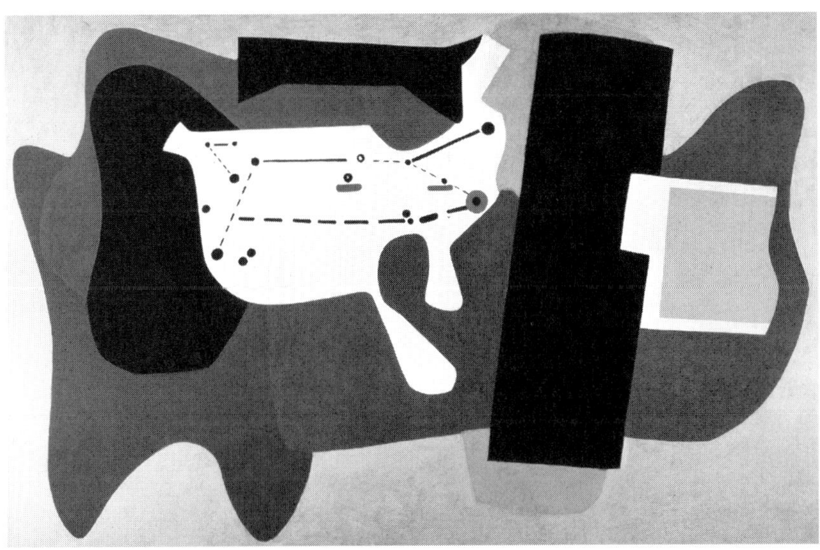

FIGURE 32
Arshile Gorky, *Aerial Map*, 1936–37. On extended loan from the Collection of The Port Authority of New York and New Jersey to the Newark Museum.

line map of the United States, all have definitely important usage in aviation, and to emphasize this I have given them importance by detaching them from their environment."[22] Gorky's process is one of deconstruction and rearticulation that creates an internal linguistic structure—with forms seemingly collaged over one another into a new visual language.

Just as if Gorky's "fungus-like, collaged English" is manifested visually,[23] in the case of the Newark murals the collage is literal. After Wyatt Davis had photographed with Gorky the airport, its functions, and its equipment, they cropped, cut up, and arranged the images interspersed with blocks of paint in order to give Gorky an idea of how to integrate object-based elements with painted abstract forms.[24] This visual collage literally displaces the foundational object, and each mechanical element that is to appear in the composition is forced into a new role within the structure of the painting, as opposed to its utilitarian role on the airfield itself. The mural format sets up metonymic shifts because the mural, as the space of the whole field (the literal landing field and viewer's field of experience), has a relationship to the parts that inhabit it—either the real-life elements on the field that serve its function or the representation of those parts within the field of the painting that serve the totality of the composition. The internal linguistic structure that Gorky created within the mural suggests that the relationship between the forms is more important than the integrity of the forms themselves. The composition bridges time and space to form an idea of flight and quote fragments of modern life. Just as one can fly from one place to another, thereby compressing time and shifting easily from space to space and culture to culture, Gorky's abstraction dislocates and reattributes elements from one composition or location to another.

The previous chapters of this study support this dialectical theory, as does Gorky's own statement about the murals, which insists on opposing photographic identification and itemizing images. Gorky used photographs to structure the image, but their purpose was only to aid in the rememoration of what he had observed. The process of Gorky's "memory portraits" and recombinations from other artists' works continues to operate here. "The realism of Modern Painting," Gorky claims, "is diametrically opposed to this concept [exact replication], since the painter of today operates on the given space of the canvas, breaking up the surface until he arrives at the realization of the entirety."[25] This statement opposes the replication and itemization of images because it exists in a world unto itself. The disjunctions that are forged within the given space of the canvas must be considered within the compositional whole. This relationship is Modernist and eventually contributes to the development of the "all-over" painting of Abstract Expressionism.

Unfortunately, responses in Newark to Gorky's philosophy of modern painting were vehemently negative. The American mainstream had viewed modern art with skepticism, distaste, and accusations of foreignness even before the 1913 Armory Show had catapulted it into the country's consciousness. Local papers made fun of Gorky's murals, and one obviously staged photograph depicted a man who appeared to dodge an oncoming plane over a caption that jested about Gorky's "supposed conception of an airplane" (fig. 33).[26] There was even an attempt by the locals to have the murals removed, which was averted through a clandestine midnight meeting of artists and townsmen on the airfield itself.[27] Despite the abstraction of the image and the uproar over the murals, they engaged their subject in a unique manner. Yet people in Newark, arguably like most Americans, were not ready for art that was ambiguous, and similar reactions to abstraction would continue even after Abstract Expressionism had become part of an art-historical canon in the 1950s. By that time, though, Gorky's murals had disappeared from the Newark Airport.[28]

Because of WPA funding in the 1930s, which both kept artists employed and by extension acknowledged art and artists as a significant part of American society, communities of artists began to form. Gorky desperately wanted to be part of a fellowship that addressed the formal elements of art. At the second meeting of the American Abstract Artists in 1937, a group that Gorky had helped to found, he proposed that they hold a workshop in which they would compose pieces subject to a predefined set of parameters. As Balcomb Green recalls, "we were each to do a canvas using only black, white, and red, and all working the same size. We would then meet and discuss what we had achieved within the limitations.[29] The group, however, believed instead that they should advance the plight of American artists against the museums and galleries that remained enamored with European artists or American reactionaries like Maurice Sterne and Thomas Hart Benton. Despite the group's concerns about negative reac-

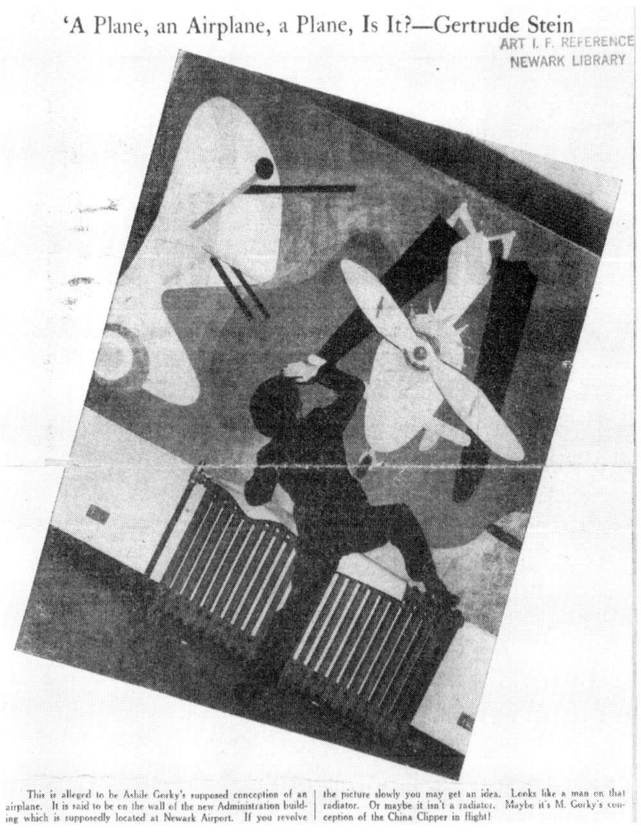

'A Plane, an Airplane, a Plane, Is It?—Gertrude Stein

This is alleged to be Ashile Gorky's supposed conception of an airplane. It is said to be on the wall of the new Administration building which is supposedly located at Newark Airport. If you revolve the picture slowly you may get an idea. Looks like a man on that radiator. Or maybe it isn't a radiator. Maybe it's M. Gorky's conception of the China Clipper in flight!

FIGURE 33
Newark Ledger, Thursday, June 10, 1937.

tions from the American public, like those Gorky suffered in Newark, Gorky walked out. Shortly thereafter, he declared to Greene that there was no such thing as abstract art, that abstraction and nonobjectivity in abstract art were "fatal directions," and that he himself was headed for a big change.[30]

Shortly thereafter, however, Gorky composed a mural that was akin to the Newark compositions. Gorky had since become aware of Picasso's *Guernica*, and *Man's Conquest of the Air* (fig. 34), despite its figural qualities, signaled Gorky's ongoing movement toward abstraction. Created for the Aviation Building at the 1939 World's Fair, this design employed elements of technological advancement similar to those in the Newark murals, while tending toward fanciful shapes, slight biomorphism, and a less graphic, less hard-edged composition. Consistent with a Surrealist style developing in his studio work, the airplanes here have an anthropomorphic personality.[31] The Newark murals had exhibited American progress and given Gorky the chance to work out some of his aesthetic ideas, but here he connected more to the mutable natural world. Gorky believed more in praxis, that if others had already said or done something that was useful, one should liberally reuse it. There was no need to waste one's time

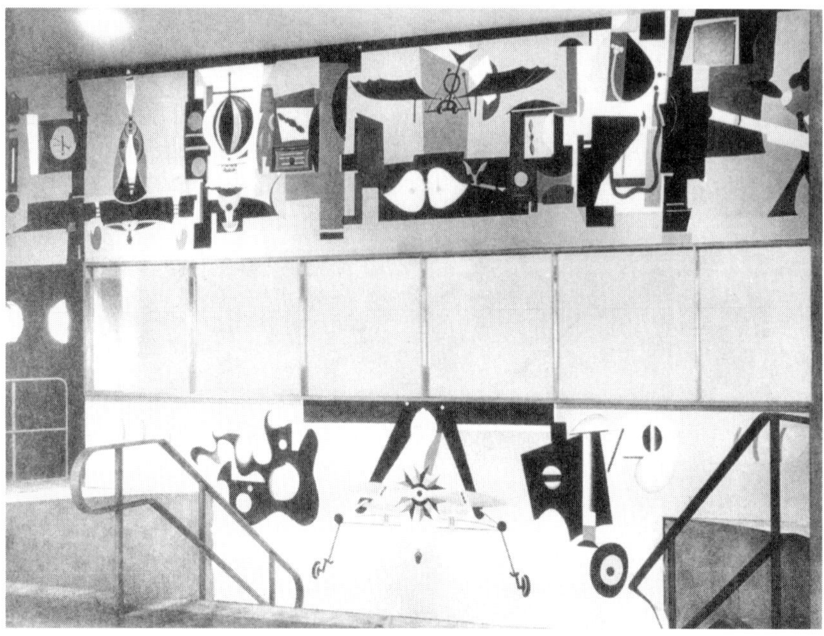

FIGURE 34
Arshile Gorky, *Man's Conquest of the Air,* 1939. Aviation Building, New York World's Fair. Destroyed.

reinventing a technique when effort could be directed into reconfiguring forms that existed already, natural or man-made.

Gorky had been having some success in his career. Since 1936 his work had appeared in the Whitney Museum annually or twice annually, with the exception of 1938–39. In 1939, Gorky, along with Sidney Janis, held an exhibition of Cubist works in Dorothy Miller's penthouse. These private exhibitions were in vogue at the time, and Gorky helped behind the scenes with organization and assisting Mrs. Janis on a presentation analyzing the Cubist works of Picasso.[32] At the same time, however, Gorky seems to have been suffering. Gorky's widow notes that "toward the end of the 1930s he felt a terrible isolation which no amount of subsequent friendliness on the part of the Surrealists or anyone else could eradicate. He often said that, if a human being managed to emerge from such a period, it could not be as a whole man and that there was no recovery from the blows and wounds of such a struggle to survive."[33] Although it is unclear why Gorky fell into such suffering, it could have been related to the artist's continued struggles to find companionship, personally and professionally, as well as figure out exactly what direction he wanted his art to go in the midst of the continued criticism that it was nothing more than derivative of other artists. Gorky was also likely still haunted by the Genocide. Survivors, even when they progress with their lives after danger has passed, can still be affected, particularly when overcome with feeling lost and alone. Viktor Frankl, the psychiatrist and concentration camp survivor whose struggles were some of the most extreme that humanity has had to endure, believed that suffering is a task: "When a man finds that it is his destiny to suffer, he will have to accept his suffering as his task; his single and unique task. He will have to acknowledge the fact that even in suffering he is unique and alone in the universe. No one can relieve him of his suffering or suffer in his place. His unique opportunity lies in the way in which he bears his burden."[34]

Surrealism, however, may have offered Gorky a respite for his suffering through the license it gave to dreams and the imagination. Surrealism seemed quite compatible with the artist's tendency to shift between past, present, and imaginary time, place, and space. This connection, along with meeting the woman who would become his wife and have his children, seemed to have invoked a necessary shift in the artist's disposition. Gorky's new direction is markedly evident in the 1941 murals for Ben Marden's Riviera nightclub in Fort Lee, New Jersey (fig. 35).[35] The murals, now destroyed, consisted of amoeba-like, starburst shapes floating in an undefined background like constellations in the sky.[36] The year 1941 is often considered to mark the inception of Gorky's mature style, which embraced biomorphic abstraction.[37] When Gorky spoke about the Riviera project in an interview, he emphasized its relationship to the natural world, declared it nonobjective art despite a relationship to the natural world and his earlier dismissal of such an aesthetic, and labeled it surrealistic:

> I call these murals non-objective art, but if labels are needed this art may be termed surrealistic, although it functions as design and decoration. The murals have continuity of theme. The theme—visions of the sky and river. The coloring likewise is derived from this and the whole design is contrived to relate to the very architecture of the building.
>
> I might add that though the variations all had specific meanings to me, it is the spectator's privilege to find his own meaning here. I feel that they will relate or parallel mine.

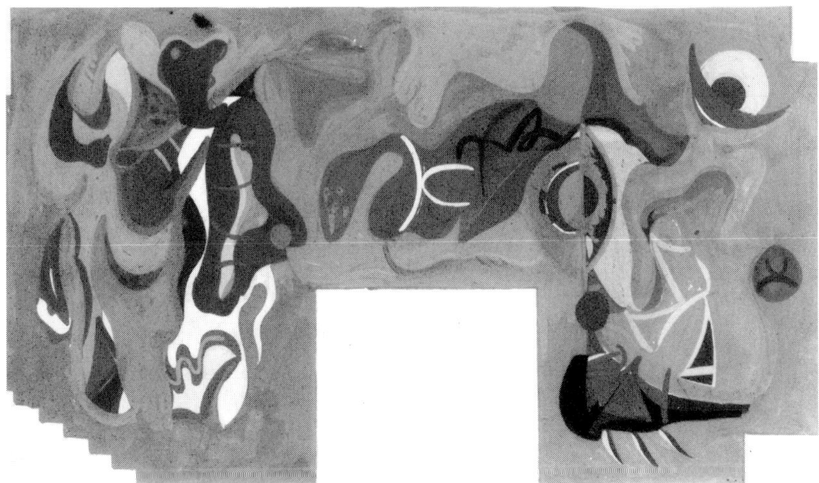

FIGURE 35
Arshile Gorky, *Mural Study for Ben Marden's Riviera Club*, ca. 1938–39. Private collection.

> Of course the outward aspect of my murals seemingly does not relate to the average man's experience. But this is an illusion! What man has not stopped at twilight and on observing the distorted shape of his elongated shadow conjured up strange and moving and often fantastic fancies from it? Certainly we all dream and in this common denominator of everyone's experience I have been able to find a language for all to understand.[38]

Just as Gorky had embraced a new name and entered into an artistic community to address his displacement, it seems that dreams and common experience resolved Gorky's loneliness and despair by linking him with his viewer. Exploiting his interest in verisimilitude, Gorky favored the viewer's own understanding of the work through the common experience of vibrancy, phantasm, and the fanciful.

Referring to illusions and distorted shapes that seem part science and part art, Gorky's published statements reflect advances evident in his oeuvre. The exchange between mural making and studio practice seems to have moved his work forward and brought to fruition the objective, which he had been developing on a more limited level since his early career, of communicating with his audience in a common language. Mexican muralists like Diego Rivera had made murals a prominent medium for such communication. In what Gorky wrote about the nightclub project, he explicitly states his desire to find a language that considered how his own and the viewer's own relation to an experience could correspond. It is not the specific experience that is important to Gorky, but emotions, reactions, or interests that intersect time, space, and place. This universal humanism, therefore, is not a specific narrative reading of a work that is shared by maker and viewer alike, but rather is a common understanding of its underlying structure or the emotion it evokes.

Indeed, the theories of Modernism learned from the Mexican muralists, Hofmann's conceptions of push-pull, Cézanne's practice of visual slippage, the faceting of Cubism, Léger's machine aesthetic, and the utopian plasticity of Mondrian percolate throughout Gorky's art and underscore a belief in the connectivity of all art. In addition, like so many who wished to enact the myth of the American Dream, Gorky endeavored to work toward something that would be as significant as the advances made by those artists, foreshadowing how art-making in America was to become the quintessential maverick and heroic process in the 1950s. Redirecting his life in this way seemed to offer Gorky purpose since his existence was interconnected to the world of artmaking and a group of likeminded artists who held color, line, and texture as sacred as any religious text. Indeed, by reassembling discontinuities and interpreting form into a revised structure in his artwork, Gorky perhaps obtained the "heightened perception of the society and culture of which he had only recently become a part" as Duncan Macmillan asserts.[39]

Despite Gorky's proximity to and reverence for his influences, his abstraction also dematerializes forms through impression and improvisation in the

Kandinskian compositional sense. Gorky had been conscious of Wassily Kandinsky at least as early as his arrival in America, if not before in Yerevan or Tiflis. At around the same time that the young Armenian changed his name to the Russian Gorky, he also claimed that he had been a student of the Russian Kandinsky. The interior dimension of the common denominator of experience between the Russian and the Armenian may have been at the heart of Gorky's interest in the older artist, but Gorky's move to more poetic, ethereal, and spiritual representations after his mural work may have been influenced by Kandinsky's work as well. Like many modern artists, Gorky had a copy of Kandinsky's *On the Spiritual in Art* in his library, and he would have encountered the artist's works, such as *Improvisation VII* (fig. 36), in the museums, galleries, and bookshops he was always exploring.

Like Gorky, Kandinsky had lived a spirited past. Before choosing to move to Munich to study art, Kandinsky was an ethnographer in Vologda Province in northern Russia. Through his travels he saw the vast Russian countryside and visited many rural villages, and the culture of the region had a lifelong impact on him. For instance, Kandinsky became aware of leshies, the woodland spirits that haunt his early works, and of the myth of a Zyrian monster that, it was said, had recently kidnapped a boy, prompting villagers to leave offerings in a bowl on their windowsills to pacify it. This fanciful folk tradition is similar to Gorky's, which featured, for example, the "tree of wish fulfillment"—passersby would tear off strips of their clothing, tie the scraps to the tree, and make a wish. Both artists were raised Orthodox, and both had a connection to the East; Kandinsky claimed that his great-grandmother had been a Tartar princess. Indeed, the Orthodox foundation is significant for understanding concepts of likeness in their art, since the icons in Orthodox churches were meant as impressions of spiritual individuals, much like the impressions of images in the works of Kandinsky and Gorky.

Just as our own understanding of Gorky has worked its way through the rudimentary biographical and methodological trappings of his career and must now illuminate the more interpretive and tangential, Gorky tuned in to the lyrical and improvisational aspects of Kandinsky's work. He elucidated the essence of Kandinsky's compositions in a nonspecific and nonrepetitive manner in his own work. It is precisely the foundations of improvisation that Gorky elicits from Kandinsky's work, which is why a readable debt to Kandinsky in Gorky's oeuvre is less pronounced than the more obvious allegiances to Cézanne, Picasso, and Léger. This accords with Gorky's understanding that Kandinsky's aesthetic was most effectively absorbed in a peripheral rather than direct manner. Connections generally had to be ethereal, not methodical, because the seeds of spirituality in Kandinsky's art, and the combination of destruction and resurrection infused in its fugue-like form, moved it toward a new vision of reality. Kandinsky's early work resembled a deluge, in which recognizable figures floated

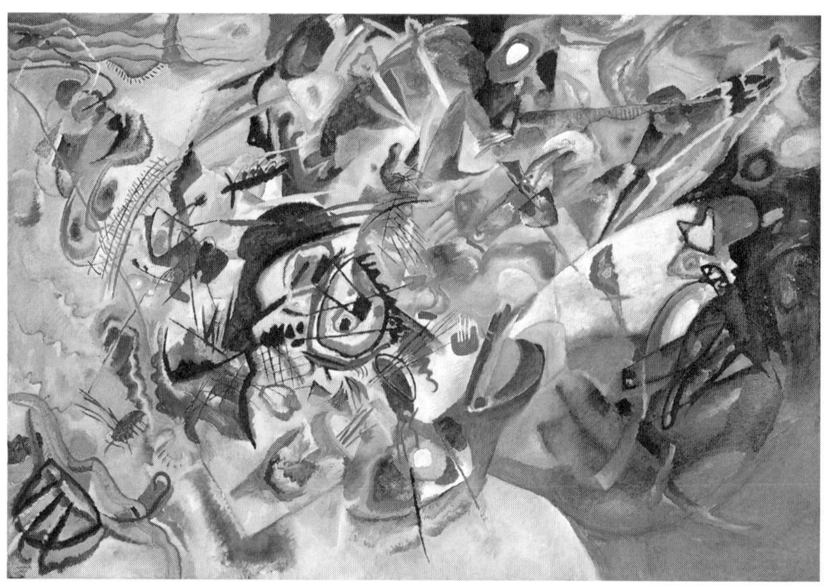

FIGURE 36
Wassily Kandinsky, *Improvisation VII (Composition VII)*, 1913. Tretyakov Gallery, Moscow.

through masses of color and form. As his work became more abstract, the color and form became contrapuntal.

Kandinsky's aesthetic theories too were perhaps as much a foundation for Gorky as those of Léger or Mondrian. *On the Spiritual in Art* outlines a process of dematerialization that is extremely important to Gorky's work because it is similar to the gradations from representational to abstract in his own work. Kandinsky labels works keyed to the outside world "impressions"; works derived from an uninhibited inspiration of nature are "improvisations"; and works that release the tangible and are formed from a conception in the mind are "compositions." Kandinsky believed that there was an inner necessity for forms to be shaped by an idea. Comparably, Gorky's drive, motivated by displacement, takes impressions of others' work while he improvises his own vision during the art-making process. For Gorky such a necessity, like Kandinsky's "compositions," was shaped by the culmination of the observed and imagined or remembered. Gorky's career follows a similar triadic trajectory.[40] Embracing the musicality in Kandinsky's abstraction, Gorky believed that "you must analyze abstract art like you analyze a fugue by Bach."[41] In addition, the three types of works that Kandinsky proposes are similar to Armenian concepts of which Gorky was likely aware. The first, *makrutyun* (simplicity), can apply to Gorky's figural works. The second *danjank* (confusion and the search for truth), can include his vast studies of art and other artists. The last, *hasnutyun* (the mastering of extreme complexity), reflects Gorky's mature abstract work. In fact, Gorky's progression follows closely Kandinsky's analysis of his own work as elaborated in his "Cologne Lecture," a summary of his work and his development that he sent to the opening of a 1914 exhibition in response to an invitation to give a lecture. Although this work was not widely available, the ideas in it floated around the European and American art communities. Kandinsky discusses three stages in his development, focusing on color, line, and spirituality; his desire not to banish the object from his work; his love of nature; his urge to create (described as an inner impulse or the creating spirit); and flatness in painting and inner depth created through layers. He concludes that he wants only "to paint good, necessary, living pictures, which are experienced properly by at least a few viewers."[42] That became a mantra for Gorky himself.

Gorky's association with the Surrealists also contributed to his art. Although only one component in a combination of artistic styles that contributed to Gorky's development, art practice, and aesthetic philosophies, Surrealism was the final and most significant one in his late career. The Surrealists did not necessarily share his processes of altering the observed, but they used memory and dreams and created compositions through free association. Surrealism began as an adaptation of psychoanalytic methods, and its leader, André Breton, expanded its basis in the unconscious to a broader understanding of "surreality." In 1924, surreality was considered a development beyond time and space, and by 1929, as the conjunction of opposites. The former implied that a work, such as a painting, was removed from narrative or temporal constraints. The latter, expressed in the second Surrealist Manifesto, allowed for the possibility that what was represented could simultaneously depict the real and imaginary, and that that which could be considered living could coexist with conceptions of death. Although it is not clear when Gorky first encountered Surrealist theory, a thread of it runs through the statements about his murals and his work of the late 1930s and early 1940s.

As Gorky developed, he always seemed to find just the right artist, artwork, or movement to fit his needs at that time. Being such a "Geiger counter of art," it seems inevitable that he would have channeled the Surrealists. Indeed, their presence in America because of World War II made encountering them unavoidable. But Surrealist theory and the embracing of his work by such well-known artists must have had a strong effect on him. Interesting, too, was that American culture was newer to these foreigners than to Gorky himself, and Gorky must have felt some pride in being able to share with them his experience, knowledge, and adaptations to American society. At the same time, their own yearnings for home, particularly in the case of Breton, who was very much a Francophile, may have stirred in Gorky his own remembrances. Aesthetic possibilities were reopening for the artist.

Gorky's marriage to his second wife, Agnes Magruder, brought him stability, at least initially, and, like Aram in *Beast on the Moon*, he began to rebuild his life after so many years of being focused on his personal and professional identities. With his wife and children he was reborn once again, but more importantly, this alliance released him from the pressing pace and modernity of the city.[43] Shifting to his in-laws' farm in Virginia during the summers in the 1940s and eventually moving to rural Connecticut prompted Gorky to look toward the landscape or domestic scenes for his inspiration. Despite his past reliance on other artists, it was likely that the new surroundings instigated his biggest artistic developments yet. The natural world, because it was itself transient and ever-changing, was more easily mutable than real people or the fixed compositions of other artists. Gorky was aware of the American landscape tradition that interpreted nature as sublime. Nature energized Gorky because he recognized its transformative powers and constant changes, and since Gorky's practice had always embraced natural processes, here was an opportunity to push the boundaries past what he had done before. Gorky more vehemently combined what he observed with scenes from his memories, which were also transient, to construct spaces that existed only in his paintings.

Gorky's development, and that of other American artists who were, as Rosenberg had attested, immigrants and sons of immigrants, was enhanced by the influx of European exiles during World War II. Although Fernand Léger, Piet Mondrian, Walter Gropius, André Masson, André Breton, and Max Ernst, unlike Gorky, were welcomed into the United States as part of the European intellectual and/or artistic community, his connection with many of them was crucial precisely because they were recognized figures in the world of art and he was flattered to have their attention.[44] Imagine, for instance, using the methodologies of a famous artist as one toiled with one's own compositions, and then meeting the artist. Even though his connection with many of these artists occurred after he had already studied and moved somewhat beyond their styles, this must have been significant to Gorky and his career. The last decade of Gorky's career has recently been labeled the "breakthrough years" because the abstract paintings and drawings from this era seem to represent a release from a self-imposed, imitative style and move toward one that becomes more individualized.[45] Far from derivative, however, Gorky had been accumulating a visual vocabulary that crystallized in the 1940s because he had reached the end of his art-historical study and had learned just about everything he could from previous artists.

Before the Surrealists began arriving in America in force, Gorky had already been absorbing what he could from them. He frequented Julien Levy's gallery, which was the first in America to show the European Surrealist movement. Levy had even written a book, *Surrealism*, which Gorky read in a back room of the gallery during his many visits to try to convince Levy to represent him.[46] In 1941, Gorky had attended Onslow Ford's lecture series, Surrealist Painting: An Adventure into Human Consciousness, at the New School for Social Research. When Levy held his first exhibition of Gorky's work, it was Bre-

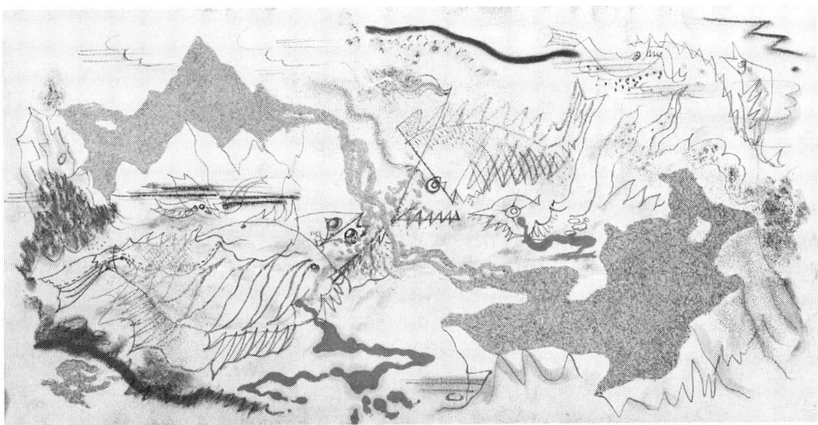

FIGURE 37
Andre Masson, *Battle of the Fishes*, 1926. The Museum of Modern Art, New York.

ton who wrote the catalogue essay. Gorky was the only American artist to be claimed by Breton as a member of the movement, even though he takes care to point out that Gorky is the only Surrealist whose compositions were based directly on nature. Gorky met the Surrealist André Masson in Connecticut in 1942, after Masson's 1941 article "Art Is a Wager," which discusses the limits of automatism, was published and Masson had severed his ties with Surrealism, although he still maintained in his work many of the stylistic devices that had characterized the movement.

Automatism had served an important purpose in the Surrealist movement and for Masson's early career. In an Exquisite Corpse, for instance, Masson was able to free his mind from the control of his drawing.[47] In most of his works, Masson had let the unconscious guide his hand, then looked at the images afterward and decided through free association what the image contained or suggested. Masson had then developed the work into an image. In a work such as *Battle of the Fishes* (fig. 37), the forms suggested mountains that Masson later enhanced by affixing sand to those sections of the work. Masson's shift from automatism occurred through drawing that was not entirely unconscious but rather often derived from observed forms. Masson's son recalled that Gorky seemed very impressed by the later drawings.

Like Masson, Gorky allowed an apparently free-flowing line to meander through his compositions, but it was based in observed or remembered objects. Gorky's *Nude* (plate 15) is a superb example of how the line ambles to evoke a form. Although free and unconstrained by recognizable space in the canvas, it is not fully autonomous. Since Gorky had a tendency to meld his influences, the fluid line may also have derived from his study of Ingres and Picasso. Ingres's serpentine line played into an eroticization of bodies in much the same way that Picasso's line was a metonymic characteristic of Cubist abstraction.[48] Appropriate to both, Gorky's *Nude* attains the same sensuality of line and surface while only hinting at form.[49] Gorky himself explained the significance of lines, saying, "People want joy and gaiety but they do not know that art is only drawing, a combination of lines and it is not important what colors burliuk [painter David Burliuk] will use to paint my portrait."[50] Gorky did not speak of or use lines in the sense that we most often understand—as coloring book–style definitions, outlines, and barriers. As Robert Hughes observes, "Gorky's sense of draftsmanship was bound up, as that sense must be, in consideration of the 'speed' of a line, its whip and springiness, its ability to convey an edge and the volume behind the edge."[51] Gorky's line was poetic, lyrical, and even calligraphic to the point that it sometimes functions as if it were an overlaid script of its own.[52]

One of Gorky's most important Surrealist connections occurred in 1943–44, when it is believed that Matta Echaurren, known for his 1938–42 series of biomorphic landscapes called "psychological morphologies" or "inscapes," encouraged Gorky to dilute his paint with turpentine. Not only did the technique further Gorky's interest in picture surface as a landscape in itself, but it allowed works such as *Waterfall* (plate 16) to mimic their subjects. The green background of *Waterfall,* which at the right drips over the other colors, is layered with washes of sienna, tan, and white, making the medium an indexical sign for the subject of the waterfall itself. Gorky absorbed images in a Cubist scrim, captured their spiritual essence by enlisting Kandinsky, and subjected them to an association both in the mind and in the physical characteristics of the painting, portraying them on canvas within a sheaf of washes and dry paint. In *Waterfall,* demarcations between objects and nonobjectivity are combined in one work, with the "idea" of the waterfall emerging from the act of painting itself. Like the erosion in his drawing *Summation,* in which the drawing is no longer on the paper but the paper is in the drawing, the drip of Gorky's diluted paint creates a waterfall down the face of the canvas. Just as a waterfall distorts through a prismatic scrim the vegetation and rocks that flow beneath it, Gorky distorts the forms and shapes in his version of one. *Waterfall* contains hints of nature's underbelly jutting out of the spilling water. Branches and boulders and earth shift from side to side and slide forward and back in the picture plane, mimicking nature. Although based on a waterfall on the Housatonic River in Connecticut, this is not necessarily a specific waterfall but rather is Gorky's idea of "waterfall" as an artist's subject. Gorky explained as early as 1926 that "Twachtman painted a waterfall that was a waterfall in any country, as Whistler's mother was any one's mother. He caught the universal idea of art. Art is always universal. It is not New England or the South or New York."[53] Despite Gorky's allegiance to Modernism, he had always been aware of the traditions of art from varying eras and styles. He had looked at Twachtman, Marin, and whoever else was necessary to gain an understanding of the aesthetic possibilities from which he might draw.

Despite a number of loosely painted works primarily from 1944, Gorky continued also using stiff paint in works like *The Liver Is the Cock's Comb* (plate 17). This might indicate that Gorky preferred control to the unpredictable dripping technique, but it is also consistent with Gorky's continuing practice of adopting whatever method fit the agenda of a particular work—hence the fluidity of *Waterfall*, the solidity of works such as *Abstraction with a Palette*, and the dry-brush technique of *The Liver Is the Cock's Comb*. The mutating quality of the thinned paint enhances the painting act itself and the completed image. Gorky's artmaking approach intertwines the recognizable and the abstract, but is always, like nature, poignant and profound. Fluctuation unifies the composition and, in a way, democratizes it because all elements are just as unrecognizable and unstable as their counterparts. It would seem, then, that because of this democratization, Gorky created the quintessential American art.[54]

Many of Gorky's paintings of the 1940s were not inspired by art made by others, as those of his early career, but instead by nature or the environment around him. In his earlier compositions, Gorky had made several versions or revisions of a work until he created his own interpretation of it. Likewise, he would make numerous preparatory drawings of a scene or landscape and then recombine them into final paintings that use black line to loosely define biomorphic shapes and intermittent touches of color that create their own syntax. In *The Leaf of an Artichoke Is an Owl* (plate 18), Gorky reveals the essence of the owl/artichoke in artichoke-green wash with orange and red. As in his exploration of different styles in his early career, Gorky layered and manipulated space to solve artistic problems. His interest was highly technical, as he considered how objects and the spatial relationships between them, like those of the Newark airplanes, could be depicted.

In *The Leaf of an Artichoke Is an Owl*, Gorky extrapolated a part, a leaf, from a whole, the artichoke, and transformed it into something else, an owl, by metaphor. The title, selected by André Breton from an observation Gorky had made at the dinner table, is a literal record of the visual transformation of his thought process. Abstractions such as *The Leaf of an Artichoke Is an Owl* denote this associative method. The leaf, shaped like an owl, becomes for Gorky literally the owl, yet the representation of it is abstract and nonliteral.[55] Gorky says, "one image leads to another, one wisdom leads to another when you look into it, like peeling an artichoke . . . the leaves lying in the plate like feathers . . . and of course the silhouette of an artichoke is quite simply that of an owl."[56] For Gorky, these leaves looked like a pile of feathers and functioned metaphorically, a metonym. Yet the similarity to the shape of the feather—part of a bird—to a whole bird such as an owl acts as a synecdoche. The association of the leaves and the artichoke is both semiotic and semeiotic.

The composition *Water of the Flowery Mill* (fig. 38), which refers to an old flour mill, uses the same loose medium. In addition to the analogy in the formal aspects of the painting, Gorky likens the homonyms *flour* and *flower*.[57] Gorky's

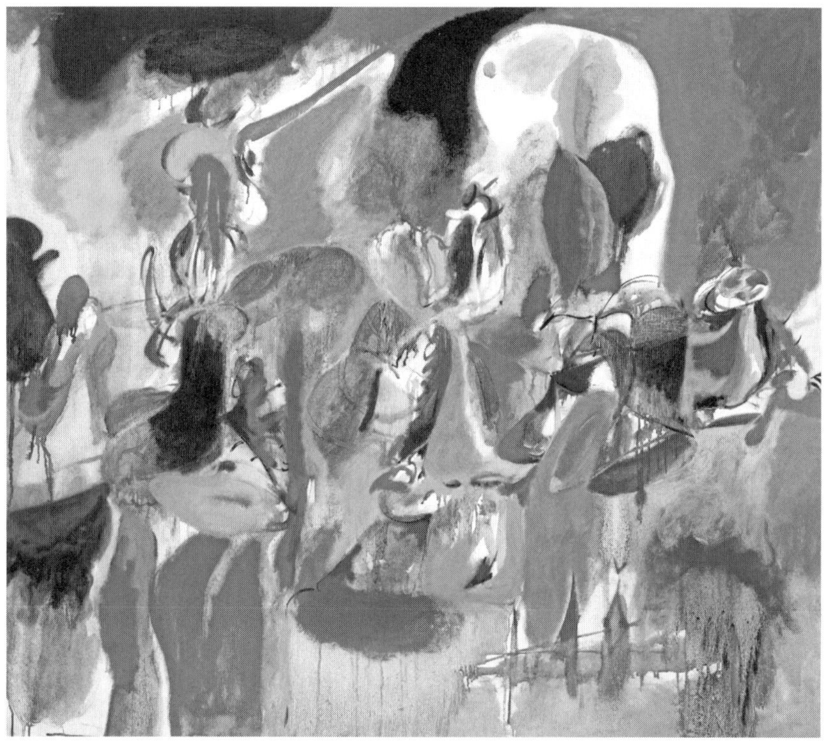

FIGURE 38
Arshile Gorky, *Water of the Flowery Mill,* 1944. The Metropolitan Museum of Art, New York.

interest in likeness incorporates aspects of Kandinsky's improvisations and Surrealist free association important to Gorky's abstraction, which is a culmination of these approaches and styles. Because Gorky's late work was based on something that had occurred or did exist in the world and did not banish all control exerted by reason, as was necessary according to the Surrealist Manifesto, it escaped the Surrealist definition of pure psychic automatism. The element of recall in Gorky's work, however, might be related to the Surrealist dream.

In his discussions of *Dada and Surrealism,* William Rubin popularized the term "dream painting," referring to the Surrealist use of Freudian dream interpretation. In psychoanalysis, it is believed that dreams are not entirely imaginary because they include aspects of one's conscious life that find meaning when they emerge through the vehicle of the unconscious. Salvador Dalí is perhaps the most well-known Surrealist practitioner of this technique, but artists such as Joan Miró, who combined free association and dream, seemed to be of the most interest to Gorky. Miró's *Harlequin's Carnival* (fig. 39) consists of automatic images that the Spaniard drew and expanded into likenesses of organisms, or "personnages," that existed in a "dream-like" space. Miró's creation of imaginary words may also have appealed to Gorky as a way to express his own duality.

Gorky's dreams, however, were mostly based on images from a past world. These "memory dreams," like his memory portraits that referred to a person, referred to a place or space. As in memory and dream, the renditions were not exact. For instance, both *The Artist and His Mother* and *Portrait of Myself and*

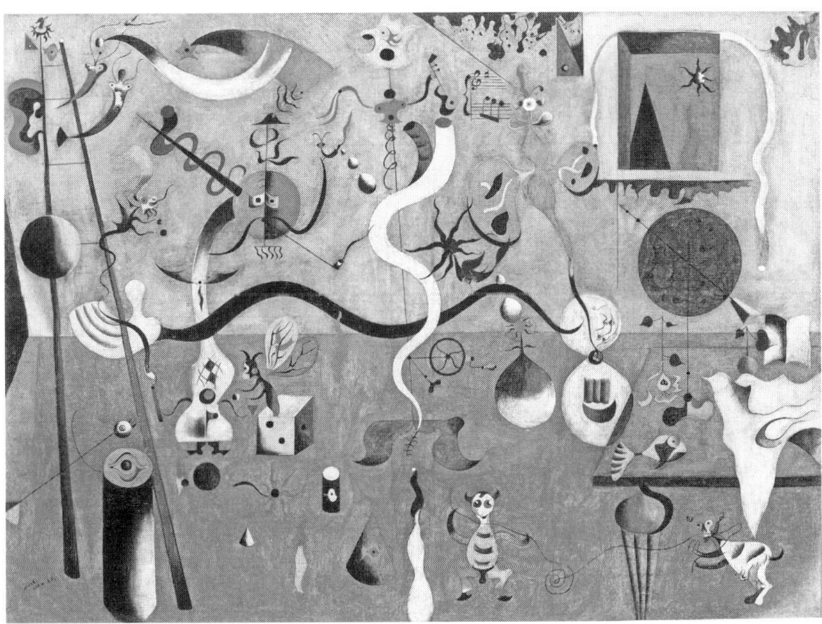

FIGURE 39
Joan Miró, *Le Carnaval d'Arlequin (Carnival of Harlequin)*, 1924–25. Albright-Knox Art Gallery, Buffalo, N.Y.

My Imaginary Wife are representative of an imagination that reflects a kind of magical thinking consistent with Surrealist philosophy. The alchemical, magical, and dream states are embedded in Surrealism, which manifests an image that is interchangeable with the art. But although it is useful to connect Gorky to the Surrealist movement, particularly since Breton claimed him as a member, Gorky, because of the connection of his work to the outside world, could never actually be a Surrealist. Despite his embrace of European art, the conditions of Gorky's own life as an artist were distinctly American. Harold Rosenberg wrote, "What makes any definition of a movement in art dubious is that it never fits the deepest artists in the movement—certainly not as well as, if successful, it does the others. Yet without the definition something essential in those best is bound to be missed. The attempt to define is like a game in which you cannot possibly reach the goal from the starting point, but can only close in on it by picking up each time from where the last play landed."[58] Surrealism was the last play in art history for Gorky up to that point, but by maintaining a connection to the world around him and using it as a foundation for his compositions, he mined the unconscious without falling victim to it. Perhaps this was because Gorky already had enough living dreams, myths, and memories (or nightmares) from his childhood in Turkey and Armenia that, if left to the unconscious entirely, he would have been overwhelmed by the struggles of or with his past.

The Surrealists offered, however, an infinite number of possible worlds for Gorky. They displaced themselves and objects through automatism and dreams.

This method was useful to the displaced Gorky, who displaced observed elements of the natural world. And yet his murals serve as a foundation in relating Gorky's subjective response to reality, in which his art is a meeting point between his worlds and identities and between the experiences of himself and his viewers. Gorky's painting is multidimensional, intended to function on many different levels—past, present, recognizable, abstract, real, imagined, remembered, and experiential. Gorky was ultimately a synthesizer; hence the term "Abstract Surrealism," invented partially to describe him. Adolph Gottlieb said that for Gorky, "as for few others, the vital task was a wedding of abstraction and surrealism. Out of these opposites something new could emerge, and Gorky's work is part of the evidence that this is true."[59] As Gorky's art progressed, it became clear that the language of art that Gorky sought to produce was a pastiche, one that reflected an understanding and distillation of the most useful qualities of many different artists and types of art.

Because Gorky's art converted European styles into an American abstraction, it should be no surprise that it hovers between Surrealism and Abstract Expressionism. Americans have always borrowed intellectual capital from Europe, but while Gorky himself moved into a more autonomous style and practice, America too was developing a powerful modern identity that was solidified during the era that bridged the two world wars. The influx of European teachers like Hans Hofmann was crucial to the development of young artists in the New York diaspora, and the two movements that bracket Gorky's work also reflect a global shift of, arguably, the art world epicenter from Paris to New York. This shift was helped along, as Serge Guilbault has noted, not only by the fact that many Surrealists fled to the United States from Europe during World War II, but also by the fact that American capital remained steady and even increased during that time. Fledgling museums and galleries in America were largely funded by individuals from corporate families who had profited from the war.[60]

After the war, the rise of American nationalism, linked to the strength of the already industrially and technologically superior United States, contributed to the prevalence of American Modernism and later made Abstract Expressionism significant in the international art world. The device of abstraction was decisive to the development of American art in the second third of the twentieth century. In his essay "Modernist Painting," Clement Greenberg created a historical justification for American abstraction,[61] and despite its foundation in Europe, the result was quintessentially American, eventually becoming linked to American freedom through the Abstract Expressionist movement.[62] As a foreigner himself, Gorky translated abstraction into something that could be digested and embraced as American. Even if the public didn't get where he was headed, the young New York artists who became the Abstract Expressionists did. In essence, Gorky had helped translate modern abstraction and injected it with emotionality before other artists such as Jackson Pollock, Willem de Kooning,

Barnett Newman, and Mark Rothko codified it. Gorky's own progression through art history as a means to learn to paint was actually a model for Greenberg's explanation of the American trajectory of modern painting, which the critic conceptualized after Gorky's death. Gorky learned an artistic heritage and language that was foreign to him but that he felt he must master, and thereby became an active translator, rather than a passive occupant of the space between two movements. Once Gorky had caught up to and adopted the practices of his time, he became an innovator, making his work, arguably, a foundation upon which abstraction in America in the mid-twentieth century would be based.

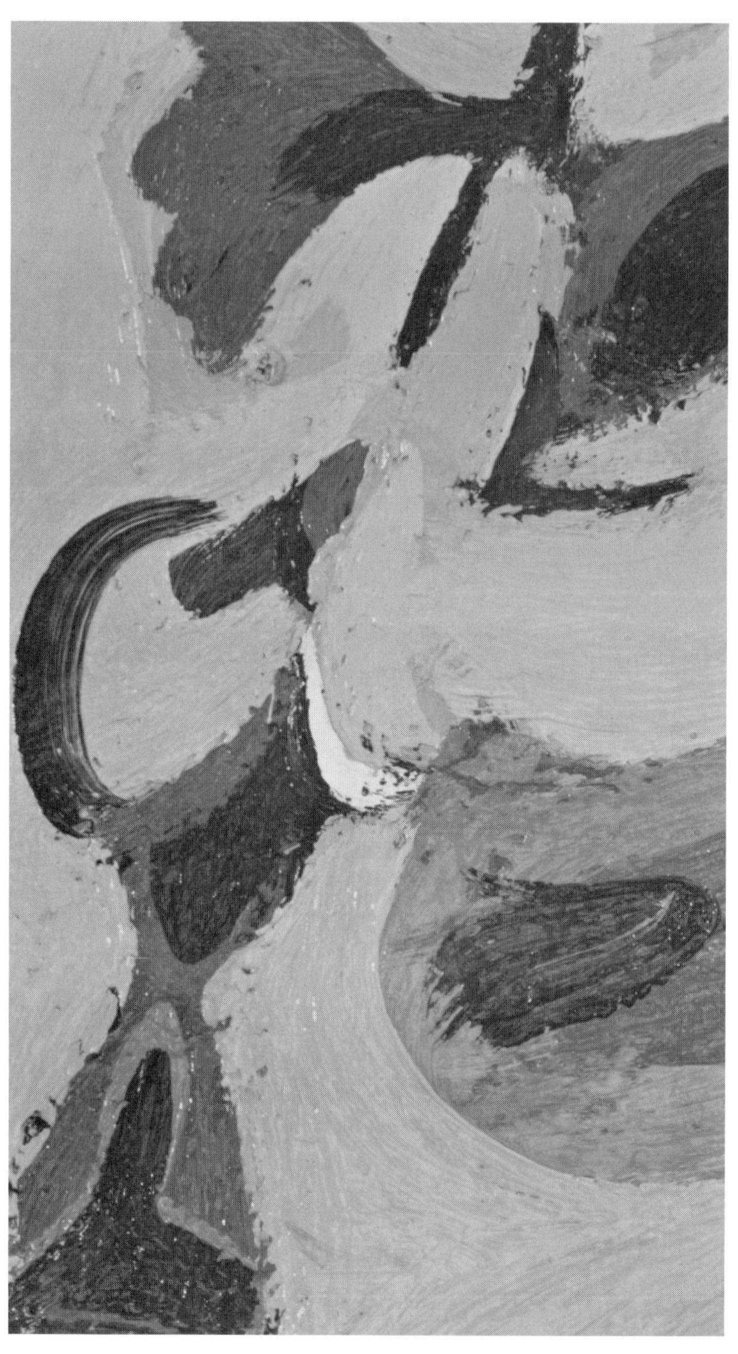

chapter 5

Difference, Likeness, and Synthesis

Those who love easy solutions will find slim pickings here: despite all warnings, they will continue their attempts to discover still lifes, landscapes and figurations in these compositions, simply because they do not have the courage to recognize the fact that all human emotions tend to be precipitated in hybrid *forms. By "hybrid" I mean to signify the end result produced by the contemplation of a natural spectacle blended with the flux of childhood and other memories provoked by an intense concentration upon this spectacle by an observer endowed with quite exceptional emotional gifts.*

—ANDRÉ BRETON

The epigraph by André Breton defines Gorky's mature images as "hybrid." The idea of hybridity certainly fits Gorky's personal displacement and his displacement of the observed world in his art, but it also harks back to the hybridity of American art and artists in general. To that point in history, American artists had characteristically been trained in Europe or, like Gorky, embraced European art movements. Even Willem de Kooning, who eventually became one of the most celebrated Abstract Expressionists, had been trained in Europe. In the early twentieth century, many were, as Harold Rosenberg noted, immigrants or sons of immigrants, often without the means to travel abroad, or interest in doing so. Stuart Davis, when attacked for his seemingly European-derived artwork, had made the defense that artists working in America were hyphenated Americans ethnically, so why should their artistic descent not be a combination as well?[1]

The words Breton uses, such as "contemplation" and "concentration," imply that Gorky's compositional methods in painting his abstractions were sim

Opening image detail of figure 40.

ilar to those he used for his memory portraits, mural work, and associative renderings. By combining forms and concentrating on surface or internal structures, Gorky addressed place, space, and time. The longer Gorky remained in America, the more he was prompted to "re-member," or reconfigure, scenes from his past while looking at the world around him. The works that resulted were the hybrid forms to which Breton refers, recombinations of memory shreds and observations. Gorky's paintings, then, became an archive of dispossession, in which what was lost, although it could never be regained, could be retrieved through disembodied memory. In the process, Gorky created something entirely new: a new space on the canvas and a new kind of art unbound by specifics but rooted in the recognizable.

Gorky sought to traverse art-historical periods, established styles, and fixed meanings in his work, making a polysemic art. Using the Modernist device, ingrained in his art, of conception over perception and idea over specificity, Gorky evoked the personal and emotional for artist and viewer alike. Memories filtered through displacement, displacing the past and present in a kind of temporal discontinuity of the observed and remembered. Like Gorky's own disjunctive speech, in which the inflection of restructured sentences held meaning for the listener in addition to the words, Gorky's art in the 1940s held implicit and explicit meanings. Just as his hybridized language was a byproduct of two different languages and grammatical structures, the structural linguistics of his paintings is a combination of styles and mutated experiences.

Gorky's practice became most evident during the summer of 1943, when during two months at his in-laws' farm in Hamilton, Virginia, Gorky worked through numerous drawings that, as they became more abstract, reconfigured and heightened the essence of an arrangement in front of him. Landscape-based works, such as the drawing *Virginia Landscape* (plate 19), began with the terrain as a point of departure and incorporated the biomorphic qualities inherent in flowers, bugs, and other living organisms. Incorporating components of the natural world into an abstract image was a continuation of Gorky's earlier methods of remaking extant works by other artists as well as expressing the musicality of compositions, which he had understood from Kandinsky. As he assembled and disassembled nature in this work, nature eventually came to have as much of a place in it as compositions by other artists had earlier in his career, a connection that Gorky makes himself. When a large area of milkweed was being removed from Crooked Run Farm, Gorky exclaimed, "They are cutting down all the Raphaels."[2] For Gorky, nature was as much a work of art as an artwork itself.[3]

As in the earlier works, Gorky's architectonics addressed the relationships between forms as much as the individual forms themselves. But in the later works the forms were less solid and recognizable and began to dematerialize as the artist created more ambiguous space and exploited the transience of natural forms and their location (or dislocation) within the entity of the canvas. In a

December 1948 letter to Ethel Schwabacher, Gorky's wife Agnes described Gorky's working process. He envisioned "fantastic animals and menacing heads in the shapes of trees and felt the earth as swell, a bosom, an expansion like a sigh. Many of the shapes in the final drawings or paintings were arbitrarily picked out or unconsciously drawn from tensions he felt between the branches of different trees for instance. The tree completely not seen as a tree. There are some drawings which I can actually see as a certain place. The fundamental arrangement of shapes in nature serving as a base."[4] Agnes noted that, although objects were somewhat recognizable in Gorky's artwork, it did not render a specific place. Gorky observed fundamental arrangements of shapes in nature that served as a basis for the compositions. He did not work from the unconscious, however. His attraction to Masson's work, significantly, had come after Masson had renounced using the unconscious as a tool.

Gorky looked at the trees in Virginia, for instance, drew between them, as he might say, and created likenesses through successive versions until he had achieved a representation that was transformational. He would, as painter and former student Walter Murch explained, "go on a drawing binge and make eighty drawings and out of those eighty he would pick five, we'll say, that really moved him and he would simply go to work and make paintings of those five or one."[5] As in his rememorations, Gorky's art was subject to a stringent editorial process of recursive repetition, making the paintings often much more abstract than the drawings from which were be derived. Gorky accessed a reservoir of images, distilling and recombining the elements of other compositions in a work. Just as he had used different Picasso works as well as ideas from artists such Mondrian, Léger, and Ozenfant in configuring *Organization*, Gorky enlisted a range of observations and mutations in his abstracted paintings because modernity itself is a disembedding and faith in the reflexivity of forms.[6] The drawings themselves, however, were still important as individual pieces. In 1946, Agnes wrote that Gorky had been "working like a madman—a happy one. I tore 50 drawings away from him to send to Julien—it took him two whole days of muttering and puttering to make up his mind to send them and now he comes home exclaiming I must write to Julien to tell him they are nothing for only today he has discovered etc. etc."[7] The drawings were significant to the development of the processes through which he always strove to discover something new.

Gorky's arrangement produced a commonality between the memories of place in his homeland, observed place in his new home, the new place created on the surface of the canvas, and the concept of place that the viewer derived. Not only does the combination of these elements go beyond hybridization, but the fundamental natural arrangements are the basis for the viewer's experience because recognition or familiarity with natural forms is shared. As Ethel Schwabacher explained, "his later painting may be better understood if we remember that he worked on several levels at once, responding to the stimuli of the immediate outside world of nature, to anterior impressions of the Caucasus, to memories of past and present art, and to the suggestions of the dreamworld or collective unconscious. His art is evocative on four levels: the senses, the psyche, the historic past and the universal level of epic symbolism."[8] Re-membering in such a manner, that is, recombining or putting together elements of images that he had observed at one point in time with those recalled through memory that such scenes evoked, is consistent with the idea of "memory portraits," which Jordan defined as the combination of what Gorky saw before him and the memory of how something looked at a particular point in time in the past.

The added element of time, freed from a linear structure, can perhaps be clarified through Stephen W. Hawking's concept of imaginary time. In *A Brief History of Time,* Hawking explains that "imaginary time is indistinguishable from directions in space . . . if one can go forward in imaginary time, one ought to be able to turn around and go backward. This means that there can be no important difference between forward and backward directions of imaginary time."[9] In Gorky's works, time and space and place are mutable and unfixed and, on some level, imaginary and constructed rather than simply hybridized.

Because the subjects of his paintings were either places that no longer existed or hybridized images of the observed and the remembered, and Gorky neither replicated a scene in front of him nor exactly depicted a place from the past, he rendered them through a nonspecific abstract style. His memories' lack of real context relates to Gorky's own identity. In keeping with his Russian pseudonym, in a series of drawings and paintings Gorky renamed his Armenian gardenland, Khorkom, as the Russian Sochi, a Black Sea resort, thus reinforcing the alterable quality of the proper name, its dispossession when removed from cultural context, and its connection to the mutable quality of landscape in his art. Khorkom itself now exists as Sochi, its Armenian homes, which Gorky had described in his Newark mural essay, populated by Muslim transplants resettled from Eastern Europe. Like the malleability of Gorky's own identity, the alterable qualities of time, space, and place in his artwork are exemplified in the *Garden in Sochi* series. Beginning around 1940, Gorky worked through several versions that became more and more abstract, eventually producing an imagined space relative only to the constraints of the canvas. By renaming *Garden in Khorkom* as *Garden in Sochi,* he essentially re-placed the identity of his homeland into something that had a different meaning for the viewer and where he himself had never been. It did not matter that Sochi was not Khorkom, because—as in Hawking's conception of time—Gorky was not necessarily trying to situate the viewer in a specific place or time. Gorky's belief in plasticity and the achievement of a common denominator for artist and viewer alike transported them both, through the visual language of color, form, and line, toward an interstitial state.

As if occupying the Cubist fourth dimension, these works are simultaneously Armenia and America. *Garden in Sochi* is not an exact depiction of a specific garden, but an abstracted impression of one, produced by a collage of elements such as memory, observation, and paint surface. In this painting, a precursor to the nonhierarchical all-over painting of Abstract Expressionism, the diversity of the numerous versions works out its internal balance. In a 1941 version (plate 20), the olive background and bright shapes float in groups across the painting. In the upper left, a cross shape is connected to a red, black, white, and yellow form that joins a shoe shape in the center of the painting. A vertical black rectangle is above the form, and a white-and-yellow vertical form is below it. To the right is a string of forms that are multicolored and biomorphic in nature. The surface of the painting is a thick impasto with a grainy texture, and each of the forms has an uneven, feathery outline from the brush moving through the thick paint, much like the surface of *Organization*.

In contrast, the 1943 *Garden in Sochi* (plate 21) is painted with a thin, dry texture, more like *The Liver Is the Cock's Comb*. The background is white, and, although the placement and general outline of the shapes are the same, the colors are bright yellow and orange and connected by a reedy ebony line. The same line surrounds each image, but colors overlap it or do not extend to the edge. Although each image has the same title and motifs, they are not exactly the same. Both paintings may be based on the garden that Gorky remembered from his home in Khorkom, but the ease with which he changed the location in the title and integrates different textures, colors, and outlines from real and remembered places, indicates how easily Gorky's work may be removed from a specific identity.[10] There is a tree-like image on the right-hand side of the painting, but we know that Gorky drew between the trees and abstracted the observed, so in the end, the work is as nonspecific as its title.[11]

According to Brian O'Doherty, Gorky was "constantly probing at the limits of expression, he analyzed and synthesized until the two processes began to mimic each other as motifs turn up so often that, like a biologist, one can recognize their morphology, partial origin, and hybridization."[12] Gorky's conception of the garden overrules the specificity of a particular garden or recognizable elements of its morphology, which illuminates Breton's idea of hybridity but simultaneously solidifies its interpretive qualities for the viewer. In Gorky's own language, he painted versions of Sochi/Khorkom over and over, working through the physical understanding of the composition in paint and emotive quality of an imagined, distant, and lost time and place. Considering this lexicon, we might hypothesize that if Gorky had, for instance, twenty words in his visual vocabulary palette, that is, twenty motifs to choose from, he might only have selected five, but these were the basis of sentences appearing in combinations of a new syntax in each new version.

The multiple meanings of the central form in *Garden in Sochi* are also significant. The composition is commonly believed to relate to a memory from

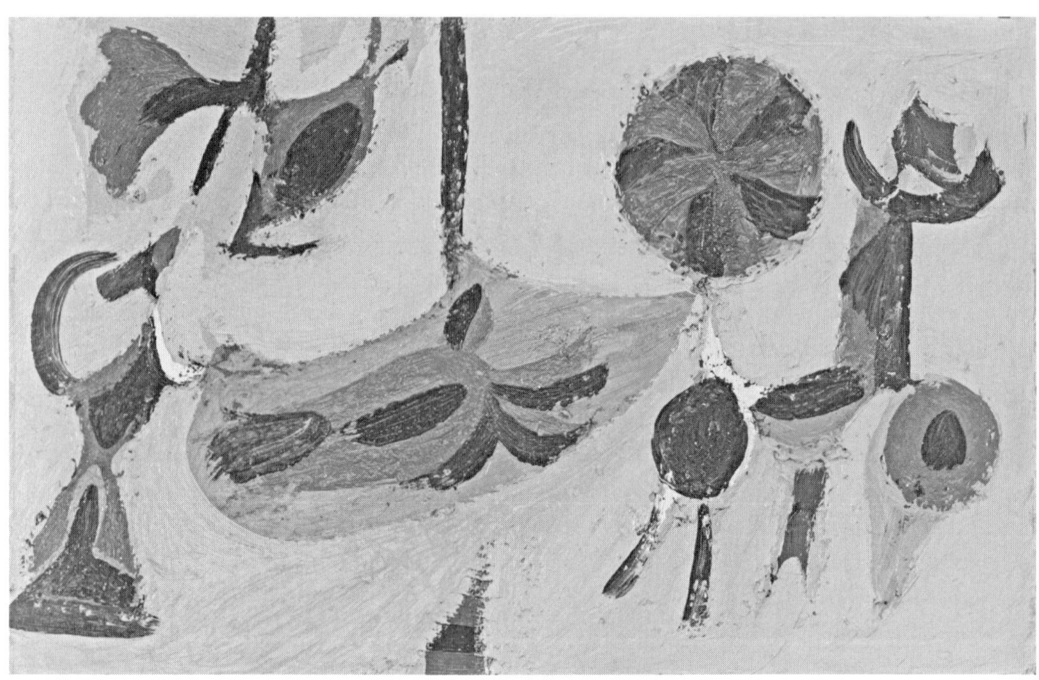

FIGURE 40
Arshile Gorky, *Argula*, 1938. The Museum of Modern Art, New York.

Gorky's childhood that included a pair of Armenian slippers that Gorky's father gave to him in the garden before leaving for America.[13] Yet the shape is more about what it evokes than what it depicts. The *Garden in Sochi* series repeats the slipper form found in *Argula* (fig. 40), one of Gorky's earlier works,[14] and harks back to the form at the center of the original *Khorkom* paintings. Multiplying the levels of interpretation, *Sochi* has also been compared to Miró's *Still Life with Old Shoe* (fig. 41), which Gorky may have used as a model. Seeing the Miró may have prompted the memory of the shoe or garden, or the shape may have reminded Gorky of the shape of the slipper, after which other associations ensued. Gorky also may have absorbed the formal qualities of the Miró and, through the association of looking at his own work, brought up associations from his own memory.[15]

As the epigraph from Breton indicates, the forms in such paintings have multiple connections. Miró's European boots are remade in Gorky's composition into Armenian slippers, just as Gorky remade himself, images of his sisters and his wife, and the dissected and reassembled visual components of airplanes. More importantly, the viewer might read the image as a shoe because it is reduced to a somewhat iconic form, even though it need not be read as Gorky's or Miró's shoe specifically, or as a shoe at all. According to the artist, it was an Armenian butter churn, a sheepskin bag, that he remembered seeing during his childhood in Armenia.[16] The act of churning butter by shaking the bag vigor-

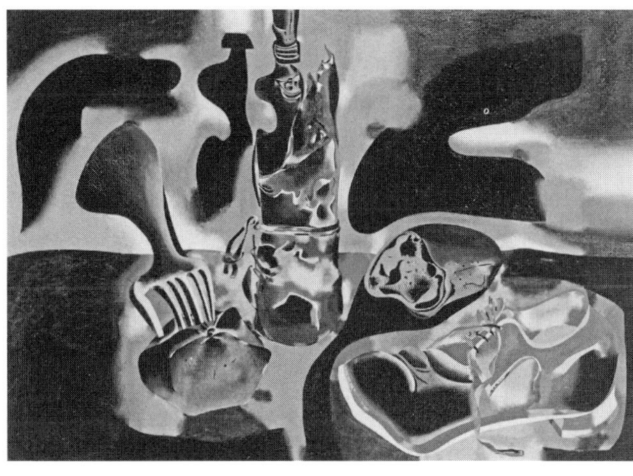

FIGURE 41
Joan Miró, *Still Life with Old Shoe*, Paris, January 24–May 29, 1937. The Museum of Modern Art, New York.

ously was often accompanied by a work song, and butter itself was considered somewhat of a magical substance—if the butter did not coagulate during the churning process, evil spirits might be at work, and talismans might be used or a priest might called in.[17]

Gorky's adaptation of *Still Life with Old Shoe* and the association of shoe forms with the butter churn underscore the free-association and stream-of-consciousness vehicles of Surrealism that were useful to the artist. Gorky never fully subscribed to the Surrealists' technique of automatism because he was never fully lost in the world he created, which, because of its basis in the remembered or the observed, was never entirely imaginary. Gorky was, however, drawn by automatism's poetic qualities of association, using free association and tangential chains of thought as part of his artmaking. The "Sochi" that Gorky referenced, was actually Khorkom, and because Khorkom, as a casualty of the Genocide, essentially no longer existed, the composition is intersubjective. The abstract plausibility of *Garden in Sochi* remains an abstraction for the viewer, embedded in a language that looks like something or someplace, but with its existence suspended like the elements floating in the composition itself. Considered in this manner, the concept of hybridity is incomplete. As Homi Bhabha would argue, because hybridity is based on rules of recognition, it is an area of conflict for the individual (who is transplanted or colonized) because identity exists within an area of conflict, margin, or in-between space.[18] The interstitial space of the canvas manifests itself like a fourth dimension, or a postnational, global space outside the canvas. If the painting of this lost place, Gorky's *Garden in Sochi*, had not been a combination of perspectives, including the viewer's, it would have become fetish.

Instead, Gorky created a mythology for the work because of its relationship to a nonexistent place, a conception that exists only in Gorky's memory and to which the viewer is not necessarily made privy, and because of displacement, which activates the internal elements in the work. The configuration of these forms in the artist's work makes it part of a narrative of art history, or mythology of it, rather than a narrative itself. The viewer, in semeiotic terms, brings his or her own connection, bank of images, and memories to the work. We know from his earlier works that visual language creation is part of Gorky's oeuvre, but here the ideas are contextualized within abstraction. This relates to Barthes, who speaks of myth in terms of creating a new language:

> Myth, indeed, must be included in the general theory of language, of writing, of the signifier, and this theory, resting on formulations of ethnology, psychoanalysis, semiology and ideological analysis must widen its object so as to take in the *sentence* or better, to take in *sentences* (the plural of the sentence). What I mean by this is that the mythical is present everywhere *sentences are turned, stories told* (in all senses of the two expressions): from inner speech to conversation, from newspaper article to political sermon, from novel (if there still are any) to advertising image—all utterances which could be brought together under the Lacanian concept of the *imaginary*.[19]

Barthes here insists that there is, in fact, a change in the object itself, an editing of sorts that is not merely a splicing together or hybridization of elements. Instead, the work is a concept of the image, which is not necessarily imagined in the manner of fantasy, but *imaged* in such a way that it becomes a repository of myth (or constructed matrix of meaning) for the society in which it exists. In this composition, Gorky tried to evoke a fanciful, happy place with flowers and birds and a tree that could fulfill wishes, but there is an ominous and staid quality that hints at loss.

It is useful here to consider Simon Schama's commentary about landscapes, which are, he says, "culture before they are nature; constructs of the imagination projected onto wood and water and rock." American landscapes in particular had always conjured an element of myth. He continues: "Once a certain idea of landscape, a myth, a vision, establishes itself in an actual place, it has a peculiar way of muddling categories, of making metaphors more real than their referents; of becoming, in fact, part of the scenery."[20] If, for example, a work like *Garden in Sochi* is based on a memory of a particular garden, what is remembered is not necessarily the garden's specifics, because memory can't be that vivid, but a "gardenness" that Gorky configures through fragmented memory and combination with the present. This sense of the garden is what Gorky hopes the viewers will recognize, not his specific garden, but an essence that will recall for them their own memories of such places.

The art historian Harry Rand's conceptions of Gorky's art support the idea of a malleable identity in his paintings. Rand discusses Gorky's *Garden at Sochi* series in terms of renaming: "In Armenian the word for poplar is Sos, or Sosi, hence Gorky was describing gardens of Sosi and clearly not gardens in Sochi. [Gorky's] mistranslation, confusing the tree with the Russian Black Sea resort, is more than a replacement of a locale for an object and he eventually acknowledged his contrived pun."[21] Gorky's supposed mistranslation is possible and could be considered a type of free association, making identity associative or interchangeable, rather than a pun.[22] The name also, of course, referenced Gorky's public identity as a Russian, and any misreading reveals that misidentification. This complicated combination of name and art is an uneasy moderator between the literal and figurative. The unification of abstraction, depiction, and memory inspired by the American landscape is part of Arshile Gorky's identity as an artist. His work may be identified as many things at once, just as Gorky is the same person but has many identities. As curator Robert Storr has pointed out, these personal and aesthetic identities are borrowed.[23] It is through this process that Gorky's multiple identities emerge and make his multivalent interpretations modern. Identity is therefore a system of relationships that functions in a manner relative to the diaspora in which it exists, whether within the world or in a painting.

Such multiplicity and combination of old and new, observation and memory, and even nature and art is elaborated in a statement by Gorky given to Dorothy Miller of the Museum of Modern Art, who needed an explanation for the museum's newly acquired version of *Garden in Sochi*. The statement exemplifies the way that Gorky's associative mind informs his compositions. Throughout it, Gorky integrates his contemporary concerns and memories of a past place into a fragmented, mostly nonnarrative exposition:

> I like the heat, the tenderness, the edible, the lusciousness, the song of a single person, the bathtub full of water to bathe myself beneath the water. I like Uccello, Grünewald, Ingres, the drawings and sketches for paintings of Seurat, and that man Pablo Picasso.
>
> I measure all things by weight.
>
> I love my mougouch. What about papa Cézanne!
> I hate things that are not like me and all the things I haven't got are God to me.
>
> Permit me—
>
> I like the wheatfields, the plough, the apricots, those flirts of the sun. And bread above all . . .
>
> About 194 feet away from our house on the road to the spring, my father had a little garden with a few apple trees which had retired from giving fruit. There was a ground constantly giving shade where grew incalculable amounts of wild carrots, and porcupines had made their nests. There was a blue rock half buried in the black earth with a few patches here and there like fallen clouds. But where came all the shadows in constant battle like lancers of Paolo Uccello's paintings? This garden was identified as the Garden of Wish Fulfillment and often I had seen my mother and other

> village women opening their bosoms and taking their soft and dependent breasts in their hands to rub them on the rock. Above all this stood an enormous tree all bleached under the sun, the rain, the cold, and deprived of leaves. This was the Holy Tree. I myself don't know why this tree was holy but I had witnessed many people, whoever did pass by, that would tear voluntarily a strip of their clothes and attach this to the tree. Thus through many years of the same act, like a veritable parade of banners under the pressure of wind all these personal inscriptions of signatures, very softly to my innocent ear used to give echo to the sh-h-h-sh-h of silver leaves of the poplars.[24]

In this collage-like format, which seems to embrace Freudian free association or Surrealist stream-of-consciousness, Gorky describes taking a bath, artistic influences, his wife, and Cézanne with no distinction between art and life. He then says that all things he does not have "are God" to him. He does not have images of Khorkom to look at—like the photograph of his mother and himself—only memories and snippets of visions, yet the statement turns into a description of the place and incidents that had occurred there. Time is liquid, and the magical, fanciful, and folk mix with art history.

Ideas of displacement, which have figured so heavily in our understanding of the artist thus far, are not lost here, since, as Gorky explains, he is influenced by a combination of past and present. The past is displaced and integrated into the present just as shapes are displaced from the compositions of other artists and incorporated into his own work, or as Gorky's observed or remembered experiences are interpreted in paint. The ethereal qualities of memory, when considered in the interpretation of paintings, release analysis of Gorky's work from the literal, giving it a sublime quality. The sublime in the twentieth century is a response not just to nature, as it tended to be in previous centuries, but to human imagination.

The form of Gorky's statement indicates that one can't really describe the visual, particularly Gorky's work, with text. Indeed, any explanation by the artist or otherwise is, as Barnett Newman writes of Adolph Gottlieb's paintings, problematic because it drains them of emotionality: "It is gratuitous to put into a sentence the stirring that takes place in these pictures."[25] What Gorky presented instead follows the form of an associative composition like the painting itself, verbally mimicking its visual form. Connections between words and images in Gorky's statement are made by analogy, similarly to the way they are connected in Gorky's mind. But the analogies are not purely about likeness, but rather about what Gorky likes and dislikes. Gorky says, "I hate the things that are not like me"; in the making of likenesses, nothing is required to be hated. Analogy becomes a mediator, and the analogies and likenesses become a formal project for Gorky, the making of things likable through likeness. And perhaps, even though they may be displaced (the images and Gorky), they can still be accepted.

The importance of this likening process is further illustrated by the story of Gorky's failed attempt to sculpt a bust of his wife in stone. Hayden Herrera gives an account that suggests that Gorky felt that likeness was as much a spiritual as a physical element of a work. After chipping feverishly away at the stone, Gorky frustratedly proclaimed, "There's no room left in it for you."[26] The sculpture was too much an object, too fixed and static. A key to understanding the latter part of Gorky's oeuvre is realizing that any object upon which it might be based is not, in fact, the whole of the painting. Like Cézanne's, Gorky's process was to reproduce not the object, but its likeness as achieved through his process of remaking. The same object could be subject to interpretation through an infinity of styles, and therefore its identity was never fixed. This allowed Gorky to reinterpret the works of others and simultaneously create his own imagery. Gorky didn't drain shapes of their referents, but rather, by not completely rendering them, allowed them to glance off one another like the shifting planes in Cézanne's work or the metalanguage of Cubism. The hovering shapes and the fluctuations of figure and ground learned from his earlier likenings exposit themselves in this mature work.

The explanation that Gorky gave a Virginia neighbor who was confused by an abstract drawing he gave her reveals Gorky's own interpretive reading and alteration of the scene:

> Pointing to a specific landscape view on Crooked Run Farm, he indicated in his drawing the converging lines of receding harvest and fencerows. At the left middle-distance of landscape and drawing he pointed to a hayrick, and he indicated that there were trees to the far left and right in both scenes, specifically a fruit tree in the upper right. The triangular funnel or cornucopia form at the center foreground in the drawing Gorky called a pool of water, acknowledging in a bemused way that it was not from the observed landscape, but was an imaginative addition.[27]

The unreality of the real underscores the flexibility of Gorky's field of experience. Gorky's alteration of a scene assumes the same poetic and compositional license that he took with images by other artists, portraits of individuals, and forms themselves.

These likenesses have been read many different ways. Breton considered them hybrid images, both of form and emotion. George Dennison believes that Breton's idea is misleading:

> They are not hybrid images, but hybrid shapes—or, more correctly, pseudo-shapes. The primary function of their ambiguity is not to refer to visible reality but to depart from it, to depart in such a way as to show us a total structure that evokes something close, something that is hard to

> come to grips with and that is neither exotic nor confined to the Unconscious. We are not released by these paintings, as we are released by classical art, but are pursued by them. They possess—and we share—a commitment to the unfinished events of life. The excitement they produce is not wholly one of fulfillment or satisfaction, but contains an element that is disturbing, an element to which we respond with gravity and meditative lingering.[28]

Dennison's point that we are pursued by these paintings is remarkably insightful; by the very virtue of their common language, Gorky's art dogs us for a meaning rather than assigning one. Indeed, one of the reasons that Gorky's art is so difficult to grasp is that it challenges what painting can be—and what the viewer may want it to be. Just as Gorky's self-creation, controlling nature, and "lack of originality" challenge our conceptions of what an artist is, his artwork challenges our conceptions of what an artist does and how he or she does it.

Although we may agree with Dennison and consider Gorky's work to consist of shapes rather than images, the shapes do suggest likenesses, and even if they are drained of specific, identifiable imagery, they are not drained of imagery altogether. The pseudo-images are often repeated likenesses, such as the recurring shoe motif in *Argula* and the *Garden in Sochi* series. Inventories by scholars such as Robert Reiff, who classified the entirety of Gorky's art created from 1943 to 1948 into five basic recurring units that he referred to as genie-from-the-bottle, oval, petal shapes, warped rectangles, and composite shapes, are reductive. Although Gorky may have wanted to drain the shapes of specific imagery, Reiff's categorizations extricate the forms from spatial and metaphoric relationships that are founded in natural forms and the viewer's interpretations of them. The fundamental premise of such an inventory—the evaluation of likenesses—is, however, as important to Gorky's process of making images as the dialogue of shape to shape in the artworks themselves. It is precisely because of Gorky's desire to form analogies, embrace free association, and invoke interpretation that prevented him from explaining his sources. When Julien Levy wanted to exhibit a drawing, instigated by observations of cows in a field, that subsequently had informed elements of Gorky's paintings, Gorky refused, wanting the viewer to experience the work in the same manner as Gorky himself had experienced it during its creation.[29]

It has been suggested that the artist purposefully camouflaged his real images to throw off the art historian and the public from what he believed was the real meaning of the work.[30] Evidence of Gorky's subterfuge is supported by a class about camouflage that Gorky conceived in 1940 in conjunction with the war effort.[31] Yet if we look at the bulletin on the class published by the Grand Central School of Art, we see references to Cubism and visual language, as well as a claim that art is in essence a vast laboratory of form, line, and color, "which are for the artist the vocabulary of his language."[32] Through his likenesses Gorky further developed an aesthetic theory that followed closely Graham's *System and Dialectics of Art*, Léger's and Mondrian's plastic art, Kandinsky's compositions, and Surrealist dream and free association. Gorky's likenesses bespeak an embryology of life.[33] Just as Breton warned against trying to find easy answers, there is a difference between hiding depictions and transforming images by creating analogies—a difference between representation and depicting likenesses.[34] Roland Barthes' *Pleasure of the Text* gives a useful warning: "There are those who want a text (an art, a painting) without a shadow, without the 'dominant ideology'; but this is to want a text without fecundity, without productivity, a sterile text. . . . The text needs it shadow: this shadow is *a bit* of ideaology, *a bit* of representation, *a bit* of subject: ghosts, pockets, traces, necessary clouds: subversion must produce its own chiaroscuro."[35] Gorky's paintings, therefore, are associative but nonnarrative. Using Surrealistic subjective space, the space of inner experience, Gorky also interpenetrates the composition with syncretic forms and the elasticity of physical nature, creating a transformative composition that is alchemical. If we recall Agnes's comment to Schwabacher that places are recognizable in Gorky's drawings, it does not necessarily mean they retain their original identity, particularly when displaced.[36] Camouflage itself is about likeness and difference. Army fatigues worn in the forest make the wearer blend in, but would make one stand out in the city. Perhaps again André Breton's essay provides a starting point for us to consider Gorky's art:

> The eye's spring . . . Arshile Gorky is, for me, the first painter to whom the secret has been fully revealed. The ultimate function of the artist is neither to compile inventories like that of a bailiff nor to enjoy illusions of false recognition like that of a maniac. It is made to cast an outline, to provide the *guiding thread* between things of the most dissimilar appearance. This perfectly ductile thread should allow one to seize, in the shortest possible time, the relations which link the innumerable physical and mental structures, even if there is no possibility of an uninterrupted passage through the labyrinth.[37]

The secret is to provide a guiding thread, either formal or emotional analogies, for the viewer, instead of representation. According to Jung, "creativeness, like the freedom of the will, contains a secret."[38] Instead of a code, perhaps what has been identified is in fact a kind of superstructure based on the natural forms that are its foundations. The superstructure, then, acts as a kind of background to the mapping of objects in Gorky's compositions. In the *Artist and His Mother* paintings, Gorky used the age-old technique of marking the composition on squared paper in order to understand how best to transfer and enlarge the photographic image to canvas. Embedded in the superstructure of his abstract works is a similar organizational system, forming and unforming shapes but also forming and unforming language. A work by Gorky then becomes like a Gaian system,[39] in that it is ultimately an organic metaphor with its own self-referential scheme.

The organic forms of *Garden in Sochi* are similar from version to version, but change and mutate like organisms themselves, growing and developing like flowers that open in daylight or visions of a scene at different times of the day. Although it is always assumed that Gorky developed and perfected a particular subject or theme in a linear fashion, multiple versions of works are explored in a spherical manner. Supported by his practice of direct observation, his interest in different physical effects and time lapses might also be explorations in the manner of Monet's *Haystacks* or versions of *Rouen Cathedral,* but represented simultaneously on one canvas rather that on different ones.

Gorky was interested in balancing different visions of subjects in different painted versions. Much of Gorky's work created analogies from specific images or landscapes that themselves were not constant. When Jim Jordan returned to Crooked Run Farm to identify landscapes that were models for some of Gorky's paintings, he reported that "no exact motifs were located. . . . It was the perishable flesh of the landscape, not its bones, which interested Gorky."[40] A composition such as *Virginia Landscape* fails to yield a pastoral scene because Gorky manipulated the "flesh of the landscape" into a manufactured landscape within the picture plane while retaining some of its colors and forms. Gorky's art sifts through the bones of the actual, exploits the perishable, and then is rebuilt into his own creation. Gorky marveled at nature and its powerful forces, but was often dissatisfied with nature's substandard comprehension of composition. In fact, Gorky had always subjected the natural world to aesthetic criticism. "Gorky would look down side streets and at groups of rocks and trees often waving his hand and saying, 'all wrong.' He meant that the given, the observed could be wrong; he criticized views that were dull, or insipid."[41] Gorky took this dissatisfaction and mistrust to his paintings and drawings and changed the specifics of the observed into something completely new—a new synthesis. If nature's compositions were all wrong, Gorky's artwork was an attempt to correct them. Perhaps, then, Gorky did not copy works of other artists, he corrected them; he did not reinterpret images of women, but made them look as they naturally should have; he did not depict nature, but, as an example of Modernist conception over perception, created an even more effective version of it.

Gorky's works were not, and were never intended to be, descriptive. If we label aspects of Gorky's compositions, we completely sterilize them and perhaps reduce them to an uninteresting collection of things (that initially *inspired* them, *might* be there, or *were* there at some earlier stage), rather than maintaining their ideas. What Gorky created was an intertext, or intersubjectivity, between elements within and outside the work, in the natural and constructed, and between memory and the observed; an alternate space. "What he felt," said

Adolph Gottlieb, "was a sense of polarity, not a dichotomy; that opposites could exist simultaneously within a body, within a painting or within an entire art."[42] This emotive quality embraces the impression of time and the spirituality and musicality that Gorky gleaned from Kandinsky's art. "Being content with classifying certain motifs," warns J. H. Matthews, "or with persuading ourselves that such motifs are indeed present, because we imagine we recognize them—leads to a very limited form of enjoyment, as we contemplate Gorky's canvas."[43] Such classifications assume that there is a right or wrong interpretation, when part of Gorky's objective was to engage the viewer in an intersubjective manner that emphasized sensation rather than representation.

Gorky's own statements throughout his career, or texts of others that he used as his own, endorse a nonspecific method of plasticity. The plasticity of time, space, and place is addressed through the physical elements of a composition within a canvas. Gorky believed that it is the spectator's privilege to find a personal meaning, in the process actually creating his or her own common language. This relates to Gorky's conception, described in his statement for the Riviera nightclub murals, of "a common denominator of everyone's experience" and "a language for all to understand."[44] This does not mean that we all see the same thing or interpret a work the same way, but rather that we all respond similarly or the work similarly evokes an emotional response in us all. We are all alike in that we have a singular view of the universe, but it is the fact of having that view, not the view itself, that is the commonality and that Gorky underscored through his work. The beckoning of the subjective experience is a universal calling, but our responses to it are different. Even if two identical twins were to look at one of Gorky's works, their response might be different because of each one's own subjective experience. Gorky's practice set forth the essence of art and life itself and the discourse between the two. Plato's Allegory of the Cave, in which prisoners mistake flickering shadows for reality, is a parable for addressing Gorky's work, which is about perception, not sight, and in which "true" knowledge is only evident in universal forms.

Adopting such an approach toward Gorky's art allows for Rand's, Lader's, Rosenberg's, the viewer's, and Gorky's interpretations of his art to exist simultaneously without requiring knowledge of the exact details of a work's foundation, the artist's biography, or its "true" meaning, which is relative and mutable. It follows then, that in order to understand the emotive qualities of the art itself, we do not need to know exact details of any object that may have informed or inspired a composition. Even if a composition is based in the artist's specific experience, through abstraction Gorky encourages the viewer to emancipate it from a specific reading and from traditional art. Fragments of the recognizable challenge the individual to construct an experience out of the encounter with the work and make it part of an internalized reality as much as to relate his or her own experience, or try to decipher the experience of the artist who produced the work in the first place. Ultimately the works become about identification—how the viewer identifies with the work, not what the viewer identifies in it—and distanciation, or how the viewer stands emotionally in relationship to it.

The cryptic qualities of objects in Gorky's paintings prevent them from being fit neatly into classifications. As they float in the canvas, they take flight in the imaginations of the viewers. This "slippage" of past and present, real and imagined, is precisely what Gorky experienced when he composed the works. Nicolas Calas, referring to Gorky's *Nude*, describes this process well: "This is not a painting of memorized images and feelings, for the forms which have been extracted from life and nature with such sensitivity are treated like precious elements and combined to form a whole whose presence was sensed on a still empty canvas and was realized through insight and labor."[45] Images, if they are recognizable, become personages with their own gestures and relationship to the composition, rather than singular readable objects. The clear, almost colorless painting style, which emphasizes black line, is related to Gorky's illustrations for André Breton's book *Young Cherry Trees Secured Against Hares.* Literal interpretation is not the point, but rather, the indirectness of the objects and the process of incorporating them into the composition is the purpose of Gorky's artmaking.

Attempting to inventory the exact components upon which a painting may be based dismantles its poetic qualities. Gorky's characteristic reinterpretation of form is readily visible in *Pirate II* (fig. 42). Although a mongrel dog that used to wander into his friend's Connecticut yard may have inspired the painting, one is hard-pressed to find an image of the dog amongst the colors and shapes in the painting; and the only recognizable feature in the painting is a likeness to a horse's hindquarters in the upper right quadrant.[46] If we know the painting's history, there are formal elements in it that might be associated with a dog. But without the artist's narrative, and without a clearer representation, we cannot know the story behind the work, and we do not necessarily need to know, because we can interpret a pleasant emotion from the washes of light colors. Gorky desired to create a suggestion in his work rather than a record of events or things. Balcomb Greene maintains that looking at Gorky's paintings is "almost as though you're seeing living things except you can't quite recognize them enough to give them names."[47] Like the chain of transformative associations in *The Leaf of an Artichoke Is an Owl,* these analogies are part of the slippage of hovering shapes and images that slid in and out of Gorky's mind. We are not necessarily meant to look backwards into the works, but to continue forward into our own new synthesis from where he himself left off.

When André Breton says that a thread in Gorky's art pulls together "things of the most dissimilar appearance," he is further clarifying Gorky's idea of creating likenesses in order to avoid "dislikeness" and, as an extreme interpretation, disliking them. Since Gorky hated "things that are not like me," perhaps, to avoid hating the location of his displacement, he tried to create likenesses

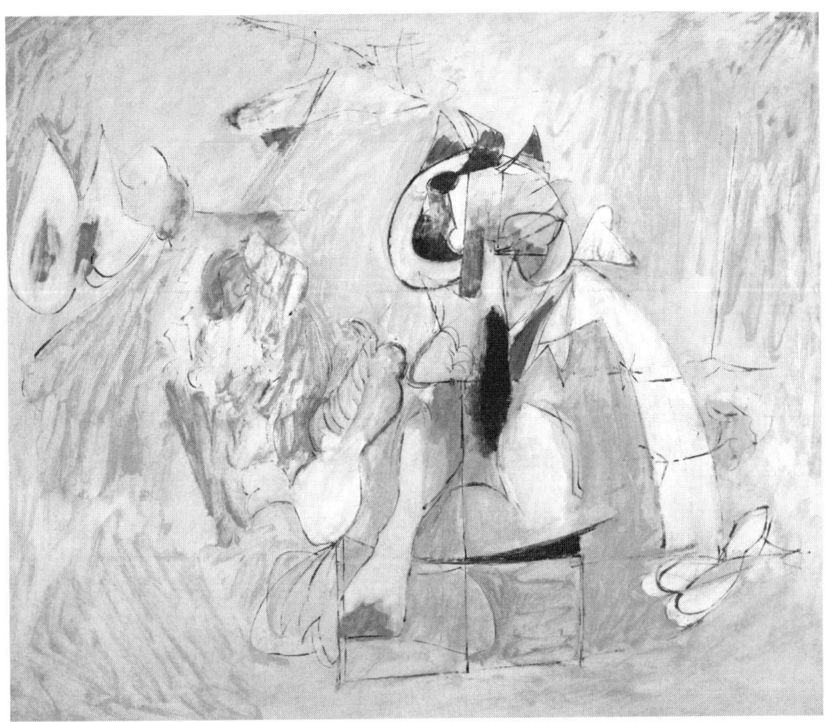

FIGURE 42
Arshile Gorky,
Pirate II, 1942–43.
Private collection.

between memories of the past, or Armenia, and the American landscape, or his surroundings in America.[48] Mina Metzger has noted Gorky's nostalgia for his native land, and it is fairly common knowledge that Gorky seemed very happy on the farm, whose landscape was quite similar to Khorkom's. Perhaps his connection to his past intensified as he got older or had children or spent more time in the country. He also became more fully a part of his new world when he married Agnes and was less of an outsider.

Gorky's associative process and rethinking has been described more fully by Ethel Schwabacher: "For instance one time, we were drawing together in the park, and I drew some trees and foliage, and he said, 'Oh Ethel, that looks like a tomato, permit me,' and he sat down and drew a tomato in my leaves. Now this is a poetic metaphor for the thing. They were leaves, and the way he drew them they were leaves plus tomato, or leaves that looked like tomato. Therefore they were tomato-leaves. And there were various levels to the meaning."[49] Schwabacher here gives important evidence of the variety of levels of Gorky's thinking that operated simultaneously. This is a key operation of abstraction; as Peter Blume says, the logic of such works "lies within their own framework, not on an outside system of thought."[50] Gorky's work, and the elements in it, like his thinking, are allusive, illusive, and elusive.

If we accept that a painting is a system of natural relationships, it becomes accessible even without our knowledge of the artist's inspiration because we become attuned to its nonliteral qualities and its identity as abstraction through its depiction of analogies. John Baur elaborated this concept just ten years after Gorky's death:

> Gorky's use of natural forms was metaphorical; it was part of the more complex method by which he dramatized the world of dreams and the obscure workings of the human heart. He did not go to nature for its own sake, but neither did he use it simply as a convenient source of symbolic form. He was endlessly fascinated by nature and found it a vital stimulus to his imagination, giving him indispensable suggestions for the visual embodiment of mental states. Gorky was introspective to a high degree, but to the extent that he found images of his own joys and sufferings in the world around him and seized upon them to illuminate personal drama on a more universal level, he escaped the extreme introspection of the private gesture.[51]

By representing memories, inspired by his immediate American surroundings, in an abstracted manner, Gorky gave his work a polysemic, plural identity similar to the way he had attained his own identity. As with Gorky's identity, elements of his artwork are not fixed but fluctuate and interchange.

Enlisting likeness, Gorky created a new vision through his abstraction. Yet intrinsic in likeness is difference, to enlist the Derridian conception. Jacques Derrida's *différance* assumes that if one can classify something as like something else, it is also different from other things. As much as Gorky's mutations are like the forms upon which they are based, they also differ from other things and the things themselves, perhaps becoming something entirely new, though not without its relationship to likeness. Derrida's definition also plays upon the concept of "defer." Gorky's creations defer the identifications upon which they are based and defer to the viewer's conception of likeness and difference.

Eliza Rathbone notes that Gorky operated a process of distillation that "simultaneously involved the creation of a form that bore an intrinsic potential to evoke layers of identity. Those layers or allusions might not be simultaneously present and constant throughout the series in each given form, but rather they grow or transform through each successive version."[52] This invocation of identity is again significant because Gorky, as we have seen in previous chapters, struggled with, manipulated, and formed his own identity. For likeness and difference, distillation and intertext, we can apply to Gorky's work, as to the artist himself, Said's borrowed term "contrapuntal," which describes the way each otherwise opposing element occurs together in a kind of döppelganger effect. This musical term stresses the musicality of Gorky's work—or its tendency to evoke response through color and form just like combinations of musical notes. This seems appropriate since Gorky, while painting, would listen to music, mostly Armenian, or sing Armenian songs to himself, such as songs about butter churning or plows. We might also consider Gorky's work within the context of time-space distanciation, which, as Anthony Giddens writes in his discussion of modernity, is the manner in which time and space are organized so as to connect presence and absence.[53] In Gorky's case, this refers to simultaneous presence and absence inherent in his condition of displacement.

For Gorky, places and names became mixed; the identities of past and present are the same but translated through time. Because through the Genocide Gorky has lost his witnesses to the past, he relearns himself and the world through his art. Earlier I noted that Anny Bakalian's research tells us that assimilation does not just happen and immigrants are not passive victims, but try to create a structure within which to live. "Armenians, like most immigrant groups in America, have established churches, schools, mass media, and myriad other organizations to enact their cultural heritage in a new land, under new conditions, as they have tried to pass their ancestral legacy onto subsequent generations. It should be noted, however, that such structures are rarely exact replicas of the ones left behind in the 'old country' or countries, as the case may be."[54] This changing same is particularly important in relation to the myth of coming to America. Typically, immigrants (including exiles) try to find a new life that they anticipate will be better than the one they left behind. Many have envisioned America as a kind of utopia. Some try to reimage the old world in America or create a new world that is not entirely different or better or worse than the old, but the best it can be. Like his American Modernist counterparts, Gorky created his new world through art, particularly through Modernist abstraction, and that new world, a contrapuntal new synthesis, was the best it could be.

Gorky's creation of a new synthesis disengaged him from his displacement and struggle for identity, both as an individual and as an artist. Rather than be assimilated into the landscape of his new culture, Gorky was the producer, the one who decided when, where, who, and what to assimilate. Gorky learned English but chose to use it in a particular manner. He painted portraits of individuals but chose to portray them more generally by changing their features. His own self-portraits, modeled after those of artists he admired, are examples of how he chose to portray himself in his new world. Gorky's lexical palette manifests in his late-career compositions almost as if he had contained in a single box a collection of his experiences that he methodically sorted through and drew from to apply to his art in the same way that he incorporated aspects of his visual vocabulary into new sentences. But then again, is this not memory itself? Do we not all have a similar box of memories and experiences, metaphorical or actual, whether we are conscious of them or not, that we bring to interpret Gorky's—or any—art we encounter?

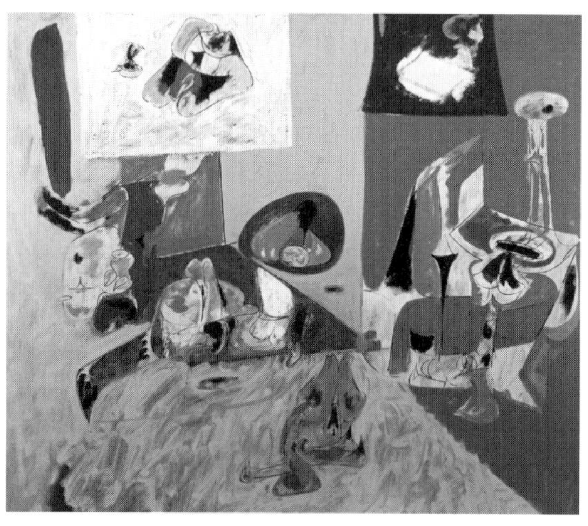

FIGURE 43
Arshile Gorky, *The Calendars*, 1946–47. Formerly in the collection of Nelson A. Rockefeller. Destroyed by fire, 1961.

The assimilation in Gorky's abstract work of selected portions of his present world relates to the assimilation of the immigrant and an intertext between past and present. Carl Jung labels this a criterion for classifying an artist as modern: "He must be proficient to the highest degree, for unless he can atone by creative ability for his break with tradition, he is merely disloyal to the past. It is sheer juggling to look upon a denial of the past as the same thing as consciousness of the present. 'Today' stands between 'yesterday' and 'tomorrow,' and forms a link between past and future; it has no other meaning. The present represents a process of transition, and that man may account himself modern who is conscious of it in this sense."[55] Jung's definition is substantiated by Clement Greenberg, writing about the modernity, originality, and syntheses visible in Gorky's late-career painting *The Calendars* (fig. 43). Contradicting his own earlier complaints about the lack of originality in and the derivativeness of Gorky's work, Greenberg says that "one should not be deceived by the familiarity of the connection of this picture, by the slightly sweet color, or by the traditional grace with which it is brushed into thinking it unoriginal. What we have here is a synthesis of a kind rare in modern painting—'mannerist' in the best sense of the term. The fluid color surfaces of Kandinsky's early abstract style are laid over Miró's neat, profiled design, and the result is a genuinely new style."[56] In many ways, Gorky's art is about dissection and articulation, or perhaps, more precisely, a rearticulation in which something is made visible that wasn't before. In essence, Gorky decomposed an image, freeing it from its recognizability, and then recomposed it—in Rosenberg's terms, unfinishing it, or in Greenberg's terms, creating a new abstract style. This is perhaps a byproduct of Gorky's displacement, since he needed to create a new structure within which his new identity could exist. Gorky's new life, and indeed his abstraction, are the new synthesis—a kind of simulacrum.

According to Gorky, the modern painter "operates on the given space of the canvas, breaking up the surface until he arrives at the realization of the entirety."[57] The new ideas that he chose to pursue were calculated according to an aesthetic that re-members. The entirety, whether or not it is representational or distorted as some might have us believe, is a larger concept than the image on the canvas because it is both personal and universal. Camus said that "the ideal of universal communication is indeed the ideal of any great artist. Contrary to the current presumption, if there is any man who has no right to solitude, it is the artist. Art cannot be a monologue."[58] For Gorky, the catalyst was his own human condition, which he portrayed for the purpose of making others aware of their own states of existence. Such objectives prefigured and perhaps helped to germinate the forthcoming primacy of the Abstract Expressionist existential struggle.

As André Breton said, Gorky was "not concerned, however, with extracting from it [an image] sensations capable of acting as *springboards* towards the deepening, in terms of consciousness as much as enjoyment, of certain spiritual states."[59] The specifics of Gorky's work, like other abstract work, actually become referenceless because they enlist analogy, likeness, and mutability. Breton foresaw such pitfalls for those who would "continue their attempts to discover still lifes, landscapes and figurations in these compositions."[60] We will never see visual reality as Gorky did, nor will we see into his memories, but we do not have to, since this is part of the social experience of Modernism. The contrapuntal, collage-like nature of Gorky's art incorporated many styles of making and was conceptually and visually global in nature. Gorky's own words about plasticity, nonobjectivity, and his desire to give the viewer an experience parallel to his own thwart those "looking for easy solutions,"[61] as Breton warned so long ago.

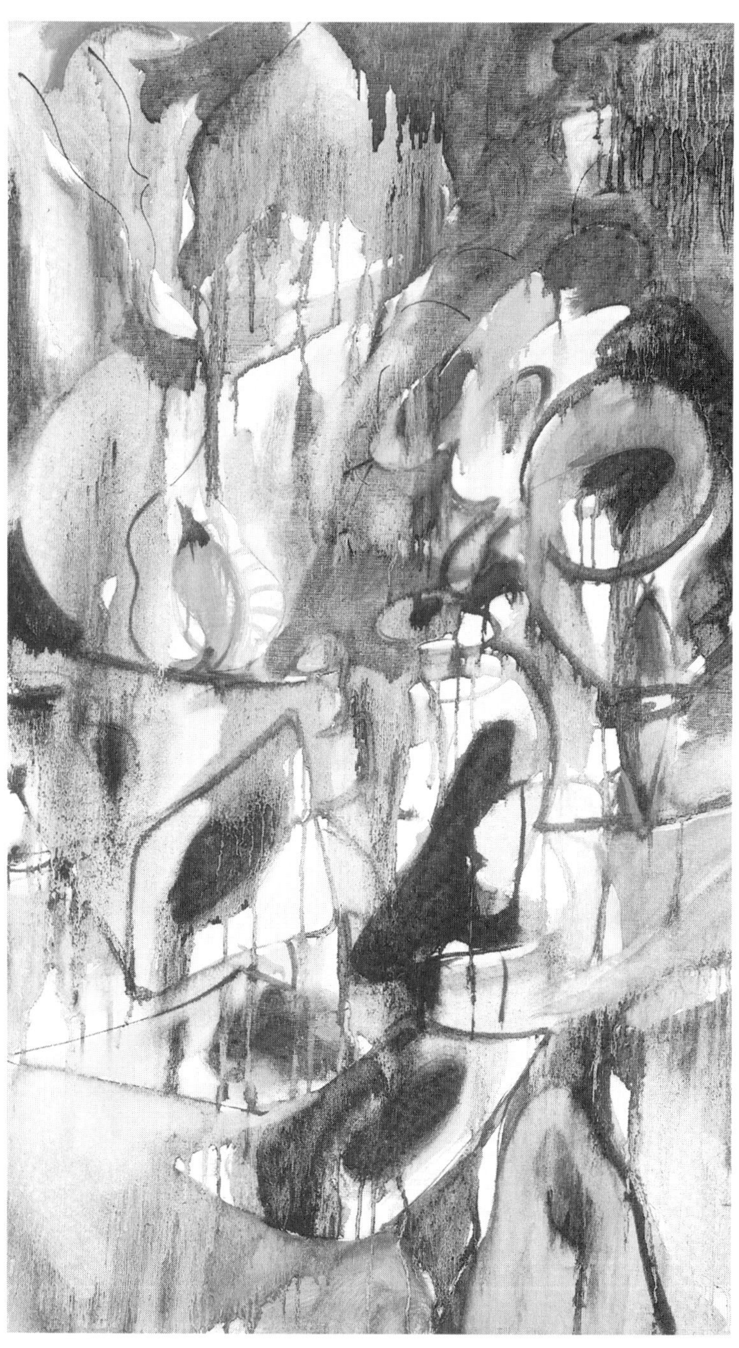

chapter 6

Conflation, Re-membering, and Indeterminacy

His provocative and allusive shapes affect us like agents or actors—yet they are in process of giving up their identities and roles. They are sensuous, but we think less of visible reality than of inward events. In addition to dreams and reveries, the referential context includes the creative act itself, certainly a more crucial becoming *to the artist. It is an act which, like the paintings themselves, is both abstract and sensuous, which recapitulates and at the same time ventures into the open. Like paintings, too, it suspends the conflict between the real and the imagined in favor of an* actuality *which is the simulacrum of both.*

—GEORGE DENNISON

Using the real without falling victim to it,[1] Gorky manipulated layering, color, and line until natural shapes retained only a hint of their original form. In Gorky's work, images, desires, and language circulate freely and without bounds. Dennison denotes that Gorky's actualizations are the simulacrum of vague or shadowy resemblances or hazy and fleeting imaginations instigated through mediated and unmediated channels. Although Gorky's abstractions are often connected to the past, in each of them he manifests something new. The Khorkom garden that was the basis for his *Garden in Sochi* series was inspired by memories triggered by catalysts in his new world. If it had ever existed in the form it did in Gorky's remembrance, it likely no longer did when the artist made his painting. And even if it did still exist, it was someone else's garden now.[2] Closely related to the unconscious, but not necessarily Surrealist, the fluidity of Gorky's work, both in terms of the media handling and the concept of time, traversed finite experiences. As Edward Said has explained, exiles "regard experiences as if they are about to disappear. What is it that anchors them in reality?

Opening image detail of figure 44.

What would you save of them? What would you give up? Only someone who has achieved independence and detachment, someone whose homeland is 'sweet' but whose circumstances make it impossible to recapture that sweetness, can answer those questions. (Such a person would also find it impossible to derive satisfaction from substitutes furnished by illusion or dogma.)"[3] Because memories are at best only reflections, Gorky mined his memory for old-country experiences in a way that often combined the past and present in abstract terms.

Gorky's *Garden in Sochi* series is an example of referencing a sweet past and the impossibility of ever fully recapturing it. Gorky's homeland remained a part of his psyche, and he often used it as a yardstick with which to measure new-world experiences. He was fond of telling people how much more beautiful the trees, mountains, and land were in "his country" than in America. As in a dream, however, things in memory become distorted. Margaret Bedrosian comments: "The most significant features of this life lie beyond objective documentation; only fleeting snatches of memory and the springs of dream and nightmare can point toward what no longer exists. Elusive as the taste of pure water or the scent of ripe apricots on a summer breeze, the memories of the Armenian immigrant nevertheless shaped his interior life concerns with the power of myth that replaces actuality after uprooting."[4] These words are actually illustrated in Gorky's 1944 *Scent of Apricots on the Fields* (plate 22), which is an orange-pink wash of atmospheric abstraction that refers to the essence of apricots. Truly ripe apricots, like those from Turkey or Armenia, are almost orgasmic in their honey-like sweetness, and it is sensation, along with their scent, that Gorky recalls in this work. The remembered apricots are literally the sweetness of which Said speaks; the memory is transformed itself and transforms the present. As poet Stephen Spender eloquently said, "A memory once clearly stated ceases to be a memory, it becomes perpetually present, because every time we experience something which recalls it, the clear and lucid original experience imposes its formal beauty on the new experience. It is thus no longer a memory but an experience lived through again and again."[5]

Gorky used abstraction to produce a new reality that invokes the sweetness of the past without illustrating it. Gorky created pungent compositions of fossilized organicism—chains of images—with the present spliced into them. The butter churn, flowers, and birdlike forms in *Garden in Sochi*, which might have existed in the original garden, are, as in the relocation of the painting's title from Khorkom to Sochi, transformed. Just as time is distorted in memory, which is not necessarily linear, the links of Gorky's image chain were not always attached in sequence. In his work, a picture is conceived as a system of relationships between objects and space in which parts are removed from their identity and made to function in a new manner, and then are reorganized into a new synthesis that is abstraction. Gorky's paintings act like palimpsests, visual manuscripts written over a partly erased ones in such a way that the old words can be read beneath the new.

Gorky's re-presentation functioned in terms that Andreas Huyssen, an expert on comparative literatures and society who has written widely on the recent cultural and political focus on memory, has identified:

> *Re*-presentation always comes after, even though some media will try to provide us with the delusion of pure presence. Rather than leading us to some authentic origin or giving us verifiable access to the real, memory, even and especially in its belatedness, is itself based on representation. The past is not simply there in memory, but it must be articulated to become memory. The fissure that opens up between experiencing an event and remembering it in representation is unavoidable. Rather than lamenting or ignoring it, this split should be understood as a powerful stimulant for cultural and artistic creativity.[6]

Because there is a split between experiencing a sublime feeling or event and remembering it representationally, it becomes, as Huyssen says, a stimulant for cultural and artistic activity.

Gorky's compositions converge personal history, memory, and the present. They also emerge out of his feelings, producing a final product that is an abstract work. Indeed, most of Gorky's viewers were and still are unaware of the artist's associations and the foundations of his work, but because images are abstract, interpretative, or emotive, the viewer's reaction parallels the artist's own. By denying a personal and specific intention bound by a specific time, place, or memory, Gorky's work could inform a transcendental experience that illustrated one of his fundamental beliefs, that one should "never put a face on an image."[7]

Just as his image of Ahko, discussed earlier, was both Gorky's impression of her in America and also a reference to how she might have looked in the past, Gorky combined multiple instances in his later abstract work. "This accidental disorder," Gorky had said, "became the modern miracle. Through the denial of reality, by removal of the object from its habitual surrounding, a new reality was pronounced."[8] *The Liver Is the Cock's Comb* contains what Ethel Schwabacher referred to as "imaginary gardens with real toads."[9] Without a clearly distinguishable image for the eye to rest upon, menacing forms float about the painting in different pictorial planes. Some are hard-edged, almost sharp-looking objects, sometimes outlined in black. The muted color field of the painting collides with the variety of bright yellow, red, and orange.[10]

The painting's title when listed in Breton's *Surrealism and Painting*, contemporaneous to the work's creation, is *The Liver Is the Cockscomb*. The divergence and similarities between the terms "cock's comb," "cockscomb," and "coxcomb" play out different connotations—a rooster's head comb and the flower referred to as the cockscomb. The flowers are often very brightly colored magenta, pinkish red, and purple and can be fairly large as well as very thick and sturdy in their stocks. Indeed, the name for the flower might have derived from its resemblance to the rooster's head comb. In an associative manner, the title may also reference the way the shape of a liver resembles these forms. A rooster, or cock, is cocky, and an ostentatious person might be referred to as such. A coxcomb is a kind of fool. The association of the liver with overconfidence can be understood by association with the term "lily-livered," which means cowardly and fearful. The liver also used to be associated with the passions. A weak person would have a pale, bloodless liver, and a courageous one a red liver.

The associations continue beyond wordplay, however, to both medical and mythological associations. The liver, as the largest organ and the one that contains the most blood, is crucial to survival, as one can only live about a day without it. It is also, however the only human organ with the power to regenerate to any great extent. It is because of this quality that in Greek mythology, as a punishment from the gods for revealing fire to humans, it was Prometheus's liver that was eaten out every day by a bird after regenerating itself. In Plato the liver represents dark passions such as jealousy and greed. The Talmud refers to the liver as the seat of anger. Interestingly, in the Near Eastern, Mediterranean, and Mesopotamian cultures, from which the Armenians derived or which they lived among, the liver was believed to contain the secret of fate. By examining the liver of a sheep or goat, one could read omens, events, and signs.

The meaning of the title and work might simply rely on image play based on the form of the liver and its relationship to the cock's comb and cockscomb. "The liver is the cock's comb (cockscomb)" simply refers to the similarity in shape between the two. Amidst the layers and hints of three-dimensional space in the painting are a number of vertical, semioutlined figures that might suggest flower-like or bird-like forms. The colors of the composition itself are bright, suggesting, along with its large size, that the painting itself is as ostentatious as the flower or rooster or the person who painted it. Despite the difference between the abstract bodies of the subject and object, the title, which is open to multiple interpretations and wordplay, and actual bodies, which are practical and fleshy, but Gorky incorporated hints of them all in his work.

While it is uncertain to what extent this work refers to Gorky's past, his references to the past are generally not entirely sweet, innocent, or uncomplicated. Often they are haunted to varying extents by the sourness of loss. The subject of a work, by virtue of its ambiguity, is a kind of absence that subverts existence.[11] In a statement about *The Liver Is the Cock's Comb*, Gorky gave an associative, and not necessarily descriptive, response: "The song of the cardinal, liver, mirrors that have not caught reflection, the aggressively heraldic branches, the saliva of the hungry man whose face is painted with white chalk."[12] This associative and disassociative definition recalls or reimagines sight, sound, and even smell, and may be part of a psychological phenomenon.

Memories of Gorky's past life may have been triggered by similar sensations in his new existence. Paul Ricoeur has noted that when memory is reduced to recall, it operates in the wake of imagination.[13] Memory is not faithful to the past, but merely a representation, like art itself. Gorky's memory, by virtue of its transformation qualities, is a quasipresence of magical operation, like Gorky's art. According to Henri Bergson, successful actualization of memory is acted rather than represented.[14] Gorky acts his memory through his art, which itself eludes representation. In painting, or repainting, subjects, Gorky actually dispels his displacement and dissipates alienation, loneliness, and dissatisfaction. This re-membering, or the combining or putting together of elements that he observed at one moment with those recalled through memory and the imaginings that such scenes evoked, becomes the essence of his artwork.

Nicolas Calas, in his essay for the exhibition entitled Bloodflames at the Hugo Gallery in 1947, explained that "with Gorky one can understand how art is neither invention nor imitation but primarily an assertion of existence."[15] Gorky's works became a site of re-embedding his existence, or recasting fragments of real and imaginary time. As Gorky addressed his displacement through his pursuit of art, these exilic landscapes and forms that were re-membered through abstraction became metaphorically a mechanism of reconciliation. When the poet John Ash, traveling in Turkey near Gorky's home village, showed his guide some reproductions of Gorky's mature paintings, the guide "responded immediately, 'Yes, these were the colors of Van in spring and autumn,'"[16] confirming Gorky's sister Vartoosh's claim that the artist had tried to recapture the colors of Van.[17] These paintings, therefore, are both of place and displacement. Just as "Arshile Gorky" would not have existed if Vosdanig Adoian had not been an exile, it is arguable that Gorky's art, which was a culmination of his past and present lives, could not have existed either. For Gorky, dreams, remembering, and representing were at the core of his artistic production. Gorky's exilic landscapes, which were re-membered through abstraction, metaphorically became a mechanism for his developing career. Writing about Armenian literature, Vahe Oshagan believed that such endeavors were typical since "the Armenian shies away from the present, he is in love with the future, he likes to fix his gaze at a bright horizon and delight in the imagery scene he has created and forget his daily pain. He lives in the past and in the mirage of the future."[18] Gorky's creation of an actualized and metaphoric space helped him forge ahead in his existence in America and reassemble his displacement.

The conflation of time, the observed and remembered, and the concrete, associative, and the imagined is most evident during the last decade of Gorky's career. This flipping back and forth and trying to merge snippets of different times, places, and objects on a canvas is perhaps indicative of Gorky's psychological state and an uneasy, rather than nostalgic, relationship to his past. Certainly, such a view is substantiated by Gorky's own evasion of the subject—very few people, including his second wife, were initially aware of his history. A study of Armenian Genocide survivors concludes that individuals, as a result of not being able to express rage or resist it when it occurred, did not speak about their experience, leaving them feeling impotent against their circumstances; or they were afraid they would cry, be judged as weak, or be devalued or stigmatized because they had been victimized.[19] Those like Gorky who lived separately from their communities were even less likely to discuss or share their feelings.[20] Gorky did not discuss the Genocide, nor did he necessarily depict it specifically in his work. Perhaps avoiding the painful parts of his past, Gorky painted lyrical works that on some level paid homage to his homeland, without acknowledging the Genocide. In addressing or not addressing the Genocide through abstraction, Gorky still exposes the trauma of genocide because his art prompts people to wonder about the places and backstory in his art.

That Gorky does not refer explicitly to genocidal actions in his artist statements or recognizably incorporate it into his work could be interpreted as a characteristic phenomenon of the aftermath of surviving the inhumanity of ethnic cleansing. This phenomenon is manifested in what cannot be read or what is unrecognizable in these works just as much as in what is visible. The reactions of Jewish Holocaust survivors were similar. According to Matthew Baigell, in his study of Jewish American artists and critics, "even the most articulate became inarticulate. Through the 1940s and well into the 1950s, Jewish intellectuals and literary figures had trouble facing the Holocaust directly. The reasons vary, but all center on a few basic notions: fear of anti-Semitism; embarrassment about being Jewish; the desire not to identify as Jewish in a parochial sense, which is not the same thing; the desire to identify as American; and the inability to comprehend the murder of six million people."[21] Just as the inability to comprehend the Holocaust invaded the psyche of Jews in America, and incomprehension of the Genocide likely plagued Gorky. His works, therefore, are both a remembrance of a sweetness and trauma, even if neither is represented in them.

Ignoring the Genocide and hiding his reaction to it might reveal just how traumatized Gorky was by it. Such a reaction is understandable when contextualized within what is known of the psychological effects of aftermath, such as post-traumatic stress disorder, memory repression, and instances where the brain actually physiologically buries trauma in the folds of the cerebrum.[22] Yet Susan Sontag reminds us that "memory is, achingly, the only relation we have with the dead,"[23] Gorky's portrait of his mother and self represents a time both before and in some ways, too, after the Genocide. It is both the moment when the photograph was created and the moment when the artist gazes upon the photograph that remains of her. This is the simultaneous time, forward and back, to which Hawking referred, which seems to operate in Gorky's paintings. Hal Foster explains trauma in relation to memory, believing that one's memory of trauma dislocates the consistency of one's identity, thereby undermining narrative sequencing.[24]

It can be useful for Gorky to engage with memory because it brings the past, like Khorkom and his mother, back to him in an intermediate place that is neither past, present, living, nor dead. A painting that is simultaneously about the before and after of an event is one that is about the event, or one that at least acknowledges it, because the event becomes a marker or reference point for what surrounds it. It is also, however, a painting that leads away from and denies the event through outward multiple associations and lack of reference or depiction. Like trauma, something always remains in Gorky's work to link it to the world, such as a picture of his mother, a piece of a plane, or hint of organic form. The viewer floats amidst the pseudorecognizable shapes on the artist's paper and canvas and hovers amidst a possible network of meanings and lack of definitive interpretation. Gorky's project was never the depicting of physical wounds of genocide, nor the replication of compositions or landscapes, but rather a not entirely deliberate attempt to reestablish an internal framework in order to mend a psychological or unseen gash. His point was to make art and be an artist, and everything else was a means to support that endeavor. Gorky tried to create a formal harmony out of the destabilization of the past, while undercutting the present. He fixed his gaze on a bright horizon, delighted in the imagery of the scene he created, and perhaps forgot his daily pain.[25]

Trauma is forever part of a survivor's psyche,[26] but, as Susan Sontag argues, that trauma cannot be depicted.[27] The no-man's-land of Gorky's art reflects a subtle silence of trauma and affects the viewer just as it did Gorky because the viewer becomes like Gorky—caught in suspension between the recognizable and the abstract, the past and the present, and living and dead. Genocide itself is not decipherable, but any genocide is human loss in universal terms.

Through abstraction, George Dennison has said, "a crucial dissolution can be enacted and a crucial *becoming* apostrophized."[28] Gorky's abstraction, then, on some level addressed the Genocide through its refusal to do so. Just because there has been a loss does not necessarily mean that there is a lack of any reference to it; it can, in fact, exist through its nonexistence.[29] What is representable in Gorky's work is the decay, erosion, and processes of the natural world, which are in a perpetual cycle of birth and death. The organic, like the body, is woundable. The recognizable exists in the three-dimensional world, but its metaphysical nature is a result of process and hints at cultural overlay. Like nature, trauma itself is unstable.[30] Memory is mutable, but traumatic memory is just as much so. Memory in these works is the result of exactly how Gorky extracts it and in what order. To lessen the impact of the image, to ensure that it was not overwhelming to the viewer, Gorky meant it to reveal itself to the viewer in layers.

With impeccable form, Gorky enacted the conceptual aspects of modern art and creative birthing of artmaking. At the same time, he was acutely aware of the depth of human suffering caused by genocide. The artwork that he created was not a representation of a nostalgic yearning for home, but a record of joy and tragedy of the in-between space of exile and the in-betweenness of art itself. Gorky's work unraveled the three-dimensional world in two dimensions through the immateriality of memory and imagination.

In Gorky's late career, from approximately 1941 until his death in 1948, he increasingly used his technique for splicing past and present. This is partly due to the time he spent outside of New York City in Virginia and Connecticut, as many have noted, but psychobiographically it can be directly related to the permanence of Gorky's situation in America. It was during this era that Gorky married and began having a family. The need to form families was, just as succeeding at a chosen profession, extremely important to survivors of trauma because it served as physical evidence—not only to others but also to the survivors themselves—of having overcome the past, which was never actually fully possible.[31] Survivors of genocide had deep scars, often both visible and psychological, such as guilt, anxiety, and reactive depression.

In his memoir *Black Dog of Fate*, Peter Balakian describes how his grandmother, an Armenian Genocide survivor who never discussed her ordeal, had a breakdown upon hearing about the bombing of Pearl Harbor because the thought of her safety being threatened by the instability of war was too reminiscent of her experience in the Genocide.[32] Few Armenians spoke of the old country, and assimilation (such as being an industrious factory worker in Watertown) became a way to bury the past and build a future, but the past always remained simmering under the surface, waiting only for the appropriate trigger to rise again. Memory itself is a chain of triggers. It is possible, for instance, that World War II and the unsettling nature of war and rationing triggered some trauma for Gorky and made its way into his work in an encrypted and allusive emotionality. Gorky's move toward abstraction coincided with the advent of World War II, and some of his most abstract works coincided with the revelation of the Holocaust. Whether or not there is a direct connection to these events, abstraction very well might have been a way to work through the world of his past and escape from the onslaught of the present.

In Gorky's visual presentations, the recognizable and unrecognizable slide in and out of his mind like the past and present and produce an abstract slippage on the canvas. Robert Hughes connects Gorky's process to Surrealist metamorphosis: "The sliding of identity, the merging of separate layers of experience . . . was the ideal way for Gorky to convey his permeable sense of the world, drenched in childhood memory, skewed and shuffled by fantasy."[33] These works are not either/or a subject but are metonymic, reflecting a contiguous linkage of related objects creating a metapicture that is at once one thing and something else. When asked about his past during a dinner with Fernand Léger, Gorky talked of his childhood and of looking at angels painted on the walls of a church. "They are all green. And in my country in the mountains of the Caucasus is a famine. I see gigantic stones and snow on the mountain peaks. And there is a murmur of a brook below, a voice sings. And this is the song."[34] Gorky told stories that evoke the oral tradition of his native Armenia. One thought leads to another in these stream-of-consciousness narratives. In this one he described experiences of his country nonspecifically through snippets of memory. He could have been speaking of any stones, any mountain peaks, any brook. The famine does most likely refer to the effects of the Genocide, but famine, like hunger, is an often-shared human tragedy.

Gorky's artwork is a simulacrum of life, dissected and rearticulated in abstract visual terms. Because Gorky's psyche was tied up with memory and denial, he forged a kind of selective remembering and forgetting. This is important to consider when addressing the Genocide as the precipitant of Gorky's artwork, because denial was a mechanism that influenced Gorky's ever-tenuous position in a new culture. Gorky not only challenged memory as a knowable object, but showed through his work that memory is selective—we choose to remember some things and leave others out. He thus made a deliberate attempt to construct a new life and to withstand the trauma of the old one. As his fellow Armenian William Saroyan wrote, "you remember only what your memory refuses to forget, and our memory will always refuse to forget that which delights or enriches it. Our memory—except in cases of amnesia—always forgets what deserves to be forgotten."[35] In Gorky's case, individual memory is tied to a cultural memory, and re-presented as part of a collective memory that selectively avoids memories related to genocide. The snippets of the past and displacement of images in his art that mimic Gorky's own displacement in poetic terms were an attempt to disengage from the unpleasant or traumatic. The splicing together of selective memory and the observed present created abstract compositions that formed Gorky's new reality. The new reality was, in fact, subjective to the viewer, and the multiple interpretations were embraced by the artist. In response to an inquiry about an abstract composition entitled *Landscape Table*, Gorky replied, "no, the black spot is not Hitler's mustache. But imagine all those generals sitting before a map and carving the landscape as if it were food."[36] Gorky did not dispel the interpretation suggested by the viewer; rather, it spawned a new association in the artist's mind.

Gorky's poetic drive was in some ways an extension of a personal unconscious that produced what was one continuous pseudoreality for the artist, a surreality, because much of it was nonexistent. In essence, Gorky, in concert with the Surrealist tradition of the "marvelous," created a dreamworld in his paintings, one that was not necessarily idyllic. Surrealist dreamworlds could be foreboding or ominous, offering the sense of something just outside the frame, as in De Chirico's *Mystery and Melancholy of a Street* or Dalí's *Persistence of Memory*, in which the properties of the recognizable world are altered and the space in the canvas depicts something of an otherworld. In creating the otherworld, Gorky may also have used lessons learned from depictions of space in works by

Yves Tanguy and Peter Blume. Tanguy created ambiguous creatures within a seemingly infinite but recognizable space, and Blume created strange combinations of objects and hybrid creatures in a definitive space. Gorky's paintings are, as we have seen, places where identities are created, revised, or rearticulated.

While Gorky often worked out the possibilities of a composition in several versions of the same work, he also processed past experiences in a psychoanalytic sense through stages and approaches. In some ways, this practice followed the Freudian explanation of dreaming, which includes four mechanisms: representability, condensation, displacement, and symbolization. Through this process, an event or observation is encoded into memory and the mind accesses it through a cue-based retrieval, that is, something triggers its emersion. The result is then condensed, or reduced to an essential form, and relocated from its original context and inserted into the dreamworld, where it symbolizes a feeling, fear, or key to a desire; a dream-façade. In the case of Gorky's art, dreams related to Gorky's practice of free association and a visual stream of consciousness that began with the re-presentation of the observed. Just as he had mutated the works of other artists and used elements of them as a basis for his own work, and replaced the identities of women, like his non-Armenian wife with Armenian attributes, he re-placed environments in his work through association.

Dreams are clearly distortions, and although the Freudian view that dreams are fulfillments of suppressed wishes is generally considered outmoded, Gorky's paintings may somewhat play such a role. Through the Surrealists, Gorky was certainly aware of Freud, and even though he rejected the psychoanalytic aspects of Surrealism, as the Abstract Expressionists did after him, and thought little of psychoanalysis itself,[37] he seemed to like the idea of wish fulfillment, which he related back to an Armenian folk practice. In his Museum of Modern Art statement about the *Garden in Sochi* series, Gorky said that the garden of wish fulfillment was central to the community, particularly the holy tree, at which people tore off strips of their clothing as they passed to tie onto it while making a wish. This still occurs in Armenia today and is similar to the age-old tradition of throwing coins into fountains while making a wish. In the case of Gorky's art, "dreams" related to Gorky's practice of *re*-presentation of the observed, but there is also an aspect of the imagined dream state within the space of the painting like the garden and the enchanted tree. In this way, the painting itself might be charmed,[38] but it also represents Gorky's existential reality of displacement.

Carl Jung has said that a painter "can give form to his own inner experience by painting it. For what he paints are active fantasies—it is that which activates him."[39] Although Gorky did not subscribe to Jung's ideas either, his work seems to be activated by a triangulation of inner and outer experience with fantasy as well as the Jungian conception of the "collective unconscious" and "universal archetypes." A prime example of the simultaneous forces at work in

Gorky's art can be explored through the 1944 painting *How My Mother's Apron Unfolds upon My Life* (plate 23). Gorky incorporated in this work the memory of his mother's self-embroidered apron, his relationship to it, his relationship to her, and his experience of painting in America years later as well as the viewer's relationship to the painting, the idea of "mother," definitions of "apron," and the viewer's interpretations of the painting.

The apron has a specific cultural meaning as part of the national costume worn by Armenian women, and in a universal sense recalls the idea of being tied to one's mother by her apron strings. Gorky, it seems, was tied to his mother through his remembrances of the stories she told him, which he reimagined in his paintings. "My mother told me many stories while I pressed my face into her long apron with my eyes closed," he said. "Her stories and the embroidery on her apron got confused in my mind. All my life her stories and her embroidery keep unraveling pictures in my memory."[40] Further underscoring the fantastic nature of Gorky's compositions, this storytelling method is useful to understanding Gorky's process. In addition to telling stories to himself while he painted, he listened to Armenian music and recalled scenes from his past, so that he worked in an unreal story state, like a trance. Amidst the lyrical black line that wraps loosely around and between diluted and dripping rainbow colors that bleed through the lines. Indeed, there may be a hint of two figures outlined in the lower center of the painting, one with his head pressed into the lap of an apron. *How My Mother's Apron Unfolds upon My Life* has a metaphoric and fantastic quality to it and might be a part of the exile's past that he remembers sweetly. This follows Breton's idea of the eye's spring: "the ultimate function of the eye is neither to compile inventories like that of a bailiff nor to enjoy illusions of false recognition like that of a maniac. It is made to cast an outline, provide a *guiding thread* between things of the most dissimilar appearance."[41] Gorky's painting is about analogy; the analogy continues with the vision of the viewer, and yet the skeins of line reflect the embroidery and literally become a guiding thread like the disjunctive stories he remembers from his past.

The vibrant colors in the painting are typical of Armenian stitchery, which often mixes flowers, birds, and objects in a nonnarrative arrangement. The white of the apron, like the white of Gorky's canvas, is an ambiguous space. Even though Gorky's painting is about storytelling, the pseudo- and distorted imagery make it nonnarrative. Interestingly, his mother's craft, the stitchery and the storytelling, imprint themselves onto Gorky's painting like the stories in his mind. Perhaps this means that his own stories—about his background, training, and life—are an equally important art form in Gorky's oeuvre. Dickran Tashjian points out that

> *his* life and *her* art are intimately connected, as Gorky brings the consequences of the Story into the present. He emphasizes that her stories and embroidery together unravel pictures in his memory. Pictures in Gorky's

> mind's eye unravel while her stories and embroidery remain intact. "Unravel" here is extremely ambiguous. It suggests first that her art forms threaten his. Unraveling becomes a specific form of confusion. But "unravel" can also mean disentangle, so that her art might clarify his. Finally, there is the imminent disintegration of her art, for its preservation depends upon his memory.[42]

Despite the connections between the painting and the apron, art and language, his and her art, and even a center motif that resembles a male figure in front of a skirted female form, neither is actually a narrative of the other. Integrated into Gorky's work is what Melvin Lader describes as the "lack of clear cut and consistent identification of the subject matter making it nearly impossible to read shapes as either animate or inanimate, natural or manmade. For Gorky these were universal shapes that characterized both worlds, evincing the continuity between the two."[43] For instance, *How My Mother's Apron Unfolds upon My Life* is a depiction not of a particular story that his mother told, but of the act of storytelling itself and his relationship to her. Yet, too, the strands of color and layers of washes happily intertwine the viewer in a similar experience—that of confused stories mixed up in the viewer's head by color and line. The idea of the scrim extends in connection to the mother. In addition to stitchery and embroidery, Armenian women also crocheted intricate lace to be used as tablecloths or curtains. The scrim-like quality of the composition reveals itself almost as if the viewer is looking through the lace or embroidery; hence the hint, recognizable in the center of the composition, of the figural outlines of aproned mother and kneeling son with his head in her lap. Gorky washed over the figures, partially erasing them, but they still remain as apparitions, like the past and Gorky's memories of his mother's stories. He doesn't note the specific story she told, probably because he couldn't completely recall it, but he recalls the act of the telling. The viewer is left with a partial vision in which to contemplate his or her own fantastical stories and confuse then with the vision of the painting.

One Year the Milkweed (fig. 44) similarly addresses issues of abstraction and transformation with its semirecognizable milkweed pods. Ultimately, so much was involved in the artist's work—internal, external, dream and fantasy—that it became larger than the artist himself and whatever specific inspiration instigated it. Abstraction, which Gorky was still developing in this work (it still had a few still recognizable elements), made the work nonspecific to the viewer and removed it from being only about and in relation to the artist. For Gorky, abstraction was the vehicle toward universal expression.

The tendency of art history to be divided nationally and temporally leaves little space for a transplanted artist such as Gorky or American art, but the concept of universality opens up possibilities. First, it breaks the closure of specific national or identifiable interpretation because it allows for multiple influences

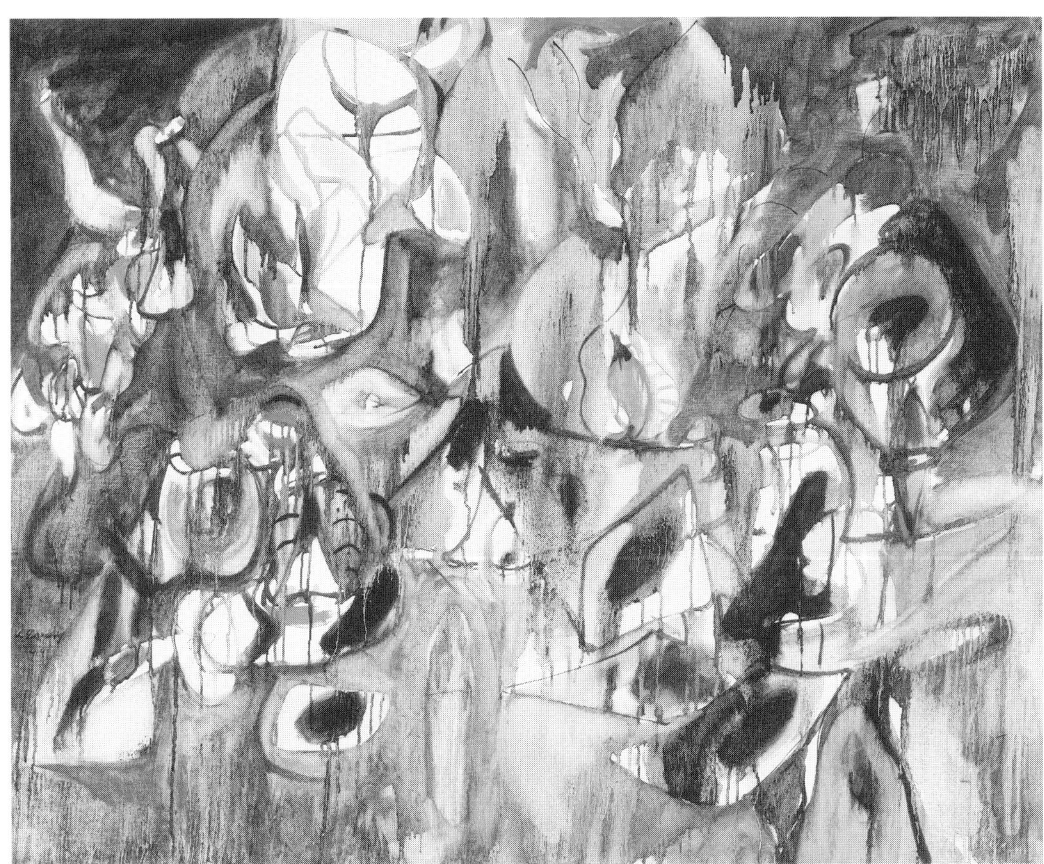

FIGURE 44
Arshile Gorky, *One Year the Milkweed,* 1944. National Gallery of Art, Washington, D.C.

to contribute to the work, such as early Modernism and Armenian culture. Abstraction kept the work from becoming too nationally specific. Gorky's state of displacement as an exile, as an Armenian who paints, and as a painter in America is therefore an inclusive one. Second, universality creates a dialectic that opens into a universal human experience, suggesting that although Gorky's specific life experience cannot be shared, the emotions, feelings, desires, and impressions can be because they are presumed universal to all of humanity. Since Gorky's work is partially self-referential, abstraction allows the viewer to create his or her own likenesses—analogies—to formal and emotional components in the art.

Meyer Schapiro described "feelings of love and fragility and despair—for which there had been little place in his art before"[44] that he believed to exist within the 1945 *Diary of a Seducer* (fig. 45). The painting contains a collection of black hues and forms that Gorky had not enlisted before to such an extent, with accents of red and yellow. The gray and charcoal give the painting a dark, tragic, and foreboding emotionality. The space of the canvas is compressed and

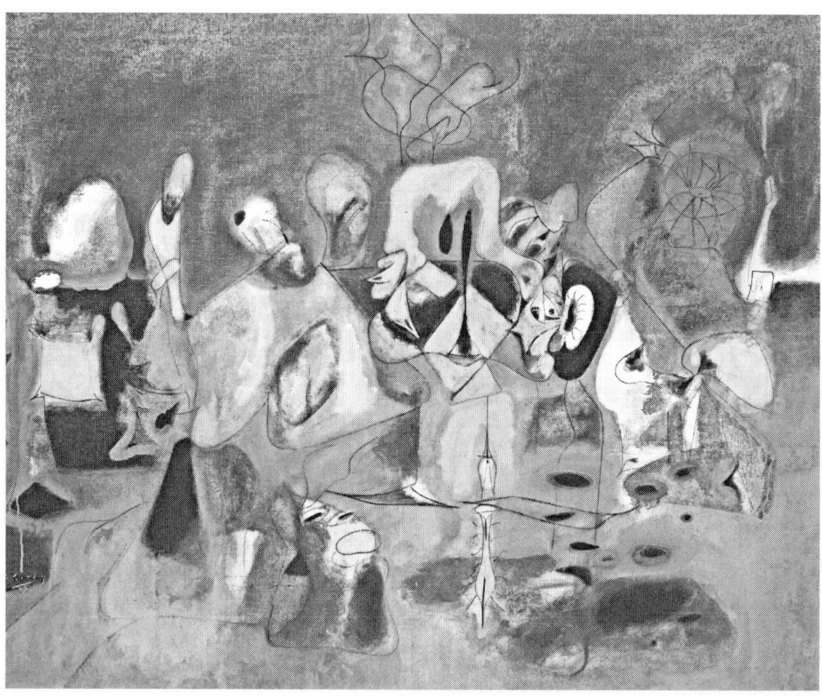

FIGURE 45
Arshile Gorky, *Diary of a Seducer,* 1945. The Museum of Modern Art, New York.

is partially read through the swatches of red that float through it. In the center of the white quadrant is a form that fluctuates between resembling an eye with a red pupil, orifice and a reddish-black, centipedal personage. The multivalent readings and subdued tones suggest something ominous and unknown. The title, which is almost sinister but also slightly sexual in nature, is believed to have been suggested by Max Ernst from a chapter title by Kierkegaard. It fits Gorky's work because the philosopher and theologian argued that one should find self-relevant truth, that once something is labeled it is negated, and that it is painful to remember a future one will never have.

The composition of *Diary of a Seducer* is structurally similar to that of *The Liver Is the Cock's Comb,* with some of the more vertical, bird-like forms more embedded into the background. It is quite possible that Gorky was working through compositional and tonal variations that he began with the earlier work. Abstract space in *Diary of a Seducer* acts like a subject, working in a highly complex way. Within the painting and in exchange with the viewer is a dialogue that implies reciprocity.[45]

While viewing the retrospective of Gorky's work at the Whitney Museum in 1981, Theodore F. Wolff of the *Christian Science Monitor* remembered the adage that "the opposite of beauty is not ugliness, but despair": "The notion that beauty as art reflects not only order and sensibility but also a positive judgment on life, that it represents a rejection of despair, that it is living proof of the transcendent nature of spirit over death, seemed particularly relevant to Gorky's struggle to find his unique voice and, having found it, to use it to create paintings that sing about the beauty of life despite increasing pain, fear, and loss."[46]

When Gorky remembered in his paintings, and re-membered as he combined his old and new worlds, he dis-membered the past. But there was more than memory that linked him and his work to the past and present. As Cathy Caruth has noted, trauma acts as a link between cultures.[47] This repetition of similarities from composition to composition, like his repetition of compositions that are adapted in a manner that reinterprets a composition, is very much like the process of working through trauma and that actually propelled it forward. In Freudian psychoanalytic terms, this is a form of displacement, in which the painfulness or intensity of an idea, image, or event is mitigated by transference through a chain of associations.

Gorky lost over three dozen paintings and drawings in a studio fire in January 1946 and underwent a colostomy operation to remove cancer a month later. Many of the lost paintings are believed to have been in the light style of works such as *Nude*,[48] but it would be interesting to see Gorky's development at this time through the transitions between types of work. For Gorky, dreams, remembering, imagining (or reimagining), and representing (or re-presenting) had been at the core of his artistic production. In the summer of 1946, Gorky produced almost three hundred drawings and twenty paintings. Like *Nude*, the *Charred Beloved* series represents Gorky's simplified style; the simplification may have been due in part to the need to replace the lost paintings in time for his next exhibition at Julien Levy's gallery. With the positive commentary these simplified works received from Clement Greenberg, it seemed logical for Gorky to develop it further.[49] The title of this series refers back to the works lost in the fire; his paintings are seemingly as beloved to him as individuals.

Despite his setbacks, Gorky still enlisted analogy and likeness in works such as the *Plow and the Song II* (plate 24), which may have been constructed from images of a Connecticut landscape that Gorky sketched while living there. But the title can be linked to memories of the songs that Gorky remembered the farmers singing while tilling the fields in Armenia. It is commonly understood that the central motif of the composition is based on the unique form of the Armenian plow, whose rudder-like shape negotiated rocky soil (fig. 46). In his statement for the Newark Airport murals, Gorky had explained that manipulation of identifiable forms produced a disorder through which a new reality could be produced. The removal

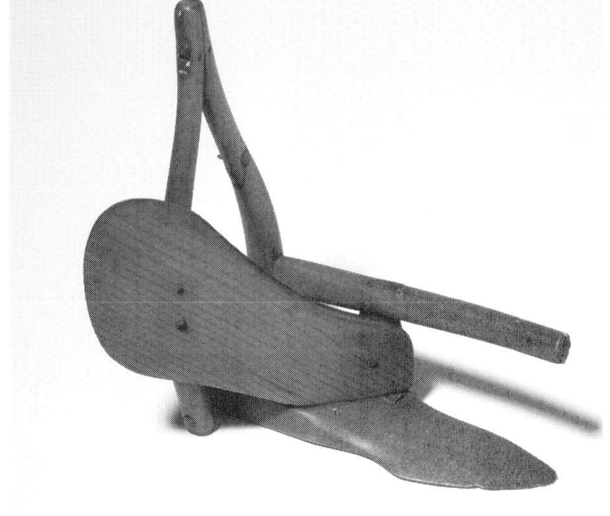

FIGURE 46 Arshile Gorky, *Haikakan Gutan I (Armenian Plow I)*, 1944.

of the plow shape from Armenia and its context as a plow and the re-presentation of it as a formal element in the painting achieves this new reality, just as Gorky's own displacement, on a fundamental level, makes this possible.

As Jim Jordan discovered, Gorky used the transient flesh of landscape in his paintings as inspiration, but Gorky also combined this with memory. Just as Gorky had found in Modernism spatial complexities that reminded him of Armenian art, he found that the American landscape reminded him of his homeland and facilitated the memory of impressions that he superimposed in his paintings. The transience of memories filtered through years of exile and childhood recollections combined with the observed American landscape into a mutation of the familiar. These "memory-scapes" were a combination of different impressions of visual reality transformed into a universalized aesthetic entity in his abstraction. Duncan Macmillan believes that Gorky needed to produce something universal because "he realized that he could not make his work American by changing superficial features. Instead he got right inside a European style, and by making it express something authentically his own and authentically American he changed it irretrievably. It was only as it became wholly American that New York painting became universal."[50] Gorky's idea of universality was something that he pursued from the beginning of his career, and it was embodied through the incorporation of Gorky's own personal story into the work, combined with what the viewer brings to it.

Carl Jung's ideas of the collective unconscious and universal archetypes was an influence on the Abstract Expressionists, and Gorky would likely have been aware of the ideas, which had been floating around New York at least as early as the 1933 publication of *Modern Man in Search of a Soul.* That work included revisions of dream theory and an expansive interpretation of the work of art and the artist's role of creation:

> Being essentially the instrument for his work, he [the artist] is subordinate to it, and we have no reason for expecting him to interpret it for us. He has done the best that in him lies in giving it form, and he must leave the interpretation to others and to the future. A great work of art is like a dream; for all its apparent obviousness it does not explain itself and it is never unequivocal. A dream never says: "You ought," or: "This is the truth." It presents an image in much the same way as nature allows a plant to grow, and we must draw our own conclusions . . . able to let the work of art act upon us as it acted upon the artist. To grasp its meaning, we must allow it to shape us as it once shaped him. Then we understand the nature of his experience. We see that he has drawn upon the healing and redeeming forces of the collective psyche that underlies consciousness with its isolation and its painful errors; that he has penetrated to that matrix of life in which all men are embedded, which imparts a common

> rhythm to all human existence, and allows the individual to communicate his feeling and his striving to mankind as a whole.[51]

Jung here seems to explain both the intention and the effect of Gorky's art. Gorky's unification of traditions and multinational characteristics acted as a link for him to world art. The apparent paradox of this attempt, however, is that by universalizing, Gorky actually removed the specific ethnic and life experiences that led him to create his art.

As a transnational artist, Gorky can then be seen as traversing national and ethnic boundaries to create a new art that retains some of its original component identities while synthesizing them into a new expression. Not only are Gorky and his art the products of a specific experience, but experience itself creates a new product that transfigures the visible and implied. Abstraction is used as a means to resolve the conflict of historical reality. Gorky portrayed images through abstraction because this was the only artistic mode that could include all of his worlds and resolve the contradiction between the present and the remembered so there was ultimately no time-space distanciation between the present life and the past. This also means that the composition is readable by the viewer not in specific terms that repeat Gorky's experience, but in terms of the viewer's own experience, so that it resonates for the viewer in a similar way. As a large drawing on the theme shows (fig. 47), the *Plow and the Song* was a compendium of fertility with intestinal shapes, flowers, and plow upon a disembodied earth. Its many versions were inspired by the observed Virginia landscape and American plows, while reminiscent of Armenian plows and the songs men sang while in the fields using them. Gorky's statement about the work indicates melancholy and a sense of loss. "What I miss most," he explained, "are the songs in the fields. No one sings them anymore. . . . And there are no more plows. I love a plow more than anything else on a farm."[52] One wants to ask, where have the plows gone and why does no one sing anymore? The answer, of course, is the Genocide.

Although Raphael Lemkin, as early as the 1920s, described the deliberate extermination of an identifiable category of people (sharing national, racial, or religious proclivities) as a recurring phenomenon of human history, the term "genocide" did not exist until he coined it in the 1940s. Without a word for it, the victims of genocide had no coherent way of explaining what had happened to them. The growing recognition of the concept of genocide coincided with the course of Gorky's career and solidified, with the coining of the term, at almost exactly the same time that Gorky's art passed into its most mature phase, that of abstraction. It is interesting to note that an alternative definition of the "uncanny" describes the nonhuman, machine-like killing of the Holocaust, or the kind of killing that does not, or is unable to, distinguish animate from inanimate, human from inhuman form.[53] In the uncanny, subjects and objects

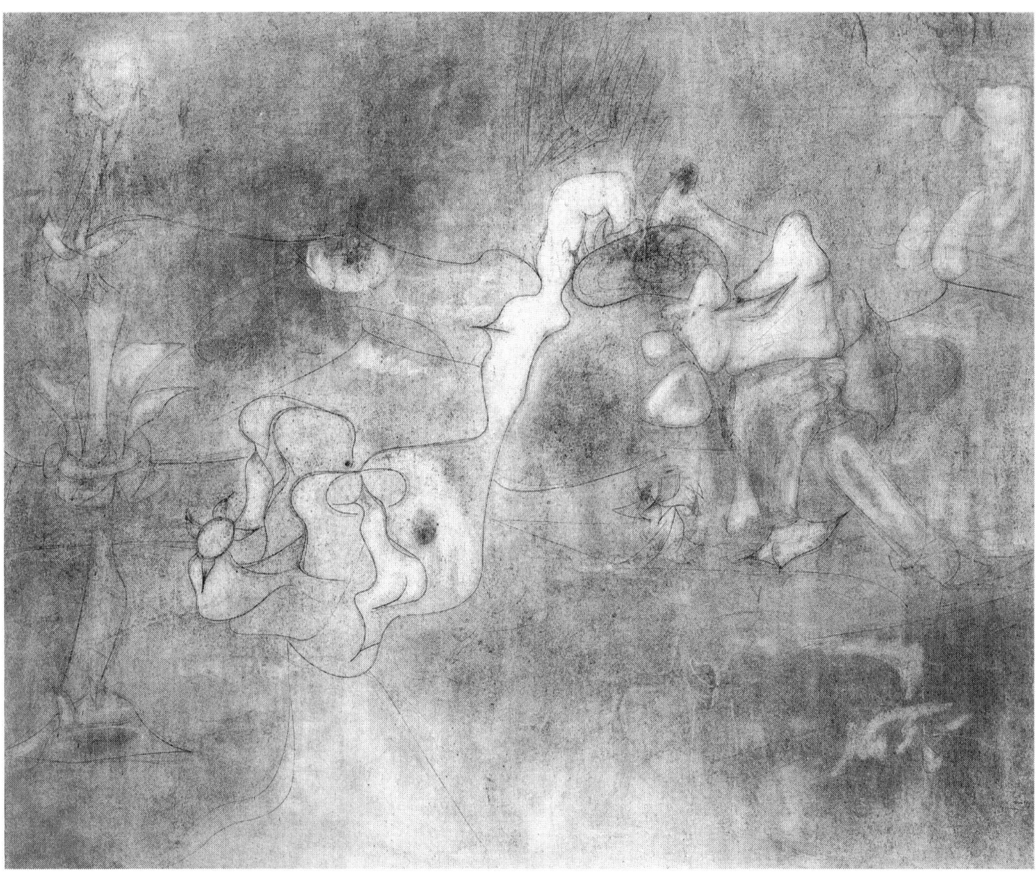

FIGURE 47
Arshile Gorky, *The Plow and the Song*, 1946

appear out of time and place in order to destabilize the boundaries of subject and object, which is exactly what Gorky's work achieves.

The lack of a definition for the Armenians' trauma had a number of implications. First, although Turkey had clearly carried out the organized mass killing of a particular ethnic and religious group, accusations were addressed as isolated and individual incidents, despite the outcry of some individuals such as the U.S. ambassador to Turkey at the time, Henry Morgenthau, who witnessed the Genocide. Second, after the Genocide, few in the world community acknowledged it, the perpetrators were not held accountable, and the victims had no way to explain what they had experienced except in individual and very personalized terms. Although Gorky's memory was perhaps never repressed, it was not always articulable. It is difficult to explain something when there is no space within which to discuss it or words to use. Julia Kristeva notes that "when one is unable to define an object, the abject stands in, neither subject or object, turns suffering into beauty."[54] Gorky's art linked a personal trauma to collective memory and universal interpretations of emotion that ultimately become beautiful as works of art.

The pursuit of an expansive human condition through art breaks the closure of specificity in art while simultaneously placing its creation at a particular historic moment that was initiated by genocide, displacement, and reconciliation. "Emotion, which is suffering," as Viktor Frankl has noted, "ceases to be suffering as soon as we form a clear and precise picture of it."[55] The ethereal quality of Gorky's art is a somewhat poetic manifestation of the creative process. Gorky had to proceed through stages in which he explored all avenues of a particular piece so that each represented a different aspect of the idea, until finally pulling together his work into a painting that reflected a universality. His artistic process was a ritual—drawing, painting, and repainting—much like an Orthodox liturgy with an invariable structure. This structure was necessary for Gorky to define himself in reference to the past or to transform his world.

Balcomb Greene observed that in looking at Gorky's compositions it is "almost as though you are seeing living things except you can't quite recognize them enough to give them names."[56] The perspective in Gorky's later abstract works is similar to those in which he used the metaphor of flight. Flying above the clouds, we are in our own reality; we know which way is up and which is down and have a sense of the world on the ground as it peeks through openings below us, but we are never quite in that world. Gorky's art was Armenia, America, and imaginary. There is an intended meaning in a work for the artist and the viewer, and a significance that is larger than both. According to Dennison, Gorky suspended himself in his compositions during their creation, as the Abstract Expressionists would during their existential struggle on the canvas, and the viewer, in experiencing them, is meant to be suspended as well, and to try to deduce a personally relevant meaning: "There is a unifying element in the various responses to Gorky's work, the references to dreams, reveries, nostalgic memory (memory under the bittersweet guise of loss), magic (but the magic of the anthropologist's excitement). In all of these actions the Self is seeking beyond its own boundaries. The *locus* of such actions may be described very aptly as the boundary of the Self and the Other. As regards the kind of experience he invokes, this is the locus of Gorky's art."[57] For Gorky, universality reflected an art that anyone could access and understand on his or her own terms. The Abstract Expressionists in general—many of whom were immigrants or came from immigrant families—also embraced the concept of universality.

Brian O'Doherty noted that Gorky worked "to transpose things symbolically as a method of dealing with experiences impossible to handle with explicit associations (i.e. realism)."[58] Abstract objects, ideas, and themes were related to both of his worlds, but were meant to create a world for the viewer. As the aesthetics of Gorky's pictures reveal themselves, we unravel unique and varied compositions. Influences of exile, visual language, and artistic vision imprint themselves through his art onto our senses. If we allow the ethereal qualities of his meditations to traverse our need for finite meanings, we grasp the analogies and a vibrant understanding of a new direction in American art. Perhaps it is the existence of a multitude of explanations for Gorky's art that contributes to his universality and is evidence of his success.

If we enlist an ethnographic Modernism to explain Gorky's development, we might see Gorky's abstraction as a means to avert the trauma of genocide. He resolved formal depiction—or nondepiction—through referential and nonreferential elements that reflect a social experience. Gorky essentially suspended any pain and destruction associated with the places that he drew upon for images, but his creation of a new synthesis that combined potentially opposing elements could very well be the result of his Armenian experience and the Genocide in particular.

Abstraction, then, served an important purpose for Gorky in the development of his identity and his art: like his renaming, it was a response to displacement. In addition to keeping him at the front of the development of Modernist art and in what he believed was the continuum of art history, abstraction kept his work from being too nationally specific. Gorky displaced images through abstraction because this was the only artistic mode that could include all of his worlds and not only balance the interaction between the real, the remembered, and the created, but allow for the viewer's understanding of the work's concept through his or her interpretation. Gorky the exile used abstraction to resolve the conflict of his historical situation. Perhaps Gorky even used abstraction as a means to avoid the trauma of genocide, displacing it as it had displaced him. In his pursuit of modern art, Modernism, and universal interpretations, his art was his salvation.[59]

Some suggest that Gorky does, in fact, depict the Genocide, and that his abstractions consist of body parts that Gorky may have seen during it.[60] But if the Genocide exists in any form for Gorky in his work, it is by association or absence. The paintings are not depictions of genocide, but another dimension of it. It exists through being left out. This argument parallels what we know of his conceptions of difference and likeness. Like Foucault in *The Order of Things*, Freud derives meaning from the gaps of silence in his patients' testimony; silence often has more meaning than what is said. This fits Gorky's method if we recall that he drew between the trees, showing the negative spaces between objects rather than the objects themselves, in a kind of visual reading between the lines. His art, like his position between cultures and art movements, exists in the in-between of a third space. Specifically representing the Genocide, however, would not only conflict with Gorky's artistic theory, but also remove the viewer's ability to interpret the artist's work according to his or her personal experience. Although Gorky's method of abstraction would not allow the literal, but a viewer could certainly perceive in the work a hinted absence or yearning.

Gorky is unique in that he uses forms as the means to perhaps escape, and therefore address, the trauma of the Genocide. The paintings are not representations but are likely, as Margaret Bedrosian proposes, surrogates for people or re-presentations of lost individuals and places.[61] Perhaps Gorky's engagement with memories and emotions had been fragmented by genocide, and this fragmentation informs his artwork as much as the compositions of other artists and nature, making slippage, analogies, likeness, and difference nonvisual manifestations of struggle. Gorky's paintings are a manifestation of the hyphenated worlds of all of the styles, identities, and experiences he had accumulated up to that point. His technique combines elements—real and imaginary, recognizable and abstract—so that even if they contrast, they work together. Said's idea of the contrapuntal makes Gorky a counterpoint himself: even though his work contrasts with Surrealism and Abstract Expressionism in some ways, it incorporates their elements as well. Not only was he of two worlds, but he simultaneously existed in many worlds and drew from many artistic and social influences. Gorky is contrapuntal art historically through his fluctuating biography, the interpretations of his paintings, and his relationship to his era.

If we subscribe to an analysis in which Gorky's abstract work solely represents the blood, guts, and body parts witnessed in the Genocide, or each painting is actually an elaborate code for a recognizable scene, or Gorky's lines make forms that resemble an alphabet or shapes that we should try to read, or even in which his compositions are imbued with overt sexuality, then we severely limit the understanding of his work. According to Gorky's own philosophy, these might be elements, but no single one should ever take precedence. Under the concept of *différance*, when you assert one identity, you simultaneously exclude all others. If we have to know Gorky's history to obtain meaning from the work, and have to experience that same history to fully respond to it, we will forever be condemned to a singular reading that opposes the intent of abstraction. This opposes Gorky's methodology of the universal, in which he wishes the viewer to experience something that is similar or parallel to his own experience, but does not necessarily replicate it. His concept of universality also does not say that we must all interpret a painting the same way.

Gorky's art, therefore, became a place to resolve his individual identity, trauma, and life in a relatively covert way. It thus reflects a typically Modernist endeavor by which existential angst works itself out through a struggle recorded on the canvas, so that the paintings are substitutes for society and societies in and of themselves.[62] Ultimately, though, Gorky's painting is about the act or process of painting itself. Even though *Garden in Sochi* has patches of reality embedded in it, it is not a visual diary. But it is marvelous in the Surrealist sense that it juxtaposes the real and the imaginary. It is perhaps because of Gorky's association with the Surrealists that he was not initially recognized for his contributions, in his mature work, to Abstract Expressionism. At first the critic

Clement Greenberg did not like Gorky's work because he felt it too close to Surrealism. This association was a handicap for Gorky at a time when American artists were trying to distinguish themselves from the European tradition. Perhaps not by coincidence, in 1947, the same year in which Gorky disenfranchised himself from the Surrealists, Greenberg lauded Gorky as one of the best American painters.

Although Gorky has been classified with the Abstract Expressionists, his practice of painting according to external visual stimuli created an uneasy relationship with the movement; Diane Waldman believes that that practice alone separated him from both the Abstract Impressionists and the Surrealists. Rosenberg called Abstract Expressionism "the usual catching up of America to European art forms," but noted that the movement was also about newness and differentiation;[63] these artists wanted to move beyond what Europe had offered thus far in art. They also differentiated themselves somewhat from Gorky, whose work was linked to the tradition of art history. Yet Gorky, in his late work, produced an abstract, though not completely nonobjective, style that was as indeterminate in its subject as the modern condition itself.

By the time of his death, Gorky had long been familiar to the individuals who became known as the Abstract Impressionists. Jackson Pollock was well aware of his work through Gorky's 1951 memorial exhibition at the Whitney Museum, if he wasn't already before then. And Gorky influenced others, such as Willem de Kooning, who had been one of Gorky's closest friends throughout the 1930s and whose own art was often imitative of Gorky's compositions or indebted to the same influences, such as Ingres. De Kooning's *Self-Portrait with Imaginary Brother* was titled after Gorky's *Portrait of the Artist and My Imaginary Wife*, and De Kooning himself, in an interview with Peter Schjeldahl, admitted the influence. "You can see the connection when you look at Gorky," De Kooning says as he pages through the Gorky catalogue; "it's the same—so quiet. It was very good for me to meet him at that particular period.'"[64] The themes of Gorky's art, as well as his style, were consistent with many developments of Abstract Expressionism.

Particularly in their early work, Abstract Expressionist artists such as Barnett Newman, Adolph Gottlieb, and Mark Rothko came to be known as the "mythmakers" for the way that they adapted and often abstracted mythological themes and subject matter. Perhaps as a gesture of emancipation from the Surrealists as well as Gorky, they eventually came to believe that memory, association, nostalgia, legend, and myth—devices of European painting—must be removed so that they could make paintings "out of ourselves, out of our own feelings."[65] Mark Rothko, whose large works are often seen as landscape horizons, stated that "the romantics were prompted,"[66] but that a modern artist must free art from the recognizable so his work may become a transcendental experience. Such a move away from depiction to an art that is more emotive and transient is very much in keeping with Gorky's ideas on plasticity, dissection of the recognizable, and interest in impressions from nature and personal experience. Adolph Gottlieb argued that "if the models we use are apparitions seen in a dream, or the recollections of our pre-historic past, is this less part of nature or realism, than a cow in a field? I think not. The role of the artist, of course, has always been that of image-maker. Different times require different images. . . To my mind certain so-called abstraction is not abstraction at all. On the contrary, it is the realism of our time."[67] Because for the Abstract Expressionists a painting was not a description but an action or event, it was completed when the artist ceased painting. The work itself was also a self-contained composition. Ann Gibson notes that a number of these artists claimed that "meaning was determined in their work not by external factors but by a kind of transcendental transfer of emotional power from the artist to the art. For this transfer to take place unimpeded, it was necessary to establish a kind if cultural vacuum around the work. Social function and historical necessity had to be ignored so that meaning could be determined by the artist's intentions alone."[68] This was a method of liberating the object but also liberating the artist from the object, which is very much what Gorky had been doing through his developing process of displacement.

Gorky created his own world order, based on displacement and his past, and this translated into the hermetic Abstract Expressionist canvas. Harold Rosenberg solidified this concept when he asserted that "the lone artist did not want the world to be different, he wanted his canvas to be a world,"[69] which is exactly what Gorky had achieved. It is perhaps not a surprise that the Abstract Expressionists also created a language, based on a combination of classical and primitive archetypes, that was ambiguous and out of context. A fascination with the primitive informs their work. Adolph Gottlieb, Franz Kline, Mark Rothko, and Jackson Pollock colonized mythology and symbolism into their work without an interest in actual meaning. The Abstract Expressionists, particularly Jackson Pollock, were followers of Jung, whose words perhaps hold a key for the abstraction that these artists created. The Lascaux caves outside Montignac, France, discovered in 1940, had become part of modern consciousness, like the Tuc d'Audubert and Trois Fréres caves, discovered just before World War I, because they gave insight into the mind of primitive man:

> In his [primitive man's] world mind and matter still interpenetrate each other, and his gods still wander through forest and field. He is like a child, only half-born, still enclosed in a dream-state within his own psyche and the world as it actually is, a world not yet distorted by the difficulties in understanding that beset a dawning intelligence. When the primitive world disintegrated into spirit and nature, the West rescued nature for itself. It was prone to a belief in nature, and only became the more entangled in it with every painful effort to make itself spiritual. The East, on the

> contrary, took mind for its own, and by explaining away matter as mere illusion (*maya*), continued to dream in Asiatic filth and misery. But since there is only *one* earth and *one* mankind, East and West cannot rend humanity into two different halves. Psychic reality exists in its original oneness, and awaits man's advance to a level of consciousness where he no longer believes in the one part and denies the other, but recognizes both as constituent elements of one psyche.[70]

Although the mythmakers attempted to create a universal experience, Abstract Expressionism has always been about personal subjectivity. The universal language that enacted a pictography of the primordial human condition remained somewhat introverted, so that it was also about a personal inner experience, just as Gorky's work was based on his own displacement and mutations of what he remembered, envisioned, or witnessed. His personal struggle between two worlds reflected, in fact, an aspect of humanity, tapping the universal meanings of beauty and struggle that Gorky intended to capture in his work. It seems, however, that Gorky's adoption of the catchphrase "universality—like his adoption of "plasticity" and "nonobjective"—is perhaps inaccurate. Because the work could mean differently for different viewers, it is more about indeterminacy.

The myth to which Gorky subscribed was not a particular story, but an intimate combination of remembered and natural forms—perhaps the myth that people and places still existed, although they did so only in his memory. According to Barthes' reading of myth, via Marx, the meaning of "myth consists in overturning culture into nature or, at least, the social, the cultural, the ideological, the historical into the 'natural.' . . . Contemporary myth is discontinuous. It is no longer expressed in long fixed narratives but only in 'discourse'; at most, it is *phraseology*, a corpus of phrases (of stereotypes); myth disappears, but leaving—so much the more insidious—the *mythical*."[71] Here the idea of myth is redoubled. Gorky created his own myth—of the artist—and created works that house a kind of myth. Myth, or interpretations by the artist "Gorky," are creations that are to be applied by viewers because myth, and in particular prototypical mythical stories, is common across different cultures and eras. For instance, most cultures have some form of creation myth to explain their existence, so myth itself is closely tied to identity. Many of the Abstract Expressionists, like Gorky, were also searching for an identity. Perhaps this prompted their embrace of the classical, primitive, and mythical. Michael Leja classifies a broader vision:

> What defines and characterizes New York School art (its "subject") is its effort to devise a form of Modernist visual representation that could accommodate and enrich developing models of the human individual, models that attributed new importance to irrational others within human beings. These models were historically conditioned and ideologically

> charged: the Modern Man subject was largely a refurbishing of the culture's prevailing model of self as essentially autonomous, integral, rational, and effectual which was faltering under pressure from historical cataclysm and social change.[72]

The Modern Man, which Leja defines, relied on an inherent otherness. Artists shared a group identification: they knew each other and embarked on a similar endeavor, although their styles varied. Regardless, there was a ritual to their painting, based in a belief in a kind of collective identity, Gorky included. Although Jean-Paul Sartre's existentialist ideas were not widely known until his writings were translated into English in the 1940s, the struggle inherent in Abstract Expressionist work—that is, when is the painting complete and where does the artist fit in relation to society—became part of the movement's mantra, just as the struggle of displacement had been important in Gorky's oeuvre. Perhaps this is because so many of the Abstract Expressionists, like him, were immigrants or the sons of immigrants and sensitive to displacement and the desire to belong. The dilemma of the Modern Man as defined by Jung, however, was unsolvable because it was so universal that no one individual could grasp it.[73]

Gorky's primary concern was producing a viable modern art. Story after story told by Gorky's friends indicates that he spared nothing for his art and was consumed by it. Dennison brilliantly concludes that in that way, Gorky's work does reflect life. "We are not released by these paintings, as we are released by classical art, but are pursued by them. They possess—and we share—a commitment to the unfinished events of life."[74] Displacement, trauma, and memory are all unfinished and without parameters, indeterminate like trauma itself, which has no real end. Gorky's work is ultimately a phenomenon that turns art on its heels because the art begins to pursue us. Dennison continues, "The excitement they produce is not wholly one of fulfillment or satisfaction, but contains an element that is disturbing, an element to which we respond with gravity and a meditative lingering."[75] Because it is indeterminate, Gorky's art is part of the larger modern human condition as well as of modern art. It follows, then, that Gorky's compositions should defy logic and labels, because it is their unfinishedness and unsettling nature that pursue us, leaving us as uneasy in the world as the artist himself. Wilhelm Worringer argued that the history of art is about how artists have chosen to deal with the interrelationships of humankind and the universe. In turn, we, as viewers, attain an understanding of the artist's work based on our relationship to it. This explains why different interpretations can simultaneously be true for Gorky's art.

Solidifying the tragic storying of Arshile Gorky, in January 1946 he lost most of his newest work in a studio fire, had a colostomy operation for rectal cancer that March, and finally, after a car accident in June 1948 that temporarily paralyzed his painting arm, hanged himself in July. Coincidentally, that same

June, the Displaced Persons Act of 1948 was passed, establishing a policy on refugees and victims of fascist regimes, so that Gorky's original status as an outsider became somewhat of a nonissue. Indeed, by that time Gorky had already become a significant part of an artistic community. There were a great many people in his orbit who cared about him as an artist and an individual. When he had his colostomy, mosaicist Jeanne Reynal sold securities to give him a large sum outright; Serge Chermayeff sent a round-robin letter to other artists asking for help; Wolf Schwabacher (Ethel's husband) secured him a grant from a foundation; and Mina Metzger lent the care of her own physician, Dr. Harry Weiss.[76] When he was bedridden again after the accident, Agnes tried to remain upbeat, remarking in a letter to Ethel Schwabacher on June 29, 1948, just before the artist's suicide, that "I am constantly surprised at how well he looks with this incredible apparatus around his head and his enormous brown hands folded on his chest . . . but then of course he was in the pink of condition when this bit of luck caught him."[77]

With his new family, like Aram in *Beast on the Moon*, he had attempted to rebuild his life as he did with his painting. After his body was broken by surgery and the accident and he could not paint, it became even more evident how necessary they were to him.[78] Perhaps Gorky was overcome by trauma. Gorky's wife wrote the following letter to the Schwabachers to explain why she had left him:

> At the moment he [Gorky] is in no shape to make any decisions regarding the children nor do I know what we will be able to do with the future, even as to where we should live. . . . But as I say, Gorky is going through such a total turmoil that all plans are futile—I came down here without even a toothbrush on the advice of Dr. Weiss who warned me that this kind of situation can create the most serious psychic trauma in the life of a child and must be halted immediately. I think in a few days or a week I will take them up to Castine [Maine] until I can come to some understanding with Gorky . . . for this thing is far beyond me now, and all his friends with all their warmth and affection can only help him if he can help himself. . . .
>
> Believe me, my heart has been totally engaged even to the exclusion my instinctive nature and if I could have I would have spared him this but my love was not strong enough I guess.[79]

The re-placing of family that Gorky had achieved, and the subsequent suspension of trauma, weakened by the studio fire, cancer, and colostomy, were lost entirely when his wife left. Gorky was likely thrown into a despair that triggered his past trauma and loss of family. Although his wife and children were only absent, it registered for Gorky as loss. Gorky went to his good friend the sculptor Isamu Noguchi with his children's rag dolls, saying, with tears streaming down his face, "This is all I have. This is all I have left."[80] The loss of his present family dredged up the loss of his past family—repeating a withdrawal of love and stability as well as disintegrating the rest of the social capital that he had gained in his adoptive country, the remainder of which had disappeared when he became unable to paint.

Gorky began to lose faith, and with it his will to live. Viktor Frankl has written of concentration camp victims that "the prisoner who had lost faith in the future—his future—was doomed. With his loss of belief in the future, he also lost his spiritual hold. . . . He simply gave up."[81] Since, as Oshagan and Bakalian have both testified, life for Armenians like Gorky was tied up in a creation of the future, when that future dissipated or became uncertain, Gorky fell apart. His desire for life had been in its remaking—and once it had been unmade, Gorky lost his will to go on. He tried several times to commit suicide, but his wife was able to stop him. It was almost as if he wanted to be stopped, rescued from his despair. He would frequently call his friends, who, alarmed by the tone of his voice, would frantically call his neighbors in Connecticut and ask them to check on him.[82] But on July 21, 1948, with his wife no longer there, he finally succeeded.

Those last moments are perhaps crystallized in *Agony* (plate 25), which he painted after his colostomy operation. The operation was a violation of his bodily space that was a source of embarrassment for the fastidiously clean Gorky. The deep red, with a slightly rough surface, exudes a quality of fermentation. It is a chimera of the fantastic and the grotesque, of intestinal and empty space. In this, as in other late works, past and present seem to intersect. In retrospect, *Agony* becomes a memento mori, reflecting the emotion of his impending end with the use of glaring reds and black lines, incised into the painting, that cut out imprecise outlines of sections of the painting. Thin and curved, these nervelike lines reflect the stretched, almost snapped nerves of Gorky's life. The security of the new world he had tried to build around him was gone, he was no longer able to cope with exile through art, and he had reached the end of art history. Gorky had lived through his art, and since he could no longer do art, his death, like his art, was by his own hand. Arshile Gorky was extinguished by the will of the artist just as he had been created, a necessary resolution to the completion of his exilic oeuvre.

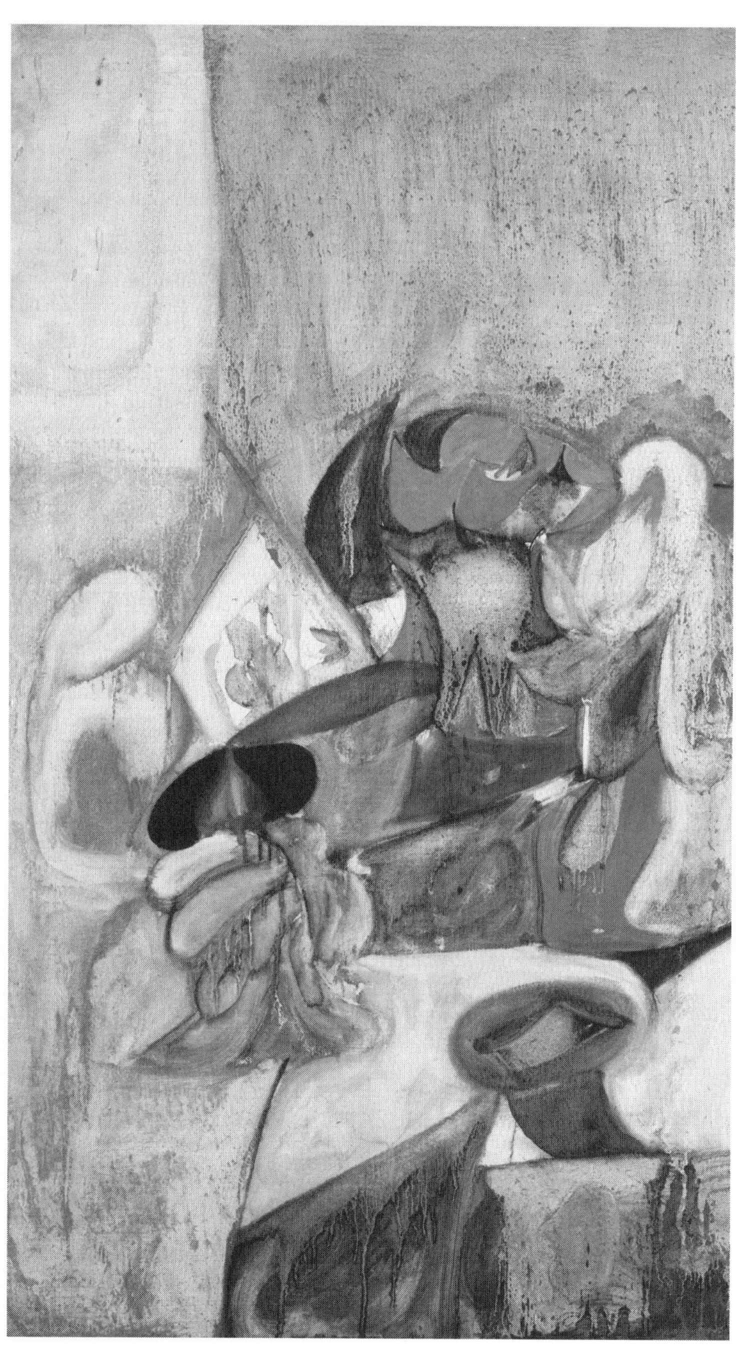

chapter 7

Primitivism, the Feminine, and Orientalization

Gorky, spirit of Europe in body of the Caucasus, getting the feel of American soil. Unswerving, critical reason seeks the quintessence of Picasso-Miró, drunkenly to absorb them, only to exude them again in a deep slumber, after such feast. This Caucasian stranger, having just quenched his hunger and thirst, is ready to shoulder down the doors into a land of his own—for those who wait without threshold. The genius of Asia celebrates his marriage to the spirit of Europe. Such an event is rare. We are fortunate to be witnesses. Tourists of the American, Asiatic and European Continents are invited. Tickets are free and at popular prices. All depends on you. The earlier you come, the longer your pleasure will last.

—FREDERICK KIESLER

Ethel Schwabacher, in the first comprehensive examination of Arshile Gorky's life and art, begins, "It occurred to me in the spring of 1948 that I might write a book about Arshile Gorky and thus bring his work, as yet insufficiently known, before the public."[1] In 1950, Gorky's work was shown at the Venice Biennale, which introduced an international audience to his brand of abstraction. Even after his death, some critics still did not hold Gorky in high esteem—Emily Grenauer quipped, after the 1951 Arshile Gorky Memorial Exhibition at the Whitney Museum, that "the only thing worse than the idolatry of second-rate artists while they're living is idolatry of second-rate artists after they're dead."[2] But by the time Schwabacher published her book in 1957, knowledge of contemporary art was growing and an acknowledgment of the first truly internationally significant American art, Abstract Expressionism, had taken hold. Although Gorky was not fully part of the movement and was thus never really considered one of the greats of the era, some did recognize his contributions to the progress of American art.

Opening image detail of plate 22.

As it became more and more evident that Gorky might have influenced some of the Abstract Expressionists, some gallery owners and critics followed Schwabacher's lead in trying to establish Gorky as a significant force within the development of modern art in America. Harold Rosenberg eventually hailed Gorky as "a typical hero of Abstract Expressionism[;] his personality as well as his work refute generally accepted myths concerning this mode of painting, particularly the myth of an art that is an eruption of mindless energy."[3] In stressing the intellectual aspects of Gorky's work, Rosenberg added credibility to the Abstract Expressionists' methods. Rosenberg's classification of Gorky as a typical hero of the movement, however, appeared well over a decade after the artist's death, and at the time Abstract Expressionism was already becoming iconic, the artists involved were attaining fame, and the style was becoming widespread.

For the most part, Gorky had always tried to avoid the critics. The more he shunned them, however, the more he became a lightning rod for their skepticism. Early in his career he had been condemned as a copyist, and that label seemed to haunt him throughout his life. Later on, he didn't fare too much better. In a 1944 letter to Gorky's wife from Jeanne Reynal, Reynal imagined the impending opening of Gorky's first one-man show: "You will see Papa Rosenberg will tootle around. Everybody, and Arshile will escape them through another channel."[4] In another letter a few months later, Reynal spoke bitterly of the "authorities" and "art racket" who had chastised Gorky for being derivative early in his career, but who took notice of him only after he had been hailed by André Breton. "But you know," she complained, "there has always been a cabal against Arshile and once when I said this he was quite cross with me. To me it becomes clear. They overlooked Gorky, and now they are too small to admit it. . . . And if one cares to embroider the point THEY ARE INCAPABLE OF MAKING THE EMOTIONAL RESPONSE that his painting requires."[5] She was likely responding to Clement Greenberg's March 24, 1945, review of Gorky's first one-man show, in which he accused Gorky of taking "the easy way out" because of his dependence on other artists.[6] Greenberg grumbled that the significance of Gorky's work was in its formal elements rather than its concept. Reynal remarked that the problem was the critic's abilities rather than Gorky's. "I have met this young man and the impression at the time was that Arshile would not listen to one word he had to say about painting, painting in general," she recounts, "so why in gods name need one take seriously what he says."[7] Greenberg eventually spoke favorably of the artist, but his commentary was never completely complimentary.

In his review of Gorky's 1948 show at Julien Levy's gallery, however, the last in the artist's lifetime, Greenberg wrote that Gorky was "among the very few contemporary American painters whose work is of more than national importance."[8] Such praise followed Greenberg's earlier declaration that Gorky's *Calendars* was the best painting in the Whitney Annual and "one of the best pictures ever done by an American."[9] Despite these compliments, his critical comments were often somewhat underhanded. In the same review in which he praised *Calendars*, Greenberg still insinuated that Gorky's work was derivative: "[He is] the only artist in America to have completely assimilated French art—an assimilation that reveals itself in the fact that, whatever else his painting may be, it is never dim or dull, and never unfeeling in touch or texture. The Frenchness of *The Calendars* is astonishing, yet it is not a question simply of felicity and taste; it also gives us a wealth of sensations, a plentitude of matter, all under a control as firm as it is delicate."[10] Here Greenberg never actually lauds the work, but compliments the artist on his complete assimilation of French style, the painting's "wealth of sensations," and characterizes what the painting is not, saying that "it is never dim or dull, and never unfeeling in touch or texture." After Gorky's death, Greenberg admitted in a letter to Ethel Schwabacher's husband, Wolf, that he regretted "a good many of the of the things" that he had written negatively about the artist's work; as a mature critic, it seems that he finally understood it.[11]

Despite Gorky's having been embraced by his fellow artists, the critics had indeed been slower to recognize Gorky's significance during his lifetime, and while Gorky showed his work frequently in museums such as the Whitney, it took him a while to find a gallery to represent him. Dichotomies often arise when one tries to understand the artist: he used French aesthetics in his development of an art in America; he was both modern in his endeavors and nostalgic in his subject; he was both plagued by self-doubt (perhaps one reason why it took so long to work through paintings) and often arrogant in his personal and professional relationships. In evaluating what Gorky's art does, and particularly what it sets in motion, the answer for Gorky, like the inseparability of his art from his life, is complicated. Even more complicated is considering how the artist has been addressed and evaluated throughout his career, because such a discussion arguably involves definitions of the "primitive," feminist critiques, and applications of Orientalist stereotypes. The negative attention that Gorky's personality has drawn from critics, as well as their unwillingness to give him credit for his art, may reflect complications of race.

Gorky's exoticism has often been referenced, most notably in terms of his broken English and party dancing, but also in relation to his art. Gorky's friend Frederick Kiesler, in his introduction to the 1934 exhibition at the Mellon Galleries in Philadelphia, alluded to Gorky's displacement, his study of other artists, his identity mystique, his synthesis of artistic styles, the significance of the viewer's interaction with his work, and his creation of "a land of his own" in his art. Although Kiesler respected Gorky a great deal and celebrated Gorky's otherness, this statement reflects the carnivalesque manner in which Gorky and his art seem sometimes to have been addressed and perceived. Unfortunately, Gorky became a caricature of a Middle Easterner, whose imagery, because it was abstracted, was used to prove that the artist himself was shifty.[12] Even Rosenberg, who understood why Gorky as an immigrant constructed his identity, sometimes subscribed to an image of Gorky as a stereotype.[13] Gorky was largely perceived as a Borat-like figure who, whether entertaining or repelling, was revered or reviled, respected for what he revealed about the world or denounced because in doing so he made fools of those who envisioned themselves as having authority. Following this particular manner of discourse, it becomes evident that Gorky and his art are often marginalized by primitivistic, feminized, or Orientalized judgments.

Primitivism, a vehicle in modern art at least since the nineteenth century, was precipitated by the desire of artists to escape the Industrial Revolution in search of what they believed was a genuine aesthetic more directly related to emotion than academy-driven practices or the structures of proper society. Artists such as Paul Gauguin fled to places like Tahiti, and Picasso embraced the apotropaic qualities of African masks. Michael Leja states that the "widespread US cultural interest in the primitive developed in the wake of World War I" in an effort to comprehend twentieth-century history.[14] Interest in primitivism grew with the publication in 1922 of Sir James George Frazer's abridged edition of the 1890 *The Golden Bough,* which elaborated the development of primitive man from savagery to civilization. At the same time, people were wondering what it meant to be a "modern man," as in Harvey Fergusson's 1936 *Modern Man: His Belief and Behavior,* which suggested that the primitive was a mirror image of the modern.

The 1939 World's Fair, full of the promise of new technology, also put on display live specimens of people from non-Western and primitive cultures. With the same irony, artists were enamored with the primitive as an experience that would yield a deeper understanding of and connection to their modern world. The tragedy of the modern man, then, was that he needed to remain connected to the initial essence of things and his primordial feelings. Carl Jung addressed this dilemma in *Modern Man in Search of a Soul,* which was available in English by 1933, and which was of great interest to the artists in New York. Jung argues that the experience of the primitive is the essence of creativity, but since such a state is overwhelming, it needs myth to become understandable:

> The primordial experience is the source of his creativeness; it cannot be fathomed, and therefore requires mythological imagery to give it form. In itself it offers no words or images, for it is a vision seen "as in a glass, darkly." It is merely a deep presentment that strives to find expression. It is like a whirlwind that seizes everything within reach and, by carrying it aloft, assumes a visible shape. Since the particular expression can never exhaust the possibilities of the vision, but falls far short of it in richness of content, the poet must have at his disposal a huge store of materials if he

> is to communicate even a few of his intimations. What is more, he must resort to an imagery that this is difficult to handle and full of contradictions in order to express the weird paradoxicality of his vision.[15]

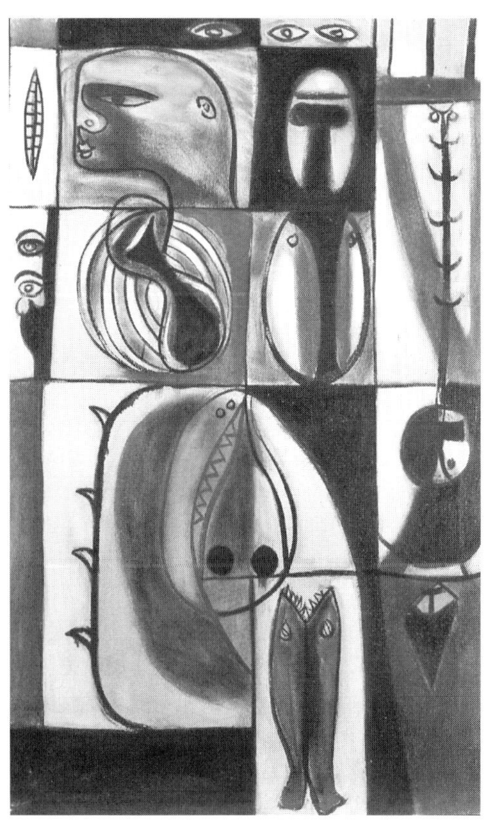

FIGURE 48
Adolph Gottlieb, *Expectation of Evil*, 1945.

The Abstract Expressionists had embraced such an idea using symbols and mythology and the primitive and archaic, removed from their original context.[16] The adopted symbols were thus displaced from their original meaning, which, not unlike Gorky's use of forms from other artist's compositions and shreds of memories from his past, created a personal mythology.

According to David and Cecile Shapiro, the goal for Abstract Expressionists like Mark Rothko and Adolph Gottlieb became a universal symbolism for a timeless art. Like Gorky's art, however, which can sometimes be unintelligible to the viewer who looks for the artist's meaning rather than trying to discover his or her own, the work of the Abstract Expressionists often expresses the personal rather than the universal, as the Shapiros point out: "Symbols removed from their cultural context become merely abstracted signs or elements of formal design if the fragments borrowed are not integrated as symbols evoking newly relevant myths."[17] While Gorky adapted forms from other compositions and took memories out of their context, the Abstract Expressionist adaptation of symbols could be interpreted as a cultural appropriation in that they actually colonized the symbols and exploited them for their own purposes, regardless of the symbols' illegibility after they had so. Gottlieb's use of pictographs, for instance, does not necessarily reference the Native American and African languages from which they were derived (fig. 48). Such a practice could reflect the opposite of its intentions—power or control over these disenfranchised cultures. Mistranslation can connote power, but the in-betweenness of image and sign that such misuse instigates is actually part of minority discourse. At the same time, disengaging the symbols from specific meanings and cultures and combining them with those of others also reflects a universality and commonality between cultures that Jung and others advocated as timeless. Gorky had long subscribed to such an understanding, having been introduced by John Graham to Henri Focillon's *The Life of Forms in Art* after the Russian artist, who had spent time in France, likely distilled the French text for him. Focillon validated for Gorky the interdependency of art—that various forms and aesthetic interests recur throughout history and across different cultures. Gorky's own visual language was multicultural and transcended time, like Modernism itself.

Mythmakers like Rothko, Gottlieb, and Kline were attracted to the lack of history in primitivist visual Modernism.[18] For Rothko, memory, history, and geometry were "obstacles between the idea and the observer."[19] The artist, then, strove to recover the status of original man but also believed that ultimately we all have some common past history since all cultures have similar myths.[20] Throughout the history of Modernism, artists often used elements from marginalized cultures as a vehicle for attaining originality. This is most popularly evident in works such as Picasso's *Les Demoiselles d'Avignon,* in which he incorporates masks into the composition. The interesting twist here is that the appropriators were not themselves part of the hegemonic center. Gottlieb, Rothko, and Barnett Newman were Jewish and were either immigrants or the children of immigrants. They tended initially to choose as their inspirations variations of ancient myth from the classical era—looking to a part of Western civilization that was further from their own Jewish heritage. This act reinforced their connection to accepted art forms by virtue of association and gave them legitimacy. As the mythmakers moved toward abstraction and searched for timeless symbols, they expanded their vocabulary of symbols removed from their context. As a direct reaction to what they saw as the evil of the time, they began to pursue abstraction, perhaps as a means to escape trauma. As Adolph Gottlieb explained, "Today when our aspirations have been reduced to a desperate attempt to escape from evil, and times are out of joint, our obsessive, subterranean and pictographic mages are the expression of the neurosis, which is our reality."[21] Abstraction, however, operated differently for artists whose otherness was marked by race rather than ethnicity. African American painter Norman Lewis, who was a member of the New York School and used recognizable and pictograph-like imagery in his art, is generally left out of mainstream discussions of Abstract Expressionism, perhaps because he was linked directly to the primitive. Ann Gibson has explained the predicament: "White Abstract Expressionists, for instance, could strip themselves in the eyes of others of adopted alliances with so-called 'primitives.' African Americans could not. Even if, like so many whites, African Americans had been brought up with an awareness of Western art and culture . . . and may have similarly yearned for an escape into immediacy, represented by 'the primitive' . . . they could hardly escape noticing that in the eyes of most of American society, they *were* the 'primitive.'[22]
Lewis, therefore, could not simply "go away" like Paul Gauguin, who escaped French industrialism and social and familial obligations by running off to Tahiti; appropriate African masks like Picasso; or adopt the pictographs of the Native Americans like Gottlieb. He was already attuned to folk practices and cultures, as revealed by his statements about *Garden in Sochi* to the Museum of

Modern Art and about his Newark murals, which describe a method of keeping time using feathers. Gorky, whose status as Middle Eastern hovered in between race and ethnicity and whose skin color was dark but not black, worked in a way that was opposite to the typical Abstract Expressionist method of appropriation. Gorky recontextualized the dominant art forms of Western art and very subtly integrated imagery and themes from his foreign background. He often complicated his art further by mixing ethnicities, such as by shifting his name and the name of his home village to Russian, thereby adopting an Eastern European instead of a Middle Eastern identity. He also created compositions that appropriated the new world in which he lived as a means to express the old, drawing the landscape or images around him but transforming them through memory and imagination into a composition that reflected his real past.

For Gorky, as for Lewis, race was another complication. Armenians had been denied naturalization because they were classified as "mongoloid Turks." This marginalization separated the Armenians somewhat from other immigrants. Gary Gerstle has summarized the effect of appearance in immigration history. He positions immigration, which is generally perceived as a particular self-contained experience, comparatively to ideas of ethnicity, effectively linking both to constructions of race.[23] Especially helpful is his understanding of ethnicity as related to "blackness." The "whiteness debate" revealed itself through a number of immigration acts in the 1920s. To actually be black in the first half of the twentieth century was to be considered below the status of the immigrant, at the very bottom of the social and economic ladder.

Immigrants, therefore, benefited from differentiating themselves from any form of blackness. Being categorized in such a hierarch as "less white" than another group was detrimental to one's social position. One example of such discrimination against Armenians occurred in Fresno, California, where a land covenant devised before World War I restricted land use or purchase by "any Negro, Chinese, Japanese, Hindu, Armenian, Asiatic or native of the Turkish Empire, or descendent of the above named persons, or anyone not of the white or Caucasian race."[24] Not only was Gorky an exile who became an immigrant—both categories that were not completely accepted into society—but his relation to blackness placed him on the fringes of society at large.

Few ethnic minorities, however, were marginalized to the extent that African Americans like Lewis were. Gorky, as an Armenian, was not denied service at lunch counters or treated as poorly as African Americans. Because of his dark, foreign features, however, he was once suspected, while in the American West, of being Mexican, another marginalized group, and almost deported to Mexico.[25]

As Gorky continued to live in the United States, one might have expected him to have appeared less ethnic and become more assimilated, particularly since he lived outside Armenian communities. As Gorky's career proceeded, however, he outwardly relied more on his ethnic roots, particularly for artistic themes. During the 1940s he began to construct a pre-Genocide Armenia around him. Several of his works during this period were linked to Armenian motifs, such as the gardens at his native home. "And as facts are sifted from fictions," said Elaine de Kooning, "his cherished childhood in the mountains of Northern Armenia remains as exotic, if less tranquil, than the ones he invented."[26] Gorky's style abstracted his past and present worlds so as to make them unplaceable. As Gibson suggests, "abstraction offered the status of the 'universal' for ancestral imagery by protecting it from the racialization."[27] Gorky's abstraction allowed him, in an inherently Modernist strategy, to erase his racialized lines and contours.

During the 1940s Gorky also began to apply identity to others. As discussed above, he called his wife, whom he married in 1941, by the name Mougouch, which may be Armenian but which he told her was Russian; his first daughter he named Maro, after an Armenian revolutionary fighter in his family; and his younger daughter, although originally he gave her the name Yalda, became Natasha, a Russian name. This cultural inversion is related to displacement and identity, especially how Gorky straddled worlds in his own identity and was prompted to assert it onto his family. Gorky was also known for bringing Armenian or Russian records with him to gatherings, dinners, and parties so that he could dance. A number of his friends have commented that Gorky would often turn his jacket inside out, making it look like a peasant outfit, and dance Armenian dances that he remembered from his boyhood. Traditionally, Armenian festive gatherings include dancing, in which groups of people organize into circles or lines follow a repeated series of steps, sometimes with a male leading the procession or in the center dancing with a handkerchief, which is what Gorky does in a photograph from the 1940s, although he is the only one dancing (fig. 49).

Alice Scourby discusses such behavior in relation to Greek culture in America: "In order to relieve the pressure of rejection and the subsequent feelings of inferiority, the immigrant overidentified with the Old World customs and traditions. The Old World's style of life became the only stabilizing pattern. Any deviations, by either himself or his children became a threat to his identity."[28] Yet while Gorky acted out his ethnicity, the bemused expressions of his audience, as evident in the photograph, perhaps make him appear the fool, the exotic.

Handkerchief dancing was not something that people did at New York parties in the 1930s. Stuart Davis told Gorky once, "we don't do that here" when Gorky began pulling out his records to sing and dance, indicating that Gorky's self-expression and ethnic identification were unacceptable in such circumstances. Davis recalled how Gorky "would go into a routine derived from the song and folk-dances of his native land. This performance took up a lot of room,

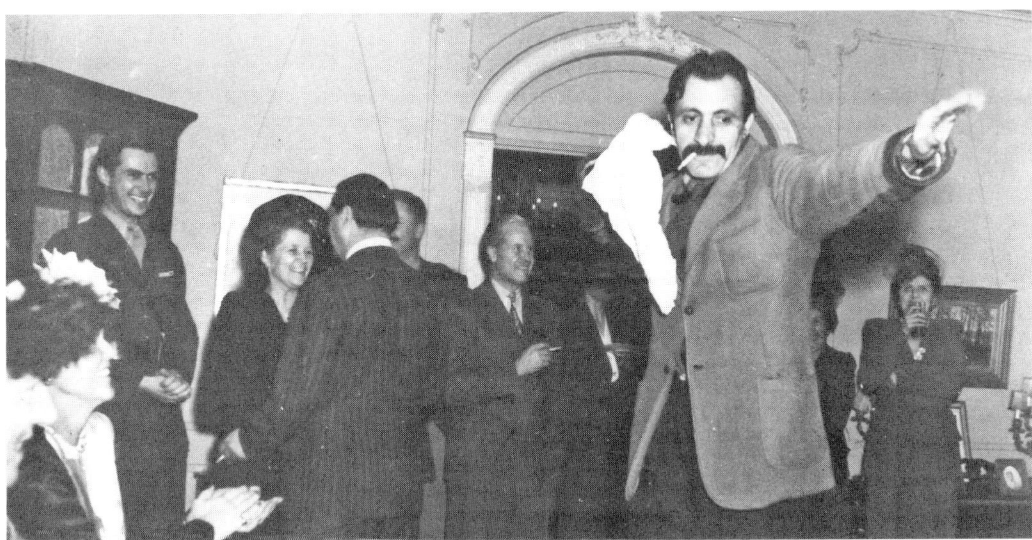

FIGURE 49
Photograph of Arshile Gorky, 1945.

and the accompanying vocalizations drowned out all competitive conversations. The idiosyncrasy was frowned on by us, who would not tolerate musical deviations of any kind from our profoundly hip devotion to American jazz. Gorky became aware of this ban very fast, and respected it after being properly indoctrinated in its rationale. He reserved his routine for other circles where it was appreciated and continued to go over big."[29] Although trying to commune with a group, Gorky was still not "at home," and his authentic self was still somewhat separate from his public self. He was perpetually, it seemed, both insider and outsider, someone who existed both at the periphery and center of social and artistic communities.

Reactions to Gorky's dancing expose a problematic component of American abstraction in early twentieth-century society. Davis, like so many middle- and upper-class whites, went to jazz clubs, and even played jazz records while painting, but just as some of the Abstract Expressionists appropriated mythic symbols and used them out of context, Davis embraced a conglomeration of fringe art forms for the purpose of his own self-expression. The experience of jazz, for example, was much different for African Americans, since, as Gibson suggests, "blacks could see jazz's structure but also lived with the inheritance of its social roots."[30] For Gorky, the Armenian music to which he wanted to dance and to which he often painted was a part of his genuine displaced heritage and not solely an affected self-expression or background music, as jazz may have been for Davis. The American Modernist use of jazz was in some ways an inauthentic acculturation. European and American Modernists colonized African art, and whites embraced the black aesthetic, such as jazz, even though black people remained segregated. As was the case with Lewis, Gorky could not co-opt his own culture. Primitivization could underlie the manner in which Gorky has been repeatedly singled out for using the work of mainstream Western artists as inspiration. Because he was not of the dominant culture, while artists such as Picasso were seen as revolutionary for adapting non-Western art forms and revising quotations of work by the old masters, Gorky, as an outsider, was seen merely as a mimic. In other words, he was not quite entitled to draw on sources that for insiders were part of their cultural inheritance.

In addition to the way that marginalized artists were seen as pursuing art, they were also often subject to descriptions that reflected race or ethnicity. The critical reception of Afro-Cuban and Chinese artist Wilfredo Lam in the United States during the 1940s often differed from that of his contemporaries, despite his thematic and formal continuities with the early New York School. Michael Leja notes that "the fact that he was from Cuba, and more important, that he was partly black—his mother was an African Cuban and his father was Chinese—often led critics to treat his work differently. Usually his exotic heritage was mentioned prominently at the start of the review; the *Art Digest*, for example opened its review of his 1942 exhibition by noting that Lam was a Cuban painter 'in whose veins runs both Chinese and Negro blood.'"[31] It was important for critics to point out Lam's ethnicity as a way to explain his art.

Even though Gorky, like Lam, was part of an artistic community, he was separated ethnically from the European immigrants with whom he kept company. Breton addressed this separation, while not directly connecting it to Gorky's ethnicity. In his 1945 introduction to Gorky's solo show at Julien Levy's gallery, Breton speaks of Gorky's work as hybrids of real and remembered forms. It is also significant that Breton notes that Gorky is the only Surrealist inspired directly by nature, which further connects him to the primitive. But his relationship with nature is also a product of Gorky's own displacement from rural past and modern present. Breton had claimed Lam too as a Surrealist, but on the same terms: as nature. Therefore, the Afro-Cuban-Chinese artist was in fact, like Gorky, still set outside of the mainstream of the Surrealist movement.

For some American modern artists, racial and ethnic identity was not necessarily linked to self-identification. Amid the numerous immigrant types that made up the new American art, one nonimmigrant was singled out above the others. Jackson Pollock was the epitome of the American Modernist artist. De Kooning, initially European, would not have been an appropriate icon, and Rothko and Newman were Jewish (and Newman was also an anarchist). Even had he lived, Gorky, with his thick accent and affectations, could never have assumed that role. As Milton Resnick said,

> This country's art world always wanted original American artists. And when Gorky died, it was very lucky for a lot of other people. With Gorky out of the way, it was very easy to say that Motherwell is original, de Kooning's original and Pollock is very original. Of course, it is not true. As a matter of fact, it has

> been the policy to have an American, people they can feel are wholesomely American. Gorky would have been a stumbling block and his being dead and out of the way gave them a chance to kind of start something and falsify things and go along and make a kind of conspiracy that would be acceptable. In other words, Gorky has been given a kind of dubious honor eternal and thrown in the closet, whereas the other boys are right now and give them a break. And so his contributions have that way of being withheld.[32]

According to Gibson, "the work of African Americans and women was often denigrated for its lack of originality."[33] The irony that when a white man used the characteristics of subcultures or "primitives," he was perceived as original, but that the members of the community who lived a version of the colonized aesthetic were perceived as unoriginal, reflects the social structure of the time. It might be said that in some ways Gorky was Orientalized by society and art history not unlike the women in Ingres's harem paintings. To apply Edward Said's terms, he was feminized as a subject:

> Orientalism is a praxis of the same sort as male gender dominance, or patriarchy, in metropolitan societies: the Orient was routinely described as feminine, its riches as fertile, its main symbols the sensual woman, the harem, and the despotic—but curiously attractive—ruler. Moreover, Orientals, like housewives, were confined to silence and to unlimited enriching production. Much of this material is manifestly connected to the configurations of sexual, racial, and political asymmetry underlying mainstream modern western culture, as illuminated respectively by feminists, by black studies critics, and by anti-imperialist activists.[34]

While he was alive, Gorky, because of his dark skin and heavy accent, could never be entirely assimilated in America, even though he eventually married an American. Gorky's artistic practices were a way to enter into high culture by completely immersing himself so as not to be rejected by it. While at the same time, because he would always remain somewhat of an outsider, celebrating that difference by references to his past in his work.

Critics often also feminized Gorky through his perceived lack of originality. This too, of course, elucidates the connection between the Orient and the feminine that Said notes above. Clement Greenberg referred to Gorky's work as "charming" and concluded that "he has trouble freeing himself from influences and asserting his own personality. . . . Because Gorky remained as long a promising painter, the suspicion across time that he lacked independence and masculinity of character."[35] He described Gorky as having "folkloric quaintness," which further undercut his masculinity because it emphasized a folk or low culture as opposed to the high culture of the European or American art worlds.

Gorky's practice opposed the developing idea of the modern American artist as maverick. His identity as an artist in the New York art world became feminized. According to Griselda Pollock, "art history itself is to be understood as a series of representational practices which actively produce definitions of sexual difference and contribute to the present configuration of sexual politics and power relations."[36] The power relations of early twentieth-century American society subjugated Gorky because of his displacement just as it did Lewis and Lam because of their race.

The sexism, racism, and xenophobia that were commonplace in the 1920s and 1930s were propagated by critics such as Thomas Craven and Meyer Schapiro, who made it part of the critique of artists.[37] As Gibson points out, such classification has a specific agenda. "One way that patriarchy as well as white supremacy was constructed and maintained was by feminizing (and thus trivializing) the African (or the Native American, or the Chinese, and so on), while reaffirming racializing aspects of the past."[38] This statement intersects with the concept of "other," which is at once an object of desire and derision. Gorky and Lam's embrace of nature in their work was perceived as feminine.

Even though he was very much a central figure in New York in the 1930s and 1940s, art-historical accounts of the time tended to feminize him. Meyer Schapiro speaks of Gorky as a disciple of the Surrealists and says that he yielded to their seduction. Perhaps most revealing is Schapiro's conclusion, which distinctly notes feminine characteristics: "Yet in the best of his last pictures, very beautiful ones like *Agony* and the *Diary of a Seducer*, he seems to us truer to himself than in his most austerely considered early work; at least he was able to realize then in a delicate style an important, perhaps feminine, part of his nature-feelings of love and fragility and despair—for which there had been little place in his art before."[39] Gorky's feminized disposition, elaborated by Greenberg and Schapiro, was similar to the literal predicament of Gorky's female contemporaries such as Lee Krasner. Writing about a visit to Krasner and Pollock at their studio, *New Yorker* writer Berton Roueché was sure to point out that although Krasner was also a painter, she was in the kitchen making jelly.[40] One might wonder why, with a reporter from a major magazine visiting, Krasner would have been executing such a feminine task anyway. Anne Wagner makes a point of contrasting the manner in which Pollock and Krasner are portrayed in the *New Yorker* article.[41] As Pollock is described as shrugging, grunting, and scowling, she "laughs merrily" and "smiles."

Perhaps it was a kinship with Gorky's predicament that led Krasner to work through a phase of her style that drew upon Gorky's work of the 1930s, emulating Gorky in the same manner as he had emulated the early modern masters. She was included in a group that he formed to execute a collaborative painting that never materialized.[42] For Krasner, it was her gender that led to her marginalization. Identity was an important issue for Krasner, who masculinized her name through numerous permutations, shifting it away from the feminine

Lenore to the more masculine Lee. Similarly, Gorky's one-time lover Michael West, at Gorky's urging, had changed her name from Corinne.

Krasner married Pollock, but West, afraid that her work would suffer if she were married, particularly to another artist, did not marry Gorky. "I was obsessed with my own work," said West; "it stood in the way."[43] Anne Wagner described Krasner's predicament in being a woman artist while at the same time being Mrs. Jackson Pollock. Krasner had been heavily involved in the New York art scene, taking classes with Hans Hofmann and spending time with other artists, to the extent that it was likely she who introduced Pollock to some of the artistic theories floating around at the time and to some of the artists who became the Abstract Expressionists. But like so many other artists' wives, she was still called upon to stuff envelopes at Pollock's gallery for his show and to keep a record of his paintings' titles, prices, and buyers.[44] In most respects, Krasner had to lose her identity as a painter so that Pollock could expand his. Even though she was already an accomplished artist, Krasner's own oeuvre was always placed in relation to his, her paintings often compared to, or even mistaken for, for Pollock's work.[45] In a similar way, formal elements of Gorky's art were traced back to the artists who inspired him rather than as showing how he created new forms out of initial inspirations.

Appropriation can be viewed as both feminine and primitive, indicating an artist who can only make art by copying others. The same characteristic has also been attributed to Middle Easterners, as is dishonesty or sly behavior, a perception that has continued until the present day. Exchanges with Europeans through trade, colonization, and war have formed in the Western imagination in such a way that Middle Easterners are viewed as sneaky, somewhat barbaric, and sexualized. These peoples held such a fascination for the West that the transgressive nature of opium and harem women became a main subject in late nineteenth-century Romantic painting. This romanticization was an idealization of male power, but the Orientalized male was marginalized in society as Edward Said has discussed, becoming ultimately primitivized and feminized in comparison to his Western counterparts.[46]

Criticism of an artist is always subject to the vantage point and environment of the critic himself. Eventually, the marginalization of specific artists by considering them as feminine within the art world gave way to the generalized identification of artists and artmaking as feminine. Despite the maverick qualities eventually attributed to Jackson Pollock and many of the Abstract Expressionist artists, the modern American artist became feminized. The artist June Wayne notes that because art is about creation, it is ultimately considered feminine:

> It appears to me that society unconsciously perceives the artist as a female. . . . Obviously the artist makes art and the woman makes babies, but the word *create* is commonly used to describe both processes. . . . After I had

> noted the interchangeability of "artist" with "woman" I played with feminist literature, substituting artist for woman and found myriad examples where the substitution worked perfectly. . . . Next I rearranged the actors of the art milieu according to sexual roles: artists as women regardless of actual gender: dealers, collectors, curators, patrons, critics, public functionaries, et al., as men regardless of gender. Now the passivity of artists and the aggressiveness of these other categories became logical and predictable.[47]

Such a technique can be used to identify how the primitive, feminine, or Oriental was applied to Gorky's work. His own stream-of-consciousness artist statements, however, allude to a pastoral past, colorful stories and experiences, and folk culture. Gorky's endeavor can likely be summed up with an anecdote, related by the poet Henry Taylor, that reflects the "innocent eye" of the primitive who precedes history and culture or the child who expresses with direct emotion, but also the perspective of someone outside the culture in which he exists. The innocent eye, which John Ruskin identified in his *Elements of Drawing,* views the world as if for the first time, afresh, and often with wide-eyed wonder. Gorky was fascinated by the process of association, particularly in children's art,[48] in which unrecognizable and ambiguous forms read as objects and stories—a red circle could be a face, a collection of blue lines might be defined by the child as a house. If we add the concept of a house, whose form can differ somewhat from culture to culture and whose name is always different, what appears to be an ambiguous visual language means something to the child just as the abstract forms in Gorky's paintings mean something to the artist, even if their specifics are undecipherable to the viewer. Ruskin's innocent artist's eye is regressive, seeing the world and objects in it regressively, before objects and their uses are comprehended. Gorky's interest in pure essential expression and the tactility of materials, and his embrace of the act of painting, are illustrated in Taylor's anecdote. As a child, Taylor lived within walking distance of Crooked Run Farm, where the artist spent a few summers in the 1940s. Because Gorky died when Taylor was four, Taylor's memories of the artist are sketchy like Gorky's own childhood memories that informed his work, but one recollection, which reflects Gorky's oeuvre, remained vivid:

> When I was very young, I shared a bedroom with my younger sister. My parents had remodeled this old house, and had the walls re-plastered (this was before the wide use of sheetrock) and, in most places, papered. But our room was left unprepared; we had the white plaster to do with as we wished, as long as no crayon passed beyond the doorsill. Once we pushed a bureau into the middle of the room, climbed up on it, and melted

> crayons on the light fixture. Anyway, on seeing this room, Gorky good-humoredly remarked, "Bot! This is what I try to do!"[49]

The relationship of the artist's method to that of innocents such as children is akin to the authentic expression that the Abstract Expressionists were trying to achieve by embracing the primitive. Their ultimate goal, like Gorky's, was to evoke pure emotion through pure, unadulterated form. And like theirs, Gorky's trajectory as an artist—the times of great production, recognition, setback, and personal growth—followed the existential survival of the exile and the endeavor of the Modernist artist. Like his life, Gorky's paintings might ultimately be unknowable; Gorky remains compelling because despite the answers we find, we continue to have questions.

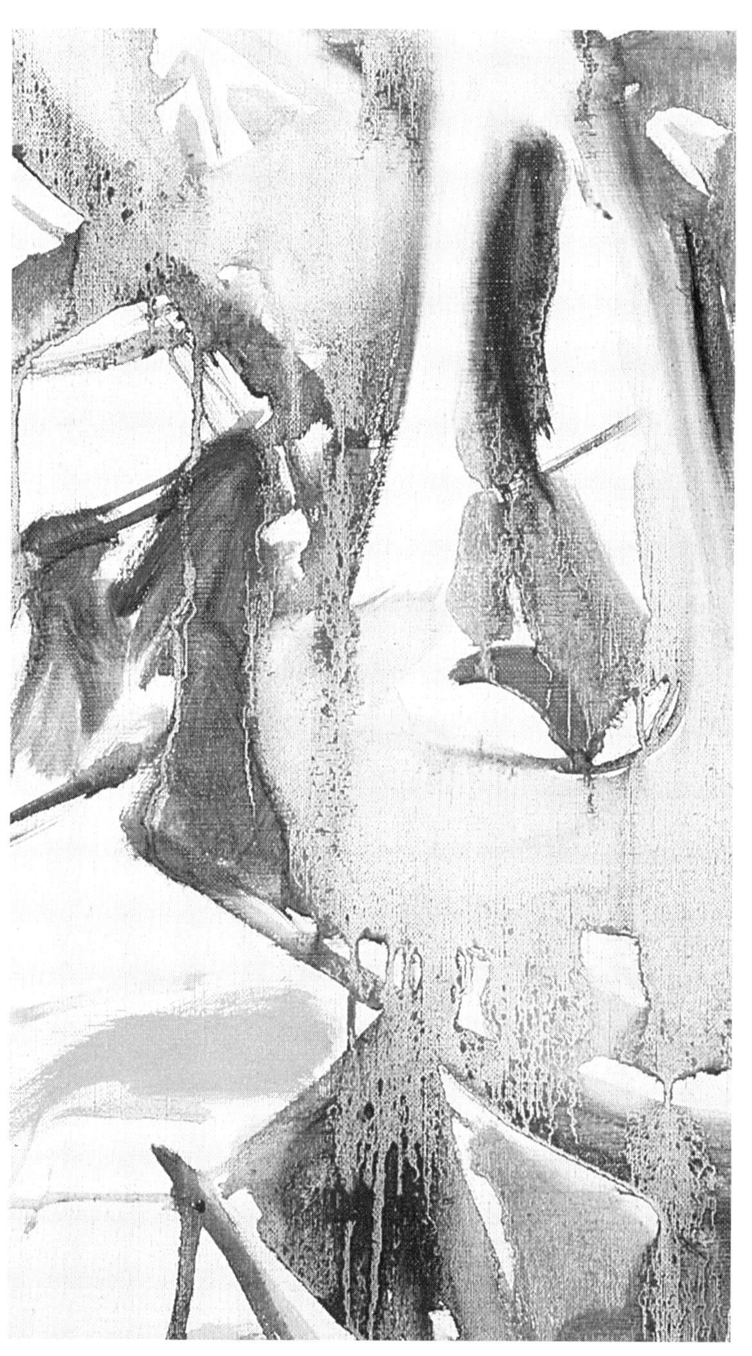

chapter 8

Enigma, Erasure, and Arshile Gorky's Afterlife

Is any of this important? Isn't it just gossip? We probably ought to feel ashamed at taking the voyeuristic, van Gogh's-ear interest in artists' lives that we do. But such interest needn't be entirely frivolous, especially at a time like the present when the questions of what an artist is and what an artist does have taken on renewed mystery and urgency. The dignified textbook stories of Gorky and early abstract expressionism—formalist à la Clement Greenberg, "heroic" à la Harold Rosenberg and others—have paled. Now we need our *Gorky.*

—PETER SCHJELDAHL

The simultaneously heroic and tragic details of Gorky biography form a grand narrative despite being built upon a foundation of indeterminacy. We do not know, for instance, the exact year and day of Gorky's birth. Like someone relating an oral history in a storytelling culture like that of his own Armenia, Gorky initiated a contrived history that has progressed to parabolic proportions. Critical interpretation of the artist, as evidenced in the previous chapter, is certainly itself subject to social conditions and cultural beliefs. In addition, biographies of the artist offer varying accounts, which, when examined, perhaps contribute to the creation of a new abstraction of the artist rather than a clarification. In the aftermath of his career, Gorky becomes a floating signifier within the history of modern painting, and his story, like modern art, becomes a process in itself.

In the contemporary world, we are fond of tracing trajectories that reveal an arc—the arc of a story, the arc of a life—but Gorky's art and life are not that tidy. Littered with bits and pieces of the real and remembered, present and past,

Opening image detail of plate 23.

and explanation and complication, the artist's work and life elude definition, a solid sequence, and even a singular theoretical model through which to explain them. Gorky slipped in and out of identities based on his audience; he floated back and forth between figural and abstract painting (his work often combining both); and he continued to revise compositions that remained in his studio regardless of what phase of his career they had been initiated, as he often used the most recent technique to improve older works. This book has tried to preserve Gorky's subtleties while forging an understanding of the artist based on explanations, analyses, and criticisms that address Gorky within a particular context and collection of themes that allow the artist and his art to be understood in an open-ended manner. "Creative man," as Carl Jung has declared, "is a riddle that we may try to answer in various ways, but always in vain."[1] Ultimately, Gorky's pursuit of Modernism drove him to produce art that made him significant enough in art history to bring attention to details of his biography, especially the Armenian Genocide, whether or not that was his intention. Gorky's contact with the canvas, then, has an immense sociopolitical meaning, and our encounters with his work reveal our perspectives as well.

Continuing attempts to explain both Gorky's art and life are evidence that he certainly has engaged us, although Gorky would probably be uncomfortable with the attention being paid to his personal struggles. Roland Barthes, in discussing the role of the author, says that "the *explanation* of a work is always sought in the man or woman who produced it, as it were always in the end, through more or less transparent allegory of the fiction, the voice of a single person, the *author* 'confiding' in us."[2] Gorky as the self-aware exile was measured and careful about what he confided. In a letter to Ethel Schwabacher, Gorky's wife noted his refusal to discuss personal details with others: "Once or twice in a letter to you and Wolf [Schwabacher's husband] I would make an allusion or write in a vein that was too personal, admitting too much of the difficulty of even just human discouragement or not even that. The letter had to be rewritten, Gorky would not allow it."[3] It was, his widow believed, a result of Gorky's cultural upbringing that he deemed it impolite to introduce personal difficulties into relationships with friends. Gorky's life, like his art, is revealed through a series of identity veils, neo-nostalgia, and the residues of a modern condition. Like his art, Gorky the individual lies outside specific depiction, allowing many often-competing theories about his art to coexist without collapsing the integrity of any. Perhaps, too, because of interest in Gorky's biography, the artist is more alive in his death than he was during his life.

The mutating nature of Gorky's biography makes evaluations of the artist and his art open-ended, making the supposition questionable that Gorky's work is, or ever can be, completely defined. Andrew Solomon refers to Gorky as "a mystery wrapped in an enigma";[4] an appropriate description, since it is hard to tell exactly where fiction ends and reality begins, or vice versa, which is exactly why champions of very different and sometimes opposing agendas claim him. The literature about Gorky, which includes biographical and art-historical studies as well as numerous exhibition catalogues, is diverse in breadth and point of view. Like his drawings and paintings, which fluctuate between the observed and the created, Gorky's performance of self and interpretations of him are perhaps *versions* of other coherencies.

The relationship of Gorky to his art and it to us is, however, exactly as it should be—vexed, complicated, and even ironic. In addition to asserting that Gorky is a spurious figure, Solomon notes how "there do not seem to be any people who had neutral feelings about Gorky, and so there is no one who speaks of him directly and honestly."[5] That Gorky is an enigma, that no one has neutral feelings about him, is just as much a part of his artwork as the indeterminacy of his biography or the contents of his paintings. As early as 1976, the art critic Hilton Kramer opined that there was indeed a need to separate the artist from the desire to mythologize him.[6] Only half a decade later, Peter Schjeldahl recounted Gorky's tragedies, but as the epigraph to this chapter indicates, he also wondered how such information could be used in redefining the idea of artist without mythologizing him. Schjeldahl admits that there is insight to be gained from entrenching Gorky's representation of our definition of an artist within the critical discourse of our time.

That Arshile Gorky is an enigma is due partially, as we have discussed, to his own self-fashioning in the form of his adoption of a pseudonym and portrayal of bohemian affectations. Contemporary explanations of the artist contribute to exaggerated characterizations. His biographers, for instance, portray Gorky variably as an exotic (in an Orientalizing vein), a prodigy, a con artist, and a genius.[7] Gorky is even depicted in a feature film, Atom Egoyan's *Ararat*, which exploits him as a tragic figure and victim. These renderings have perhaps cheapened Gorky's accomplishments and stigmatized him in the same way that Van Gogh's identity is tied to his cut ear, or that Frida Kahlo's tragedy has been emphasized to such a point that she has become a cult figure who appears on keychains, coasters, and napkins. In *Ararat*, for instance, Gorky is shown as a haunted individual in the tradition of Michelangelo in *The Agony and the Ecstasy*, Van Gogh in *Lust for Life*, and Jackson Pollock in *Pollock*. As Dore Ashton has observed, the fascination with Gorky is often tied to exoticism.[8]

Gorky's entry into popular culture compounds misunderstandings about his life and work that already exist, but examining the foundations of the mythologizations of artists may be useful here, since we need to deconstruct that myth before being able to elaborate upon it. Perhaps the intention of Gorky's biographers is, on some level, to address Gorky's myth—the one that he initially created himself through self-fashioning. The main problem with Gorky's biographies, however, in addition to their failing for the most part to consider *why* Gorky fashioned himself as he did, is that the narrative form of biography works against Gorky's own collage-like existence and the indeterminate qualities of his work. Addressing Gorky in a linear manner perhaps substantiates his continued mythologization. Embracing a postmodern turn, we see that Gorky's identity—like his art—emerges out of both the artist's state of mind and what others perceive that state to be. Discussions about Gorky are imbued with twentieth-century perpetuations of the "tragic artist" rather than restorying the experience of Arshile Gorky in a critical manner.

Initially, Gorky's life reflects a fairly standard rendition of an artist myth that adheres to a rubric through which greatness is measured. Ernst Kris and Otto Kurz have deconstructed the typical artist-narrative by establishing that stories about artists follow certain similar leitmotifs.[9] For instance, those whom we have deemed "great artists" are often described as child prodigies who are compelled to make art and forge ahead despite often being misunderstood because of their moody or brooding temperaments. Indeed, Gorky follows that formula: he supposedly didn't speak for years as young child; was exposed to and absorbed manuscript art; was gifted without training; was such a good artist when he came to America that he was offered a teaching position; worked incessantly, often feverishly drawing upon any surface available to him; and had extreme moods. Artists also have been instigated by tragic events to make art. If one adds to this mix Gorky's trauma from the Armenian Genocide, he fits this formula perfectly.

The first biography of the artist, published independently in 1978 by Gorky's nephew Karlen Mooradian, established the very characteristics that Kris and Kurz describe. Revealing at length Gorky's Armenian background, Mooradian wanted to rectify misinformation provided in Ethel Schwabacher's *Arshile Gorky*, the first study of the artist, and in numerous articles, whose authors Mooradian indicts even though their misinformation may have been provided to them by the artist himself. In a letter to Schwabacher from Gorky's widow, dated about six months after Gorky's death, it is evident that even she was unsure of his background, however. At one time, it appears, Gorky told her that his mother had died of a dog bite. In a reply to Schwabacher's inquiries about obtaining information from Gorky's sisters (one of whom was Mooradian's mother, Vartoosh), Agnes replied, "the sisters are rather mixed up and naturally there is a false pride and jealousy rampant among them, which was one reason G. hated to go see them."[10] Of course, Gorky might not have wanted to see them as well because they knew his true history, which he preferred not to be divulged to his wife.

It is this precarious situation that informs Mooradian's own inquiry. Mooradian was told stories by his mother, who had her own vantage point and possible agenda. Indeed, the recent biographies of the artist reveal that, depending on which sister was interviewed, it was she who claimed credit for financially supporting and encouraging Gorky, not the others. This contrast actually makes evident another crucial point that lines Gorky's antitrajectory: at some point he seems to have wanted to get away from his Armenian family, whether as a response to trauma, to continue hiding his true identity, or from a desire to start over, as suggested in earlier chapters.

Included in Mooradian's books are numerous letters allegedly written by Gorky to his sister and translated by Mooradian from Armenian. These letters provide some of the only statements by Gorky explaining his aesthetic theory and have been used by scholars to elucidate claims about Gorky's work. Because Mooradian refused to allow them to be seen and read in their untranslated form, they had been questioned for some time by the Armenian community, both for their authenticity and for the accuracy of Mooradian's translations. The letters, therefore, represent a crisis in Gorky scholarship, but they also further elaborate the effects of the Armenian Genocide on Gorky's story. Despite Gorky's ambitions, family was family, and Gorky did write letters to his sister Vartoosh. Any elaboration by Mooradian reflects a generational desire to reclaim his own heritage by enforcing a strict connection between Gorky's work and Armenia, but also perhaps his own need to be linked to his famous uncle. Regardless of whether the most significant letters that describe Gorky's connection to his heritage, and his debt to it in creating his art, actually exist, Mooradian changed the way that Gorky was ethnically identified and how his work was interpreted as linked to Armenia.[11] Mooradian's conjectures challenge what is authentic in the same way that Gorky's art does. Mooradian's letters, then, are not necessarily useless, because they offer an interpretation of the artist that fits so easily and well that scholars relied on them for decades without question. Mooradian's construction of Gorky's identity as an artist—insisting that his uncle's sources were solely Armenian rather than European—reflects Gorky's dilemma, and that of the Armenians, quite effectively. Certainly, the subject of Gorky is politically and emotionally charged because of the Armenian Genocide and Turkey's continued denial of it, and this too affects both remembrances of Gorky and interpretations of his art.[12] Mooradian's writings are nationalistic in tone, including arguments that Gorky's work is Armenian and almost exclusively based on Armenian manuscript painting rather than on the compositions of modern artists that Gorky studied and admired.

Nouritza Matossian's biography of Gorky reads like a flowery novel as she imagines scenes in Gorky's life. Matossian takes great liberties to define the thoughts and feelings of Gorky's dead mother toward him, and describes experiences that Gorky may have had, writing things like, "Hand in hand, the small boy walked with his tall, slender mother, she dressed in headscarf and long skirt, down the dirt track, along the lake, to the neighboring village of Koshk. He was lucky to be able to attend school, she told him."[13] Matossian's poetic fiction is used as the basis for an imaginary Gorky in Atom Egoyan's *Ararat* and her own one-woman show, in which she plays all of the people in Gorky's life, including the artist himself. The subjectivity of such interpretations, particularly of a biographer whose task should be to rectify the misinformation about the artist, not produce more, is ironic, and maybe even appropriate, because it mimics Gorky's own self-fashioning and ambiguous compositions. The Armenian biographer refashions the self and the narrative of Gorky's life in the same spirit as the artist had, Gorky's reasons being both self-serving and linked to the traumatic aftereffects of genocide. Matossian and Egoyan, who embraces her interpretation in his film, dramatize and fictionalize the artist who dramatized and fictionalized himself. These acts, like the artist's own self-fashioning and reference to the Genocide through both hints of a pre-Genocide world and the nondepiction of Genocide, move closer to, not further away from, the truth, because they move closer to Gorky's Armenian heritage and genocide trauma, even if the biographer and filmmaker can never know exactly what Gorky really experienced.

The myth that Mooradian, Matossian, and Egoyan perpetuate actually enforces Gorky's ethnic connection and therefore is a link to the Genocide and a culture that has all but disappeared. Such an attitude on the part of the Armenians who depict Gorky is itself quite ironic in light of Gorky's position in the Armenian community when he was alive. It does not seem that many Armenians of Gorky's generation took him seriously as an artist or even liked his art. Gorky was sometimes given a little financial help by Armenian restaurateurs or doctors, which he repaid with works of art. In most cases, that art was lost or destroyed because, despite Mooradian's claims for its kinship to Oriental carpets and medieval manuscript painting, it was not at all understood. Modernity was puzzling to the traditionalist Armenian diaspora, despite Armenians' past embrace of modern societies and cultures and relationship to industrialized society. In one instance, Gorky thanked a couple for a meal at their Armenian restaurant by giving them a drawing, which they referred to as scribbles and subsequently used to wrap fish.[14]

Recently, however, because of his recognition by the art world, Gorky has been used as a vehicle to support nationalism in the Armenian Republic. There has been a movement to disinter the artist and move his remains to Armenia, and the fraudulent letters Mooradian published have been republished in Armenia in earnest.[15] For Armenians, because of the continued denial of the Genocide, Gorky has become an emblem of Armenian perseverance and success. In order to understand the direness of the need for Armenians to make an Armenian connection, it is important to understand the generational aftereffects of the Genocide. Mooradian hails from the first post-Genocide generation of Armenians, those born or largely raised outside their homeland. Matossian, too, has an idyllic relationship to her homeland and to the Armenian diaspora who survived ethnic cleansing.

The pain suffered by Gorky's generation, however, was marked by attempts to assimilate even while connecting with other Armenians and feeling rightfully proud to be descended from a historic culture that had suffered so much. Such a reaction reflects a desire to escape from the victimization of an unrecognized or deemphasized injustice such as genocide, slavery, or rape.[16] Because its perpetrators have still not recognized the Armenian Genocide, victimization continues in the subsequent generations to which Mooradian, Matossian, and Egoyan belong. The generation that was physically victimized by acts so horrible that they could not talk about them is given a voice later by their children and grandchildren. The nature of memory creates a chain of experiences that passes from one generation to the next. This "postmemory" can be imbued with melancholia, which according to Judith Butler, conflates absence and loss and gives social power to the lost object. Matossian and Mooradian's generation brings the Genocide out into the open, and Egoyan's next generation insists on recognition and, in some cases, reparations.[17]

The disorienting effects of the Genocide, while evident in the discussion of Gorky thus far, culminate in the work of Atom Egoyan. A devotee of Gorky to the extent that he named a son Arshile, Egoyan represents a generation of Armenians both at odds with and trying to reclaim his heritage. Half Armenian, born in Cairo but raised in Canada, and having married the fellow–Armenian immigrant Arsinée Khanjian, who stars in most of his films, Egoyan has an awareness of his own intermediate status that plays out in his 1993 film *Calendar*.[18] *Calendar* is a loosely autobiographical account, starring Egoyan, in which he tries to come to terms with his Armenian heritage after a trip back to the old country with his wife, played by his real-life wife Khanjian. It is a physical and emotional search for reconciliation with one's displaced heritage. Juxtaposed with Gorky's negotiation of his identity in a new world is the question of how descendants reconcile their connection with the old world as a product of the new—how much of the past and traditions and identification with it does one retain? That was also Gorky's quest—how much does one retain of the past in the present, and to what extent can the viewer identify, or identify with, within the parameters of his or her own experience and context?

A short film he completed in 1998, *A Portrait of Arshile Gorky*,[19] is perhaps a foundation for Egoyan's inclusion of Gorky in the later *Ararat*. *A Portrait of Arshile Gorky* is essentially a home movie of Egoyan's son, Arshile, named in honor of the dead artist. This bizarre conflation of past and present extends the semeiotic analysis of Gorky's name change discussed earlier. The Armenian immigrant family gives their son a name that is a pseudonym chosen by an artist from the name of another artist, who took it himself as a pseudonym.

Through *A Portrait of Arshile Gorky*, Arshile Egoyan becomes the signifier for the artist Arshile Gorky. As the young Arshile, old enough to walk but not to speak, is filmed close-framed, the narrator, his father, explains to him the significance of his name: that he was named after a great artist who had suffered but who had painted a beautiful portrait of himself and his mother. A female speaking voice, that of young Arshile's mother (appropriate to the subject of the painting, *The Artist and His Mother,* that is being discussed), repeats the narration in Armenian. The child moves in and out of focus in extreme close-up and touches the camera lens, thereby both blocking the camera's voyeuristic gaze and often assaulting it with smudgy fingerprints, as if wanting to deny this heritage or protest against being saddled with such an imperative name history. The voices speak over haunting music, an occasional barking dog, the "ga-ga's" of the child, or street noise:

> "Arshile. You are named after a man who painted a portrait of himself and his mother."
>
> "You are named after a man who based this portrait on a photograph taken in 1912 in Van, Armenia."
>
> "The boy was eight."
>
> "His mother was a devoutly religious mother named Shushanik de Marderosian Adoian."
>
> "Her son, the person you're named after, was called Vosdanik. Your name is Arshile."
>
> "You are named after a man who adored his mother and was inspired by her love of nature and her pride in Armenian language."
>
> "You are named after a man who seven years after the photograph was taken would hold his mother in his arms and she died of starvation. The city was Yerevan."
>
> "The boy was fifteen."
>
> "You are named after a man who would look at his mother's face in this photograph and was afraid of disappointing her."
>
> "So Vosdanik Adoian changed his name to Arshile Gorky."
>
> "You are named after a man who changed his name because of what he thought he felt he remembered in his mother's face . . . because of what he felt when he remembered his mother's face."
>
> "His mother's face which now stares from a gallery wall into a land she never dreamed of."

The film was created after, as Egoyan explains in the DVD commentary, he and other directors were asked to meditate on a painting that meant a lot to them. It is, however, the persona of Gorky, understood through the biography of the artist, that Egoyan explores in *Portrait of Arshile,* and that he pushes further in his film *Ararat.*

Egoyan's *Ararat* is very much about the Genocide and denial of it. A film within a film, it is the story of a number of individuals whose lives become intertwined through the making of a film about the Armenian Genocide. Ani (played by Khanjian), an art historian who lectures about Gorky, is the main character.

After hearing one of her lectures, a movie producer and the director of a movie about the Genocide decide to incorporate Gorky into it as a character. Gorky appears in the movie as a mature painter working on *The Artist and His Mother* and as a boy during the siege by the Turks of the town in which Gorky, his mother, and his sisters were staying after his father left. Here Gorky is portrayed as a revolutionary fighter, and his close relationship to his mother is explained. The director of the film-within-the-film in *Ararat*, Saroyan (played by Charles Aznavour), and the producer, Rouben (Eric Bogosian), explain to Ani that they will take poetic license with Gorky in order to weave him into the events. In keeping with that approach, it is no surprise that aspects of the Egoyan film are based on Matossian's conjectural dramatized biography. *Ararat*, ironically, is like a Gorky painting: it encompasses multiple times, places, and perspectives and does not force a conclusion about Genocide onto the viewer, but allows the viewer to come to his or her own realization of his or her relationship to it. Each character in the movie has a very personalized reaction to the intersection of the past with the present.

The most significant and valuable scene in *Ararat* is one that is, in fact, deleted. Like many deleted scenes that are available on special-edition DVDs or in the "special features," it enlightens us on the motivations of the director in much the same way as the movie-within-a-movie plot explores the motivations of its own director and producer characters. In this scene, entitled "A Cruel Joke," Ani enters the portion of the set that represents Gorky's studio and begins speaking with the actor who plays Gorky. Because it reveals the randomness of Gorky's inclusion in the movie, if the scene had been included, it likely would have negated Gorky's purpose in the movie. The conversation is spoken in Armenian.

Ani asks the actor, "What's the matter?"

The actor replies, speaking as himself, "I feel this is a cruel joke. This man heard you give a lecture. He got excited about fitting Gorky into his film." And he continues from the vantage point of his character, "The coincidence over my childhood and the history he wanted to tell are irresistible. But the truth is that I don't need to be in this."

"That's not true," Ani protests.

"What is true?" he retorts, "My meaningful stories at the canvas I am painting? The picture I am looking at? I am conjured for a few days of shooting, then I will be discarded. No other artist has suffered what I have. Now, my life is reduced to a few scenes in a movie about someone else."[20]

Egoyan, in the commentary about the scene, explains that he wished to keep the scene in the movie and that people liked the argument, but they felt that the nature of the commentary was pretentious.[21] The audience's view of the scene as pretentious could be because it fingers the myth of the artist and audience's desire to think of Gorky as a mythological rather than self-aware character. And yet the power of this scene is that the Gorky character refers to himself as a constructed image. Gorky constructed an image of himself in life, which in death has been reconstructed by his biographers. This new version of Gorky is then presented to a mass audience in both the film *Ararat* and the fictional film within it, reinforcing the constructed image of the artist. We *want* the image of Gorky as a tragic artist. We want that myth. We want him to fit whatever needs we have for him and points we wish to make. We want the mythological, not the self-aware, Gorky. As Schjeldahl explains, "we need *our* Gorky."[22] Again, Egoyan himself is aware of his own reason for needing Gorky in the film: it helps him expose the Genocide and its lack of recognition, which is a significant part of his own identity as a second-generation displaced Armenian.[23]

The passages in the film that depict Arshile Gorky are themselves almost complete fictions, except that Gorky did paint the image of *The Artist and His Mother* from a photograph and sometimes painted to Armenian music in his studio. The nondepiction of the mother's hands in the work is explained in a dramatization that has the artist on his knees wiping them out in a fit of mourning and loss. Although Gorky was in Van during the siege, almost all actions depicted in the film are likely suppositions on the part of Egoyan, through the director, Saroyan, and from the biographical information from Matossian and Mooradian that Egoyan consulted. Just as the art historian Ani questions Rouben regarding the poetic license in making Mount Ararat visible from Van (which it is not), Rouben argues that the inclusion of the Gorky character in the film helps to tell the story. This seems to underscore Egoyan's reason for including the artist and Saroyan's rationalizations for doing so, and substantiates an argument that one cannot directly depict the horrors of a real genocide, but rather must story it through indirect images. Such storying provides the viewer adequate escapes from witnessing trauma while acknowledging that genocide is perpetuated by denial and is ever-present within the psyche of the individuals who had experienced it and their descendants.

Despite the difficulty of addressing the Armenian Genocide, non-Armenian scholars, writers, and biographers do try do deal with Gorky's background, which could hardly be avoided in a bibliography. Matthew Spender, married to Gorky's eldest daughter, Maro, focuses his biography, *From A High Place*, on Gorky's life in America, and particularly Gorky's life with Maro's mother, Agnes. Spender's tone suggests that he somewhat reluctantly includes information about the Armenian Genocide, and he gives little credit to the influence of Gorky's ethnic background. This is in direct contrast to Mooradian, for instance, who asserts that Gorky is motivated exclusively by his background. Spender's version of Gorky's life reads as if he doesn't quite trust the object of his research and almost as if he continues the Orientalizing critiques of the past.

Spender does, however, suggest at times a broader empathetic response to genocide and denial, as when he writes about *The Artist and His Mother* that

"Armenians of the Diaspora recognize in these works degrees of suffering about which those who are not Armenian know nothing. . . . As does no other work by an Armenian artist, it bears witness of the genocide of 1915."[24] Those affected by individual crimes, as well as crimes against humanity such as genocide, are often met with a lack of empathy from the unaffected, who can't understand why they don't just "get over" it. The Armenian Genocide happened almost a century ago, and still Armenians commemorate it every year on April 24, the day when the large-scale assault on the Armenians began in 1915. The point for Armenians is to keep marking the date until the Turkish government admits that it happened. Such a day acts as a memorial, activist statement, and designated time of mourning.

Despite Spender's tone,[25] in his book, because of its focus on Agnes, we find out about a great deal of Gorky's life in the 1940s, including previously unknown components of his private life such as Agnes's abortion and what appears to have been Gorky's abuse of her.[26] In a letter to Ethel Schwabacher just before the dissolution of the marriage, Agnes writes:

> It was a long struggle and possibly a wrong one before I realized that it was not one but three lives at stake. . . . Until the end I was still snatching at any straw that fell our way, money or a house, then a studio that would create the security he needed and relax his inner tension so that our problems could be solved more sanely and safely. The accident put an end to that effort, of that there can be no doubt . . . whether it would have failed anyway everyone but me seems to know. Perhaps I have said all these things to you . . . that our life . . . was what it seemed to be, it was love and painting and roses and thorns and dark and light, all the things that get lost in a survey of facts and analysis.[27]

Although Agnes does not speak in direct terms, she does give a telling indication of the troubled dynamics of the marriage and the artist's mental state.[28]

Hayden Herrera tries to differentiate her biography from other books and biographies on Gorky by analyzing some of Gorky's art in addition to cataloguing his life. In an earlier biography of Frida Kahlo, Herrera was clearly enticed by the tragic life of her exotic subject. As she did with Kahlo, Herrera objectifies Gorky, suggesting an Orientalist fascination similar to that of the nineteenth-century romanticists who were drawn to the sensuality of the Middle East. Much like Matossian, Herrera begins her biography like a melodramatic movie, recounting the story of the studio fire in 1945 that claimed many of Gorky's works. Then she jumps back to relate Gorky's early life chronologically, reiterating common information about the Armenian Genocide, family information originally provided in Mooradian's biography, and accounts of Gorky's life quoted from Matossian and Spender. Indeed, it is almost as if the narrative of

Gorky's early life was written by a different author or was a later addition after Herrera discovered its significance to the artist's oeuvre. Much of what the latter part of Herrera's book, like Spender's version, has to tell was provided by Gorky's widow from her private archives, and is reiterated by Herrera unquestioningly. Like Spender, whose proximity as Gorky's son-in-law, even though he never met the artist himself, affords him automatic credibility, Herrera has a certain status as Gorky's widow's goddaughter and former stepdaughter.

The ideas that both Spender and Herrera argue often appear to be Agnes's, and in a way, because she supplied so much information from her own perspective and because her life overlaps his late career, they end up writing her biography as much as Gorky's. "Mougouch" is often blamed for Gorky's suicide because of her fling with Umberto Matta Echaurren, the young, charming, and also married Surrealist painter. Although Mougouch was an asset and source of strength for Gorky even while she did not seem to fully understand him, likely because of his own dishonesty with her, a point that both biographers establish well, Gorky was jealous and volatile prior to the affair. Herrera and Spender rightly exonerate Agnes of any responsibility for Gorky's suicide.[29] As the discussion in this book suggests, Gorky's issues were deep-seated and existed long before he ever met the woman who would become the mother of his children. Indeed, his previous relationships with women, recounted especially well in Matossian's, Spender's, and Herrera's biographies, appear to establish a history that worked against any hope of the relationship with his Mougouch succeeding.

Despite any shortcomings and biases, and the impossibility of pigeonholing Gorky into a single narrative, each of these recent biographies may ultimately have a positive effect on Gorky scholarship. Matossian, Spender, and Herrera all try in some way to rectify the misinformation about Gorky's background, caused in a large part by the artist himself. It may be that only through so many different biographies, each in its own form with its own version of the truth, can Gorky's story can be told. It is the combination of these fractal identities that makes Gorky's biography part dream, linking it to Surrealism, and part struggle, exhibiting Abstract Expressionist angst.[30] As Harold Rosenberg writes, painting on canvas becomes an event or action.[31] This means that Gorky's life is just that—a struggle that is constantly working itself out. Gorky's life exists as a collage of pieces that are combined and overlaid through the action of the artist and the subsequent biographies that try to explain him, just as his artworks consist of various influences, shifting planes, and coagulations of different times and places.

A common pitfall in interpreting Gorky and his work is to believe that there is only one answer or one possible meaning to a painting or drawing. The same is true of his biographies. Unlike Mooradian and Herrera, both Spender and Matossian seemed to have realized that because much of Gorky's life cannot be verified, their biographies would likely not be definitive. Perhaps this is why they differ on some points about Gorky's life and why they are both subtitled "A" (not "The") *Life of Arshile Gorky*. Peter Schjeldahl expresses the dilemma of Gorky's biography:

> What is the significance of Gorky's biography for his art? In a familiar way—promulgated by T. S. Eliot as the "dissociation" of "the man who suffers" from "the mind that creates"—there is none. Even in as explicit a painting as *Agony*, it is the mind's joy in creation, not the ghastly suffering of the man, that we mainly feel. In another way, though, Gorky's horrible personal insecurity, locked in tension with his aesthetic idealism, is what grips our artistic as well as human interest. No detached, problem-solving spirit motivates someone to undergo first the abject self-effacements and then the huge risks that Gorky embraced.[32]

Against everything, we may want to continue to adhere to a myth of the artist's brilliance and tragedy. If we insert Gorky into such a role, founded upon a narrative into which he does not neatly fit, we can produce a myth. As Schjeldahl has declared, "we need our Gorky."[33] We desire closure, we want to know his narrative for certain, but the very nature of Gorky's life and his position in the world and art history defy that—as does the very nature of his art itself. Gorky's biography—and varying versions of it—will just have to suffice toward that purpose, but the most truthful and accurate story is perhaps reflected in our readings of his art.

Gorky, his life, and his art were evanescent. He left Watertown, Massachusetts, and changed his name as a way to remove himself from being Armenian; he went to New York City to become an artist as a way of not becoming American; he used but did not repeat exact images in his art; and he addressed but never expressed visual reality in his work. Any purportedly definitive biography will perhaps be an ill-fated attempt to pinpoint an artist whose irreconcilable nature reflects the social experience of Modernism.

As Harold Rosenberg observes, "no doubt art took on for Gorky so total a function because there was little else in his life."[34] Embracing a postmodern turn, we see that Gorky's identity—like his art—emerges out of both the artist's state of mind and what others perceive that state to be. Discussions about Gorky are imbued with twentieth-century constructions of the "tragic artist" perpetuated by various authors. The recent biographies of the artist, which are attempts to clarify misinformation provided by the artist himself, perhaps muddy Gorky's own attempts at self-definition and the myth that is inherent in his biography. But maybe that, too, fits what Gorky wanted. Maybe in terms of Gorky's life, as of his art, there is no one resolution, nor one story or linear narrative. Gorky's own stories about himself, and others about him, also act contrapuntally and also collage an identity of not only Gorky the artist, but the general conception of "the artist." Like the floating forms in Gorky's art, which hint at the presence of figures and ground but do not seem anchored to an identifiable space or appear to be nameable, Gorky's life floats in and out of the verifiable and the constructed. His identity is malleable, and his biography is equally so, making each, along with his paintings, part of a semeiosis that is relative to whoever is looking at the painting or telling the story. Perhaps, then, Gorky's art is truly American not only because of his immigrant history, but because it is the ultimate universal experience, an experience that is democratized because everyone has the opportunity to read his or her own meaning from it. Similar to a Peircian traveling sign, Gorky's significance travels through time and, as the biographies establish, is relative to an individual's experience. In the end then, we do, each of us, have *our* Gorky.

While I address the particular vantage points of the biographers, critics, and art historians, I am not immune to bias myself. If Gorky has been discussed in many different ways because he is a vehicle for a variety of people and groups, then for some, perpetuating Gorky's myths about himself was useful, and for others, discounting them was equally so. Our views about his work are part of our biases—my own included. My grandparents were of Gorky's generation and, like him, escaped the Armenian Genocide. Only my mother's side of the family is Armenian, I was not raised as part of an Armenian community (although not far from Gorky's Watertown, Massachusetts, which I frequented while growing up), and both during childhood in a largely working-class town and in my professional life as an academic I have lived under a French Canadian, not an Armenian, name. My background has allowed me to recognize the effects of the Armenian Genocide on Gorky yet maintain some distance from it. Although I am likely driven by the second-generation Armenian's desire for justice and clarity, I am also driven as an art historian to see Gorky's story as a subject that enlightens us to a style of art and an era of great significance within the discipline.

Agony reflects the emotion of Gorky's late career not through recognizable images, but with the use of glaring reds and his tensile black line, thinned and curved, connecting the composition like exposed nerves. The black lines act as inaccurate boundaries to sections of the painting, incised into the painting, cutting in and out of it. These thin nerve-like lines reflect the stretched, almost snapped nerves of Gorky's life. But Gorky was neither hero nor victim; he was perhaps, in the words of Paul Brach, an artist of mythic proportions: "For me, Gorky was the last mythic artist. . . . He was mythic because of his flamboyant personal style, his self-invented name and life story and his tragic suicide. . . . Most of all he was mythic because he was gone before he arrived."[35] Gorky's self-fashioning, personal style, and suicidal end, rather than his tragic biography, seem to be part of an elaborate process of becoming in which each successive stage of a drawing or subsequent painting in a series is part of earlier or later ones.

André Breton remarked that "living and ceasing to live are imaginary solutions. Existence is elsewhere."[36] Could it be that the answers to Gorky's art lie elsewhere, outside of his paintings? Not in his biography, but in the misrepresentation and misinterpretation of it. Not in his paintings, but in the discourse between the many interpretations of them. We have observed—or have unobserved or extricated—that what is significant in Gorky's art is often what is not there: the abstraction, the painting outside of the lines rather than the definition of them, the nonrepresentation of the literal, the conscious forgetting of history or overlooking the present in lieu of some sweet past that in itself likely did not exist. Gorky had lived through his art, and since he could no longer do art, his death was by his own hand. Arshile Gorky was extinguished by the will of the artist just as he had been created, in a necessary resolution to his complicated exilic oeuvre.

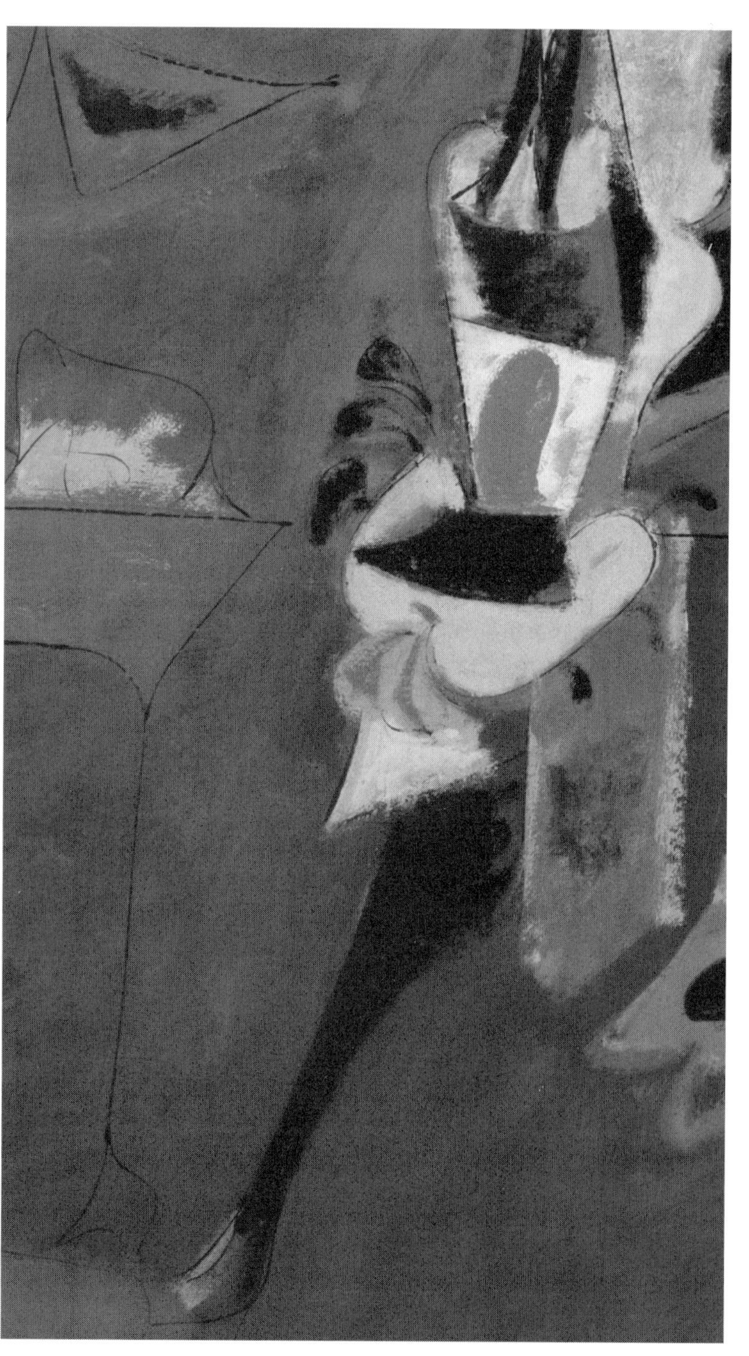

Conclusion

I am an individual—Gorky—and it is my individual feeling which counts the most. Why? I do not know nor do I wish to know. I accept it as a fact which does not need explanation.

—ARSHILE GORKY

A long time has passed since Gorky's sister Vartoosh insisted to the staff of the Museum of Modern Art in the mid-1950s that the artist's nationality on the wall label to the 1947 painting *Agony* was incorrect and should be changed from "Russian" to "Armenian." Currently, most museums label Gorky's works something like "Arshile Gorky, American, born Armenia," and some list his original surname, but for the Armenian community it is quite understandable that this often is not enough. Gorky has become an icon for Armenians, proof that Turkey has not yet succeeded in removing them from the world, even though it has effectively removed them from Turkey. Like the story of David and Goliath, or the similar success of the Armenian David of Sassoon, Gorky has become a metaphor for Armenians' ultimate triumph over the Turks, in which intellect, culture, and civilization overcome ignorance, barbarism, and oppression.

The stories of other survivors are useful in analyzing Gorky's conduct and its relationship to the Genocide as well as his place in new world culture. Mariam Davis, a good friend of Gorky's who was married to the photographer

Opening image detail of plate 25.

Wyatt Davis (brother of Gorky's one-time friend Stuart Davis), was also Armenian, and spoke of the experience as one she was expected to forget. Orphaned in the Genocide and subsequently adopted by an American family, she was told never speak of her experience, but to leave it behind and become Americanized. Clearly suffering from posttraumatic stress disorder, Mariam had nightmares as her memories of the Genocide welled up in her subconscious.[1]

Because the perpetrators of the Genocide, the Turkish government, still deny that the Armenian Genocide ever happened, it continues to affect the Armenians. This denial, therefore, perpetuates trauma for the survivors and descendants of the Genocide. Like the families of missing persons or the victims of rape or other crimes where the criminal is never caught, they have had no closure and no peace of mind. The situation is worsened by the fact that Turkey funds research, publications, and propaganda (often through top American research institutions) actively denying that the Genocide ever happened.[2] Ultimately, Gorky's objective was never activist, to bring attention to the Genocide, nor was it dismissive, to elude his past or his background entirely. As we have seen, he embraced it as a subject for his work. The artist Robert Jonas explained that

> Gorky's Armenian past saturated his consciousness. You felt it all the time, as if he was never really here, as if his umbilical cord to his past was never broken. Gorky's works have Armenian warmth and dancing quality. Artists were for a long time stuck with cubism. They wanted to break through it, to free themselves from its rigors and strictures. It had imposed upon them a strict, planned discipline. It was Gorky who first broke through cubism with his poetic imagery. It was the poetic-laden shapes of his brushes that opened the way. Gorky never reached the public. He had a passionate love for the past, a love for art of the past. And he had to break through and translate what he knew as an Armenian before he became Gorky and the germinating force behind the abstract expressionist movement.[3]

Gorky marked the beginning of a shift in consciousness in the art world, where European art had always taken precedence over American art. Gorky was on the cutting edge of a transition that he helped to create and that would eventually solidify after World War II and, unfortunately, the artist's death.

In Abstract Expressionism, the artist is the subject of the painting, but as Howard Singerman has pointed out, "the artist, or again this life of the artist, is always out of time and place."[4] Gorky's stories about himself and the conflations of time, space, and place in his art perhaps emerge out of the same desire to forget or insistence on forgetting. Although Gorky was indicted for his tall tales, as we ourselves could indict his biographers, such misinformation, whether intentional and accidental, is perhaps part of the legacy of genocide. One observant woman, Florence Chakerian, who married an Armenian man, has explained that her husband, like Gorky, "also told tall tales (especially to wide-mouthed children who believed every word). He, too, would give directions to women to do this or that. He, too, loved singing, and flying about brandishing a shish kebab poker, leaping upon chairs—(one fine piece broke down). And he, too, had that old world dignity, reticence and yes, innocence. And underlying it all was a melancholy for he too was orphaned very young."[5] Gorky's relationship to his own tall tales may be similar because he too had a compulsion to perpetuate them. Gorky asserted his individuality by co-opting the words of someone else. Repeating Gaudier-Brzeska,[6] Gorky claimed precedence for the feelings of the individual, which, in contemporary society in particular, take precedence. Eventually, like the main character in *Beast on the Moon*, Gorky was overcome by loss. Raoul Hague said that Gorky, on their last encounter, sadly revealed his operation to his old-country friend and that Hague did not believe him, thinking he was joking, in the way that the city-born Hague and the country-born Gorky often teased each other back and forth. The downward spiral of the artist, his jealousy over his young wife and the mask of security about his art that he forged at a time when Abstract Expressionism was gaining hold, seemed to be a continuation of a turbulent internal dialogue. Margaret Osborne believed that Gorky

> had a very curious combination of absolute confidence and tremendous doubt. It was part of his makeup. He had a terrific streak of humility but it was a terrible punishment. He inflicted a great deal of punishment on himself. He went through periods of great despair about his work, and great despair about whether people were really paying any attention to it and how it went. I don't think he ever was vain or conceited about his work. But I think he must have intuitively known what an extraordinary artist he really was. When he spoke about painting, he spoke with a great deal of confidence and understanding, and sometimes with a considerable amount of arrogance. Gorky was a very complicated man.[7]

Indeed, Gorky always felt a longing and loneliness, even, it seems, when he was successful. As early as spring 1939, Gorky's works in Paris were received well and published in *Cahiers d'Art*, and he welcomed the attention of André Breton. Still, he seems often to have felt as if there was no place for him in the world and that people were unreliable and unable to understand.[8]

Perhaps this is part of what Cathy Caruth explains as evidence of a "wound culture:

> The nature of losses varies with the nature of events and responses to them. Some losses may be traumatic while others are not, and there are variations in the intensity or devastating impact of trauma. There are of course also particular losses in all societies and cultures, indeed in all

> lives, but the ways in which they might be confronted differ from the responses more suited to absence. When absence and loss are conflated, melancholic paralysis or manic agitation may set in, and the significance or force of particular historical losses (for example, those of apartheid or the Shoah) may be obfuscated or rashly generalized. As a consequence one encounters the dubious ideas that everyone (including perpetrators or collaborators) is a victim, that all history is trauma, or that we all share a pathological public sphere or a "wound culture."[9]

In the case of denial, Armenians are left with an open wound. Remembering, as Susan Sontag would argue, is an ethical act. The impact of trauma on Gorky, it seems, is reflected in his eventual suicide and his conflation of absence and loss upon his wife's departure. Scrawling "Goodbye My Loveds" on a nearby wall, Gorky's act repeats the battle between a broken body and death that was revealed in Anton Chekhov's "The Black Monk," which Julien Levy has noted that Gorky was reading at the time.[10]

Gorky's situation, trajectory, and myth go far beyond the artist himself or the plight of the Armenians, however, especially if we understand that Gorky's primary drive was produce art. He may have come to that through his traumatic or immigration experience, but his predicament is actually a marker for twentieth-century art, which is an individual expression, often of personal identity and trauma, particularly in the art of the 1980s and 1990s, when diversity and multiculturalism came to the fore and artists directly expressed their experiences rather than couching them in abstraction.

The majority of articles, studies, and books on Gorky have appeared only within the last thirty years, with increasing frequency.[11] This resurgence is due partly to renewed interest in abstraction and reevaluations of the Abstract Expressionists in American art, reflecting a new art history conscious of ethnic, social, and political influences.[12] As a vehicle for many different people and groups, Gorky has been linked to America, modern art, and his Armenian background in various ways. Harold Rosenberg placed Gorky with the Abstract Expressionists, Gorky's nephew Karlen Mooradian separated him from the modern tradition and highlighted Gorky's Armenian roots (which, as we have seen, are not mutually exclusive, but complementary), and still others, such as Harry Rand and Peter Balakian, have read Gorky's abstractions iconographically[13] Both of the latter interpretations are Aesopian in the way that they see Gorky as conveying innocent forms to the outsider and a hidden meaning to the initiated. The art historian may well be privy to Gorky's code or his camouflaged places, and the Armenian may be privy to images that reflect the Genocide, but Gorky wanted everyone to connect to his work on a fundamental level so that it could be a reflection of ourselves and our own experience. "Understanding" the pictures on Gorky's terms gives us power over them as well as the artist we have revealed,[14] but if we understand them on our own terms, the connection is personal and emotional and mimics the artist's own connection. The Genocide, Gorky's experience as an immigrant, and his longing and loneliness in the world translate into painting in many ways—likeness/difference, recognizable/abstract, and remembered/invented—but perhaps the foremost quality of his work that originated in his experiences was empathy. Reuben Nakian, Gorky's good friend and fellow Armenian, explained the empathy that Gorky attained in his work and that he wanted to convey to the viewer:

> Once in the good old days, maybe around 1938 or so, Gorky and I were sitting on a bench by the lake in Central Park. And there were pigeons around, and one of them was hurt and about to drown. And we watched as a man from a nearby peanut stand waded in the water to rescue it. So when it was over, Arshile turned to me and said, "My God, I felt the agony you had." I had been worried and felt we should jump in the water to save it, when we saw the other man doing it. But I didn't say a word and just sat there, and he felt my alarm just as though he had the ability to feel right through me. He had that uncanny, that mystic quality, an amazing ability to perceive things deep down inside.[15]

The quality of empathy that Gorky's work achieves makes it readable to the viewer on personal terms, and the "true meaning" of his work seems to escape only the art historians, biographers, and viewers who cannot experience it on an empathetic level or solely experience it in reference to Gorky.

Any approach to Gorky's work must also embrace his approach to painting as an act of discovery that should produce a similar act of discovery in those who encounter it. One might see aspects that look identifiable, but also embrace the shapes, line, and color that are Gorky's visual vocabulary. During a cross-country road trip with his soon-to-wife and Isamu Noguchi, Gorky wanted to play a game that identified images in the shape of the clouds. For Noguchi, the clouds were nothing more than clouds, but for Gorky they could be anything, and he tried hard to find similarities to the recognizable from his point of reference. Such a game for Gorky was an act of discovery and possibility, just like his painting. Dore Ashton has explained that painting, especially its physical properties, was for Gorky an act of discovery and, like his embrace of Surrealist analogy, a manifestation of the marvelous, the magical, and the alchemical. The medium and his imagination were his methodology. "These sensuous effects, endemic to the art of the oil painter, are more telling than any identification of a Turkish slipper or Armenian plough, or Virginia fireplace."[16] Gorky's friend Milton Resnick made a keen observation about the artist's poetic and personal objectives: "One thing was very important to Gorky. And that is that whatever it was that he was doing, there was always a moment when his picture suddenly spoke to him. It was a moment of breathlessness. It was that moment when it gasped with life. That kind of instantaneous quality seemed more important to Gorky than any of the categories that people later credited him with creating or influencing."[17] Gorky often painted in series, developing an idea through many versions, but these can be viewed as thematic explorations rather than historic progressions. Gorky's work, although it may be based on observed forms, transforms objects and images through abstraction so that they have new roles and meanings that have attained that moment of crystallization. Perhaps Gorky's biographers and the scholars who write about him do the same thing; that is, each of their works is a thematic exploration offering interpretations that together shed light on the artist. We are left now with a plethora of material to combine and interpret. Just like Gorky, we can't go back, we can only go forward, but we have to do so with snippets of images and themes that may never yield an entirely coherent revelation of the artist and his work. In the end, we must take the information contained in scholarly analyses, biographies, films, and the works themselves and synthesize them into a new understanding of Gorky's art—itself a new synthesis that represents a universal story.

My nonlinear, collage-like study relies on many types of sources and writers who have gone before, but it has also recombined their findings into new interpretations. As we have seen throughout this book, these interpretations, like our insistence that Gorky's art be read in its full plasticity, are plastic in themselves, meant to be read differently by different people, but ultimately, to enlighten each reader to the essence of Arshile Gorky and his art so that everyone's understanding of the artist is "universally individual." We all need not hold the exact same interpretations of the artist and his art, but rather the art should resonate with us all in some manner regardless of the different personal experiences that we bring to the encounter with the art.

Gorky the individual is, as I suggested in the introduction to this book, a punctum that opens up and out to many ideas about representations of the idea of "artist." As this study has revealed, Gorky's art acts as punctum in other ways as well. As Barthes has said, the significance of a punctum, in Barthes' case a photograph, is revealed only after the fact, when it is no longer present. This is perhaps the reason that, with artists like Gorky, we fail to see their significance until long after their passing. Gorky was, however, punctal in the truest sense because his work gave way to and opened up possibilities to other artists—the Abstract Expressionists; second-generation New York School artists such as Helen Frankenthaler, Sam Francis, and Joan Mitchell; and, I would also argue, Postmodern artists, especially those practicing in the 1970s and 1980s, whose work focused on identity, particularly their own. Furthermore, Gorky is a punctum because through his work, which is a combination of times, places, and spaces, he opens viewers to many and simultaneous interpretations of it. Gorky's work is not linear but punctal in its form of semitransparent veils of color that also shadow veils of artist's history, emotions, and life. It is my hope that this book is also a punctum in the way that it opens study of the artist's life and art to many possibilities that can exist simultaneously. The indeterminacy of the artist and his art are wonderfully freeing in the end, producing universality through their manner of engaging the individual, and that is the ultimate point that the artist was trying to make.

In the epigraph that opened this study, Peter Schjeldahl asked if Gorky had made it. Had he joined the ranks of the masters? What exactly constitutes greatness? And in the end, does any of that matter? Are we the ones to appreciate his self-inventing, reckless grace? "The attainment of individuality against ridiculous odds," says Schjeldahl, "is right up our alley." Our exploration of Gorky's journeys, our interpretations of the artist and his oeuvre, and our *own* attainment of individuality against ridiculous odds are perhaps a version of grace. An individual and perhaps deeply personal understanding of the artist and his art, is indeed, right up our alley.

Notes

Introduction

1. The resolution to Gorky's placement in art history, as well as his significance, however, was somewhat mitigated by Paul Schimmel in his 1986 exhibition The Interpretive Link, in which he categorized Gorky as an Abstract Surrealist. Schimmel defines Abstract Surrealism, which was not a recognized stylistic movement, as a tendency in art that used or was inspired by aspects of Surrealism while it developed an abstract vocabulary. Paul Schimmel, *The Interpretive Link: Abstract Surrealism into Abstract Expressionism: Works on Paper, 1938–48* (Newport Beach, Calif.: Newport Harbor Art Museum, 1986).

2. Diane Waldman, *Arshile Gorky, 1904–1948: A Retrospective* (New York: Harry N. Abrams, 1982), 60.

3. Nouritza Matossian, *Black Angel: A Life of Arshile Gorky* (London: Chatto and Windus, 1998); Matthew Spender, *From a High Place: A Life of Arshile Gorky* (New York: Knopf, 1999); and Hayden Herrera, *Arshile Gorky: His Life and Work* (New York: Farrar, Strauss and Giroux, 2003).

4. The major studies are those completed by the late Melvin P. Lader, the foremost scholar on the artist, particularly in his seminal *Arshile Gorky* (New York: Abbeville Press, 1985).Other scholarship includes Harry Rand in *Arshile Gorky: The Implications of Symbols* (Montclair, N.J.: Allanheld and Schram, 1980), and Waldman, *Arshile Gorky*.

5. This is the premise of the first book ever written on the artist, Ethel Schwabacher's *Arshile Gorky Memorial Exhibition*, exh. cat. (New York: Whitney Museum, 1951), which was revised into her book *Arshile Gorky* (New York: Macmillan, 1957). This point is further illustrated by Gorky's friend and colleague Balcomb Greene, who remembers a lecture by Schwabacher in which she said, "Gorky wouldn't want us to write about him personally. He wouldn't care to become a legend. After one is gone, it's the paintings that count." See Balcomb Greene, "Memories of Arshile Gorky," *Arts Magazine* 50, no. 7 (1976): 108.

6. Elaine de Kooning, "Gorky: Painter of His Own Legend," *Art News* 49 (January 1951): 40.

7. There are numerous stories of Gorky taking over the floor at artists' meetings and pontificating about this or that artist, and according to Elaine de Kooning, he "loved to have a spectator or two while he painted." Ibid.

8. For instance, when Mooradian's mother Vartoosh allowed Nouritza Matossian to look at the letters, Matossian could not find evidence that many of the letters existed. See Matossian, *Black Angel*, 496–98. These letters were significant because although written in Armenian, which Mooradian supposedly translated himself, they enumerate Gorky's aesthetic theories and philosophy about art, whereas very little exists otherwise.

9. Some article-length inquiries apply theory to Gorky's work. The most notable is Jack Ben-Levi, "A Sadomasochistic Drama in an Age of Traditional Family Values," in *Abject Art: Repulsion and Desire in American Art* (New York: Whitney Museum, 1993), 17–32.

10. There have been a number of exhibitions of various sizes in both art museums and private galleries, including, a 1995 exhibition of Gorky's late abstract paintings at the National Gallery of Art in Washington, D.C., two shows at the Gagosian Gallery in New York City (which represents the artist's estate), and a comprehensive exhibition of drawings at the Whitney Museum of American Art in November 2003, organized by the late Melvin P. Lader. Michael Taylor of the Philadelphia Museum of Art recently organized a major retrospective of the artist's career.

11. Dore Ashton appears to agree with Schimmel's conception by suggesting that perhaps we should stop trying to pin Gorky to a particular art movement, allow him to be an Abstract Surrealist, and finally move on to other examinations of his oeuvre. See Ashton, "Crisis and the Perpetual Resolution," in Schimmel, *Interpretive Link*, 29–32; and Ashton, "A Straggler's View of Gorky," in *Arshile Gorky: The Breakthrough Years*, ed. Michael Auping (New York: Rizzoli, 1995), 39–61.

12. Jim Jordan explores this sequencing somewhat, and redates some works. See "The Paintings of Arshile Gorky: New Discoveries, New Sources, and Chronology," in *The Paintings of Arshile Gorky: A Critical Catalogue*, by Jim Jordan and Robert Goldwater (New York: New York University Press, 1982), 7–103. Although some museums and scholars have on occasion reconsidered dates given by the artist, we likely have the most to learn about the artist's process through scientific methods. A few paintings have thus far been subjected to X ray, mostly for the purpose of conservation, but there are promising possibilities for scholars as these works are reexamined in this manner.

13. E. de Kooning, "Gorky," 40.

14. This is discussed in detail in the subsequent chapters, but Gorky seems to have been a proponent of indeterminate art that precipitated multivalent and universal interpretations.

15. It is significant to note that my serious inquiry into

Gorky in the fall of 1992 and the initial undertaking and ideas presented here predate the publication of most contemporary material on the artist. My theories about the artist, therefore, predate the publication of all three biographies of the artist and the Peter Balakian essay that relates Gorky's work to the Armenian Genocide (although my approach was somewhat different, I wrote a paper for during my master's degree that identified some of the issues that Balakian raised). All of my work has been available through a thesis, dissertation, and public presentations, and on at least one occasion I spoke directly with one of the biographers. In that case, I inspired a fundamental shift in the author's thinking and resulting publication by insisting that just because Gorky did not discuss the Armenian Genocide with Mougouch, it did not mean that it was not a significant aspect in his life.

16. See Hayden V. White, "Historical Emplotment and the Problem of Truth in Historical Representation," in *Figural Realism: Studies in the Mimesis Effect* (Baltimore: Johns Hopkins University Press, 1999), 27–42.

17. "Stuart Davis," *Creative Art* 9 (September 1931): 217.

18. See Herschel B. Chipp, "Contemporary Art," in *Theories of Modern Art: A Source Book by Artists and Critics*, ed. Herschel B. Chipp, Peter Selz, and Joshua C. Taylor (Berkeley: University of California Press, 1968), 510–19.

19. Dorothy C. Miller, ed., *Fourteen Americans* (New York: Museum of Modern Art, 1946), 8.

20. Harold Rosenberg, "The American Action Painters," in *the Tradition of the New* (New York: Horizon Press, 1959), 27.

21. Saying, for instance, that he had studied with Wassily Kandinsky, when in fact he had no training.

22. All translations of Armenian names follow the Western Armenian conventions since this is true to Gorky's original dialect. With the exception of Nouritza Matossian, biographers and writers use the Eastern dialect of Armenian, which tends to exchange the "g" for "k" in words and names. The original translation, and possibly mistranslations, occurred because Gorky did spent some time in Eastern Armenia and because Karlen Mooradian used the Eastern dialect in his biography of Gorky. Karlen's mother was Gorky's sister Vartoosh and along with his father, Moorad, frequented Eastern Armenia as it became the Armenian Republic.

23. We can trace these types of fictions at least all the way back to the Renaissance in the words of others, such as Michelangelo, as well. Vasari, for instance, often made up anecdotes about artists in his *Lives of the Artists*. A detailed, enlightening, and entertaining discussion of Vasari's fictions can be found in Paul Barolsky's *Why the Mona Lisa Smiles and Other Tales by Vasari* (University Park: Pennsylvania State University Press, 1991). Michelangelo's self-creation is discussed extensively in Barolsky's *Michelangelo's Nose: A Myth and Its Maker* (University Park: Pennsylvania State University Press, 1990).

24. Identity is defined by critic Harold Rosenberg in "The American Action Painters" (31) as a paramount theme, conceptualizing art as a creation that "brings the artist literally into the picture." See Rosenberg, "Arshile Gorky: Art and Identity," in *The Anxious Object* (New York: Horizon Press, 1964), 100–101.

25. Meyer Schapiro, interview by Karlen Mooradian, in *The Many Worlds of Arshile Gorky* (Chicago: Gilgamesh Press, 1980), 200.

26. Schwabacher, *Arshile Gorky*, 49.

27. See Maurice Merleau-Ponty, "Eye and Mind," in *Art in Theory, 1900–1990: An Anthology of Changing Ideas*, ed. Charles Harrison and Paul Wood (Cambridge, Mass.: Blackwell, 2000), 751.

28. Peter Schjeldahl, "The Great Gorky," *Village Voice*, May 13–19, 1981, 101.

29. André Breton, "Arshile Gorky," in *Surrealism and Painting*, trans. Simon Watson Taylor (New York: Harper and Row, 1972), 200.

30. Margaret Osborne, "The Mystery of Arshile Gorky: A Personal Account," *Art News* 61, no. 10 (1963): 42.

31. Some misinformation about the artist stemmed from his own statements that writers such as Ethel Schwabacher, Harold Rosenberg, and others repeated. In addition, a collection of letters that has been used by art historians to substantiate interpretations of Gorky's art was likely forged by their publisher and Gorky's nephew, Karlen Mooradian. See sources listed in subsequent note for elaborations.

32. Homi K. Bhabha, *The Location of Culture* (New York: Routledge, 1994), 10.

33. See Roland Barthes, *Camera Lucida: Reflections on Photography*, trans. Richard Howard (New York: Hill and Wang, 1981).

34. Ibid., 57.

35. Ibid., 59.

36. E. de Kooning, "Gorky," 63.

37. This refers to Jacques Derrida's theory of *différance*. See Jacques Derrida, "Différance," in *Critical Theory Since 1965*, ed. Hazard Adams and Leroy Searle (Tallahassee: Florida State University Press, 1986), 120.

Chapter 1

1. Duncan Macmillan, "The Outsider: Gorky and America," *Art International* 23, nos. 3–4 (1979): 105.

2. Howard Singerman, *Art Subjects: Making Artists in*

the American University (Berkeley and Los Angeles: University of California Press, 1999), 26–27.

3. Janet Wolff, *Resident Alien: Feminist Cultural Criticism* (Cambridge: Polity, 1995), 7.

4. Although I disagree with the conclusion that for Gorky biography was something to hide behind, Elaine de Kooning does suggest that the specifics were not important, only the telling of the tale: "A biography, as Arshile saw it, like a beard or a moustache, was something convenient to hide behind. Thus, from various accounts, all his own, he was born in three different countries in three different years (Tiflis, Russia, 1904, was, for some reason, his favorite choice)." Elaine de Kooning, "Gorky: Painter of His Own Legend," *Art News* 49 (January 1951): 40.

5. E. H. Gombrich, *In Search of Cultural History* (Oxford: Clarendon Press, 1969), 41.

6. The term "Armenian Genocide" refers to the systematic annihilation of the Armenian population in Turkey, which occurred over an extended period of time but culminated in 1915. For contemporary accounts of what became known as the Armenian Genocide, see Henry Morgenthau, *Ambassador Morgenthau's Story* (Garden City, N.Y.: Doubleday, Page, 1918); and Clarence D. Ussher, with Grace H. Knapp, *An American Physician in Turkey: A Narrative of Adventures in Peace and War* (Boston: Houghton Mifflin, 1917). For a history of the Armenian Genocide, see Vahakn N. Dadrian, *The History of the Armenian Genocide: Ethnic Conflict from the Balkans to Anatolia to the Caucasus*, 4th rev. ed. (New York: Berghahn Books, 2003); Yves Ternon, *The Armenians: History of a Genocide*, trans. Rouben C. Cholokian, 2nd ed. (Delmar, N.Y.: Caravan Books, 1981).

7. Turkish actions manifested in different forms and often varied between towns or regions. Armenians were generally forbidden to own firearms, so that they had no protection when Turkish soldiers or individuals took whatever they wanted from them, including food, farm animals, and valuables. Armenians had no recourse against such incursions, and women could be raped or taken at will (indeed, many young girls were "saved" by being forced to marry Turkish men). Some Turkish families, recognizing the inhumanity of their leaders, took in young Armenian children as their own to save them from being abducted, killed, or forced onto death marches. The Kurds were instrumental in assisting Turkey with its genocide against the Armenians, by which they increased their own social standing with the Turks and gained financially. While the Turks took Armenian land and wealth, the Kurds acted as mercenaries, attacking towns as marauding bands of government-sanctioned thieves or, during the forced marches, taking food, valuables, and women from the starving bands of travelers.

8. For a detailed account of the conditions of the Armenian Genocide and documented survivor accounts, I highly recommend Donald E. Miller and Linda Touryan Miller, *Survivors: An Oral History of the Armenian Genocide* (Berkeley and Los Angeles: University of California Press, 1993). Torture and executions were often public, and women were often raped in front of their families for the purpose of invoking fear, causing emotional and physical pain, breaking spirits, and demoralizing the Armenian population.

9. Henry Theriault, "Rethinking Dehumanization in Genocide," in *The Armenian Genocide: Cultural and Ethical Legacies*, ed. Richard Hovannisian (New Brunswick, N.J.: Transaction, 2007), 27–40.

10. The international community, with the exception of Russia, which had a strategic interest in the land that bordered Turkey, ignored pleas from missionaries, international observers, and the American ambassador Henry Morgenthau, who recognized what was happening, calling it race extermination, but was not able to stop it. Turkey still, to this day, not only vehemently denies that genocide against the Armenians ever occurred, but takes action against anyone who makes the accusation. This has included funding scholars to write rebuttals against the accusations, threatening to sanction governments, such as the United States, every time a resolution to recognize the Armenian Genocide arises, or murdering, imprisoning, or threatening the safety of any individuals, including their own citizens, who might try to expose this unflattering aspect of Turkish history. Orhan Pamuk alluded to the Armenian Genocide and the great Turkish coverup regarding it, in his book *Snow*, which contributed to his receiving the Nobel Prize in 2006. Despite this international honor, Pamuk was prosecuted by the Turkish government for his honesty.

11. Karlen Mooradian, *Arshile Gorky Adoian* (Chicago: Gilgamesh Press, 1978), 148.

12. Gorky's story is similar to the plight of many Armenians. By World War I, sixty thousand Armenians had fled to the United States. After the war, in the aftermath of the Genocide, more Armenians left, and in 1920, the year of Gorky's arrival, a record number of over ten thousand Armenians were admitted. See Anny Bakalian, *Armenian-Americans: From Being to Feeling Armenian* (New Brunswick, N.J.: Transaction, 1993), 10.

13. Gorky's biographers seem to agree that there was some animosity between Gorky and his father and stepbrother for a number of reasons. First, there is some question as to why it took Setrag so long to compile an insufficient amount of money to retrieve the whole family,

suggesting that perhaps, since he was living with Hagop, his eldest son had interfered. Another common belief is that Setrag and Hagop disapproved of Gorky's desire to make art rather than make a living by working in factories as they themselves did out of necessity.

14. This is implied in Matthew Spender's biography, and similar reactions are recorded in Miller and Miller, *Survivors.*

15. Dominick LaCapra, "Trauma, Absence, Loss," *Critical Inquiry* 25, no. 4 (1999): 703.

16. It is useful to consider Charles S. Peirce's semeiotic theory in defining the traveling sign. Peirce wrote a devastating critique of Saussure's binary of signifier-signified, arguing instead that all cognition is irreducibly triadic and that the nature of a sign is fallible because it is thoroughly immersed in a continuing process of interpretation. Peirce's term "semeiotic" (not semiotics, which is simply a term for the various studies of signs) refers a general theory of logic, with language as a portion of semeiosis.

17. It is likely that many Turkish citizens who deny the Armenian Genocide are, because of this practice, ethnically Armenian, or born from other nationalities that over the centuries Turkish invaders had ravaged. In present-day Turkey, Armenians are identified as such, even though they consider themselves Turkish citizens and many are Muslims.

18. An interesting discussion of the types of immigrants and exiles and the coping choices available to them during World War II, when the numbers of displaced peoples increased in a short amount of time and included Europeans who had been less likely to emigrate in large numbers in the past (such as the French), can be found in Stephan Lackner, "Reflections on an Exile in France and the United States," in *Exiles and Émigrés: The Flight of European Artists from Hitler,* ed. Stephanie Barron (Los Angeles: Los Angeles County Museum of Art; New York: Harry N. Abrams, 1997), 363–73.

19. Edward Said, "Reflections on Exile," in *Reflections on Exile and Other Essays* (Cambridge, Mass.: Harvard University Press, 2000), 173.

20. See Bakalian, *Armenian-Americans.*

21. Cathy Caruth, introduction to *Trauma: Explorations in Memory,* ed. Cathy Caruth (Baltimore: Johns Hopkins University Press, 1995), 4.

22. Anie Kalayjian and Siroon P. Shahinian, "Recollections of the Armenian Survivors of the Ottoman Turkish Genocide," in "Resilience in Ethnic Experiences with Massive Trauma and Violence," ed. Flora Hogman, special issue, *Psychoanalytic Review* 85, no. 4 (1998): 494.

23. Although the American government was aware of the mass murder of Armenians in Turkey, it refused to intervene. It did allow immigration, which met with local opposition. Mixed up with considerations of ethnicity and difference is that of race, which is tied to immigration and naturalization. The question first emerged in 1909, when Judge Francis Cabot Lowell of the United States Circuit of Massachusetts determined that the Armenians were Caucasian (as opposed to "yellow" or "Mongoloid") due to their predilection to European culture, their Indo-European language, and their Christian religion. The eligibility of Armenians to become American citizens was raised again in the 1924 case *United States vs. Cartozian,* in which the Armenians were finally determined to be "white persons" and thus allowed to become naturalized. See Robert Mirak, *Torn Between Two Lands: Armenians in America, 1890–World War I* (Cambridge, Mass.: Harvard University Press, 1983), 282. This type of court action separated Armenians from other immigrants and likely affected Gorky.

24. Joshua Freeman, *Who Built America? Working People and the Nation's Economy, Politics, Culture, and Society,* vol. 2, *From the Gilded Age to the Present* (New York: Pantheon Books, 1992), 41. For more extensive discussions, see Milton M. Gordon, *Assimilation in American Life* (New York: Oxford University Press, 1964); Philip Gleason, "American Identity and Americanization," in *Harvard Encyclopedia of American Ethnic Groups,* ed. Stephan Thernstrom, Ann Orlov, and Oscar Handlin (Cambridge, Mass.: Harvard University Press, 1980); and Oscar Handlin, *Immigration as a Factor in American History* (Englewood Cliffs, N.J.: Prentice-Hall, 1959).

25. Stuart Davis, "Arshile Gorky in the 1930's: A Personal Recollection by Stuart Davis," *Magazine of Art* 44 (February 1951): 57.

26. Bakalian, *Armenian-Americans,* 349.

27. See Werner Sollors, *Beyond Ethnicity: Consent and Descent in American Culture* (New York: Oxford University Press, 1986).

28. Mirak, *Torn Between Two Lands,* 282.

29. Homi K. Bhabha, *The Location of Culture* (New York: Routledge, 1994), 55.

30. I wish to thank Samina Hadi-Tabassum for the introduction to this tripartite concept as well as her elaborations on Peirce.

31. His Armenian ancestors were named Aivazian, although his father used the name Haivazosky. Along with his brother, the artist decided on the name Aivazian or Aivazovsky, although occasionally he apparently signed works Hovhannes Aivazian, writing in Armenian.

32. David Anfam, "Arshile Gorky: Tradition and Identity," *Antique Collector* 61, no. 2 (1990): 27.

33. Bakalian, *Armenian-Americans,* 6.

34. Ernst Kris and Otto Kurz, *Legend, Myth, and Magic in the Image of the Artist: A Historical Experiment* (New Haven: Yale University Press, 1979), 30.

35. Gorky was sympathetic to the socialist system being developed in Soviet Armenia at the time, particularly because of the Russian involvement in rescuing the Armenians from the Turks and offering his family, like so many other Armenians, refuge after the Armenian Genocide.

36. See Bhabha, *Location of Culture*, for additional discussion on this concept.

37. Harold Rosenberg, *Arshile Gorky: The Man, The Time, The Idea* (New York: Horizon Press, 1962), 36.

38. Ibid., 22–23.

39. Matthew Baigell, *Jewish-American Artists and the Holocaust* (New Brunswick, N.J.: Rutgers University Press, 1997), 24.

40. See Aharon Applefeld, "The Awakening: On a Pervasive Feeling," in *Shapes of Memory*, ed. Geoffrey Hartman (Oxford: Oxford University Press, 1992).

41. See Bakalian, *Armenian-Americans*; Kalayjian and Shahinian, "Recollections"; Miller and Miller, *Survivors*; and Anie S. Kalayjian, Siroon P. Shahinian, Edmund L. Gregerian, and Lisa Saraydarian, "Coping with Ottoman Turkish Genocide: An Exploration of the Experience of Armenian Survivors," *Journal of Traumatic Stress* 9, no. 1 (1996): 87–97.

42. Laura Mulvey, "Visual Pleasure and the Narrative Cinema," in *Film Theory and Criticism: Introductory Readings*, ed. Leo Braudy and Marshall Cohen (New York: Oxford University Press, 1999), 833–44. First delivered as a paper given in the French Department at the University of Wisconsin–Madison in spring 1973.

43. Arthur C. Danto, "Art After the End of Art," in *The Wake of Art: Criticism, Philosophy, and the Ends of Taste*, ed. Gregg Horowitz and Tom Huhn (Amsterdam: Gordon and Breach, 1998), 121.

44. Harold Rosenberg, "Arshile Gorky: Art and Identity," in *The Anxious Object* (New York: Horizon Press, 1964), 99.

45. Harold Rosenberg says, "There is one unique fact that each individual anxiously struggles to hide from himself, and this is the very fact that is the root of his identity." "Notes on Identity: With Special Reference to the Mixed Philosopher, Søren Kierkegaard," *View* 6 (May 1946): 8.

46. Michel Foucault, "What Is an Author?" in *Critical Theory Since 1965*, ed. Hazard Searle (Tallahassee: University of Florida Press, 1986), 142.

47. Bakalian, *Armenian-Americans*, 352.

48. Said, "Reflections on Exile," 177.

49. Susie Hoogasian Villa and Mary Kilbourne Matossian, *Armenian Village Life Before 1914* (Detroit: Wayne State University Press, 1982), 24.

50. According to Gorky's family, his mother, Shushan der Marderosian, hailed from a line of intellectuals including priests, knights, and artists who maintained an ancestral *vank*, or religious academic complex. See Mooradian, *Arshile Gorky Adoian*.

51. Even before becoming an exile, Gorky was fractured between two places. Such a duality, or multiple identities, is underscored by the various translations of Gorky's Armenian names: Manoog, Manuk, Manouk, Vosdanig, and Vostanik. The interchangeability of the "g" and "k" sounds is consistent with differences between the western and eastern dialects of Armenian, respectively, and further underscores the mutable quality of the name. Gorky himself had existed in both regions: he was born in Turkey and spoke Western Armenian, but, because of the Genocide, fled to Eastern Armenia, and the dialect he spoke was likely a combination of the two.

52. Susan Gubar, *Poetry After Auschwitz: Remembering What One Never Knew* (Bloomington: Indiana University Press, 2003), 245.

53. Maurice Blanchot, *The Writing of Disaster*, trans. Ann Smock (Lincoln: University of Nebraska Press, 1986), 2.

54. Bhabha, *Location of Culture*, 19.

55. For a complete discussion of this concept, see Edward Soja, *Postmodern Geographies: The Reassertion of Space in Critical Social Theory* (New York: Verso, 1989).

56. Matthew Spender claims that this is derivative of the Armenian word *aysaharel*, meaning "accursed." See *From a High Place: A Life of Arshile Gorky* (New York: Knopf, 1999), 60.

57. The transcript of Gorky's federal service lists an "Arsmile Gorky, DOB 4/15/05" on an office payroll note. Hirshhorn Museum and Sculpture Garden archives.

58. Since public assistance for artists during the 1930s, through the Works Project Administration, was need-based, he may have maintained this bank account to keep some of his savings hidden.

59. Paul Barolsky, *Why the Mona Lisa Smiles and Other Tales by Vasari* (University Park: Pennsylvania State University Press, 1991), 43–44.

60. Stephen Greenblatt, *Renaissance Self-Fashioning: From More to Shakespeare* (Chicago: University of Chicago Press, 1983), 2.

61. Kris and Kurz, *Legend, Myth, and Magic*.

62. Ibid. At the Grand Central School of Art, where Arshile Gorky taught, he was identified as Maxim's cousin in a published interview. See "Fetish of Antique Stifles Art Here Says Gorky Kin," *New York Evening Post*, September 15, 1926, 17.

63. This was confirmed to me by the artist's widow in a conversation on June 23, 2008. Even though she was not

married to the artist at the time, discussions with her husband had yielded such conclusions. The painter also looked quite a bit like a writer, wearing his hair parted in the middle and a similar mustache.

64. I wish to thank Howard Singerman for pointing this out.

65. If the defense had been successful, the family likely would have stayed in Van. See Nouritza Matossian, *Black Angel: A Life of Arshile Gorky* (London: Chatto and Windus, 1998), for a detailed account.

66. Julian Levy, *Arshile Gorky* (New York: Harry N. Abrams, 1966), 18.

67. It is possible that Gorky might not have known that his assumed name was a pseudonym. In 1946, when one of his mother-in-law's friends, who had lived for a few years in Tiflis, pointed out that because Maxim Gorky's name was an alias, Arshile's must be too, Gorky flew into a rage and blurted out that she really knew nothing about his country. See Spender, *From a High Place*, 317. Of course, it is unclear to which country Gorky was referring (Armenia or Russia). As the meaning of the name passes in and out of appropriate translation, so, too, did Gorky's identity, and it is no surprise that he was sometimes the immigrant, sometimes the educated foreigner, or sometimes declared that he had studied with this or that artist when he had only studied the artist's works in reproductions or galleries. The claim to be Maxim's cousin is in this vein. Even if Gorky did not realize he had taken on a pseudonym that was a pseudonym, the act is similar to the way Gorky co-opted imagery from works by other artists.

68. Rosenberg speaks of the American painter in as reborn through the act of painting. "The American Action Painters," in *The Tradition of the New* (New York: Horizon Press, 1959), 23–39. See David Shapiro and Cecile Shapiro, eds., *Abstract Expressionism: A Critical Record* (New York: Cambridge University Press, 1990), 79.

69. William Saroyan, "A Note on Hilaire Hiler," in *Why Abstract?* (New York: New Directions Press, 1945), 30.

70. Spender, *From a High Place*, 223.

71. Bakalian, *Armenian-Americans*, 6.

72. Gorky actually despised Saroyan, anyway. Interview with the artist's widow, June 23, 2008.The writer's statements are likely due to his own distance from the 'old country' because unlike Gorky, he was born in the United States, hence a different generational attitude.

73. Bakalian, *Armenian-Americans*, 371.

74. Baigell, *Jewish-American Artists and the Holocaust*, 18.

75. Baigell relates a similar response by Jewish-American artists to the Holocaust (ibid, 18). For specifically Armenian accounts, see Miller and Miller, *Survivors*.

76. See Barbara Rose, *American Painting Since 1900: A Critical History* (New York: F. A. Praeger, 1967).

77. Raymond Williams, "The Metropolis and the Emergence of Modernism," in Edward Timms and David Kelley, *The Unreal City: Urban Experience in Modern European Literature and Art*, edited by Edward Timms and David Kelly (Manchester: Manchester University Press, 1985), 21.

78. Milton Resnick, interview by Karlen Mooradian, in *The Many Worlds of Arshile Gorky* (Chicago: Gilgamesh Press, 1980), 196.

79. Margaret Osborne, "The Mystery of Arshile Gorky: A Personal Account," *Art News* 61, no. 10 (1963): 59.

80. Davis, "Arshile Gorky in the 1930's," 57.

81. Kate Bornstein asserts that this makes one malleable because one can take on an identity easily and even change identities like outfits in one's wardrobe. *Gender Outlaw: On Men, Women, and the Rest of Us* (New York: Vintage, 1995).

82. E. de Kooning, "Gorky," 40

83. Rosenberg, *Arshile Gorky*, 101–2.

84. Although David Anfam speaks only of Gorky ("Arshile Gorky," 27), I believe that this is part of a larger modern condition related to the Abstract Expressionists.

85. From Michael FitzGerald, "Arshile Gorky and the Whitney Museum of American Art," Whitney Museum Gorky Archive Project, http://www.whitney.org/www/research/gorky/index.html.

86. Ibid.

87. Lorne Shirinian, "Part Three: A Study of the Texts. The Armenian Immigrant: Sourian, Hagopian, and Hacikyan," in *Armenian-North American Literature: A Critical Introduction: Genocide, Diaspora, and Symbols* (Lewiston, N.Y.: Edwin Mellen Press, 1990), 207.

Chapter 2

1. According to Gorky's widow, he had worked on the National Gallery version as late as 1942. Conversation with Agnes Gorky Fielding, June 23, 2008.

2. Melvin P. Lader, "Arshile Gorky's *The Artist and His Mother*: Further Study of Its Evolution, Sources, and Meaning," *Arts Magazine* 58, no. 5 (1984): 102.

3. Lader, "Arshile Gorky's *The Artist and His Mother*," 97.

4. Although Gorky used graph paper to map the photograph and transfer it to the canvas with an underlying structure, he altered it in the painting.

5. Raphael Sawyer has explained that it was a drunken De Kooning who commented on portraits at the 1951 Arshile Gorky Memorial Exhibition. Interview by Raphael

Soyer, 1981 (Oral History Project, Archives of American Art, Smithsonian Institution, Washington, D.C.).

6. Letter from Vincent van Gogh to his brother Theo, Arles, September 8, 1888, in *Theories of Modern Art: A Source Book by Artists and Critics*, ed. Herschel B. Chipp, Peter Selz, and Joshua C. Taylor (Berkeley: University of California Press, 1968), 36. Excerpted from *The Complete Letters of Vincent Van Gogh*, vol. 3 (Greenwich, Conn.: New York Graphic Society, 1958), 28–29.

7. Lader has compared her to the Virgin Mary, who is often cloaked in blue, a convention with which Gorky might have been familiar from Armenian manuscripts and numerous works he viewed in art museums. See Lader, "Arshile Gorky's *The Artist and His Mother*," 100.

8. Hans Belting, *Likeness and Presence: A History of the Image Before the Era of Art*, trans. Edmund Jephcott (Chicago: University of Chicago Press, 1996), 99.

9. Conversation with artist Jeffery Cote de Luna, March 4, 2004.

10. Roland Barthes, *Camera Lucida: Reflections on Photography*, trans. Richard Howard (New York: Hill and Wang, 1981), 93.

11. See Lader, "Arshile Gorky's *The Artist and His Mother*."

12. Edward Said, "Reflections on Exile," in *Reflections on Exile and Other Essays* (Cambridge, Mass.: Harvard University Press, 2000), 186.

13. Robert A. Neimeyer, Holly G. Prigerson, and Betty Davies, "Mourning and Meaning," *American Behavioral Scientist* 46, no. 2 (2002): 239.

14. Melvin P. Lader, *Arshile Gorky* (New York: Abbeville Press, 1985), 35.

15. Hal Foster, "Death in America," *October* 75 (Winter 1996): 42.

16. Melvin P. Lader suggests that she takes the form of a martyr in the work. See Lader, "Arshile Gorky's *The Artist and His Mother*," 97.

17. Ethel Schwabacher, *Arshile Gorky* (New York: Macmillan, 1957), 25.

18. Ellen Handler Spitz, *Art and Psyche: A Study In Psychoanalysis and Aesthetics* (New Haven: Yale University Press, 1985), 77.

19. Ibid., 78.

20. Ibid.

21. Vartoosh felt that when she saw the work it was as if her mother was talking to her. See Karlen Mooradian, "Arshile Gorky," *Armenian Review* (Summer 1955): 49–58.

22. Conversation with Agnes Gorky Fielding, June 23, 2008.

23. Harold Rosenberg, "Arshile Gorky: Art and Identity," in *The Anxious Object* (New York: Horizon Press, 1964), 100.

24. Ibid., 74.

25. Said, "Reflections on Exile," 181.

26. Ibid.

27. Spitz, *Art and Psyche*, 77.

28. Ruth Mussikian, interview by Karlen Mooradian, in *The Many Worlds of Arshile Gorky* (Chicago: Gilgamesh Press, 1980), 223. I would like to add here that my grandmother, Servart Ayanian Sielian, who is from the same region of Turkish Armenia as Gorky and who arrived in America at around the same time, settling in Massachusetts as Gorky initially did, also used the word "vulgar" quite frequently—often to describe American behavior.

29. Karlen Mooradian makes an extensive argument that Gorky's works were based on these precedents almost exclusively. *Arshile Gorky Adoian* (Chicago: Gilgamesh Press, 1978). It was, however, the similarity between the iconicity of the older ethnic styles and the Modernist ones that he encountered that formed the basis for his own aesthetic. He was drawn to the familiarity of the later styles perhaps because of his affinity for the earlier ones.

30. During which Gorky lost almost all of the work he had produced for a one-man show at Julien Levy's gallery.

31. Jack Ben-Levi, "A Sadomasochistic Drama in an Age of Traditional Family Values," in *Abject Art: Repulsion and Desire in American Art* (New York: Whitney Museum, 1993), 21.

32. Later, however, he used reproductions, images from books, works he viewed in galleries and museums, and the observed world as a basis.

33. Schwabacher, *Arshile Gorky*, 35.

34. Dominick LaCapra, *Writing History, Writing Trauma* (Baltimore: Johns Hopkins University Press, 2001), 69.

35. Balakian, "Arshile Gorky and the Armenian Genocide," 66.

36. Harry Rand, *Arshile Gorky: The Implications of Symbols* (Montclair, N.J.: Allanheld and Schram, 1980), 16.

37. Aristodemos Kaldis, interview by Karlen Mooradian, in *Many Worlds of Arshile Gorky*, 155.

38. The interesting thing here, whether or not Gorky or Eluard understood it, is that in Islamic love poetry "beloved" often refers to a male. If it refers to a woman, she is likely a prostitute or slave. See Walter G. Andreas and Mehmet Kalpakh, *The Age of Beloveds: Love and the Beloved in Early-Modern Ottoman and European Culture and Society* (Durham: Duke University Press, 2005).

39. Julien Levy, *Surrealism* (New York: Black Sun Press, 1936), 114.

40. Although the date of the painting seems to precede Gorky's involvement with West, the imaginary wife may look a bit like her.

41. Richard Kalinoski, *Beast on the Moon*, in *Humana Festival '95: The Complete Plays*, ed. Marisa Smith (Lyme, N.H.: Smith and Kraus, 1995).

42. Many of the surviving children of the massacred were kept in orphanages and adopted by well-meaning American families, or in the case of girls who came of age in the system, were mail-order brides for Armenian men who had escaped.

43. Kalinoski, *Beast on the Moon*, 106–7.

44. See Mae Henderson, introduction to *Boundaries, Boundaries, and Frames: Cultural Criticism and Cultural Studies*, ed. Mae Henderson (New York: Routledge, 1995), 1–30.

45. Carl G. Jung, *Modern Man in Search of a Soul*, trans. W. S. Dell and Cary F. Baynes (San Diego: Harvest Books, 1933), 75.

46. Hayden Herrera, "Gorky's Self Portraits: The Artist by Himself," *Art in America* 64 (March 1976): 56.

47. William James, *The Principles of Psychology*, vol. 1 (New York: Henry Holt, 1890), 295.

48. See Lader, *Arshile Gorky*, 28–30.

49. Ibid., 29.

50. Stephen Greenblatt, *Renaissance Self-Fashioning: From More to Shakespeare* (Chicago: University of Chicago Press, 1983), 1.

51. A notorious contemporary example is Thomas Kinkade, who often wears a black beret, an outmoded popular culture cliché that represents "artist."

52. At one time, Gorky had a job entertaining moviegoers by quick-drawing caricatures of American presidents during intermissions.

53. "Fetish of Antique Stifles Art Here Says Gorky Kin," *New York Evening Post*, September 15, 1926, 17.

54. This is discussed in Clement Greenberg, "Byzantine Parallels," in *Art and Culture: Critical Essays* (Boston: Beacon Press, 1965), 167–74.

55. Belting, *Likeness and Presence*, 10.

56. John Ash, "Arshile Gorky: How My Mother's Embroidered Apron Unfolds in My Life," *Artforum* 34, no. 1 (1995): 79, 121.

57. Many, especially Mooradian, have compared Gorky's portraiture to Armenian manuscript illustrations and his abstraction to Oriental carpets. An example of the interpretations of the art of other cultures would be Picasso's use of masks in such works as the 1907 *Les Demoiselles d'Avignon*.

58. Matisse may have been looking at similar stylistic iconic representations when making his own work. Mooradian has established the comparison to manuscript painting. Comparisons to modern artists like Matisse have been made most markedly by Lader and Rand and repeated by Herrera.

59. Melvin P. Lader, "Graham, Gorky, De Kooning, and the 'Ingres Revival' in America," *Arts Magazine* 52, no. 7 (1978): 94–99.

60. See ibid. for a more detailed discussion of this phenomenon.

61. See ibid., and John Graham, *System and Dialectics of Art*, ed. Marcia Epstein Allentuck (Baltimore: Johns Hopkins University Press, 1971), 238.

62. John D. Graham, "Primitive Art and Picasso," *Magazine of Art* 30 (April 1937): 238.

63. See Carol Ockman, *Ingres's Eroticized Bodies: Retracing the Serpentine Line* (New Haven: Yale University Press, 1995).

64. Mary Burliuk, "Arshile Gorky," *Color and Rhyme* 19 (1949): 3.

65. Vartoosh Mooradian, interview by Karlen Mooradian, in *Many Worlds of Arshile Gorky*, 41.

66. In response to charges that Gorky aped artists such as Picasso, and in an attempt to define Gorky as an Armenian hero, Gorky's nephew addressed this issue by enlisting the letters that Gorky had supposedly written to Vartoosh; these are now believed to be fabricated. Despite Mooradian's overemphasis on Gorky's reliance on Armenian precedents, there is evidence in Gorky's work to support the term. Mooradian's conclusions about the Armenian eye are shared by the Armenian culture; Armenians identify other Armenians through the observation of prominent dark eyes often with dark circles underneath them, dark hair, and olive complexions. Whether or not Gorky actually penned these sentences, he is likely to have made the observation himself: "Mother's Armenian eyes they call Picasso's, Armenian melancholy they term Byzantine and Russian. And if I correct them and say, 'No, dear sirs, you err for these are Armenian eyes.' They thereupon view one strangely and pronounce that such corrections are mere exaggerations of 'small nation chauvinism.' Imagine the audacity! The corrector is condemned by the corrected. Our eyes. The eyes of the Armenian speak before the lips move and long after they cease to." In Mooradian, *Many Worlds of Arshile Gorky*, 281.

67. See in particular Rand, *Implications of Symbols*, for a more extensive discussion of this source.

68. See Mooradian, *Arshile Gorky Adoian*.

69. Graham, *System and Dialectics of Art*, 238.

70. Judi Freeman, *Picasso and the Weeping Women: The Years of Marie-Therese Walter and Dora Maar* (New York: Rizzoli, 1994), 14.

71. Karlen Mooradian, Gorky's nephew, has discussed this in detail. See Mooradian, *Arshile Gorky Adoian.*

72. Homi K. Bhabha, *The Location of Culture* (New York: Routledge, 1994), 41.

73. Jim Jordan and Robert Goldwater, *The Paintings of Arshile Gorky: A Critical Catalogue* (New York: New York University Press, 1971), 56–57.

74. Ibid.

75. Paul Ricoeur, *Memory, History, Forgetting*, trans. Kathleen Blamey and David Pellauer (Chicago: University of Chicago Press, 2006), 56.

76. Martica Sawain, "The Cycloptic Eye, Pataphysics, and the Possible: Transformations of Surrealism," in *Interpretive Link: Abstract Surrealism into Abstract Expressionism: Works on Paper*, 1938–48, ed. Paul Schimmel (Newport Beach, Calif.: Newport Harbor Art Museum, 1986), 37.

77. It is unlikely that Gorky painted anything while escaping the Armenian Genocide or was able to carry any thing with him on his ragtag travels.

78. Jordan and Goldwater, *Paintings of Arshile Gorky*, 56–7

79. Ibid.

80. Mooradian, *Many Worlds of Arshile Gorky*, 39.

81. Schwabacher, *Arshile Gorky*, 61.

82. See Schwabacher, ibid., for accounts.

83. Although Gorky was clearly and deeply affected by the escape of his father, the siege of Van, the flight to Yerevan, and starvation, we are not entirely aware of exactly what he had witnessed. On Sirun's life, see Nouritza Matossian, *Black Angel: A Life of Arshile Gorky* (London: Chatto and Windus, 1998). Also, Sirun's father had shot her twice, in order to spare her from the Genocide (ibid., 181).

84. An old Armenian woman (name withheld, conversation, November 1992), once remarked to me that if only Gorky had married an Armenian woman he wouldn't have killed himself because she would have understood. Clearly, as his relationship with Sirun shows, this was likely not the case.

85. Schwabacher, *Arshile Gorky*, 59.

86. Ibid., 61.

87. Agnes Gorky, letter to Ethel Schwabacher, December 28, 1949 (Archives of American Art, Whitney Museum Papers, Smithsonian Institution, Washington, D.C.).

88. Agnes Gorky, letter to Ethel Schwabacher, n.d. (post-1948) (Archives of American Art, Whitney Museum Papers, Smithsonian Institution, Washington, D.C.).

89. For more detail on Agnes's background, see Arshile Gorky biographies, particularly Spender and Herrera.

90. She has remarked that before she married Gorky she was "ready to lend my support to Mao." Conversation, June 23, 2008.

91. Mooradian believed this nickname was related to his own mother's name, Vartoosh, which is an abridged version of Vartanouch.

92. Agnes Gorky, letter to Ethel Schwabacher, summer 1946 (Washington, D.C., Archives of American Art, Whitney Museum Papers).

93. Conversation with Agnes Gorky Fielding, June 23, 2008.

94. Gorky explained, "Too many American artists paint portraits that are portraits of a New Yorker, but not a human being." See "Fetish of Antique Stifles Art Here."

95. Willem de Kooning, interview by Karlen Mooradian, in *Many Worlds of Arshile Gorky*, 132.

96. Agnes Gorky, letter to Ethel Schwabacher, December 28, 1949 (Washington, D.C., Archives of American Art, Whitney Museum Papers).

97. Conversation with Agnes Gorky Fielding, June 23, 2008.

98. Agnes Gorky, letter to Ethel Schwabacher, December 28, 1949 (Washington, D.C., Archives of American Art, Whitney Museum Papers).

99. Elaine de Kooning, interview by Phyllis Tuchman, August 27, 1981.

100. Author conversation with Agnes Gorky Fielding, the artist's widow, June 23, 2008.

101. Ibid.

102. Said, "Reflections on Exile," 186.

103. See Spender, *From a High Place*, Matossian, *Black Angel*, and Herrera, *Arshile Gorky*, for additional views and varying information regarding this relationship and Gorky's disclosure.

104. It is well known that Breton blamed Matta for Gorky's suicide and excommunicated him from the Surrealists, at least for a while. The affair with Matta, although well known in Surrealist and Abstract Expressionist circles, was kept fairly quiet until Gorky's recent biographies because, I believe, many blamed Agnes for Gorky's death. Also, because of the status of women in the 1950s, the world would have been shocked by mention of an affair, particularly if a woman was the transgressor, and Agnes would have greatly suffered because of it. It seems that people wanted to disavow the incident, which was a messy reality amidst the struggle of Gorky's art to be accepted in the mainstream. In a letter to Ethel Schwabacher responding to her book on Gorky in 1957, Barnett Newman said, "I am, however, pleased to see you have eliminated a discussion of the Matta-Agnes situation which would have reduced the tone of the book." Letter to Ethel Schwabacher, ca.

November 1957 (Washington, D.C., Archives of American Art, Ethel Schwabacher Papers). Newman also wrote in a letter to Lloyd Goodrich, then curator at the Whitney Museum of American Art, that although he differed on some of its content, "it is an outstanding work on an American painter. . . . At a time when books on artists are involved in the gutter of smear and gossip, Mrs. Schwabacher's book is like a breath of fresh air." November 22, 1957 (Washington, D.C.: Archives of American Art, Whitney Museum Papers).

105. Kalinoski, *Beast on the Moon*, 108.

Chapter 3

1. These facts are already widely discussed in the literature on Gorky.

2. It is highly probable that John Graham influenced this tendency, as it was he who may have first been familiar with these techniques.

3. Interview with Balcomb Greene (Oral History Project, Archives of American Art, Smithsonian Institution, Washington, D.C.).

4. Harold Rosenberg speaks of "Gorky's transactions with his personal and aesthetic identity" and how Gorky used this theme to bridge the distance between the child represented in the painting *The Artist and His Mother* and his life as a vanguard painter. "Art and Identity: The Unfinished Masterpiece," *New Yorker*, January 5, 1963, 70–77.

5. David Anfam, "Arshile Gorky: Tradition and Identity," *Antique Collector* 61, no. 2 (1990): 27.

6. Robert A. Neimeyer, Holly G. Prigerson, and Betty Davies, "Mourning and Meaning," *American Behavioral Scientist* 46, no. 2 (2002): 1. "Major losses, however, undercut our efforts to maintain a coherent self-narrative as the significant others on whom our life stories depend are removed, prompting substantial revisions of our daily and long-range goals if our lives are once again to achieve a measure of predictability and direction. Moreover, the losses of those who have been the intimate witnesses to our past—our partners, parents, grandparents, siblings, or long-term friends—can undermine even our basic self-definition as no one any longer occupies the special relational stance toward us needed to call forth and validate the unique fund of shared memories that sustains our sense of who we have been. Thus, the death of a spouse at the point of retirement, perhaps after a protracted period of caregiving in the face of chronic illness, confronts the partner with more than symptoms of separation distress. This relatively normative form of bereavement also introduces the need to reorganize the daily plot of the survivor's life, to relinquish jointly formulated postretirement plans that promised to structure the remaining chapters of their shared life narrative, and to recruit new social validation for the survivor's characterization of who he or she is beyond the marital role relationship. In all of these senses and more, bereavement therefore prompts us to 'relearn the self' and 'relearn the world' in the wake of loss." See also Thomas Attig, *How We Grieve: Relearning the World* (New York: Oxford University Press, 1996).

7. Donald Kuspit, "Arshile Gorky: Images in Support of the Invented Self," in *Abstract Expressionism: The Critical Developments*, ed. Michael Auping (New York: Harry N. Abrams, 1987), 53.

8. Harold Rosenberg, *Arshile Gorky: The Man, the Time, the Idea* (New York: Horizon Press, 1962), 25–26.

9. Edward Said, "Reflections on Exile," in *Reflections on Exile and Other Essays* (Cambridge, Mass.: Harvard University Press, 2000), 186.

10. According to Thomas F. Mathews, Armenians were commonly open to other influences, often amalgamating both new materials and folk practices in their arts. "The Art of the Armenian Manuscript," in *Treasures in Heaven: Armenian Illuminated Manuscripts*, ed. Thomas F. Mathews and Roger S. Wieck (Princeton: Princeton University Press, 1994), 50–52.

11. James Etemkjian, "Western European and Modern Armenian Literary Relations up to 1915," *Review of National Literatures* 13 (1984): 78.

12. Ibid., 84.

13. As the distinguished scholar Roger Stein pointed out to me, this was typical of some Turkish individuals as well and was part of the larger issue of early twentieth-century Modernism's center being located in Paris. In addition, I would note that some Orthodox Armenians became Catholic, particularly since some of the missionaries assisted in the escape from the massacres.

14. Vahe Oshagan, "Self-Image of Armenians in Modern Literature," in *The Armenian Image in History and Literature*, ed. Richard G. Hovannisian (Malibu: Undena, 1981), 207.

15. Matthew Spender, *From a High Place: A Life of Arshile Gorky* (New York: Knopf, 1999), 30.

16. I would like to thank Roger Stein for enhancing this line of discussion.

17. Among others, Max Weber had visited Russia and Paris, and the Russian immigrant Graham had frequented Paris. I suspect that Gorky's initial attraction to Russian culture was a result of his time in Armenia, the Armenian camaraderie with Russia as a necessary defense against annihilation by the Turks, and an affection for it he may have absorbed from the Armenian community in Watertown during his early years in America. Although he was

aware of French culture and art, I believe that his full introduction to modern art, primarily French, occurred after his move to New York.

18. The American Regionalists of the 1930s Thomas Hart Benton and Grant Wood, who both eventually rejected European art, painted in the Cubist style while in Paris, and their Regionalist work still owes a debt to Cubist organization, flatness, and spacing.

19. For an expanded discussion, see Melvin P. Lader, *Arshile Gorky* (New York: Abbeville Press, 1985).

20. Amédée Ozenfant, "Notes on Cubism," in *Art in Theory: 1900–1990: An Anthology of Changing Ideas*, ed. Charles Harrison and Paul Wood (Cambridge, Mass.: Blackwell, 2000), 224. Originally published in *L'Élan*, no. 10 (1916), the final issue of the magazine that Ozenfant had founded in Paris a year earlier.

21. See Homi K. Bhabha, *The Location of Culture* (New York: Routledge, 1994), 120–21 for a discussion of mimicry that relates to postcolonial discourse.

22. Ibid., 19.

23. This recalls Henry Ford's Americanization efforts and the literacy requirement passed in 1917, which that are discussed in chapter 1.

24. Stuart Davis, "Arshile Gorky in the 1930s: A Personal Recollection," *Magazine of Art* 44 (February 1951): 57.

25. Balcomb Greene, "Memories of Arshile Gorky," *Arts Magazine* 50, no. 7 (1976): 108.

26. The case of my Armenian grandfather, who worked in shoe factories with French Canadian women, is a good example of this language acquisition. The women assumed that because he spoke broken English, he could not understand their often very private conversations in French. However, years of practice deciphering English words had given him the ability to uncode other languages.

27. For instance, if I wanted to declare an action in English, I would say something like "I am going home." In Armenian, I would say, "Doon gertam gor," or "Home I am going."

28. Margaret Osborne, "The Mystery of Arshile Gorky: A Personal Account," *Art News* 61, no. 10 (1963): 59.

29. The artist is known to have rewritten others such as Eluard and Gaudier-Brzeska. See Nick Dante Vaccaro, "Gorky's Debt to Gaudier-Brzeska," *Art Journal* 23 (Fall 1963): 33–34.

30. Davis, "Arshile Gorky in the 1930s," 58.

31. Gorky kept an extensive library of books, journals, and exhibition catalogues throughout his career. These included books in German, Italian, English, and French on Ingrés, Picasso, Matisse, Uccello, Arp, Mondrian, Léger, Giotto, David, Cézanne, African art, Degas, Lorain, Michelangelo, De Chirico, Klee, Renoir, Japanese painting, Corot, Daumier, Egypto-Roman portraiture, Seurat, Toulouse-Lautrec, Grünewald, El Greco, Massaccio, Greek Sculpture, Da Vinci, Van Gogh, Goya, Calder, Carpaccio, Dalí, Turner, Bosch, Rousseau, Bonnard, Kirchner, Modigliani, Gris, and Braque. He also kept many reproductions, including most of the aforementioned artists plus Tintoretto, Cranach, Bronzino, Bellini, Dürer, Lippi, Pisanello, Simone Martini, Rubens, Van Dyck, Gainsborough, Raphael, Rembrandt, Picabia, Dufy, Gleizes, and Copley. Found in his studio as well was Armenian embroidery. This list excludes the books, journals, exhibition catalogues, and reproductions lost in the 1945 studio fire.

32. Raymond Williams, "The Metropolis and the Emergence of Modernism," in *The Unreal City: Urban Experience in Modern European Literature and Art*, ed. Edward Timms and David Kelley (Manchester: Manchester University Press, 1985), 22.

33. Interview, 1963 (Oral History Project, Archives of American Art, Smithsonian Institution, Washington, D.C.).

34. Edward Sapir, *Selected Writings in Language, Culture, and Personality*, ed. David G. Mandelbaum (Berkeley: University of California Press, 1949), 162.

35. Jacob Kainen, "Memories of Arshile Gorky," *Arts Magazine* 50, no. 7 (1976): 97.

36. Ibid.

37. Ethel Schwabacher, *Arshile Gorky* (New York: Macmillan, 1957), 93.

38. Harold Rosenberg, "Arshile Gorky: Art and Identity," in *The Anxious Object* (New York: Horizon Press, 1964), 100.

39. Jim Jordan and Robert Goldwater, *The Paintings of Arshile Gorky: A Critical Catalogue* (New York: New York University Press, 1982), 18.

40. See Lader, *Arshile Gorky*, for a fuller discussion of this and subsequent "still life" works.

41. George Dennison, "The Crisis-Art of Arshile Gorky," *Arts Magazine* 37, no. 5 (1963): 17.

42. Howard Singerman, *Art Subjects: Making Artists in the American University* (Berkeley and Los Angeles: University of California Press, 1999), 137.

43. Ibid., 138.

44. Ibid.

45. See ibid., 97–99, for theoretical and historical development of reformist educational theory from which these concepts derive.

46. Dore Ashton, "A Straggler's View of Gorky," in *Arshile Gorky: The Breakthrough Years*, ed. Michael Auping (New York: Rizzoli, 1995), 41.

47. Donald Kuspit, "Arshile Gorky in the Thirties," in

Arshile Gorky: Paintings and Drawings, 1929–1942, exh. cat. (New York: Gagosian Gallery, 1998), 9.

48. In a review of Davis's work, critic Henry J. McBride implies that he followed Picasso because he was unable to think of a style of his own. See Stuart Davis, "Is There an American Art?" in *Theories of Modern Art: A Source Book by Artists and Critics*, ed. Herschel B. Chipp, Peter Selz, and Joshua C. Taylor (Berkeley: University of California Press, 1968), 521.

49. Milton Resnick, interview by Karlen Mooradian, in *The Many Worlds of Arshile Gorky* (Chicago: Gilgamesh Press, 1980), 192–93.

50. Leo Hamalian, "The Armenian Genocide and the Literary Imagination," in *The Armenian Genocide in Perspective*, ed. Richard G. Hovannisian (New Brunswick, N.J.: Transaction Press, 1987), 155.

51. William C. Seitz, *Arshile Gorky: Paintings, Drawings, Studies* (New York: Doubleday, 1962), 13.

52. This is a recurring motif. Manifested as a palette here, it appears in works such as *Organization* and in a hybridized form in *Image in Khorkom*, and transforms into a shoe shape in *Garden in Sochi*.

53. Walter Murch, Archives of American Art, interview by Dorothy Seckler, June 6, 1967.

54. Richard Wollheim, "Kitaj: Recollections and Reflections," in *R. B. Kitaj: A Retrospective*, ed. Richard Morphet, exh. cat. (London: Tate Gallery, 1994), 38.

55. On one occasion Gorky incorporated a piece of cheese into a work, which a mouse subsequently ate during the night. Jordan and Goldwater, *Paintings of Arshile Gorky*, 258.

56. Ibid.

57. Objects were quite as difficult to manipulate as women, but paint was nevertheless much easier to control.

58. See the discussion below. This includes many works, such as *Organization, Image in Khorkom*, and *Garden in Sochi*.

59. For an introduction to Hofmann's theories, see Hans Hofmann, "Excerpts from His Teaching," in Chipp, Selz, and Taylor, *Theories of Modern Art*, 536–44.

60. Davis, "Arshile Gorky in the 1930's," 57.

61. Kainen, "Memories of Arshile Gorky," 97.

62. See Lader, *Arshile Gorky*.

63. Fernand Léger, *The Aesthetic of the Machine* (1924), in Chipp, Selz, and Taylor, *Theories of Modern Art*, 277.

64. Fellow artists and biographers have commented that Pollock seemed to be jealous of Gorky's abilities and that Krasner's work had been informed by Gorky's.

65. Nan Greacen, interview by Matthew Spender, March 18, 1995, in Matthew Spender, "Paintings in the Exhibition," in *Arshile Gorky: Paintings and Drawings*, 20.

66. Like his name, which existed in various manifestations before Gorky settled on Arshile, the name of Gorky's hometown also existed in several versions, appearing as Xhorkom and Khorkom at various times. Although Peter Balakian has suggested that Gorky deliberately spelled it with an "X," literally x-ing out the home that no longer existed, it is more likely that Gorky, as with the various ways he tried spelling his name, was simply uncertain how to translate the Armenian sound properly into English. See Peter Balakian, "Arshile Gorky and the Armenian Genocide," *Art in America* 84, no. 2 (1996): 58–67, 108–9.

67. Schwabacher, *Arshile Gorky*, 52.

68. I am indebted to Eileen Sullivan for her clarification of this point.

69. This has been discussed in detail, most markedly by Lader, *Arshile Gorky*, and most recently illustrated in the exhibition Picasso and American Art at the Whitney Museum of American Art from September 28, 2006, to January 28, 2007. See Michael C. FitzGerald and Julia May Boddewyn, *Picasso and American Art* (New Haven: Yale University Press, 2006).

70. Roland Barthes, "The Death of the Author," in *Image, Music, Text*, trans. Stephen Heath (New York: Hill and Wang, 1977), 146.

71. Clement Greenberg, "Byzantine Parallels," in *Art and Culture: Critical Essays* (Boston: Beacon Press, 1965), 172.

72. Harold Rosenberg, "The American Action Painters," in *The Tradition of the New* (New York: Horizon Press, 1959), 35.

73. In "Arshile Gorky: Art and Identity," Rosenberg continues, "one of the lessons learned from the vanguard Europeans by American artists in the forties was that a work of art need consist of nothing more than an inscription of the artist's identity . . . the total effect is that of a unique signature" (101).

74. Jacob Kainen, interview by Avis Berman, August 11, 1982. Archives of American Art Oral History Project.

75. Elaine de Kooning, "Gorky: Painter of His Own Legend," *Art News* 49 (January 1951): 39.

76. Lader, *Arshile Gorky*, 22.

77. John Graham, *System and Dialectics of Art*, ed. Marcia Epstein Allentuck (Baltimore: Johns Hopkins University Press, 1971).

78. Ann Eden Gibson, *Abstract Expressionism: Other Politics* (New Haven: Yale University Press, 1997), xxviii.

79. Ethel Schwabacher, interview by Colette Roberts, New York City, March 1965, *Archives of American Art* microfilm (Reel 3975), 518.

80. Williams, "Metropolis and the Emergence of Modernism," 21.

81. Willem de Kooning, interview by Karlen Mooradian, in *Many Worlds of Arshile Gorky*, 128.

82. E. de Kooning, "Gorky," 39.

83. Rosenberg, *Arshile Gorky*, 66–67.

84. Meyer Schapiro, interview by Karlen Mooradian, in *Many Worlds of Arshile Gorky*, 201–202.

85. Albert Camus, "The Wager of Our Generation," in *Resistance, Rebellion, and Death* , ed. and trans. Justin O'Brien (New York: Vintage Books, 1988), 264 (interview in *Demain*, October 24–30, 1957).

86. Anne Middleton Wagner, "Lee Krasner as L. K.," *Representations* 25 (Winter 1989): 48.

87. Ellen Handler Spitz, *Art and Psyche: A Study in Psychoanalysis and Aesthetics* (New Haven: Yale University Press, 1985), 122.

88. Nicolas Calas, "Arshile Gorky," in *Calas Presenting Bloodflames 1947, ex.* exh. cat. (New York: Hugo Gallery, 1947), 8 (in conjunction with the Hugo Gallery exhibition Bloodflames 1947, New York, February 15–28, 1947).

89. I am indebted to Neery Melkonian for introducing me to this concept in 1993.

90. Schwabacher, *Arshile Gorky Memorial Exhibition*, 19.

91. "Fetish of Antique Stifles Art Here, Says Gorky Kin," *New York Evening Post*, September 15, 1926, 17.

92. Schwabacher, *Arshile Gorky*, 110.

Chapter 4

1. See Harry Rand, *Arshile Gorky: The Implications of Symbols* (Berkeley and Los Angeles: University of California Press, 1991); Melvin P. Lader, *Arshile Gorky* (New York: Abbeville Press, 1985).

2. Dickran Tashjian, *Surrealism and the Avant-Garde, 1920–1950* (New York: Thames and Hudson, 1995), 280.

3. Ethel Schwabacher, *Arshile Gorky* (New York: Macmillan, 1957), 52.

4. Elaine de Kooning, "Gorky: Painter of His Own Legend," *Art News* 49 (January 1951): 64.

5. This obsession with one subject/composition is conceptual in nature, and Gorky's process reminds me of the systems that Sol Lewitt explored in his three-dimensional works, such as those that worked through all of the possible permutations of a cube. Working through variables as Gorky did also resembles mathematical formulations and proofing, or at the very least the simultaneous analyses evident in Cubist painting.

6. Maurice Blanchot, *The Writing of Disaster*, trans. Ann Smock (Lincoln: University of Nebraska Press, 1986), 30.

7. Melvin P. Lader, *Arshile Gorky: Three Decades of Drawing* (New York: Peters, 1990), 32.

8. Martica Sawain, "'The Third Man,' or Automatism American Style," in "New Myths for Old: Redefining Abstract Expressionism," ed. Ann Eden Gibson and Stephen Polcari, special issue, *Art Journal* 47, no. 3 (1988): 181.

9. E. De Kooning, "Gorky," 40

10. Sawain, "'Third Man,'" 182.

11. Clement Greenberg, "Byzantine Parallels," in *Art and Culture: Critical Essays* (Boston: Beacon Press, 1965), 173.

12. Schwabacher, *Arshile Gorky*, 50.

13. Balcomb Greene, "Memories of Arshile Gorky," *Arts Magazine* 50, no. 7 (1976): 110.

14. See Edward Soja, *Postmodern Geographies: The Reassertion of Space in Critical Social Theory* (New York: Verso, 1989).

15. Francis V. O'Connor notes that the original manuscript seems to have been edited by Emanuel Benson, who was compiling an anthology of WPA/FAP artist statements, and that there were three versions. O'Connor accepts the original version, with the addition of an opening paragraph from the second, as authentic. See *Murals Without Walls: Arshile Gorky's Aviation Murals Rediscovered*, ed. Ruth Bowman (Newark: Newark Museum, 1978), 16.

16. Arshile Gorky, "My Murals for the Newark Airport: An Interpretation," reprinted in Bowman, *Murals Without Walls*, 13.

17. Fernand Léger, *The Aesthetic of the Machine* (1924), in *Theories of Modern Art: A Source Book by Artists and Critics*, ed. Herschel B. Chipp, Peter Selz, and Joshua C. Taylor (Berkeley: University of California Press, 1968), 277.

18. Fernand Léger, *A New Realism—the Object* (1926), in Chipp, Selz, and Taylor, *Theories of Modern Art*, 279.

19. Piet Mondrian, *Plastic Art and Pure Plastic Art (Figurative Art and Non-Figurative Art)* (1937), in Chipp, Selz, and Taylor, *Theories of Modern Art*, 349.

20. Gorky, "My Murals," 13.

21. I refer here to Charles S. Peirce's theory of semeiotics, which is triadic and continuously dependent on the process of interpretation, rather than the more commonly accepted binary semiotic theory of the signifier and signified as defined by Saussure.

22. Gorky, "My Murals," 13.

23. Joe Soloman, letter to Jacob Kainen (Kainen Papers, Archives of American Art, Smithsonian Institution, Washington, D.C.), 174, 565.

24. See Schwabacher, *Arshile Gorky*, 79.

25. Gorky, "My Murals," 13.

26. This is stated in the caption of the photograph that accompanies a local review. See Gerald Sullivan, "Gorky's Murals for the Airport They Puzzle," *Newark Ledger*, June 10, 1937, reprinted in Bowman, *Murals Without Walls*, 39.

27. See Ruth Bowman, "Arshile Gorky's *Aviation* Murals Rediscovered," in Bowman, *Murals Without Walls*, 38.

28. The murals disappeared around the time the airport was taken over by the U.S. military during World War II. See Bowman, *Murals Without Walls*, for the entire story of their disappearance and rediscovery.

29. Greene, "Memories of Arshile Gorky," 110.

30. Ibid.

31. In discussing these works, Harry Rand states that Gorky "used the opportunity to shift ever so slightly his stylistic alignment away from Léger and more toward the beribboned painting of Míro" (*Arshile Gorky*, 45).

32. Sydney Janis, interview by Paul Cummings, January 21, 1971 (Archives of American Art, Smithsonian Institution, Washington, D.C.).

33. Hayden Herrera, "Gorky's Self Portraits: The Artist by Himself," *Art in America* 64 (March 1976): 62.

34. Viktor Frankl, *Man's Search for Meaning* (New York: Pocket Books, 1984), 99.

35. Gorky had painted nightclub murals before. Roselle Davis, Stuart's second wife, recalled that Gorky painted one for a speakeasy on Sixth Avenue near Waverly Place, not for pay but for recognition; the owner who believed that he saw obscenity in the abstract forms, insisted that it be painted out. Roselle Davis, interview by Karlen Mooradian, in *The Many Worlds of Arshile Gorky* (Chicago: Gilgamesh Press, 1980), 124.

36. As Harry Rand points out, a preparatory sketch clearly reveals Gorky's move toward Surrealism and maturation of style (*Arshile Gorky*, 46).

37. See Michael Auping, ed., *Arshile Gorky: The Breakthrough Years* (New York: Rizzoli, 1995), and Lader, *Arshile Gorky*.

38. Schwabacher, *Arshile Gorky*, 79. From an interview with Malcolm Johnson, "Café Life in New York," *New York Sun*, August 22, 1941.

39. Duncan Macmillan, "The Outsider: Gorky and America," *Art International* 23, nos. 3–4 (1979): 105.

40. See Lader, *Arshile Gorky*.

41. Avis Berman, *Rebels on Eighth Street: Juliana Force and the Whitney Museum of Art* (New York: Atheneum, 1990), 376.

42. Wassily Kandinsky, "The Cologne Lecture," in *Art in Theory, 1900–2000: An Anthology of Changing Ideas*, ed. Charles Harrison and Paul Wood (Malden, Mass.: Blackwell, 2003), 93.

43. As New York emerged from the Depression in the 1930s, it became a bastion of innovation as its many new skyscrapers revised the American landscape into something ultraurban and futuristic.

44. As the exhibition Exiles + Émigrés: The Flight of European Artists from Hitler, organized by the Los Angeles County Museum of Art, points out, this recognition ensured their survival. Efforts by groups such as the Emergency Rescue Committee pleaded their cases to the American government, and Peggy Guggenheim, the famous socialite, art dealer, and collector, flew a number of these artists to the United States in her private airplane. Once here, some World War II exiles did stay, such as Max Beckmann, who taught at Washington University, and Josef Albers, who helped establish programs at Black Mountain College and Yale. Others, such as Francophile André Breton, returned to their native lands as soon as the war concluded, but their presence reflects an unmistakable surge in American art after World War II. Almost all of the Abstract Expressionists, for instance, studied with Hans Hofmann or at the very least knew his art and theories.

45. See Auping, *Arshile Gorky*, for further explanation of this term.

46. Julien Levy, *Surrealism* (New York: Black Sun Press, 1936).

47. An Exquisite Corpse is created by two artists or an entire ensemble working together. One draws on a section of paper, folds the paper to conceal all but the end lines of the drawing, and then passes it to another, who continues the drawing from the visible points. After each artist has had a turn, the entire composition is unfolded. At that point, the Surrealists artists would try to determine the meaning of the work in the same manner as in Freudian psychoanalysis.

48. See Carol Ockman, *Ingres's Eroticized Bodies: Retracing the Serpentine Line* (New Haven: Yale University Press, 1995).

49. It is commonly thought that Willem de Kooning introduced Gorky to a brush used for painting signs, which is what allowed him to render them so delicately.

50. Mary Burliuk, "Arshile Gorky," *Color and Rhyme* 19 (1949): 3.

51. Robert Hughes, "The Triumph of Achilles the Bitter: In New York City, a Definitive Arshile Gorky Retrospective," *Time*, May 11, 1981, 81.

52. Just as Gorky's work is based on the recognizable in nature but is not representative of nature, some of the lines of Gorky's work look like script, particularly Armenian letters, amidst the composition and colors. This could be a feasible component in Gorky's work, since he might have adapted something similar from Cubism and because of his history of floating his signature around the canvas. I would not delve too deeply into this component of the work, though, because it bespeaks an iconographical reading along the lines of Harry Rand's search for an underlying

code in Gorky's work or Peter Balakian's insistence that Gorky was depicting a cipher of genocide.

53. "Fetish of Antique Stifles Art Here, Says Gorky Kin," *New York Evening Post*, September 15, 1926, 17.

54. I am indebted to Eileen Sullivan for this suggestion.

55. Considering the date of the painting and the play of language, I wonder if Gorky was at all familiar with James Joyce's *Finnegan's Wake*, which contains multilingual puns.

56. Julien Levy, *Arshile Gorky* (New York: Harry N. Abrams, 1966), 34.

57. Gorky told Levy that "down the road, by the stream, that Old Mill, it used to grind corn, now it is covered with vines, birds, flowers. Flour Mill—Flowery Mill. That's funny! I like that idea" (ibid., 35).

58. Harold Rosenberg, "The American Action Painters," in *The Tradition of the New* (New York: Horizon Press, 1959), 23.

59. "Notes on the Artist," in Selected Paintings by the Late Arshile Gorky, exh. cat. (New York: Samuel Kootz Gallery, 1950).

60. Serge Guilbault, *How New York Stole the Idea of Modern Art: Abstract Expressionism, Freedom, and the Cold War*, trans. Arthur Goldhammer (Chicago: University of Chicago Press, 2000).

61. Clement Greenberg's "Modernist Painting" first appeared in 1960 as a pamphlet published by the Voice of America. It was reprinted in *Art and Literature*, no. 4 (Spring 1965): 193–201, and has appeared numerous times since, often in revised form.

62. I refer here to a government program called Art in the Embassies, which placed work by American artists in American embassies around the world, beginning with the Abstract Expressionists.

Chapter 5

1. See chap. 3, n. 48.

2. Interview with Agnes Gorky Phillips Fielding in *Arshile Gorky*, a film directed by Charlotte Zwerin and produced by Courtney Sale (Court Productions, 1982).

3. He was so fascinated by milkweed in particular—a pod with seeds inside, attached to long fuzz that when the pod opened would assist the seeds in becoming airborne—that when he discovered it, he put some in an envelope to send to Jeanne Reynal in California. Conversation with the artist's widow, June 23, 2008.

4. Agnes Gorky, letter to Ethel Schwabacher, December 28, 1948 (Papers of Ethel Schwabacher, Archives of American Art, Smithsonian Institution, Washington, D.C.).

5. Walter Murch, interview by Dorothy Seckler, June 6, 1967 (Archives of American Art, Smithsonian Institution, Washington, D.C.).

6. Anthony Giddens, *The Consequences of Modernity* (Stanford: Stanford University Press, 1990), 108.

7. Ethel Schwabacher, *Arshile Gorky* (New York: Macmillan, 1957), 121.

8. Ibid., 92.

9. Stephen W. Hawking, *A Brief History of Time: From The Big Bang to Black Holes* (New York: Bantam Books, 1988), 135.

10. Gorky was to have discussed the title change in a letter from July 1943, but Nouritza Matossian has confirmed that this letter does not exist. See *Black Angel: A Life of Arshile Gorky* (London: Chatto and Windus, 1998), 496–98. The Museum of Modern Art artist statement still illuminates the work.

11. Harry Rand, "Arshile Gorky's Armenian Sources," *Journal of Armenian Studies* 3, nos. 1–2 (1986–87): 182

12. Brian O'Doherty, "Gorky. Private Language, Universal Theme," *New York Times*, May 10, 1964, X17.

13. Arshile Gorky, statement on *Garden in Sochi*, Museum of Modern Art, Archives.

14. See Agnes Magruder Gorky, letter to Ethel Schwabacher, October 24, 1950, Papers of Ethel Schwabacher, Archives of American Art. Also discussed in Matthew Spender, *From a High Place: A Life of Arshile Gorky* (New York: Knopf, 1999), 15. Spender suggests that the title comes from the first words that Gorky spoke, "Ar gu la," meaning "he is crying" in Armenian. Based on the metaphor of *The Leaf of the Artichoke Is an Owl*, however, I wonder if the word might not also have been a variation on "arugula," the salad green whose shape the motif also resembles.

15. Gorky's relationship with Miró was poignant. On the occasion of a dinner between the two, Gorky began to sing Armenian songs and Miró began to sing Catalan songs, like dueling banjos, each responding to the other with equal emotionality. Schwabacher, *Arshile Gorky*, 122. Gorky may have been attracted to Miró's art, as he was to Kandinsky's, because of the similarities in their backgrounds.

16. Conversation with the artist's widow, June 23, 2008.

17. Irina Petrosian and David Underwood, *Armenian Food: Fact, Fiction, and Folklore* (Bloomington, Ind.: Yerker, 2006), 52.

18. Homi K. Bhabha, *The Location of Culture* (New York: Routledge, 1994), 162.

19. Roland Barthes, "Change the Object Itself: Mythology Today," in *Image, Music, Text*, trans. Stephen Heath (New York: Hill and Wang, 1977), 168–69.

20. Simon Schama, *Landscape and Memory* (New York: Vintage, 1996), 61.

21. Harry Rand, *Arshile Gorky: The Implications of Symbols* (Montclair, N.J.: Allanheld and Schram, 1980), 82. Rand bases this conclusion that Gorky later confided his intentions to his family on letters by Gorky translated by his nephew, Karlen Mooradian, which may not be entirely genuine (see note 9).

22. The revelation of this pun is itself questionable, since it is contained in Mooradian's questionable letters.

23. Robert Storr, "Fertile Mirrors," in *Arshile Gorky, 1904–48* (London: Whitechapel Gallery, 1990), 31.

24. Schwabacher, *Arshile Gorky*, 66.

25. Barnett Newman, "Adolph Gottlieb," exhibition pamphlet, New York, Wakefield Gallery, February 7–19, 1944, n.p.

26. Hayden Herrera, "The Sculptures of Arshile Gorky." *Arts Magazine* 50, No. 7 (Mar. 1976): 88–90.

27. Jim Jordan, "Arshile Gorky at Crooked Run Farm," *Arts Magazine* 50, no. 7 (1976): 101.

28. George Dennison, "The Crisis-Art of Arshile Gorky," *Arts Magazine* 37, no. 5 (1963): 14.

29. Melvin P. Lader, "Arshile Gorky: A Modern Artist in the Academic Tradition," in *Arshile Gorky: Works on Paper*, ed. Melvin P. Lader (Venice: Peggy Guggenheim, 1992): 15–54.

30. Rand, *Arshile Gorky*, 7.

31. Ibid.

32. Harold Rosenberg, *Arshile Gorky: The Man, the Time, the Idea* (New York: Horizon Press, 1962), 134.

33. Rand, "Arshile Gorky's Armenian Sources," 182.

34. According to Rand (ibid.), Gorky's abstraction consisted of a clever manipulation of scenes that the artist consciously transformed through drawings and adjusted compositions. Rand believes that "by identifying the sources for his shapes [using the drawings that led up to final work], it is possible to read the spaces surrounding each form and decide which forms and colors serve the stylistic evolution of a picture, and which the iconographic—even narrative—exposition." Here Rand is really reading likenesses, albeit to an extreme. The forms are only analogies between the works and what may be their "sources."

35. Roland Barthes, *The Pleasure of the Text*, trans. Richard Miller (New York: Hill and Wang, 1975), 32.

36. Such a belief also discounts the importance of the drawings as self-sufficient works in themselves, not merely as preparations for paintings, an argument that scholar Melvin P. Lader made for many years.

37. André Breton, "Arshile Gorky," in *Surrealism and Painting* (New York: Harper and Row, 1972), 199–200.

38. Carl G. Jung, *Modern Man In Search of a Soul*, trans. W. S. Dell and Cary F. Baynes (San Diego: Harvest Books, 1933), 167.

39. I am referring to the Gaia hypothesis, devised by James Ephraim Lovelock, in which he proposes that the earth is a "living" self-regulating and self-sustaining single system.

40. Jordan, "Arshile Gorky at Crooked Run Farm," 100.

41. Diane Waldman, *Arshile Gorky, 1904–1948: A Retrospective* (New York: Harry N. Abrams, 1981), 24.

42. Adolph Gottlieb, *Selected Paintings by the Late Arshile Gorky* (New York: Samuel Kootz Gallery, 1950).

43. J. H. Matthews, "André Breton and Painting: The Case of Arshile Gorky," *Dada/Surrealism* 17 (1988): 36.

44. Schwabacher, *Arshile Gorky*, 79. From an interview with Malcolm Johnson, "Café Life in New York," *New York Sun*, August 22, 1941.

45. Nicolas Calas, "Arshile Gorky," in *Calas Presenting Bloodflames 1947, ex.* exh. cat. (New York: Hugo Gallery, 1947), 8 (in conjunction with the Hugo Gallery exhibition Bloodflames 1947, New York, February 15–28, 1947).

46. See Rand, *Arshile Gorky*.

47. Balcomb Greene, interview by Karlen Mooradian, in *The Many Worlds of Arshile Gorky* (Chicago: Gilgamesh Press, 1980), 146.

48. Gorky once remarked, "Nineteen miserable years have I lived in America." Edward Denby, interview by Karlen Mooradian, in *Many Worlds of Arshile Gorky*, 134.

49. See Ethel Schwabacher Papers, 1940–1975, Archives of American Art, Reel 3975, interview by Colette Roberts, March 1965. Schwabacher, *Arshile Gorky*, 9.

50. Peter Blume, "Will Abstract Art Survive?" *New Republic*, April 1939, 308.

51. John I. H. Baur, *Nature in Abstraction: The Relation of Abstract Painting and Sculpture to Nature in Twentieth-Century American Art*, exh. cat. (New York: Whitney Museum, 1958), 11.

52. Eliza Rathbone, "Arshile Gorky: The Plow and the Song," in *American Art at Mid-century: The Subjects of the Artist* (Washington, D.C.: National Gallery of Art, 1978), 66.

53. Giddens, *Consequences of Modernity*, 14.

54. Anny Bakalian, *Armenian-Americans: From Being to Feeling Armenian* (New Brunswick, N.J.: Transaction, 1993), 6.

55. Jung, *Modern Man*, 199.

56. Clement Greenberg, Art, *Nation*, January 10, 1948, 52.

57. Arshile Gorky, "My Murals for the Newark Airport: An Interpretation," reprinted in *Murals Without Walls: Arshile Gorky's Aviation Murals Rediscovered*, ed. Ruth Bowman (Newark: Newark Museum, 1978), 13.

58. Albert Camus, "The Wager of Our Generation," in *Resistance, Rebellion, and Death* , ed. and trans. Justin O'Brien (New York: Vintage Books, 1988), 257 (interview in *Demain*, October 24–30, 1957).

59. Breton, "Arshile Gorky," 200.

60. Ibid.

61. Ibid.

Chapter 6

1. J. H. Matthews, "André Breton and Painting: The Case of Arshile Gorky," *Dada/Surrealism* 17 (1988): 39.

2. Some first-generation Armenian immigrants believed that their sojourn in America was a temporary displacement in order to avoid what they believed were transient problems in their homeland, to which they fully expected to return.

3. Edward Said, "Reflections on Exile," in *Reflections on Exile and Other Essays* (Cambridge, Mass.: Harvard University Press, 2000), 186.

4. Anny Bakalian, *Armenian-Americans: From Being to Feeling Armenian* (New Brunswick, N.J.: Transaction, 1993).

5. Stephen Spender, *The Making of a Poem* (London: Hamish Hamilton, 1955), 57. Sir Stephen was the father of Matthew Spender, Gorky's biographer and son-in-law.

6. Andreas Huyssen, *Twilight Memories: Marking Time in a Culture of Amnesia* (New York: Routledge, 1995), 2–3.

7. Ethel Schwabacher, *Arshile Gorky Memorial Exhibition*, exh. cat. (New York: Whitney Museum, 1951), 34.

8. Arshile Gorky, "My Murals for the Newark Airport: An Interpretation," reprinted in *Murals Without Walls: Arshile Gorky's Aviation Murals Rediscovered*, ed. Ruth Bowen (Newark: Newark Museum, 1978), 13.

9. Ethel Schwabacher, *Arshile Gorky* (New York: Macmillan, 1957), 111.

10. Ibid., 92.

11. Maurice Blanchot, *The Writing of Disaster*, trans. Ann Smock (Lincoln: University of Nebraska Press, 1986), 29.

12. Sidney Janis, *Abstract and Surrealist Art in America* (New York: Reynal and Hitchcock, 1944), 89, 120.

13. Paul Ricoeur, *Memory, History, Forgetting*, trans. Kathleen Blamey and David Pellauer (Chicago: University of Chicago Press, 2006), 5.

14. See Henri Bergson, *Matter and Memory*, trans. Nancy M. Paul and W. Scott Palmer (London: Allen and Unwin, 1950).

15. Nicolas Calas, "Arshile Gorky," in *Calas Presenting Bloodflames 1947, ex.* exh. cat. (New York: Hugo Gallery, 1947), 8 (in conjunction with the Hugo Gallery exhibition Bloodflames 1947, New York, February 15–28, 1947).

16. John Ash, "Arshile Gorky: How My Mother's Embroidered Apron Unfolds in My Life," *Artforum* 34, no. 1 (1995): 79, 121.

17. Vartoosh Mooradian, interview by Karlen Mooradian, in *The Many Worlds of Arshile Gorky* (Chicago: Gilgamesh Press, 1980), 43.

18. Vahe Oshagan, "Self-Image of Armenians in Modern Literature," in *The Armenian Image in History and Literature*, ed. Richard G. Hovannisian (Malibu: Undena, 1981), 206.

19. Anie S. Kalayjian, Siroon P. Shahinian, Edmund L. Gregerian, and Lisa Saraydarian, "Coping with Ottoman Turkish Genocide: An Exploration of the Experience of Armenian Survivors," *Journal of Traumatic Stress* 9, no. 1 (1996): 95.

20. This is evident in Bakalian's work as well as studies she cites. See *Armenian-Americans*. See also Richard G. Hovannisian, ed., *The Armenian Genocide in Perspective* (New Brunswick: Transaction, 1986).

21. Matthew Baigell, *Jewish-American Artists and the Holocaust* (New Brunswick, N.J.: Rutgers University Press, 1997), 18–19.

22. Anny Bakalian discusses this trauma and its affect on Armenian-American generations in detail (*Armenian-Americans*, 348–49).

23. Susan Sontag, *Regarding the Pain of Others* (New York: Picador, 2003), 115.

24. Hal Foster, *The Return of the Real: Art and Theory at the End of the Century* (Cambridge, Mass.: MIT Press, 1996).

25. Oshagan, "Self-Image," 206.

26. The importance of the Genocide to Gorky's oeuvre is an idea that I began exploring in 1992 and discussed in 1995 in my master's thesis. Others, such as Peter Balakian in 1996 and Nouritza Matossian in 1999, have also noted its importance. To comprehend more fully the impact of the Armenian Genocide on individuals, see Donald E. Miller and Lorna Touryan Miller, *Survivors: An Oral History of the Armenian Genocide* (Berkeley and Los Angeles: University of California Press, 1993).

27. Sontag, *Regarding the Pain of Others*.

28. Dennison, "Crisis-Art of Arshile Gorky," 18.

29. Dominic LaCapra has noted that "loss is often correlated with lack, for as loss is to the past, so lack is to the present and future." "Trauma, Absence, Loss," *Critical Inquiry* 25, no. 4 (1999): 703. LaCapra explains further "the need to explore the problematic relations between absence and loss (or lack) as well as between structural and historical trauma without simply collapsing the two or reducing one to the other. One may well argue that structural trauma related to absence or a gap in existence—with the anxiety, ambivalence, and elation it evokes—may not be cured but only lived with in various ways. Nor may it be reduced to a dated historical event or derived from one; its status is more like

that of a condition of possibility of historicity (without being identical to history, some of whose processes—for example, certain ritual and institutional processes—may mitigate or counteract it). One may even argue that it is ethically and politically dubious to believe that one can overcome or transcend structural trauma or constitutive absence to achieve full intactness, wholeness, or communal identity and that attempts at transcendence or salvation may lead to the demonization and scapegoating of those on whom unavoidable anxiety is projected. But historical traumas and losses may conceivably be avoided and their legacies to some viable extent worked through both in order to allow a less self-deceptive confrontation with transhistorical, structural trauma and in order to further historical, social, and political specificity, including the elaboration of more desirable social and political institutions and practices" (ibid., 727).

30. See Ruth Leys, *Trauma: A Genealogy* (Chicago: University of Chicago Press, 2000).

31. See Levon Z. Boyajian and Haikaz M. Gregorian, "Reflections on the Denial of Armenian Genocide," in "Resilience in Ethnic Experiences with Massive Trauma and Violence," edited by Flora Hogman, special issue of *Psychoanalytic Review*, vol. 85, no. 4 (1998): 505–16.

32. Peter Balakian, *Black Dog of Fate* (New York: Broadway Books, 1997), 286.

33. Robert Hughes, "The Triumph of Achilles the Bitter: In New York City, A Definitive Arshile Gorky Retrospective," *Time*, May 11, 1981, 80.

34. Mary Burliuk, "Arshile Gorky," *Color and Rhyme* 19 (1949): 2.

35. William Saroyan, "A Note on Hilaire Hiler," in *Why Abstract?* (New York: New Directions Press, 1945), 33.

36. Julien Levy, *Arshile Gorky* (New York: Harry N. Abrams, 1966), 35.

37. See Karlen Mooradian, *Arshile Gorky Adoian* (Chicago: Gilgamesh Press, 1978).

38. This is not the first time in modern art when an artist might have courted the idea of magic in his art. Pablo Picasso was extremely superstitious, and some of his works, like the masked *Les Demoiselles d'Avignon*, arguably have an apotropaic quality.

39. Carl G. Jung, *Modern Man in Search of a Soul*, trans. W. S. Dell and Cary F. Baynes (San Diego: Harvest Books, 1933), 70.

40. Levy, *Arshile Gorky*, 34.

41. André Breton, "Arshile Gorky," in *Surrealism and Painting* (New York: Harper and Row, 1972), 199–200.

42. Dickran Tashjian, "Arshile Gorky's Armenian Script: Ethnicity and Modernism in the Diaspora," *Bucknell Review* 30, no. 1 (1986): 154.

43. Melvin P. Lader, *Arshile Gorky* (New York: Abbeville Press, 1980), 41.

44. Meyer Schapiro, introduction to *Arshile Gorky*, by Ethel Schwabacher (New York: Macmillan, 1957), 13–14.

45. See Edward Soja, *Postmodern Geographies: The Reassertion of Space in Critical Social Theory* (New York: Verso, 1989).

46. Theodore F. Wolff, "The Many Masks of Modern Art," *Christian Science Monitor*, May 26, 1981, 24.

47. Cathy Caruth, introduction to *Trauma: Explorations in Memory*, ed. Cathy Caruth (Baltimore: Johns Hopkins University Press, 1995), 11.

48. Lader, *Arshile Gorky*, 91.

49. Ibid.

50. Duncan Macmillan, "The Outsider: Gorky and America," *Art International* 23, nos. 3–4 (1979): 106.

51. Jung, *Modern Man*, 171–72.

52. Schwabacher, *Arshile Gorky*, 128. From Talcott B. Clapp, "A Painter in a Glass House," *Sunday Republican Magazine*, February 9, 1948.

53. Saul Friedländer, *Memory, History, and the Extermination of the Jews of Europe* (Bloomington: Indiana University Press, 1993).

54. Julia Kristeva, *Powers of Horror: An Essay in Abjection*, trans. Leon S. Roudiez (New York: Columbia University Press, 1982), 2.

55. Viktor Frankl, *Man's Search for Meaning* (New York: Pocket Books, 1984), 95.

56. Balcomb Greene, interview by Karlen Mooradian, in *Many Worlds of Arshile Gorky*, 146.

57. Dennison, "Crisis-Art of Arshile Gorky," 17.

58. Brian O'Doherty, "Gorky: Private Language, Universal Theme," *New York Times*, May 10, 1964.

59. Harold Rosenberg, *Arshile Gorky: The Man, the Time, the Idea* (New York: Horizon Press, 1962), 70.

60. See Peter Balakian, "Arshile Gorky and the Armenian Genocide," *Art in America* 84, no. 2 (1996): 58–67, 108–9.

61. Bedrosian, *Magical Pine Ring*, 215.

62. This is most closely associated with Abstract Expressionism, but has its roots in German Expressionism and, in Gorky's case, Kandinsky and Marc's spirituality as much as Kirchner and Heckel's anxious work.

63. Harold Rosenberg, "The American Action Painters," in *The Tradition of the New* (New York: Horizon Press, 1959), 25–26.

64. Peter Schjeldahl, "The Great Gorky," *Village Voice*, May 13–19, 1981, 101.

65. Barnett Newman, "The Sublime Is Now: The Ideas of Art: Six Opinions on What Is Sublime In Art," *Tiger's Eye* 6 (December 1948): 53.

66. Mark Rothko, "The Romantics Were Prompted," *Possibilities* 1 (1947–48): 84.

67. Adolph Gottlieb, "Statement," *Tiger's Eye* 1 (December 1947): 43.

68. Ann Eden Gibson, *Abstract Expressionism: Other Politics* (New Haven: Yale University Press, 1997), xxiv.

69. Rosenberg, "American Action Painters," 30.

70. Jung, *Modern Man*, 191.

71. Roland Barthes, "Change the Object Itself: Mythology Today," in *Image, Music, Text*, trans. Stephen Heath (New York: Hill and Wang, 1977), 165.

72. Michael Leja, *Reframing Abstract Expressionism: Subjectivity and Painting in the 1940s* (New Haven: Yale University Press, 1993), 9.

73. Jung, *Modern Man*, 196.

74. Dennison, "Crisis-Art of Arshile Gorky," 14.

75. Ibid.

76. Schwabacher, *Arshile Gorky*, 116.

77. Ibid., 140.

78. Jeanne Reynal commented in a January 9, 1945, letter to Agnes that "I love to hear so about the children and how they are necessary to Arshile." Jeanne Reynal papers, Archives of American Art, Smithsonian Institution.

79. Schwabacher, *Arshile Gorky*, 144.

80. Isamu Noguchi, interview by Karlen Mooradian, in *Many Worlds of Arshile Gorky*, 185.

81. Frankl, *Man's Search for Meaning*, 95.

82. Agnes has explained that Gorky's mood was quite dark and he set off to kill himself numerous times. But she generally foiled him by, for example, sending the children after him to play, after which his mood would change. On one occasion, when he headed off with rope to hang himself, she told the children, "Daddy is going to build you a swing," and they promptly caught up with him and distracted him until his destructive urge had passed. See interview with Agnes Gorky in the 1997 film *Strokes of Genius: Arshile Gorky*, directed by Charlotte Zerwin.

Chapter 7

1. Ethel Schwabacher, *Arshile Gorky* (New York: Macmillan, 1957), 15.

2. Emily Grenauer, *New York Herald Tribune*, January 7, 1951. Despite the protest of sixty-nine people in an open letter denouncing Grenauer's desecration, no one would publish it in his defense.

3. Harold Rosenberg, *Arshile Gorky: The Man, the Time, the Idea* (New York: Horizon Press, 1962), 14.

4. Jeanne Reynal Papers, Archives of American Art, Smithsonian Institution, Washington, DC.

5. Jeanne Reynal, letter to Agnes Gorky, dated "April 5 or so, 1945," Reynal Papers.

6. Clement Greenberg, Art, *Nation* 160 (March 24, 1945): 331–32.

7. Jeanne Reynal, letter to Agnes Gorky dated April 7, 1945, Reynal Papers.

8. Clement Greenberg, Art, *Nation* 166 (March 20, 1948): 331–32.

9. Clement Greenberg, Art, *Nation* 166 (January 10, 1948): 52.

10. Ibid.

11. Ethel Schwabacher Papers, Archives of American Art, Smithsonian Institution, Washington, D.C.

12. This is evident at times in the tone of some of the writings of Harry Rand and Matthew Spender.

13. Rosenberg, *Arshile Gorky*, 30–31.

14. Michael Leja, *Reframing Abstract Expressionism: Subjectivity and Painting in the 1940s* (New Haven: Yale University Press, 1993), 65.

15. Carl G. Jung, *Modern Man in Search of a Soul* (San Diego: Harvest Books, 1933) 164.

16. Mark Rothko and Adolph Gottlieb elaborate upon this concept in "Art in New York," a radio interview on October 13, 1943.

17. David Shapiro and Cecile Shapiro, *Abstract Expressionism: A Critical Record* (New York: Cambridge University Press, 1999), 10. Gottlieb, Rothko and Newman used symbols and mythology, the primitive and archaic, taken out of context, abstracted, and with no connection to their original meaning. In this way they perhaps created a personal mythology.

18. Leja, *Reframing Abstract Expressionism*, 94.

19. Mark Rothko, "Statement on Painting," *Tiger's Eye* 9 (October 1949): 114.

20. See Jung, *Modern Man*, and more recently, Joseph Campbell, with Bill Moyers, *The Power of Myth* (New York: Anchor Books, 1991).

21. Adolph Gottlieb, "Statement," *Tiger's Eye* 1 (December 1947): 43.

22. Ann Eden Gibson, *Abstract Expressionism: Other Politics* (New Haven: Yale University Press, 1997), xxxvii.

23. See Gary Gerstle, *American Crucible: Race and Nation in the Twentieth Century* (Princeton: Princeton University Press, 2001).

24. Robert Mirak, *Torn Between Two Lands: Armenians in America 1890–World War I* (Cambridge: Harvard University Press, 1983), 144–45.

25. Matthew Spender, *From a High Place: A Life of Arshile Gorky* (New York: Knopf, 1999), 230.

26. Elaine de Kooning, "Gorky: Painter of His Own Legend," *Art News* 49 (January 1951): 40.

27. Gibson, *Abstract Expressionism*, 73.

28. Alice Scourby, *Third Generation Greek Americans: A Study of Religious Attitudes* (New York: Arno Press, 1980), 14–15.

29. Stuart Davis, "Arshile Gorky in the 1930's: A Personal Recollection by Stuart Davis," *Magazine of Art* 44 (February 1951): 57.

30. Gibson, *Abstract Expressionism*, 32.

31. Leja, *Reframing Abstract Expressionism*, 102.

32. Milton Resnick, interview by Karlen Mooradian, in *The Many Worlds of Arshile Gorky* (Chicago: Gilgamesh Press, 1980), 196.

33. Gibson, *Abstract Expressionism*, xxviii.

34. Edward Said, "Orientalism Reconsidered," in *Reflections on Exile and Other Essays* (Cambridge, Mass.: Harvard University Press, 2000), 212.

35. Clement Greenberg, Art, *Nation* 160 (March 24, 1945): 342–43.

36. Griselda Pollock, *Vision and Difference: Femininity, Feminism, and Histories of Art* (New York: Routledge, 1989), 11.

37. Howard Singerman, *Art Subjects: Making Artists in the American University* (Berkeley and Los Angeles: University of California Press, 1999), 39.

38. Gibson, *Abstract Expressionism*, 73.

39. Meyer Schapiro, introduction to Schwabacher, *Arshile Gorky*, 13–14.

40. Anne Middleton Wagner, "Lee Krasner as L.K.," *Representations* 25 (Winter 1989): 42.

41. Ibid.

42. Anne Middleton Wagner, *Three Artists (Three Women): Modernism in the Art of Hesse, Krasner, and O'Keefe* (Berkeley and Los Angeles: University of California Press, 1996), 158.

43. Gibson, *Abstract Expressionism*, 156.

44. Anne M. Wagner, "Lee Krasner as L.K.," *Representations* 25 (Winter 1989): 44.

45. Wagner, *Three Artists*, 154.

46. See Edward Said, *Orientalism* (New York: Vintage, 1979).

47. June Wayne, "The Male Artist as a Stereotypical Female," *Art Journal* 32, no. 4 (1973): 414–15.

48. Interest in children's art had been increasing since the second half of the nineteenth century, particularly in response to the Child Study movement of the 1880s, and became important to developing education principles in the twentieth century.

49. Henry Taylor, e-mail to the author, January 24, 1996.

Chapter 8

1. Carl G. Jung, *Modern Man in Search of a Soul*, trans. W. S. Dell and Cary F. Baynes (San Diego: Harvest Books, 1933), 167.

2. Roland Barthes, "The Death of the Author," in *Image, Music, Text*, trans. Stephen Heath (New York: Hill and Wang, 1977), 143.

3. Quoted from a 1949 letter from Gorky's widow to Ethel Schwabacher. Portions quoted in Ethel Schwabacher, *Arshile Gorky* (New York: Macmillan, 1957). Complete version in Ethel Schwabacher Papers, Archives of American Art.

4. Andrew Solomon, "His Life Was a Forgery," *New York Times Book Review*, July 11, 1999, 11.

5. Ibid.

6. See Hilton Kramer, "Gorky—Separating the Artist from the Myth," Art View, *New York Times*, February 22, 1976, D31, 33.

7. Karlen Mooradian, *Arshile Gorky Adoian* (Chicago: Gilgamesh Press, 1978); Nouritza Matossian, *Black Angel: A Life of Arshile Gorky* (London: Chatto and Windus, 1998); Matthew Spender, *From a High Place: A Life of Arshile Gorky* (New York: Knopf, 1999); and Hayden Herrera, *Arshile Gorky: His Life and Work* (New York: Farrar, Straus and Giroux, 2003).

8. Dore Ashton, "Roundtrip," *Colóquio Artes* 32, no. 84 (1990): 5–13 (English), 76–78 (Portuguese).

9. Ernst Kris and Otto Kurz have deconstructed this narrative in *Legend, Myth, and Magic in the Image of the Artist: A Historical Experiment* (New Haven: Yale University Press, 1979).

10. Copies of the letter can be found in versions of Schwabacher, *Arshile Gorky*, and the Ethel Schwabacher Papers at the Archives of American Art.

11. Although Matthew Spender's *From a High Place* and Nouritza Matossian's *Black Angel* sometimes disagree about the sequence and specifics of Gorky's life, they both question Mooradian's translation of the letters from Armenian to English. In addition, both biographers dispute the existence of some of the letters, especially those that cast light on Gorky's aesthetic theory; in them the artist links his oeuvre to his Armenian heritage almost exclusively. Hayden Herrera, in her biography *Arshile Gorky: His Life and Work*, which is largely a rewriting of Mooradian's as well as the other two, skirts the issue by using alternative translations of existing letters.

12. By "Armenian question" I refer not only to the role that Gorky's heritage played in his art, but also to Turkey's denial that there ever was a Genocide.

13. Matossian, *Black Angel*, 25.

14. As told to the author, April 1998, Richmond, Va.

15. Quoted from ARMENPRESS (Internet news list) 05/19/04.

16. I encourage the reader to examine the scholarship of Henry Charles Theriault, who connects the Armenian Genocide, slavery and racism against African Americans, injustices to the Cambodians, depopulation of the Native Americans, the Rwandan genocide, and other human rights violations to further elaborate this connection.

17. Judith Butler, *The Psychic Life of Power: Theories in Subjection* (Stanford: Stanford University Press, 1997), 197–98.

18. See the DVD of *Calendar*, distributed by Zeitgeist Video.

19. "Portrait of Arshile Gorky," a special feature on the *Ararat* DVD. All references to *Ararat* are from the DVD, distributed by Buena Vista Home Entertainment.

20. "A Cruel Joke," *Ararat* DVD special feature.

21. Director's commentary on *Ararat* DVD.

22. Schjeldahl, "Great Gorky."

23. Egoyan's family fled the Genocide and ended up in Egypt, where he lived before immigrating to Canada and ending up in Toronto.

24. Spender, *From a High Place*, 182.

25. There is an aspect of the tone that suggests that Spender is affected by his wife's own traumatic relationship to her father.

26. Matossian recounts some of his abuse of an earlier lover (*Black Angel*, 187).

27. Schwabacher, *Arshile Gorky*, 142, 144.

28. Which, arguably, was written to Schwabacher as a personal letter and not intended for publication.

29. This is a sticky subject, of course, but Agnes prevented him from committing suicide on several occasions. Ultimately it seems to have come down to her and her children's survival in contrast to Gorky's, which is why she eventually left him.

30. Paul Gilroy speaks of "fractal identities" in "It Ain't Where You're From, It's Where You're At: The Dialectics of Diasporic Identification," *Third Text* 13 (Winter 1990/91): 3–16.

31. Harold Rosenberg, "The American Action Painters," in *The Tradition of the New* (New York: Horizon Press, 1959), 23–39.

32. Schjeldahl, "Great Gorky."

33. Ibid.

34. Harold Rosenberg, *Arshile Gorky: The Man, the Time, the Idea* (New York: Horizon Press, 1962), 22.

35. Paul Brach, "Gorky's Secret Garden," *Art in America* 59 (October 1981): 122.

36. André Breton, "First Manifesto of Surrealism" (1924), in *Art in Theory, 1900–1990: An Anthology of Changing Ideas*, ed. Charles Harrison and Paul Wood (Oxford: Blackwell, 1993), 439.

Conclusion

1. Carol Stocker, "Centerpiece: A Woman of Many Identities Is Certain of Being Armenian," *Boston Globe*, April 23, 1983, 15.

2. I am indebted to Henry Charles Theriault for his extensive research on genocide and denial for much of the discussion about the Armenian Genocide that occurs in this book. Also, it is important to note that despite the historic record of the Holocaust, that too is often still denied.

3. Robert Jonas, interview by Karlen Mooradian, in *The Many Worlds of Arshile Gorky* (Chicago: Gilgamesh Press, 1980), 151.

4. Howard Singerman, *Art Subjects: Making Artists in the American University* (Berkeley and Los Angeles: University of California Press, 1999), 26.

5. Note to the author, June 29, 1999.

6. Nick Dante Vaccaro, "Gorky's Debt to Gaudier-Brzeska," *Art Journal* 23 (Fall 1963): 33–34.

7. Margaret Osborne, interview by Karlen Mooradian, in *The Many Worlds of Arshile Gorky* (Chicago: Gilgamesh Press, 1980), 186.

8. Some of this is revealed in a letter found in a Whitney Museum file and that despite many translations, it remains only snippets of words and phrases. The letter is described in detail by Matthew Spender in *From A High Place: A Life of Arshile Gorky* (New York: Knopf, 1999), 194.

9. Cathy Caruth, "Trauma, Absence, Loss," *Critical Inquiry* 25, no. 4 (1999): 712.

10. Julien Levy, *Arshile Gorky* (New York: Harry N. Abrams, 1966).

11. Books include the three recent biographies discussed in chapter 8, and exhibition catalogues such as *Arshile Gorky: The Breakthrough Years*, ed. Michael Auping (New York: Rizzoli, 1995), and Janice C. Lee and Melvin P. Lader, *Arshile Gorky: A Retrospective of Drawings* (New York: Harry N. Abrams, 2004).

12. Such as Ann Eden Gibson's *Abstract Expressionism: Other Politics* (New Haven: Yale University Press, 1997), Michael Leja's *Reframing Abstract Expressionism: Subjectivity and Painting in the 1940s* (New Haven: Yale University Press, 1993), and Ellen Landau's *Reading Abstract*

Expressionism: Context and Critique (New Haven: Yale University Press, 2005).

13. Here I am generalizing works by authors such as Karlen Mooradian, *Arshile Gorky Adoian* (Chicago: Gilgamesh Press, 1978); André Breton, "The Eye-Spring: Arshile Gorky," *Le Surrealism et la Peinture* (1945), 196–99; and Harry Rand, *Arshile Gorky: The Implications of Symbols* (Montclair, N.J.: Allanheld and Schram, 1980).

14. Timothy Mitchell, *Questions of Modernity* (Minneapolis: University of Minnesota Press, 2000), 6.

15. Rueben Nakian, "My Fellow Countryman," in *Arshile Gorky: Drawings to Paintings* (Austin: University of Texas Press, 1975), 93.

16. Dore Ashton, "A Straggler's View of Gorky," in *Arshile Gorky: The Breakthrough Years*, ed. Michael Auping (New York: Rizzoli, 1995), 40.

17. Milton Resnik, interview by Karlen Mooradian, in *Many Worlds of Arshile Gorky*, 195.

Selected Bibliography

In addition to the references listed below, I also consulted the following resources at the Archives of American Art in Washington, D.C.: Whitney Museum Papers; Oral History Project: Papers of Ethel Schwabacher; Papers Concerning Arshile Gorky.

Akiskal, Kareen K., and Hagop S. Akiskal. "Abstract Expressionism as Psychobiography: The Life and Suicide of Arshile Gorky." In *Depression and the Spiritual in Modern Art: Homage to Miró*, edited by Joseph J. Schildkraut and Aurora Otero, 221–38. Chichester, England: John Wiley, 1996.

Andreas, Walter G., and Mehmet Kalpakh. *The Age of Beloveds: Love and the Beloved in Early-Modern Ottoman and European Culture and Society*. Durham: Duke University Press, 2005.

Anfam, David. "Arshile Gorky: Tradition and Identity." *Antique Collector* 61, no. 2 (1990): 26–33.

Anon. "Old House Made New." *Life*, February 9, 1948, 90–92.

Applefeld, Aharon. "The Awakening: On a Pervasive Feeling." In *Shapes of Memory*, edited by Geoffrey Hartman. Oxford: Oxford University Press, 1992.

Aronowitz, Stanley. "Reflections on Identity." In *Dead Artists, Live Theories, and Other Cultural Problems*, 191–208. New York: Routledge, 1994.

Ash, John. "Arshile Gorky: How My Mother's Embroidered Apron Unfolds in My Life." *Artforum* 34, no. 1 (1995): 79, 121.

Ashton, Dore. "Crisis of Perpetual Resolution." In Schimmel, *Interpretive Link*, 29–32.

———. "A Straggler's View of Gorky." In Auping, *Arshile Gorky*, 39–61.

Attig, Thomas. *How We Grieve: Relearning the World*. New York: Oxford University Press, 1996.

Auping, Michael, ed. *Arshile Gorky: The Breakthrough Years*. New York: Rizzoli, 1995.

———. "Gorky's Erotic Garden." In Auping, *Arshile Gorky*, 63–76.

———. Introduction to Auping, *Arshile Gorky*, 13–26.

———. Lecture, Albright-Knox Art Gallery, Buffalo, N.Y., October 14, 1995.

Baber, Alice. "Gorky's Color." In *Arshile Gorky: Drawings to Paintings*. Exh. cat. Austin: University of Texas Press, 1975.

Baigell, Matthew. *Jewish-American Artists and the Holocaust*. New Brunswick: Rutgers University Press, 1997.

Bakalian, Anny. *Armenian-Americans: From Being to Feeling Armenian*. New Brunswick, N.J.: Transaction, 1993.

Balakian, Peter. "Arshile Gorky and the Armenian Genocide." *Art in America* 84, no. 2 (1996): 58–67, 108–9.

———. *Black Dog of Fate*. New York: Broadway Books, 1997.

Barolsky, Paul. *Michelangelo's Nose: A Myth and Its Maker*. University Park: Pennsylvania State University Press, 1990.

———. *Why the Mona Lisa Smiles and Other Tales by Vasari*. University Park: Pennsylvania State University Press, 1991.

Barron, Stephanie. *Exiles and Émigrés: The Flight of European Artists from Hitler*. Los Angeles: Los Angeles County Museum of Art; New York: Harry N. Abrams, 1997.

Barthes, Roland. *Camera Lucida: Reflections on Photography*. Translated by Richard Howard. New York: Hill and Wang, 1981.

———. "Change the Object Itself: Mythology Today." In Barthes, *Image, Music, Text*, 165–69.

———. "The Death of the Author." In Barthes, *Image, Music, Text*, 142–48.

———. *Image, Music, Text*. Translated by Stephen Heath. New York: Hill and Wang, 1977.

———. *The Pleasure of the Text*. Translated by Richard Miller. New York: Hill and Wang, 1975.

Baur, John I. H. *Nature in Abstraction: The Relation of Abstract Painting and Sculpture to Nature in Twentieth-Century American Art*. Exh. cat. New York: Macmillan, 1958.

Bedrosian, Margaret. *The Magical Pine Ring: Culture and Immigration in American-Armenian Literature*. Detroit: Wayne State University Press, 1991.

———. "The Other Modernists: Tradition and the Individual Talent in Armenian-American Literature." Ph.D. diss., University of California at Davis, 1981.

Belting, Hans. *Likeness and Presence: A History of the Image Before the Era of Art*. Translated by Edmund Jephcott. Chicago: University of Chicago Press, 1996.

Ben-Levi, Jack. "A Sadomasochistic Drama in an Age of Traditional Family Values." In *Abject Art: Repulsion and Desire in American Art*. Exh. cat. New York: Whitney Museum, 1993.

Berman, Avis. *Rebels on Eighth Street: Juliana Force and the Whitney Museum of Art*. New York: Atheneum, 1990.

Beuttner, Stewart. "Arshile Gorky and the Abstract-Surreal." *Arts Magazine* 50, no. 7 (1976): 86–87.

Bhabha, Homi K. *The Location of Culture*. New York: Routledge, 1994.

Blanchot, Maurice. *The Writing of Disaster*. Translated by Ann Smock. Lincoln: University of Nebraska Press, 1986.

Blume, Peter. "Will Abstract Art Survive?" *New Republic*, April 1939, 308.

Bodnar, John. *The Transplanted: A History of Immigration in Urban America*. Bloomington: Indiana University Press, 1985.

Bois, Yve-Alain. "Painting: The Task of Mourning." In *Endgame: Reference and Simulation in Recent Painting and Sculpture*, 29–49. Cambridge, Mass.: MIT Press, 1986.

Bornstein, Kate. *Gender Outlaw: On Men, Women, and the Rest of Us*. New York: Vintage, 1995.

Bowman, Ruth. "Gorky's Aviation Murals Rediscovered." In Bowman, *Murals Without Walls*, 34–46.

———, ed. *Murals Without Walls: Arshile Gorky's Aviation Murals Rediscovered*. Newark: Newark Museum, 1978.

Boyajian, Levon Z., and Haikaz M. Gregorian. "Reflections on the Denial of Armenian Genocide." In "Resilience in Ethnic Experiences with Massive Trauma and Violence," edited by Flora Hogman, special issue of *Psychoanalytic Review* 85, no. 4 (1998): 505–16.

Brach, Paul. "Gorky's Secret Garden." *Art in America* 59 (October 1981): 122.

Breton, André. "Arshile Gorky." In *Surrealism and Painting*, translated by Simon Watson Taylor. New York: Harper and Row, 1972.

———. "The Eye Spring." In *Arshile Gorky*. New York: Levy Gallery, 1945.

———. "Farewell to Arshile Gorky." 1948. Reprinted in *Arshile Gorky: The Man, The Time, The Idea*, by Harold Rosenberg. New York: Horizon, 1962.

———. "First Manifesto of Surrealism." 1924. In *Art in Theory, 1900–1990: An Anthology of Changing Ideas*, edited by Charles Harrison and Paul Wood. Oxford: Blackwell, 1993.

———. *Young Cherry Trees Secured Against Young Hares*. 1946. Reprint, Ann Arbor: University of Michigan Press, 1969.

Burliuk, Mary. "Arshile Gorky." *Color and Rhyme* 19 (1949): 2–3.

Butler, Judith. *Bodies That Matter: On the Discursive Limits of "Sex."* New York: Routledge, 1993.

———. *The Psychic Life of Power: Theories in Subjection*. Stanford: Stanford University Press, 1997.

Calas, Nicolas. "Arshile Gorky." In *Calas Presenting Bloodflames 1947*. Exh. cat. New York: Hugo Gallery, 1947.

Campbell, Joseph, with Bill Moyers. *The Power of Myth*. New York: Anchor Books, 1991.

Camus, Albert. "The Wager of Our Generation." In *Resistance, Rebellion, and Death*, edited and translated by Justin O'Brien. New York: Vintage Books, 1988. Interview in *Demain*, October 24–30, 1957.

Caruth, Cathy. Introduction to *Trauma: Explorations in Memory*, edited by Cathy Caruth, 3–12. Baltimore: Johns Hopkins University Press, 1995.

———. "Trauma, Absence, Loss." *Critical Inquiry* 25, no. 4 (1999): 696–727.

———. *Unclaimed Experience: Trauma, Narrative, and History*. Baltimore: Johns Hopkins University Press, 1996.

Chipp, Herschel B. "Contemporary Art." In Chipp, Selz, and Taylor, *Theories of Modern Art*, 510–19.

Chipp, Herschel B., Peter Selz, and Joshua C. Taylor, eds. *Theories of Modern Art: A Source Book by Artists and Critics*. Berkeley: University of California Press, 1968.

Clapp, Talcott B. "A Painter in a Glass House." *Waterbury (Conn.) Sunday Republican Magazine*, February 9, 1948.

Clifford, James. *The Predicament of Culture: Twentieth-Century Ethnography, Literature, and Art*. Cambridge, Mass.: Harvard University Press, 1988.

Cohen, A. P. *The Symbolic Construction of Community*. London: Tavistock, 1985.

Corn, Wanda. *The Great American Thing*. Berkeley and Los Angeles: University of California Press, 1999.

Cote de Luna, Jeffery. Discussion with the author. March 4, 2004.

Culler, Jonathan. *The Pursuit of Signs: Semiotics, Literature, Deconstruction*. Ithaca: Cornell University Press, 1981.

Daniels, Roger. *Coming to America: A History of Immigration and Ethnicity in American Life*. New York: HarperCollins, 1990.

Danto, Arthur C. "Art After the End of Art." In *The Wake of Art: Criticism, Philosophy, and the Ends of Taste*, edited by Gregg Horowitz and Tom Huhn, 115–28. Amsterdam: Gordon and Breach, 1998.

Davis, Gene. "Gorky Taught Me That: A Remembrance of Arshile Gorky." *Arts Magazine* 50, no. 7 (1976): 81.

Davis, Stuart. "Arshile Gorky in the 1930's: A Personal Recollection by Stuart Davis." *Magazine of Art* 44 (1951): 57–58.

Deleuze, Gilles, and Félix Guattari. *Anit-Oedipus: Capitalism and Schizophrenia*. Translated by Robert Hurley,

Mark Seem, and Helen R. Lane. Minneapolis: University of Minnesota Press, 1983.

De Kooning, Elaine. "Gorky: Painter of His Own Legend." *Art News* 49 (January 1951): 38–41, 63–66.

De Kooning, Willem. Letter. *Art News* 47 (January 1949): 6.

Dennison, George. "The Crisis-Art of Arshile Gorky." *Arts Magazine* 37, no. 5 (1963):14–18.

Derrida, Jacques. "Différance." In *Critical Theory Since 1965*, edited by Hazard Adams and Leroy Searle, 120–36. Tallahassee: Florida State University Press, 1986.

Dinnerstein, Leonard, and David M. Reimers. *Ethnic Americans: A History of Immigration*. 4th ed. New York: Columbia University Press, 1999.

Doss, Erika. *Benton, Pollock, and the Politics of Modernism: From Regionalism to Abstract Expressionism*. Chicago: University of Chicago Press, 1991.

Duncan, Carol. "Virility and Domination in Early Twentieth-Century Vanguard Painting." In *Feminism and Art History: Questioning the Litany*, edited by Norma Broude and Mary D. Garrard, 293–313. New York: Harper and Row, 1982.

Ellison, Ralph. *Shadow and Act*. New York: Vintage, 1995.

Etemkjian, James. "Western European and Modern Armenian Literary Relations up to 1915." *Review of National Literatures* 13 (1984): 78.

FitzGerald, Michael C., and Julia May Boddewyn. *Picasso and American Art*. New Haven: Yale University Press, 2006.

Foster, Hal. "Death in America." *October* 75 (Winter 1996): 36–59.

———. *The Return of the Real: Art and Theory at the End of the Century*. Cambridge, Mass.: MIT Press, 1996.

Foucault, Michel. "What Is an Author?" In *Critical Theory Since 1965*, edited by Hazard Searle, 137–48. Tallahassee: University of Florida Press, 1986.

Frank, Elizabeth. "How Arshile Gorky Finally Became Himself." *Art News* 80 (September 1981): 168–70.

Frankl, Viktor. *Man's Search for Meaning*. New York: Pocket Books, 1984.

Franklin, Candace Gorham. "Arshile Gorky and Surrealist Inspiration." Master's thesis, University of Virginia, 1977.

Freeman, Judi. *Picasso and the Weeping Women: The Years of Marie-Therese Walter and Dora Maar*. New York: Rizzoli, 1994.

Freeman, Joshua. *Who Built America? Working People and the Nation's Economy, Politics, Culture, and Society*. Vol. 2, *From the Gilded Age to the Present*. New York: Pantheon Books, 1992.

Friedländer, Saul. *Memory, History, and the Extermination of the Jews of Europe*. Bloomington: Indiana University Press, 1993.

———. "Trauma, Transference, and 'Working Through' in Writing the History of the Shoah." *History and Memory* 4 (Spring/Summer 1992): 39–59.

Freud, Sigmund. *Beyond the Pleasure Principle and Other Writings*. Translated by John Reddick. New York: Penguin Books, 2003.

———. *The Interpretation of Dreams*. Edited and translated by James Strachey. New York: Basic Books, 1955.

Gates, Henry Louis, Jr. Introduction to *"Race," Writing, and Difference*. Chicago: University of Chicago Press, 1986.

———. *The Signifying Monkey: A Theory of Afro-American Literary Criticism*. New York: Oxford, 1988.

Gediman, Helen K., and Janice S. Lieberman. "The Imposturous Artist, Arshile Gorky: From Identity Confusion to Identity Synthesis." In *The Many Faces of Deceit: Omissions, Lies, and Disguise in Psychotherapy*, 169–96. North Vale, N.J.: J. Aronson, 1996.

Gerstle, Gary. *American Crucible: Race and Nation in the Twentieth Century*. Princeton: Princeton University Press, 2001.

Gibson, Ann Eden. *Abstract Expressionism: Other Politics*. New Haven: Yale University Press, 1997.

———. "Abstract Expressionism's Evasion of Language." In "New Myths for Old: Redefining Abstract Expressionism," edited by Ann Eden Gibson and Stephen Polcari. Special issue, *Art Journal* 47, no. 3 (1988): 208–14.

Giddens, Anthony. *The Consequences of Modernity*. Stanford: Stanford University Press, 1990.

Gilroy, Paul. "It Ain't Where You're From, It's Where You're At: The Dialectics of Diasporic Identitification." *Third Text* 13 (Winter 1990/91): 3–16.

Gjerde, Jon. *Major Problems in American Immigration and Ethnic History*. Boston: Houghton Mifflin, 1998.

Gleason, Philip. "American Identity and Americanization." In *Harvard Encyclopedia of American Ethnic Groups*, edited by Stephan Thernstrom, Ann Orlov, and Oscar Handlin. Cambridge, Mass.: Harvard University Press, 1980.

Goldwater, Robert. "Thoughts on Arshile Gorky." In *The Paintings of Arshile Gorky: A Critical Catalogue*, edited by Jim Jordan and Robert Goldwater, 3–5. New York: NYU Press, 1982.

Gombrich, E. H., *In Search of Cultural History*. Oxford: Clarendon Press, 1969.

Gordon, Milton M. *Assimilation in American Life*. New York: Oxford University Press, 1964.

Gorky, Arshile. *Arshile Gorky, 1904–48*. Exh. cat. London: Whitechapel Gallery, 1990.

———. *Arshile Gorky: Drawings*. New York: Arts Council Museum of Modern Art, 1964.

———. *Arshile Gorky: In Memory*. Exh. cat. New York: Washburn Gallery, 1978.

———. *Arshile Gorky: Late Paintings*. Exh. cat. New York: Gagosian Gallery, 1994.

———. *Arshile Gorky: Paintings and Drawings, 1929–1942*. Exh. cat. New York: Gagosian Gallery, 1998.

———. "Aviation: Evolution of Forms Under Aerodynamic Limitations." Description of Newark Airport Murals, December 1936. Reprinted in Rosenberg, *Arshile Gorky*, 130–32.

———. "Camouflage." Course description from *The Grand Central School of Art Course Announcement*. New York, 1942.

———. "My Murals for the Newark Airport: An Interpretation." In Bowman, *Murals Without Walls*, 13–16.

———. "Stuart Davis." *Creative Art* 9 (September 1931): 213–17.

———. "Thirst." *Grand Central School of Art Quarterly* (November 1926).

Gottlieb, Adolph. "Statement." *Tiger's Eye* 1 (December 1947): 43.

———. *Selected Paintings by the Late Arshile Gorky*. New York: Samuel Kootz Gallery, 1950.

Graham, John D. "Primitive Art and Picasso." *Magazine of Art* 30 (April 1937): 236–39.

———. *System and Dialectics of Art*. Edited by Marcia Epstein Allentuck. Baltimore: Johns Hopkins University Press, 1971.

Greenberg, Clement. Art. *Nation* 160 (March 24, 1945): 342–43.

———. Art. *Nation* 162 (May 4, 1946): 552.

———. Art. *Nation* 166 (January 10, 1948): 52.

———. Art. *Nation* 166 (March 20, 1948): 331–32.

———. "Avant-Garde and Kitsch." In *Art and Culture: Critical Essays*, 3–21. Boston: Beacon Press, 1965.

———. "Byzantine Parallels." In *Art and Culture: Critical Essays*, 167–74. Boston: Beacon Press, 1965.

———. "Modernist Painting." *Art and Literature*, no. 4 (Spring 1965): 193–201.

Greenblatt, Stephen. *Renaissance Self-Fashioning: From More to Shakespeare*. Chicago: University of Chicago Press, 1983.

Greene, Balcomb. "Memories of Arshile Gorky." *Arts Magazine* 50, no. 7 (1976): 108–10.

Gubar, Susan. *Poetry After Auschwitz: Remembering What One Never Knew*. Bloomington: Indiana University Press, 2003.

Guilbaut, Serge. *How New York Stole the Idea of Modern Art: Abstract Expressionism, Freedom, and the Cold War*. Translated by Arthur Goldhammer. Chicago: University of Chicago Press, 1983.

Hall, Stuart. "Cultural Identity and Diaspora." In *Diaspora and Visual Culture: Representing Africans and Jews*, edited by Nicholas Mirzoeff, 21–33. New York: Routledge, 2000.

Hamalian, Leo. "The Armenian Genocide and the Literary Imagination." In Hovannisian, *Armenian Genocide in Perspective*, 153–65.

Handlin, Oscar. *Immigration as a Factor in American History*. Englewood Cliffs, N.J.: Prentice-Hall, 1959.

Hawking, Stephen W. *A Brief History of Time: From the Big Bang to Black Holes*. New York: Bantam, 1988.

Heidegger, Martin. *Identity and Difference*. Translated by Joan Stambaugh. New York: Harper and Row, 1969.

Henderson, Linda Dalrymple. "Mysticism, Romanticism, and the Fourth Dimention." In *The Spiritual in Art: Abstract Painting, 1890–1985*, 219–37. New York: Abbeville Press; Los Angeles: Los Angeles County Museum of Art, 1986.

Henderson, Mae. Introduction to *Boundaries, Boundaries, and Frames: Cultural Criticism and Cultural Studies*, edited by Mae Henderson, 1–30. New York: Routledge, 1995.

Herrera, Hayden. *Arshile Gorky: His Life and Work*. New York: Farrar, Straus and Giroux, 2003.

———. "The Artist's Self Image: Self Portraits by Arshile Gorky." In *Arshile Gorky: Drawings to Paintings*, 41–55. Exh. cat. Austin: University of Texas Press, 1975.

———. "Gorky's Self-Portraits: The Artist by Himself." *Art in America* 64 (March 1976): 56–64.

———. "The Sculptures of Arshile Gorky." *Arts Magazine* 50, no. 7 (1976): 88–90.

Hovannisian, Richard, ed.. *The Armenian Genocide in Perspective*. New Brunswick, N.J.: Transaction Press, 1987.

———. *The Armenian Image in History and Literature*. Malibu: Undena, 1981.

Howe, Irving. *World of Our Fathers*. New York: Harcourt Brace Jovanovich, 1976.

Hughes, Robert. "The Triumph of Achilles the Bitter: In New York City, a Definitive Arshile Gorky Retrospective." *Time*, May 11, 1981, 80.

Huyssen, Andreas. *After The Great Divide: Modernism, Mass Culture, Postmodernism*. Bloomington: Indiana University Press, 1986.

———. *Twilight Memories: Marking Time in a Culture of Amnesia*. New York: Routledge, 1995.

Ivy, Marilyn. *Discourses of the Vanishing: Modernity, Phan-*

tasm, Japan. Chicago: University of Chicago Press, 1995.

James, William. *The Principles of Psychology*. Vol. 1. New York: Henry Holt, 1890.

Janis, Sidney. *Abstract and Surrealist Art in America*. New York: Reynal and Hitchcock, 1944.

Jordan, Jim. "Arshile Gorky at Crooked Run Farm." *Arts Magazine* 50, no. 7 (1976): 99–103.

———. "Gorky, Braque, Picasso." In *Arshile Gorky: Drawings to Paintings*, 79–90. Exh. cat. Austin: University of Texas Press, 1975.

———. *Gorky: Drawings*. Exh. cat. New York: M. Knoedler, 1969.

———. "The Paintings of Arshile Gorky: New Discoveries, New Sources, and Chronology." In Jordan and Goldwater, *Paintings of Arshile Gorky*, 7–103.

———. "The Place of the Newark Murals in Gorky's Art." In Bowman, *Murals Without Walls*, 27–64.

Jordan, Jim, and Robert Goldwater. *The Paintings of Arshile Gorky: A Critical Catalogue*. New York: New York University Press, 1982.

Joseph, May. *Nomadic Identities: The Performance of Citizenship*. Minneapolis: University of Minnesota Press, 1999.

Joyner, Brooks. *The Drawings of Arshile Gorky*. College Park: University of Maryland Press, 1969.

Jung, Carl G. *Modern Man in Search of a Soul*. Translated by W. S. Dell and Cary F. Baynes. San Diego: Harvest Books, 1933.

Kahan, Mitchell Douglass. "Subjective Currents in American Painting of the 1930's." Ph.D. diss., City University of New York, 1983.

Kainen, Jacob. "Arshile Gorky's Iconography." *Arts Magazine* 50, no. 7 (1976): 82–85.

———. "Memories of Arshile Gorky." *Arts Magazine* 50, no. 7 (1976): 96–98.

Kalayjian, Anie, and Siroon P. Shahinian. "Recollections of the Armenian Survivors of the Ottoman Turkish Genocide." In "Resilience in Ethnic Experiences with Massive Trauma and Violence," edited by Flora Hogman. Special issue, *Psychoanalytic Review* 85, no. 4 (1998): 489–504.

Kalayjian, Anie S., Siroon P. Shahinian, Edmund L. Gregerian, and Lisa Saraydarian. "Coping with Ottoman Turkish Genocide: An Exploration of the Experience of Armenian Survivors." *Journal of Traumatic Stress* 9, no. 1 (1996): 87–97.

Kalinoski, Richard. *Beast on the Moon*. In *Humana Festival '95: The Complete Plays*, edited by Marisa Smith. Lyme, N.H.: Smith and Kraus, 1995.

Kandinsky, Wassily. "The Cologne Lecture." in *Art in Theory, 1900–2000: An Anthology of Changing Ideas*, edited by Charles Harrison and Paul Wood, 89–93. Malden, Mass.: Blackwell, 2003.

Karp, Diane Rosenberg. "Arshile Gorky: The Language of Art." Ph.D. diss., University of Pennsylvania, 1982.

Kern, Stephen. *The Culture of Time and Space, 1880–1918*. Cambrdge, Mass.: Harvard University Press, 1983.

Khatchaturian, Shahen. *Armenian Artists: 19th and 20th Centuries*. New York: National Gallery of Armenia USA, 1993.

Kiesler, Frederick. "Murals Without Walls: Relating to Gorky's Newark Project." In Bowman, *Murals Without Walls*, 30–33. Orig. pub. *Artfront* (December 1936).

———. "Statement." In *Exhibition, Arshile Gorky*. Exh. cat. Philadelphia: Mellon Galleries, 1934.

Klein, Melanie. "Mourning and Its Relation to Manic-Depressive States." In *Contributions to Psycho-Analysis, 1921–1945: Melanie Klein*, edited by Ernest Jones. International Psycho-Analytical Library 34. London: Hogarth Press and the Institute of Psychoanalysis, 1973.

Kramer, Hilton. "Artview: Gorky—Separating the Artist from the Myth." *New York Times*, February 22, 1976, 31, 33.

Krauss, Rosalind E. "In the Name of Picasso." In *The Originality of the Avant-Garde and Other Modernist Myths*, 23–40. Cambridge, Mass.: MIT Press, 1985.

Kris, Ernst, and Otto Kurz. *Legend, Myth, and Magic in the Image of the Artist: A Historical Experiment*. New Haven: Yale University Press, 1979.

Kristeva, Julia. *Desire in Language: A Semiotic Approach to Literature and Art*. Edited by Leon S. Roudiez. Translated by Thomas Gora, Alice Jardine, and Leon S. Roudiez. New York: Columbia University Press, 1980.

———. *Powers of Horror: An Essay in Abjection*. Translated by Leon S. Roudiez. New York: Columbia University Press, 1982.

Kuspit, Donald. "Arshile Gorky: Images in Support of the Invented Self." In *Abstract Expressionism: The Critical Developments*, edited by Michael Auping, 49–63. New York: Harry N. Abrams, 1987.

———. "Arshile Gorky in the Thirties." In Gorky, *Arshile Gorky: Paintings and Drawings*.

LaCapra, Dominick. *History and Memory After Auschwitz*. Ithaca: Cornell University Press, 1998.

———. "Trauma, Absence, Loss." *Critical Inquiry* 25, no. 4 (1999): 696–727.

———. *Writing History, Writing Trauma*. Baltimore: Johns Hopkins University Press, 2001.

Lackner, Stephan. "Reflections on an Exile in France and

the United States." In Barron, *Exiles and Émigrés*, 363–73.

Lader, Melvin P. *Arshile Gorky*. New York: Abbeville Press, 1985.

———. "Arshile Gorky: A Modern Artist in the Academic Tradition." In *Arshile Gorky: Works on Paper*, edited by Melvin P. Lader, 15–54. Venice: Peggy Guggenheim, 1992.

———. "Arshile Gorky's *The Artist and His Mother*: Further Study of Its Evolution, Sources, and Meaning." *Arts Magazine* 58, no. 5 (1984): 102.

———. *Arshile Gorky: The Early Years*. Los Angeles: Jack Rutberg Fine Arts, 2004.

———. *Arshile Gorky: Three Decades of Drawing*. New York: Peters, 1990.

———. "Graham, Gorky, De Kooning, and the 'Ingres Revival' in America." *Arts Magazine* 52, no. 7 (1978): 94–99.

———. "What the Drawings Reveal: Some Observations on Arshile Gorky's Working Method." In Lee and Lader, *Arshile Gorky*, 15–54.

Landau, Ellen. *Reading Abstract Expressionism: Context and Critique*. New Haven: Yale University Press, 2005.

Lang, Berel. *Act and Idea in the Nazi Genocide*. Chicago: University of Chicago Press, 1990.

Lee, Janice C., and Melvin P. Lader. *Arshile Gorky: A Retrospective of Drawings*. New York: Harry N. Abrams, 2004.

Lefebre, Henri. *The Production of Space*. Translated by Donald Nicholson-Smith. Malden, Mass.: Blackwell, 1991.

Leja, Michael. *Reframing Abstract Expressionism: Subjectivity and Painting in the 1940s*. New Haven: Yale University Press, 1993.

Levy, Julien. *Arshile Gorky*. New York: Harry N. Abrams, 1966.

———. *Surrealism*. New York: Black Sun Press, 1936.

Leys, Ruth. *Trauma: A Genealogy*. Chicago: University of Chicago Press, 2000.

Lynch, H. F. B. "The Russian Provinces." In *Armenia: Travels and Studies*, vol. 1. Beirut: Khayats, 1965.

Macmillan, Duncan. "The Outsider: Gorky and America." *Art International* 23, nos. 3–4 (1979): 104–6.

Mathews, Thomas F. "The Art of the Armenian Manuscript." In *Treasures in Heaven: Armenian Illuminated Manuscripts*, edited by Thomas F. Mathews and Roger S. Wieck, 38–53. Princeton: Princeton University Press, 1994.

Matossian, Nouritza. *Black Angel: A Life of Arshile Gorky*. London: Chatto and Windus, 1998.

Matthews, J. H. "André Breton and Painting: The Case of Arshile Gorky." *Dada/Surrealism* 17 (1988): 36–45.

McCabe, Cynthia Jaffe. *The Golden Door: Artist-Immigrants of America, 1876–1976*. Washington, D.C.: Smithsonian Institution Press, 1976.

Melkonian, Neery. Discussion with the author, March 14, 1994.

Melville, Robert. Introduction to *Arshile Gorky: Paintings and Drawings*. Exh. cat. London: Tate Gallery, 1965.

Merleau-Ponty, Maurice. "Eye and Mind." In *Art in Theory, 1900–1990: An Anthology of Changing Ideas*, edited by Charles Harrison and Paul Wood. Cambridge, Mass.: Blackwell, 2000.

Miller, Donald E., and Lorna Touryan Miller. *Survivors: An Oral History of the Armenian Genocide*. Berkeley and Los Angeles: University of California Press, 1999.

Miller, Dorothy C., ed. *Fourteen Americans*. New York: Museum of Modern Art, 1946.

Miller, Nancy. *Bequest and Betrayal: Memoirs of a Parent's Death*. New York: Oxford University Press, 1996.

Miller, Nancy, and Jason Tougaw. *Extremities: Trauma, Testimony, and Community*. Urbana: University of Illinois Press, 2002.

Mirak, Robert. *Torn Between Two Lands: Armenians in America, 1890–World War I*. Cambridge: Harvard University Press, 1983.

Mitchell, Timothy. *Questions of Modernity*. Minneapolis: University of Minnesota Press, 2000.

Mitchell, W. J. T. *Picture Theory*. Chicago: University of Chicago Press, 1995.

Mooradian, Karlen. "Arshile Gorky." *Armenian Review* (Summer 1955): 49–58.

———. *Arshile Gorky Adoian*. Chicago: Gilgamesh Press, 1978.

———. "Arshile Gorky: Image from Armenia." In *An Exhibition of Drawings by Arshile Gorky*, 3–13. Exh. cat. Oklahoma City: Oklahoma Art Center, 1973.

———. "The Gardener from Eden." *Ararat* 9 (Winter 1968): 2–13.

———. *The Many Worlds of Arshile Gorky*. Chicago: Gilgamesh Press, 1980.

———, ed. "A Special Issue on Arshile Gorky." *Ararat* 12, no. 5 (1971).

———."The Unknown Gorky." *Art News* 66, no. 5 (1967): 52–53, 66–68.

———. "The Wars of Arshile Gorky." *Ararat* 24 (Autumn 1983): 2–6.

Mulvey, Laura. "Visual Pleasure and the Narrative Cinema." In *Film Theory and Criticism: Introductory Readings*, edited by Leo Braudy and Marshall Cohen, 833–44. New York: Oxford University Press, 1999.

Nakian, Reuben. “My Fellow Countryman.” In *Arshile Gorky: Drawings to Paintings*, 93–94. Exh. cat. Austin: University of Texas Press, 1975.

Neimeyer, Robert A., Holly G. Prigerson, and Betty Davies. “Mourning and Meaning.” *American Behavioral Scientist* 46, no. 2 (2002): 240.

Nercessian, Nora. “Beyond the Armenian Self-Image: The Art of Minas Avetesian and Arshile Gorky.” In Hovannisian, *Armenian Image*.

. “The Defeat of Arshile Gorky.” *Armenian Review* 36, no. 1 (1983): 89–99.

Newman, Barnett. “The Sublime Is Now: The Ideas of Art: Six Opinions on What Is Sublime in Art.” *Tiger's Eye* 6 (December 1948): 53.

Nochlin, Linda. “Art and the Conditions of Exile: Men/Women, Emigration/Expatriation.” In “Creativity and Exile: European/American Perspectives I,” edited by Susan Rubin Suleiman. Special issue, *Poetics Today* 17, no. 3 (1996): 317–37.

Ockman, Carol. *Ingres's Eroticized Bodies: Retracing the Serpentine Line*. New Haven: Yale University Press, 1995.

O'Connor, Francis V. “Arshile Gorky's Newark Airport Murals: The History of Their Making.” In Bowman, *Murals Without Walls*.

O'Hara, Frank. Introduction to Gorky, *Arshile Gorky: Drawings*.

Osborne, Margaret. “The Mystery of Arshile Gorky: A Personal Account.” *Art News* 61, no. 10 (1963): 59.

Oshagan, Vahe. “Self-Image of Armenians in Modern Literature.” In Hovannissian, *Armenian Image*.

Ozenfant, Amédée. “Notes on Cubism.” In *Art in Theory, 1900–1990: An Anthology of Changing Ideas*, edited by Charles Harrison and Paul Wood. Cambridge, Mass.: Blackwell, 2000.

Park, Marlene, and Gerald E. Markowitz. *Democratic Vistas: Post Office and Public Art in the New Deal*. Philadelphia: Temple University, 1984.

Peroomian, Rubina. *Literary Responses to Catastrophe: A Comparison of the Armenian and Jewish Experience*. UCLA Studies in Near Eastern Culture. Atlanta: Scholars Press, 1993.

Petrosian, Irina, and David Underwood. *Armenian Food: Fact, Fiction, and Folklore*. Bloomington, Ind.: Yerker, 2006.

Pollock, Griselda. *Vision and Difference: Femininity, Feminism, and Histories of Art*. New York: Routledge, 1989.

Rand, Harry. “Arshile Gorky's Armenian Sources.” *Journal of Armenian Studies* 3, nos. 1–2 (1986–87): 175–88.

———. “Arshile Gorky's Iconography.” In *Arshile Gorky: Drawings to Paintings*, 61–71. Exh. cat. Austin: University of Texas Press, 1975:

———. *Arshile Gorky: The Implications of Symbols*. Montclair, N.J.: Allanheld and Schram, 1980.

———. “The Calendars of Arshile Gorky.” *Arts Magazine* 50 (1976): 70–80.

———. “Great Expectations (of Style).” *Arts Magazine* 60, no. 3 (1985): 58–59.

Rathbone, Eliza. “Arshile Gorky: The Plow and the Song.” In *American Art at Mid-century: The Subjects of the Artist*, 58–90. Exh. cat. Washington, D.C.: National Gallery of Art, 1978.

Reiff, Robert. “Arshile Gorky's Object Matter.” *Arts Magazine* 50, no. 7 (1976): 91–93.

———. *A Stylistic Analysis of Gorky's Art from 1943–1948*. New York: Garland, 1977.

Reynolds, Dee. *Symbolist Aesthetics and Early Abstract Art: Sites of Imaginary Space*. New York: Cambridge University Press, 2005.

Ricoeur, Paul. *Memory, History, Forgetting*. Translated by Kathleen Blamey and David Pellauer. Chicago: University of Chicago Press, 2006.

Roediger, David R. *Working Toward Whiteness: How America's Immigrants Became White: The Strange Journey from Ellis Island to the Suburbs*. New York: Basic Books, 2005.

Rose, Barbara. *American Painting Since 1900: A Critical History*. New York: F. A. Praeger, 1967.

———. “Arshile Gorky and John Graham: Eastern Exiles in a Western World.” *Arts Magazine* 50, no. 7 (1976): 62–69.

———. “Arshile Gorky and the Genesis of a Master.” In *Arshile Gorky and the Genesis of Abstraction*, edited by Matthew Spender and Barbara Rose. Exh. cat. New York: Mazoh, 1994.

Rosenberg, Harold. “The American Action Painters.” In *The Tradition of the New*, 23–39. New York: Horizon Press, 1959. Orig. pub. *Art News* 51, no. 8 (1952).

———. “Arshile Gorky: Art and Identity.” In *The Anxious Object*, 99–106. New York: Horizon Press, 1964.

———. *Arshile Gorky: The Man, the Time, the Idea*. New York: Horizon Press, 1962.

———. “Art and Identity: The Unfinished Masterpiece.” *New Yorker*, January 5, 1963, 70–77.

———. “Notes on Identity: With Special Reference to the Mixed Philosopher, Søren Kierkegaard.” *View* 6 (May 1946): 8.

Rosenblum, Robert. “Arshile Gorky.” *Art Magazine* 32 (January 1958): 30–32.

Rosenzweig, Phyllis. *Arshile Gorky*, Washington: Hirshhorn

Museum and Sculpture Garden, 1979.

Rothko, Mark. "The Romantics Were Prompted." *Possibilities* 1 (1947–48): 84.

Rubin, William. "Arshile Gorky, Surrealism, and the New American Painting." In *New York Painting and Sculpture, 1940–70*, edited by Henry Geldzahler, 372–402. New York: Dutton, 1969.

Said, Edward. *Orientalism*. New York: Vintage, 1979.

———. "Orientalism Reconsidered." In Said, *Reflections on Exile*, 198–215.

———. "Reflections on Exile." In Said, *Reflections on Exile*, 173–86.

———. *Reflections on Exile and Other Essays*. Cambridge, Mass.: Harvard University Press, 2000.

Saroyan, William. "A Note on Hilaire Hiler." In *Why Abstract?* 30. New York: New Directions Press, 1945.

Sawain, Martica. "The Cycloptic Eye, Pataphysics, and the Possible: Transformations of Surrealism." In Schimmel, *Interpretive Link*, 37–41.

———. "'The Third Man,' or Automatism American Style." In "New Myths for Old: Redefining Abstract Expressionism," edited by Ann Eden Gibson and Stephen Polcari. Special issue, *Art Journal* 47, no. 3 (1988): 181–86.

Schaffner, Ingrid, and Lisa Jacobs. *Julien Levy: Portrait of an Art Gallery*. Cambridge, Mass.: MIT Press, 1998.

Schama, Simon. *Landscape and Memory*. New York: Vintage, 1995.

Schapiro, Meyer. Introduction to *Arshile Gorky*, by Ethel Schwabacher. New York: Macmillan, 1957.

Schildkraut, Joseph J., Alissa J. Hirshfeld, and Jane M. Murphy. "Depressive Disorders, Spirituality, and Early Deaths in the Abstract Expressionist Artists of the New York School." In *Depression and the Spiritual in Modern Art: Homage to Miro*, edited by Joseph J. Schildkraut and Aurora Otero, 196–220. New York: John Wiley, 1996.

Schimmel, Paul. "Images of Metamorphosis." In Schimmel, *Interpretive Link*, 17–28.

———. *The Interpretive Link: Abstract Surrealism into Abstract Expressionism: Works on Paper, 1938–48*, edited by Paul Schimmel. Newport Beach, Calif.: Newport Harbor Art Museum, 1986.

Schjeldahl, Peter. "The Great Gorky." *Village Voice*, May 13–19, 1981, 101.

Schwabacher, Ethel. *Arshile Gorky Memorial Exhibition*. Exh. cat. New York: Whitney Museum, 1951.

———. *Arshile Gorky*. New York: Macmillan, 1957.

Scourby, Alice. *Third Generation Greek Americans: A Study of Religious Attitudes*. New York: Arno Press, 1980.

Searle, John. *Speech Acts: An Essay in the Philosophy of Language*. New York: Cambridge University Press, 1969.

Seitz, William. *Arshile Gorky: Paintings, Drawings, Studies*. New York: Doubleday, 1962.

———. Foreword to *Arshile Gorky*, by Julien Levy. New York: Harry N. Abrams, 1978.

———. "Spirit, Time, and 'Abstract Expressionism.'" *Magazine of Art* 46 (1953): 80–88.

Shapiro, David, and Cecile Shapiro, eds. *Abstract Expressionism: A Critical Record*. New York: Cambridge University Press, 1990.

Shirinian, Lorne. "Part Three: A Study of the Texts. The Armenian Immigrant: Sourian, Hagopian, and Hacikyan." In *Armenian–North American Literature: A Critical Introduction: Genocide, Diaspora, and Symbols*. Lewiston, N.Y.: Edwin Mellen Press, 1990.

Singerman, Howard. *Art Subjects: Making Artists in the American University*. Berkeley and Los Angeles: University of California Press, 1999.

Smith, Robert. *Derrida and Autobiography*. New York: Cambridge University Press, 1995.

Soja, Edward. *Postmodern Geographies: The Reassertion of Space in Critical Social Theory*. New York: Verso, 1989.

Sollors, Werner. *Beyond Ethnicity: Consent and Descent in American Culture*. New York: Oxford University Press, 1986.

Solomon, Andrew. "His Life Was a Forgery." *New York Times Book Review*, July 11, 1999, 11.

Sontag, Susan. *Regarding the Pain of Others*. New York: Picador, 2003.

Spender, Matthew. "Arshile Gorky's Early Life." In *Arshile Gorky: The Breakthrough Years*, edited by Michael Auping, 27–37. New York: Rizzoli, 1995.

———. "Arshile Gorky: Themes for the Mural '1934.'" In *Arshile Gorky and the Genesis of Abstraction*, edited by Matthew Spender and Barbara Rose, ix–xii. New York: Mazoh, 1994.

———. *From A High Place: A Life of Arshile Gorky*. New York: Knopf, 1999.

———, ed. *Papers Concerning Arshile Gorky, 1957–1991*. Washington, DC: Archives of American Art, 1992.

Spender, Stephen. *The Making of a Poem*. London: Hamish Hamilton, 1955.

Spitz, Ellen Handler. *Art and Psyche: A Study in Psychoanalysis and Aesthetics*. New Haven: Yale University Press, 1985.

Storr, Robert. "Fertile Mirrors." In *Arshile Gorky, 1904–48*, 27–33. London: Whitechapel, 1990.

Tashjian, Dickran. "Arshile Gorky's Armenian Script: Ethnicity and Modernism in the Diaspora." *Bucknell Review* 30, no. 1 (1986) 144–61.

———. *Surrealism and the Avant-Garde, 1920–1950*. New York: Thames and Hudson, 1995.

Tedeschi, R. G., and L. G. Calhoun. "Posttraumatic Growth: Conceptual Foundations and Empirical Evidence." *Psychological Inquiry* 15 (2004): 1–18.

Theriault, Henry. "Rethinking Dehumanization in Genocide." In *The Armenian Genocide: Cultural and Ethical Legacies*, edited by Richard Hovannisian, 27–40. New Brunswick, N.J.: Transaction, 2007.

Theriault, Kim S. "Arshile Gorky as an Example of a Twentieth Century Armenian Immigrant." Paper delivered at Society for Armenian Studies 20th Annual Conference, Los Angeles, November 1994.

———. "Arshile Gorky: Immigration and Universality in American Art." Master's thesis, State University of New York at Buffalo, 1995.

. "Arshile Gorky's Self Fashioning: The Name, Naming, and Other Epithets." *Journal for the Society of Armenian Studies* 15 (2006): 141–56.

———. "Consideration of Genocide and Denial: Arshile Gorky in the History of Art." 1992.

———. "Images of Women in Arshile Gorky's Art." Paper delivered at Middle Atlantic Symposium in the History of Art, National Gallery of Art, Washington, D.C., April 1998.

———. "It's What Isn't There That Is: Memory, Trauma, and Abstraction in Arshile Gorky's Art." In "Catastrophe and Representation," edited by Peggy Schaller. Special issue, *Florida Atlantic Comparative Studies Literary Journal* 9 (2007): 85–108.

———. "Re-Placing Arshile Gorky: Exile, Identity, and Abstraction in Twentieth-Century Art." Ph.D. diss., University of Virginia, 2000.

Vaccaro, Nick Dante. "Gorky's Debt to Gaudier-Brzeska." *Art Journal* 23 (Fall 1963): 33–34.

Villa, Susie Hoogasian, and Mary Kilbourne Matossian. *Armenian Village Life Before 1914*. Detroit: Wayne State University Press, 1982.

Wagner, Anne Middleton. "Lee Krasner as L.K." *Representations* 25 (Winter 1989): 42–57.

———. *Three Artists: (Three Women): Modernism and the Art of Hesse, Krasner, and O'Keeffe*. Berkeley and Los Angeles: University of California Press, 1996.

Waldman, Diane. *Arshile Gorky,1904–1948: A Retrospective*. New York: Harry N. Abrams, 1981.

Wayne, June. "The Male Artist as a Stereotypical Female." *Art Journal* 32, no. 4 (1973): 414–16.

White, Hayden V. "Historical Emplotment and the Problem of Truth in Historical Representation." In *Figural Realism: Studies in the Mimesis Effect*, 27–42. Baltimore: Johns Hopkins University Press, 1999.

Whitehead, Anne. *Memory*. London. Routledge, 2009.

Williams, Raymond. "The Metropolis and the Emergence of Modernism." In *The Unreal City: Urban Experience in Modern European Literature and Art*, edited by Edward Timms and David Kelley, 13–24. Manchester: Manchester University Press, 1985.

Wolff, Janet. *Resident Alien: Feminist Cultural Criticism*. Cambridge: Polity, 1995.

Wollheim, Richard. "Kitaj: Recollections and Reflections." In *R. B. Kitaj: A Retrospective*, edited by Richard Morphet. Exh. cat. London: Tate Gallery, 1994.

Worringer, Wilhelm. *Abstraction and Empathy: A Contribution to the Psychology of Style*. Translated by Michael Bullock. Chicago: Ivan Dee, 1908.

Index